Taking SIDES

Clashing Views on Controversial Issues in World Politics

Seventh Edition

Edited, Selected, and with Introductions by

John T. Rourke
University of Connecticut

Dushkin Publishing Group/Brown & Benchmark Publishers
A Times Mirror Higher Education Group Company

*For Mimi Egan: From whom I learned much about
clashing views on controversial issues.*

Photo Acknowledgments

Part 1   United Nations/A. Holcombe
Part 2   USDA Soil Conservation Service
Part 3   United Nations/UN Photo 41750
Part 4   United Nations
Part 5   United Nations/UN Photo 61973

Cover Art Acknowledgment

Charles Vitelli

Manufactured in the United States of America

Seventh Edition

10 9 8 7 6 5 4 3 2 1

Library of Congress Cataloging-in-Publication Data

Main entry under title:
    Taking sides: clashing views on controversial issues in world politics/edited, selected, and
with introductions by John T. Rourke.—7th ed.
    Includes bibliographical references and index.
    1. World Politics—1945–. I. Rourke, John T., *comp.*

909.82
95-83864

0-697-31296-8

Printed on Recycled Paper

PREFACE

In the first edition of *Taking Sides*, I wrote of my belief in informed argument:

> [A] book that debates vital issues is valuable and necessary.... [It is important] to recognize that world politics is usually not a subject of absolute rights and absolute wrongs and of easy policy choices. We all have a responsibility to study the issues thoughtfully, and we should be careful to understand all sides of the debates.

It is gratifying to discover, as indicated by the success of *Taking Sides* over six editions, that so many of my colleagues share this belief in the value of a debate-format text.

The format of this edition follows a formula that has proved successful in acquainting students with the global issues that we face and generating discussion of those issues and the policy choices that address them. This book addresses 19 issues on a wide range of topics in international relations. Each issue has two readings: one pro and one con. Each is also accompanied by an issue *introduction*, which sets the stage for the debate, provides some background information on each author, and generally puts the issue into its political context. Each issue concludes with a *postscript* that summarizes the debate, gives the reader paths for further investigation, and suggests additional readings that might be helpful.

I have continued to emphasize issues that are currently being debated in the policy sphere. The authors of the selections are a mix of practitioners, scholars, and noted political commentators. Also, in order to give the reader a truly international perspective on the issues of world politics, the authors represent many nations, including Burma, Egypt, Great Britain, and Singapore, as well as the United States.

Changes to this edition   The dynamic, constantly changing nature of the world political system and the many helpful comments from reviewers have brought about significant changes to this edition. There are 10 completely new issues: *Is It Wise to Admit East European Countries into NATO?* (Issue 2); *Will the Israelis and Palestinians Be Able to Achieve Lasting Peace?* (Issue 5); *Will China Become an Asian Superpower?* (Issue 6); *Should the U.S. Economic Embargo Against Cuba Be Lifted?* (Issue 7); *Is the New General Agreement on Tariffs and Trade Beneficial?* (Issue 8); *Was Dropping Atomic Bombs on Japan Justifiable?* (Issue 11); *Does the World Need to Have Nuclear Weapons at All?* (Issue 12); *Are Efforts to Promote Democracy Culturally Biased and Self-Serving?* (Issue 15); *Should Serbia Be Treated Leniently?* (Issue 16); and *Will the World Fragment into Antagonistic Cultures?* (Issue 18). Two other issues have been recast to reflect changing emphasis: *Should Foreign Policymakers Minimize Human Rights Concerns?* (Issue 14) and *Should Immigration Be Restricted?* (Issue 17). Even where issues have remained controversial and have been carried over to this edition, new events and more current views have led to the use of new readings: *Should the United States Abandon Its Superpower Role?* (Issue 3); *Is Islamic Fundamentalism a Threat to Political Stability?* (Issue 4); *Is There a Global Environmental Crisis?* (Issue 10); and *Should a Permanent UN Military Force Be Established?* (Issue 13). Of the 38 readings, 27 are new. In addition, 32 were published in 1994 or 1995, and no reading is dated earlier than 1992. My practice of searching a wide range of journals for more recent expositions on one side or the other of the various issues ensures that the readings are as fresh as the issues are current.

A word to the instructor   An *Instructor's Manual With Test Questions* (both multiple-choice and essay) is available through the publisher for instructors using *Taking Sides* in the classroom. A general guidebook, *Using Taking Sides in the Classroom*, which discusses methods and techniques for integrating the pro-con approach into any classroom setting, is also available through Dushkin Publishing Group/Brown & Benchmark Publishers.

A note especially for the student reader   You will find that the debates in this book are not one-sided. Each author strongly believes in his or her position. And if you read the debates without prejudging them, you will see that each author makes cogent points. An author may not be "right," but the arguments made in an essay should not be dismissed out of hand, and you should work at remaining tolerant of those who hold beliefs that are different from your own.

There is an additional consideration to keep in mind as you pursue this debate approach to world politics. To consider objectively divergent views does not mean that you have to remain forever neutral. In fact, once you are informed, you ought to form convictions. More important, you should try to influence international policy to conform better with your beliefs. Write letters to policymakers; donate to causes you support; work for candidates who agree with your views; join an activist organization. *Do* something, whichever side of an issue you are on!

Acknowledgments   I received many helpful comments and suggestions from colleagues and readers across the United States and Canada. Their suggestions have markedly enhanced the quality of this edition of *Taking Sides*. If as you read this book you are reminded of a selection or an issue that could be included in a future edition, please write to me in care of Dushkin Publishing Group/Brown & Benchmark Publishers with your recommendations.

My thanks go to those who responded with suggestions for the sixth edition:

Agnes Bakhshi
Richard Bland College of
   William and Mary

Blaine D. Benedict
Houghton College

Robina Bhatti
Westmont College

Michael J. Connolly
Gonzaga University

R. Crownover
Madonna University

Richard Danilowicz
Niagara University

Douglas M. Dent
Madonna University

Alistair Edgar
Wilfrid Laurier University

T. Elliott
Brigham Young University

Roy Grow
Carleton College

Ken Hall
Ball State University

Dennis Hart
Kent State University

Clinton G. Hewan
Northern Kentucky
   University

Kurt W. Jefferson
Westminster College

Yussuf F. Kly
University of Regina

Margaret Leahy
Golden Gate University

Wei-chin Lee
Wake Forest University

Anthony Lombardo
Centenary College

Joseph Lugherrmo
Northwood University

Krishan Mathur
University of DC

Chris Meindl
University of Florida

Michael O'Donnell
Clinch Valley College

Theodore Reller
Canada College

Houman A. Sadri
University of Richmond

Renee Scherlen
Appalachian State University

John L. Seitz
Wofford College

Dina Spechler
Indiana University

Kristine Thompson
Concordia College–
Moorhead

Melvin M. Vuk
New Mexico State University

Jutta Weldes
Kent State University

I would also like to thank Mimi Egan, publisher for the Taking Sides series; David Dean, list manager; and David Brackley, developmental editor, for their help in refining this edition.

John T. Rourke
University of Connecticut

CONTENTS IN BRIEF

CONTENTS

Patrick Glynn, a former official in the U.S. Arms Control and Disarmament Agency, contends that the post–cold war world is a more dangerous place. Francis Fukuyama, a consultant at the RAND Corporation, argues that the current period of political instability will not necessarily lead to a more dangerous future.

Zbigniew Brzezinski, a professor of foreign policy, argues that an expanded NATO will produce a more peaceful Europe in the future. Michael E. Brown, a fellow of the Center for Science and International Affairs at Harvard University, contends that the costs of expanding NATO outweigh any possible advantages that could be gained.

Doug Bandow, a senior fellow at the Cato Institute, argues that the United States should bring its military forces home and curtail expensive foreign aid programs. Anthony Lake, special assistant for national security affairs for the Clinton administration, maintains that U.S. national interests make full international engagement imperative.

Daniel Pipes, editor of *Middle East Quarterly*, argues that Islamic fundamentalists pose a real threat to international stability. John L. Esposito, a professor of religion and international affairs, holds that it is wrong to view Islam as an organized whole whose adherents are mostly dangerous fanatics.

Robert Satloff, executive director of the Washington Institute for Near East Policy, maintains that peace between the Israelis and Palestinians can be achieved. Clovis Maksoud, director of the Center for the Study of the Global South, predicts that current peace efforts will lead to disillusionment and strife.

Denny Roy, a professor of political science at the National University of Singapore, argues that China poses a long-term threat to Asia-Pacific security. Michael G. Gallagher, who has taught international studies in both China and the United States, suggests that concerns about China trying to dominate the Asia-Pacific region are overwrought.

William Ratliff, a senior research fellow at the Hoover Institution, Stanford University, contends that continuing the U.S. economic embargo against Cuba reduces the likelihood of a peaceful transition to democracy in Cuba. Michael G. Wilson, a senior analyst for inter-American affairs and trade policy at the Heritage Foundation, argues that the United States should maintain its economic embargo against Cuba.

Michael Kantor, U.S. special trade representative for the Clinton administration, argues that the new General Agreement on Tariffs and Trade (GATT) will provide a major boost to the global economy. Ralph Nader, a longtime consumer advocate, maintains that the new system of international governance found in the GATT will adversely affect democracy and sovereignty.

United Nations executive James P. Grant contends that one way to jump-start solutions to many of the world's problems is to extend more assistance to impoverished countries. The editors of *The Economist*, a well-known British publication, suggest that the usual ways in which international aid is distributed and spent make it a waste of resources.

Hilary F. French, a senior researcher at the Worldwatch Institute in Washington, D.C., warns that an international effort must be made now to stop environmental degradation. Julian L. Simon, a professor of economics and business administration, argues that reports of an environmental crisis are not supported by scientific facts.

Donald Kagan, a professor of history and classics, contends that using the atomic bombs on Japan was a legitimate way to bring about Japanese surrender. Political philosopher John Rawls contends that dropping atomic bombs on Japan did not satisfy the principles governing the just conduct of war.

Professor of history Alex Roland contends that nuclear weapons protect the world from conventional warfare. Joseph Rotblat, an emeritus professor of physics, contends that outlawing nuclear weapons altogether might well produce a world that is much more secure than the present world.

Lukas Haynes, a former assistant to the president of the Carnegie Endowment for International Peace, and Timothy W. Stanley, vice president for policy of the United Nations Association–National Capital Area, assert that a standing UN military force would better enable the United Nations to meet its peacekeeping mission. John F. Hillen III, a defense policy analyst at the Heritage Foundation, concludes that a permanent UN military force is unworkable.

Alan Tonelson, a fellow of the Economic Strategy Institute in Washington, D.C., contends that the United States' human rights policy ought to be jettisoned. Michael Posner, executive director of the Lawyers Committee for Human Rights, maintains that the United States should continue to incorporate human rights concerns into its foreign policy decisions.

Kishore Mahbubani, deputy secretary of foreign affairs, contends that much of the world sees the West's standards of democracy as culturally biased. Aung San Suu Kyi, the leader of Burma's National League for Democracy, maintains that the concept of democracy is alien to indigenous values.

Marten van Heuven, an analyst at the RAND Corporation, contends that future relations should be aimed at working with, rather than punishing, Serbia. Hodding Carter, a former U.S. State Department spokesman, argues that Serbia has been responsible for a great deal of suffering in the Balkans, for which it should be punished.

Economist George J. Borjas argues that immigrants to the United States are negatively affecting the economy. Economist Stephen Moore maintains that the net gains from the contributions of immigrants far outweigh any social costs.

Professor of government Samuel P. Huntington asserts that the world is entering a new phase during which culture will be the fundamental source of conflict. Professor of political science James Kurth contends that the greatest clash will be within the West itself.

Michael Lind, executive editor of *The National Interest*, writes that for reasons of principle, the United States should support legitimate efforts at self-determination. Amitai Etzioni, a professor of sociology at George Washington University, contends that self-determination movements are destructive.

INTRODUCTION

World Politics and the Voice of Justice

John T. Rourke

Some years ago, the Rolling Stones recorded "Sympathy With the Devil." If you have never heard it, go find a copy. It is worth listening to. The theme of the song is echoed in a wonderful essay by Marshall Berman, "Have Sympathy for the Devil" (*New American Review*, 1973). The common theme of the Stones' and Berman's works is based on Johann Goethe's *Faust*. In that classic drama, the protagonist, Dr. Faust, trades his soul to gain great power. He attempts to do good, but in the end he commits evil by, in contemporary paraphrase, "doing the wrong things for the right reasons." Does that make Faust evil, the personification of the devil Mephistopheles among us? Or is the good doctor merely misguided in his effort to make the world better as he saw it and imagined it might be? The point that the Stones and Berman make is that it is important to avoid falling prey to the trap of many zealots who are so convinced of the truth of their own views that they feel righteously at liberty to condemn those who disagree with them as stupid or even diabolical.

It is to the principle of rational discourse, of tolerant debate, that this reader is dedicated. There are many issues in this volume that appropriately excite passion—for example, Issue 4 on whether or not Islamic fundamentalism represents a threat to political stability or Issue 12 on whether or not the world needs to have nuclear weapons at all. Few would find fault with the goal of avoiding nuclear destruction—indeed, of achieving a peaceful world. How to reach that goal is another matter, however, and we should take care not to confuse disagreement on means with disagreement on ends. In other cases, the debates you will read do diverge on goals. Amitai Etzioni, for example, argues in Issue 19 that nationalism is destructive and that we would be better off seeking new forms of political loyalty and organization. Michael Lind, in disagreement, stresses the positive contributions of self-determination. Issue 18 is also concerned with how people will organize themselves politically and relate to one another in the future. The debate here is whether or not the world will fragment into antagonistic cultures, with Samuel Huntington arguing that it will and James Kurth predicting that it will not.

As you will see, each of the authors in all the debates strongly believes in his or her position. If you read these debates objectively, you will find that each side makes cogent points. They may or may not be right, but they should not be dismissed out of hand. It is also important to repeat that the debate format does not imply that you should remain forever neutral. In fact, once you are informed, you *ought* to form convictions, and you should try to act on those convictions and try to influence international policy to conform better with your beliefs. Ponder the similarities in the views of two very different leaders, a very young president in a relatively young democracy and a very old emperor in a very old country: In 1963 President John F. Kennedy, in recalling the words of the author of the epoch poem *The Divine Comedy* (1321), told a West German audience, "Dante once said that the hottest places in hell are reserved for those who in a period of moral crisis maintain their neutrality." That very same year, while speaking to the United Nations, Ethiopia's emperor Haile Selassie (1892–1975) said, "Throughout history it has been the inaction of those who could have acted, the indifference of those who should have known better, the silence of the voice of justice when it mattered most that made it possible for evil to triumph."

The point is: Become Informed. Then *do* something! Write letters to policymakers, donate money to causes you support, work for candidates with whom you agree, join an activist organization, or any of the many other things that you can do to make a difference. What you do is less important than that you do it.

APPROACHES TO STUDYING INTERNATIONAL POLITICS

As will become evident as you read this volume, there are many approaches to the study of international politics. Some political scientists and most practitioners specialize in *substantive topics*, and this reader is organized along topical lines. Part 1 (Issues 1 through 7) begins with a question about the present condition of the international system, currently an emphasis of many scholars. Patrick Glynn and Francis Fukuyama debate whether or not the world has become a more dangerous place since the end of the cold war. Beginning with Issue 2, the focus of Part 1 shifts to regional issues and actors. Debates here deal with Eastern Europe, the United States, Asia, Latin America, and the Middle East. Part 2 (Issues 8 through 10) focuses on international economic issues, including the new revision of the General Agreement on Tariffs and Trade (GATT) and the creation of the powerful World Trade Organization (WTO); the impact of efforts by the wealthier countries of the North to assist the less developed countries of the South; and whether or not there is a global environmental crisis. Part 3 (Issues 11 through 13) examines controversies surrounding the use of force in international relations, including whether or not the world would be wise to rid itself completely of nuclear weapons, whether or not the United States was justified in dropping two atomic bombs on Japan in 1945, and whether or not a permanent UN military force should be established. The inability of UN peacekeepers to bring about peace in Bosnia makes this last issue especially timely. Part 4 (Issues 14 and 15) examines the application of values in the global system. Issues here concern whether or not morality should be a centerpiece of foreign policy formation and whether or not efforts to promote democracy around the world are culturally biased. Part 5 (Issues 16 through 19) addresses issues of political identification. Where people live and to what or whom they give their political loyalties is in a great state of flux. The first of these debates examines whether Serbia should be offered leniency to achieve peace in the Balkans or punished with economic and diplomatic sanctions for its role in the war in the Balkans. Other issues in this part consider immigration, whether or not the world will fragment into conflicting cultures, and the wisdom of promoting unfettered self-determination.

Political scientists also approach their subject from differing *methodological perspectives*. We will see, for example, that world politics can be studied from different *levels of analysis*. The question is: What is the basic source of the forces that shape the conduct of politics? Possible answers are world forces, the individual political processes of the specific countries, or the personal attributes of a country's leaders and decision makers. Various readings will illustrate all three levels.

Another way for students and practitioners of world politics to approach their subject is to focus on what is called the realist versus the idealist debate. Realists tend to assume that the world is permanently flawed and therefore advocate following policies in their country's narrow self-interests. Idealists take the approach that the world condition can be improved substantially by following policies that, at least in the short term, call for some risk or self-sacrifice. This divergence is an element of many of the debates in this book.

DYNAMICS OF WORLD POLITICS

The action on the global stage today is vastly different from what it was a few decades ago, or even a few years ago. *Technology* is one of the causes of this change. Technology has changed communications, manufacturing, health care, and many other aspects of the human condition. Technology has also led to the creation of nuclear weapons and other highly sophisticated and expensive conventional weapons. Issue 12 frames a debate over whether or not, having created and armed ourselves with nuclear weapons, we can and should reverse the process and disarm. Technology has also vastly increased our ability to consume resources and excrete pollution, and Issue 10 examines the controversy over whether or not there is a global environmental crisis and, if so, what should be done about it. Another dynamic aspect of world politics involves the *changing axes* of the world system. For about 40 years after World War II ended in 1945, a bipolar system existed, the primary axis of which was the *East-West* conflict, which pitted the United States and its allies against the Soviet Union and its allies. Now that the Warsaw Pact has collapsed as an axis of world politics, many new questions have surfaced relating to how security should be provided for Europe and the future of the North Atlantic Treaty Organization (NATO). Some analysts advocate expanding NATO to include some or all of the countries of Eastern Europe and, perhaps, even Russia and some of the other former Soviet republics. This plan is the topic of Issue 2. Insofar as containing communism and the Soviet Union were the mainstay of U.S. post–World War II policy, the end of the Soviet threat also brings the

United States to a pivotal choice about future foreign involvement. As Issue 3 explains, there is a growing tide of American sentiment that favors limiting the role of the United States abroad, but there are also those who argue that the United States should not abandon the activist, international superpower role.

Technological changes and the shifting axes of international politics also highlight the *increased role of economics* in world politics. Economics have always played a role, but traditionally the main focus has been on strategic-political questions—especially military power. This concern still strongly exists, but it now shares the international spotlight with economic issues. One important change in recent decades has been the rapid growth of regional and global markets and the promotion of free trade and other forms of international economic interchange. As Issue 8 on GATT indicates, many people support these efforts and see them as the wave of the future. But there are others who believe that free trade undermines sovereignty and the ability of governments to regulate multinational corporations.

Another change in the world system has to do with the main *international* actors. At one time states (countries) were practically the only international actors on the world stage. Now, and increasingly so, there are other actors. Some are global actors, such as the United Nations, whose current and future role in maintaining world peace is examined in Issue 13. Other actors are regional, such as China, whose potential regional superpower status is the focus of Issue 6.

PERCEPTIONS VERSUS REALITY

In addition to addressing the general changes in the world system outlined above, the debates in this reader explore the controversies that exist over many of the fundamental issues that face the world.

One key to these debates is the differing *perceptions* that protagonists bring to them. There may be a reality in world politics, but very often that reality is obscured. Many observers, for example, are alarmed by the seeming rise in radical actions by Islamic fundamentalists. As Issue 4 illustrates, the image of Islamic radicalism is not a fact but a perception; perhaps correct, perhaps not. In cases such as this, though, it is often the perception, not the reality, that is more important because policy is formulated on what decision makers *think*, not necessarily on what *is*. Thus, perception becomes the operating guide, or *operational reality*, whether it is true or not.

Perceptions result from many factors. One factor is the information that decision makers receive. For a variety of reasons, the facts and analyses that are given to leaders are often inaccurate or at least represent only part of the picture. Perceptions are also formed by the value system of a decision maker, which is based on his or her experiences and ideology. The way in which such an individual thinks and speaks about another leader, country, or the world in general is called his or her *operational code*. Issue 3, for example, explores the role of the United States in the world. How U.S. presidents and other Americans define their country's role creates an operational code governing relations. President Bill Clinton has shown himself to have more of an internationalist operational code than the public. Clinton, for example, wanted to launch a military intervention into Bosnia and Herzegovina to assist the Muslims who were under attack by Serbian forces there. The American public was opposed to intervention in this civil war, demonstrating much less willingness than the president to cast their country in the role of defender of democracy, of human rights, or of what President George Bush called the "new world order."

Another aspect of perception is the tendency to see oneself as peacefully motivated and one's opponent as aggressive. This can lead to perceptual distortions such as an inability to understand that your actions (perceived by you as defensive) may be perceived as a threat by your opponent and, indeed, may cause your opponent to take defensive actions that, in turn, seem aggressive to you. Issue 6, for example, focuses on China and its capabilities to become an Asian superpower. Whatever China's true intention may be, there is a widespread perception that China will attempt to dominate the region. As a result, other countries in the region are building up their weapons inventories, and Asia is becoming a region of increasing military tension. Thus, perceptions could lead to conflict in Asia.

Perceptions, then, are crucial to understanding international politics. It is important to understand objective reality, but it is also necessary to comprehend subjective reality in order to be able to predict and analyze another country's actions.

LEVELS OF ANALYSIS

Political scientists approach the study of international politics from different levels of analysis. The most macroscopic view is *system-level analysis*. This is a top-down approach that maintains that world factors virtually compel countries to follow certain foreign policies. Governing factors include the number of powerful actors, geographic relationships, economic needs, and technology. System analysts hold that a country's internal political system and its leaders do not have a major impact on policy. As such, political scientists who work from this perspective are interested in exploring the governing factors, how they cause policy, and how and why systems change. The discussion of the future dimension of global conflict in Issue 18 is an example of system-level analysis

After the end of World War II, the world was structured as a *bipolar* system, dominated by the United States and the Soviet Union. Furthermore, each superpower was supported by a tightly organized and dependent group of allies. For a variety of reasons, including changing economics and the nuclear standoff, the bipolar system has faded. Some political scientists argue that the bipolar system is being replaced by a *multipolar* system. In such a configuration, those who favor *balance-of-power* politics maintain that it is unwise to ignore power considerations. The debate in Issue 3 about the future of U.S. international activity reflects the changes that have occurred in the system and the efforts of Americans to decide what role they should play in the new multipolar structure.

State-level analysis is the middle, and the most common, level of analysis. Social scientists who study world politics from this perspective focus on how countries, singly or comparatively, make foreign policy. In other words, this perspective is concerned with internal political dynamics such as the roles of and interactions between the executive and legislative branches of government, the impact of bureaucracy, the role of interest groups, and the effect of public opinion. There are a number of issues in this reader that are subject to strong domestic pressure on political leaders. To a substantial degree, whether or not the Israelis and Palestinians will be able to achieve lasting peace, as debated in Issue 5, will depend on whether or not each side can resist internal forces that are opposed to what is seen as appeasement of the enemy.

A third level of analysis, which is the most microscopic, is *human-level analysis*. This approach focuses, in part, on the role of individual decision makers. This technique is applied under the assumption that individuals make decisions and that the nature of those decisions is determined by the decision makers' perceptions, predilections, and strengths and weaknesses. Human-level analysis also focuses on the nature of humans. Issue 11 examplifies this analysis technique in that it looks into the motives of President Harry S. Truman and others who decided to drop atomic bombs on Japan in 1945.

REALISM VERSUS IDEALISM

Realism and idealism represent another division among political scientists and practitioners in their approaches to the study and conduct of international relations. *Realists* are usually skeptical about the nature of politics and, perhaps, the nature of humankind. They tend to believe that countries have opposing interests and that these differences can lead to conflict. They further contend that states (countries) are by definition obligated to do what is beneficial for their own citizens (national interest). The amount of power that a state has will determine how successful it is in attaining these goals. Therefore, politics is, and ought to be, a process of gaining, maintaining, and using power. Realists are apt to believe that the best way to avoid conflict is to remain powerful and to avoid pursuing goals that are beyond one's power to achieve. "Peace through strength" is a phrase that most realists would agree with.

Idealists disagree with realists about both the nature and conduct of international relations. They tend to be more optimistic that the global community is capable of finding ways to live in harmony and that it has a sense of collective, rather than national, interest. Idealists also claim that the pursuit of a narrow national interest is shortsighted. They argue that, in the long run, countries must learn to cooperate or face the prospect of a variety of evils, including possible nuclear warfare, environmental disaster, or continuing economic hardship. Idealists argue, for example, that armaments cause world tensions, whereas realists maintain that conflict requires states to have weapons. Idealists are especially concerned with conducting current world politics on a more moral or ethical plane and with searching for alternatives to the present pursuit of nationalist interests through power politics.

Several of the issues in this volume address the realist-idealist split. For example, the disagreement between realists and idealists on whether or not human rights considerations should play a strong role in determining foreign policy is the focus of Issue 14. In this debate, Alan Tonelson is the realist and Michael Posner is the idealist. The realist-idealist split is also reflected in Issue 15, in which Burmese democracy advocate Aung San Suu Kyi supports promoting democracy around the world, and Singapore diplomat Kishore Mahbubani opposes such promotion as culturally imperialistic.

THE POLITICAL AND ECOLOGICAL FUTURE

Future *world alternatives* are discussed in many of the issues in this volume. Issue 1, for example, debates whether or not the current world situation portends anarchy. The debate in Issue 9 on the North providing aid to the South is not just about humanitarian impulses; it is about whether or not the world can survive and be stable economically and politically if it is divided into a minority of wealthy nations and a majority of poor countries. Another, more far-reaching, alternative is if an international organization were to take over some (or all) of the sovereign responsibilities of national governments. In this vein, Issue 13 focuses on the authority of the UN Security Council to assume supranational (above countries) power in the area of peacekeeping. And Issue 8 is about the supranational authority possessed by the World Trade Organization under the recently revised GATT.

The global future also involves the ability of the world to prosper economically while, at the same time, not denuding itself of its natural resources or destroying the environment. This is the focus of Issue 20 on sustainable development.

THE AXES OF WORLD DIVISION

It is a truism that the world is politically dynamic and that the nature of the political system is undergoing profound change. As noted, the once-primary axis of world politics, the East-West confrontation, has broken down. Yet a few vestiges of the conflict on that axis remain. Issue 7 reviews the arguments for and against the United States lifting its economic sanctions against communist Cuba.

In contrast to the moribund East-West axis, the *North-South axis* has increased in importance and tension. The wealthy, industrialized countries (North) are on one end, and the poor, less developed countries (LDCs, South) are at the other extreme. Economic differences and disputes are the primary dimension of this axis, in contrast to the military nature of the East-West axis. Issue 9 explores these differences and debates whether or not the North should significantly increase economic aid to the South.

The maldistribution of wealth in the world leads many people in the impoverished South to try to emigrate, legally or illegally, to wealthier countries in an effort to find a better life for themselves and their families. The extent of this migration has caused the economically developed nations to increasingly resist the movement of people across international borders. The wisdom of severely constraining immigration is the subject of Issue 17.

Then there is the question of what, if anything, will develop to divide the countries of the North and replace the East-West axis. The possibility for tension is represented in several issues. Some believe that the remnants of the USSR, especially Russia, will one day again pose a threat to the rest of Europe. At least some of the East European countries that want to join NATO do so because of that possibility. The wisdom of expanding NATO to include these countries is debated in Issue 2. If Samuel Huntington is correct (Issue 18), then cultural divisions will form the new, multiaxial dimension of global antagonism. Expanding NATO may be one step toward the formation of one part of the axis. China, dominating parts of Southeast Asia (contemplated in Issue 6), and politically resurgent Muslims (as discussed in Issue 4) could become coherent powers themselves.

INCREASED ROLE OF ECONOMICS

As the growing importance of the North-South axis indicates, economics are playing an increased role in world politics. The economic reasons behind the decline of the East-West axis is further evidence. Economics have always played a part in international relations, but the traditional focus has been on strategic-political affairs, especially questions of military power.

Political scientists, however, are now increasingly focusing on the international political economy, or the economic dimensions of world politics. International trade, for instance, has increased dramatically, expanding from an annual world total of $20 billion in 1933 to $3.5 trillion in 1993. The impact has been profound. The domestic economic health of most countries is heavily affected by trade and other aspects of international economics. Since World War II, there has been an emphasis on expanding free trade by decreasing tariffs and other barriers to international commerce. In recent years, however, a downturn in the economies of many of the industrialized countries has increased calls for more protectionism. This is related to the debate in Issue 8 on GATT. Yet restrictions trade and other economic activity can also be used as diplomatic weapons. This is discussed in Issue 7 on the U.S. economic embargo against Cuba and in Issue 16 on whether or not economic sanctions and other methods should be used to punish Serbia for its part in the Balkan conflict.

The level and impact of international aid is another economic issue of considerable dispute. Issue 9 examines the question of whether massive foreign aid would help the less developed countries (and the developed countries as well) or actually hinder economic progress in the less developed countries.

Another economic issue is whether or not the environment can withstand current and increased levels of economic activity. For people in industrialized countries, the issue is whether or not they can sustain current standards of living without consuming unsustainable levels of energy and other resources or creating unsustainable levels of pollution. For people in less developed countries, the issue is whether or not they can develop their economies and reach the standard of living enjoyed by people in wealthy countries without creating vast new drains on resources and vast new amounts of pollution. This concern is at the core of the debate in Issue 10.

CONCLUSION

Having discussed many of the various dimensions and approaches to the study of world politics, it is incumbent on this editor to advise against your becoming too structured by them. Issues of focus and methodology are important both to studying international relations and to understanding how others are analyzing global conduct. However, they are also partially pedagogical. In the final analysis, world politics is a highly interrelated, perhaps seamless, subject. No one level of analysis, for instance, can fully explain the events on the world stage. Instead, using each of the levels to analyze events and trends will bring the greatest understanding.

Similarly, the realist-idealist division is less precise in practice than it may appear. As some of the debates indicate, each side often stresses its own standards of morality. Which is more moral: defeating dictatorship or sparing the sword and saving lives that will almost inevitably be lost in the dictator's overthrow? Furthermore, realists usually do not reject moral considerations. Rather, they contend that morality is but one of the factors that a country's decision makers must consider. Realists are also apt to argue that standards of morality differ when dealing with a country as opposed to an individual. By the same token, most idealists do not completely ignore the often dangerous nature of the world. Nor do they argue that a country must totally sacrifice its short-term interests to promote the betterment of the current and future world. Thus, realism and idealism can be seen most accurately as the ends of a continuum—with most political scientists and practitioners falling somewhere between, rather than at, the extremes. The best advice, then, is this: think broadly about international politics. The subject is very complex, and the more creative and expansive you are in selecting your foci and methodologies, the more insight you will gain. To end where we began, with Dr. Faust, I offer his last words in Goethe's drama, *"Mehr licht,"* ... More light! That is the goal of this book.

PART 1

Regional Issues and Actors

The issues in this section deal with countries that are major regional powers. In this era of interdependence among nations, it is important to understand the concerns that these issues address and the actors involved because they will shape the world and will affect the lives of all people.

- Has the World Become a More Dangerous Place Since the End of the Cold War?

- Is It Wise to Admit East European Countries into NATO?

- Should the United States Abandon Its Superpower Role?

- Is Islamic Fundamentalism a Threat to Political Stability?

- Will the Israelis and Palestinians Be Able to Achieve Lasting Peace?

- Will China Become an Asian Superpower?

- Should the U.S. Economic Embargo Against Cuba Be Lifted?

ISSUE 1

Has the World Become a More Dangerous Place Since the End of the Cold War?

YES: Patrick Glynn, from "The Age of Balkanization," *Commentary* (July 1993)

NO: Francis Fukuyama, from "Against the New Pessimism," *Commentary* (February 1994)

ISSUE SUMMARY

YES: Patrick Glynn, a resident scholar at the American Enterprise Institute and a former official in the U.S. Arms Control and Disarmament Agency, contends that post–cold war political and social fragmentation is destabilizing countries and making the world a more dangerous place.

NO: Francis Fukuyama, a resident consultant at the RAND Corporation and a former State Department official, argues that the current period of post–cold war instability does not necessarily mean that we face a more dangerous future.

The first half of the 1990s was truly remarkable. The world watched in amazement as the Soviet Union's empire in Eastern Europe disintegrated, and then as the communist and authoritarian political system of the USSR itself collapsed into 15 different countries and disappeared. For nearly three-quarters of a century, the communist Soviet Union had seemed to most in the West to loom threateningly. For 45 years an East-West rivalry had locked the Soviet Union and the United States, both militarily mighty and ideologically hostile toward each other, and their respective allies in a seeming death struggle. The two alliances never engaged one another directly in combat, or a hot war. Still, the struggle was so intense and so potentially apocalyptic, given the two superpowers' nuclear arsenals, that *cold war* became the accepted term to describe the tensions that gripped international relations.

And then the foreboding was gone! The Soviet flag was lowered from atop the Kremlin in Moscow, and the Russian flag was raised in its stead. Russian president Boris Yeltsin pledged democracy and peace with the United States. The cold war is over, U.S. president George Bush told a national audience, and the Americans have won. The world seemed so much safer. There were pledges of friendship from the capitals of most of the former enemies as well as several new arms control initiatives and treaties. There were moves in the United States and elsewhere to slash defense spending. And people debated how to spend the surplus funds, the so-called peace dividend.

There was also great optimism about changing the world system for the better. As President Bush put it at the time, "A new world order [is] struggling to be born . . . where the rule of law supplants the rule of the jungle. A world in which nations recognize the shared responsibility for freedom and justice. A world where the strong respect the rights of the weak."

Not everyone was so hopeful. Scholar John Mearsheimer, for one, in "Why We Will Soon Miss the Cold War," *The Atlantic Monthly* (August 1990), warned that we would one day look back nostalgically at the stability of the cold war. His view was determined in part by the view of many political scientists who theorize that when there are changes in the number of major powers (called poles) in the international system, or a significant shift in the strength of one or more of the poles, then several destabilizing trends may occur. One is that rising powers and declining powers may clash over territory, control of resources, or other matters. Second, areas once dominated by a fading power may fall into uncontrolled rivalries once the declining power's influence dissipates.

Soon after the cold war ended, the more dire image of the future projected by Mearsheimer and others seemed to come to pass. Nationalism was the most common cause of conflict around the world. Several of the 15 republics that established their independence by seceding from the Soviet Union now face their own secessionist movements. Elsewhere, the efforts of Kurds to break away from Iraq (and other surrounding countries), fighting between Muslims in the north of the Sudan and non-Muslims in the south, clashes among Bosnians, Croats, and Serbs in the former Yugoslavia, clan warfare in Somalia, tribal violence between Hutus and Tutsis in Rwanda, and other bloodletting have shocked the world. Such national and ethnic-based rivalries are, in the view of some analysts, part of a greater pattern of fragmentation that threatens to destroy the domestic social fabric of many countries. Whether the differences are based on race, gender, religion, language, or some other characteristic, numerous commentators argue that the national political systems that have so long been at the center of domestic order and a primary aspect of the international system are in danger of disintegrating.

There can be little doubt that there is instability in the international system as it seeks a new equilibrium. What is not certain, and what is the subject of this debate, is whether or not the current state of affairs is long-term and should make us relatively pessimistic about future global stability. Patrick Glynn and Francis Fukuyama take up this debate. Glynn argues that the world is becoming politically and socially fragmented and therefore unstable. Fukuyama contends that if we look beyond immediate distressing events, we need not be pessimistic about the future.

YES

Patrick Glynn

THE AGE OF BALKANIZATION

Today a fundamental change is under way in the character of global political life. A new era is in the making. Gone or fading are the great bipolar conflicts —between democracy and fascism, between democracy and Communism, and even perhaps between Left and Right—that shaped war and peace in the 20th century. In their place a new political struggle is emerging—more complex, more diffuse, but nonetheless global in character.

On every continent, in almost every major nation, and in almost every walk of life the overriding political reality today is that of increasing social separatism and fragmentation—a sometimes violent splintering of humanity by ethnic group, race, religion, and even (to a less dramatic extent) such characteristics as gender or sexual orientation. While the causes of this phenomenon are as yet imperfectly understood, its implications could hardly be more far-reaching.

The most dramatic manifestation of the change is found, of course, in the countries that used to be known as Yugoslavia and Czechoslovakia, and it is also showing itself in other parts of the defunct Soviet empire, not to mention the old Soviet Union itself. But the phenomenon is not merely one of Communism giving way to nationalism, nor is it confined to the old Communist world.

Indeed, everywhere one sees well-established nation-states threatened with disunion, and even in countries without explicit separatist movements, the unifying themes of political life are increasingly under attack. Canada copes with Quebec's secessionism, the United Kingdom with Scottish separatists, Italy with increasing tensions between its north and its south. In Germany, as well as in France and Britain, ethnically motivated violence has become a major factor in politics, and rebellious youths are inflamed by a puzzling new ideology of ethnic hatred.

Even in America—the proverbial melting pot—racial, ethnic, and other varieties of separatism are distinctly on the rise. Blacks assert their identity as "African-Americans"; homosexuals discover in their sexual orientation a basis for political action; Christian fundamentalists exert more and more influence as an organized political force.

Nor is this phenomenon merely political. It also finds its reflection in the highest reaches of contemporary culture and intellectual life. The controversial doctrine of "multiculturalist education" and the "postmodernist" philosophy now so current in American universities are both essentially codifications of the new experience of fragmentation.

Side by side with this splintering, paradoxically, has gone a fresh drive for unity. As the cold war was ending, George Bush, then still in the White House, hailed the advent of a Europe "whole and free," and in the lead-up to the Gulf war he spoke hopefully of a "new world order." Since then, European Community leaders have worked to forge a unitary Europe, while Germany's leadership has sought to make one nation out of two. In Russia, Boris Yeltsin fights a parallel battle, desperately trying to hold Russia together while moving toward democracy in the face of radical nationalism and mounting pressures for regional secession.

But these efforts at unification—including the effort to posit a new world order based on common democratic values—have thus far proved unable to stem the powerful counter-currents rooted in separatist identities. For this new cultural struggle is taking place not only within nations, but among them. Attempts to expand the postwar liberal trading order have been frustrated by intensified cultural conflict between America and Japan and, to a lesser extent, between America and Western Europe. Islamic fundamentalism poses a threat to moderate Arab regimes and increases the likelihood of eventual armed conflict between the West and radical Arab states.

Slowly this clash between, on the one hand, ethnic (and other types of) particularism and, on the other hand, what might be called democratic universalism seems to be replacing the old Left-Right and class polarities that have governed political life for nearly a century. It has every appearance of becoming the new bipolarity of global politics, the new dialectic of a new age.

*   *   *

What are the reasons for this great shift? The most obvious cause would seem to lie in the collapse of Soviet Communism. Communism repressed national differences; indeed, Marxist-Leninist ideology, rooted as it was in Enlightenment economic thinking, defined national and ethnic differences as epiphenomenal, stressing instead the primacy of class. Under Communism, nationalism was either disguised or stifled.

What we have seen since the breakdown of Communism—whether in the former Soviet Union, the former Yugoslavia, or the rest of Eastern Europe—is, to borrow a phrase from Sigmund Freud, a "return of the repressed," a resurgence of powerful national and ethnic feelings which had been simmering angrily beneath the surface.

But if Communist regimes ruthlessly imposed unity on their own peoples, they also evoked a more or less united response from the outside world they threatened. The unitary nature of the Communist threat inspired an unprecedented degree of cooperation—under American leadership—among heretofore uncooperative states. European adversaries laid aside age-old grudges to join NATO. New security relationships were forged among the United States and major Asian nations, including Japan.

To be sure, Woodrow Wilson and Franklin Roosevelt had earlier sought on their own initiative to structure a more or less unified world order, to export America's stated principles of ethnic tolerance, and to bring the many nations of the world together on the basis of common interests and goals. But it is far from clear that, absent the Soviet threat, so many disparate nations would have been so successful in achieving collaboration, not just on trade but on a host of diplomatic and security matters, as they were during the cold war. Long ago the sociologist Georg Simmel posited that human societies were cemented together by the need to cope with outside threats. This was clearly true of what we used to call the "free world."

Even within American politics, the anti-Communist imperative had a powerful unifying effect. It produced, albeit intermittently, bipartisanship in foreign policy. It also, at various times, unified each of the two major parties. In the early years of the cold war, the Democrats, and in the later years, the Republicans, found a basis for party solidarity in the anti-Communist cause. So much was this the case that when the Democrats and then the Republicans experienced ruinous internal division, it was owing in part to a perceived or real diminution of the Soviet threat—for the Democrats during the late 1960's and early 1970's, when many believed the cold war to have become obsolete, and for the Republicans in recent years, when it became plain that the cold war was in fact over.

The Republican case is especially interesting, for what else but fear of the Soviet threat could finally have held together the diverse elements of Ronald Reagan's winning electoral coalition: Christian fundamentalists, Jewish neoconservative intellectuals, free-market libertarians, blue-collar Democrats, and

traditional Republican voters? Should it surprise us that with the subsidence of the Soviet threat, old party alignments would weaken? Is it illogical that with external dangers reduced we would turn inward as a society and discover social and political differences among one another that we had previously been willing to overlook?

Yet while the collapse of Soviet Communism remains the signal event of our age, many of the trends we are discussing were apparent before the Berlin Wall came down. Ethnic, national, and racial awareness was already growing, on both sides of the iron curtain. Here in America, for example, the multiculturalist movement—now so famous and controversial for its advocacy of heightened ethnic and racial consciousness in schools —was already making inroads into secondary and higher education. On both sides of the iron curtain, faith in central authority was declining and had been declining for some time. Even before the advent of Mikhail Gorbachev, Western Sovietologists debated whether Communist leaders still actually believed their ideology. Ironically, a weakening in the influence of received values—society's traditional unifying ideas—was apparent in our own culture as well, observed by intellectuals and documented by opinion polls.

* * *

In other words, it is hard to say whether the demise of Soviet Communism is the ultimate cause of the change we are witnessing, or whether Soviet Communism itself fell victim to some vaster trend, some grand Hegelian shift in human consciousness.

Certainly the contemporary experience of social and political fragmentation was foreshadowed by new directions in intellectual life, long before the social consequences were apparent. One of the major proponents of "postmodernist" thinking, Fredric Jameson of Duke University, has written of the postmodern idiom in contemporary literature:

Perhaps the immense fragmentation and privatization of modern literature —its explosion into a host of distinct private styles and mannerisms— foreshadow deeper and more general trends in social life as a whole. Supposing that modern art and modernism—far from being a kind of specialized aesthetic curiosity—actually anticipated social developments along these lines; supposing that in the decades since the emergence of the great modern styles of society has itself begun to fragment in this way, each group coming to speak a curious private language of its own, each profession developing its own private code or idiolect, and finally each individual coming to be a kind of linguistic island, separated from everyone else?

Behind this new experience of cultural and intellectual fragmentation lies a loss of faith in general truths, and even, at its most radical, a loss of faith in the very possibility of general truths. Notably, the most sophisticated humanities instructors in our major universities today will no longer venture to assert that a proposition is "true," merely that it is "productive" or "intriguing," i.e., a basis for reflection or intellectual play. This premise lends a notable arbitrariness to "postmodern" modes of expression, robbing contemporary literature, criticism, and even philosophy of a certain weight, authority, or seriousness.

The same mixture of posturing and pastiche has become evident in our political discourse (think back to Bush's Gulf war speeches). However glorious the phrases—"freedom," "tyranny," "new world order"—they are uttered today with a certain self-conscious nostalgia.

We have lived through an era when people attached themselves to grand ideas—whether for good or for evil—and fought and sometimes died for them. But for some reason these ideas collectively seem to be losing their force. Such is the defining tendency of our age.

The resulting fragmentation is far from being a propitious development. At stake, one could argue, is the future of civilization itself. The struggle for civilization has always been a struggle for unity, universality, ecumenism. The great ages of civilization have been periods of concord and commonality, when large tracts of the globe were more or less united by common values, and sometimes even by a common language and common laws—the Roman empire, the era of Charlemagne, the Renaissance, the 19th-century Concert of Europe. These periods have been succeeded in turn by periods of fragmentation, factional strife, and relative barbarism: the Dark Ages, the feudal era, the Reformation with its religious wars, and of course the long "civil war" that wrenched Europe between 1914 and 1945. Looking back, one can see that Western history has been marked by a cyclical pattern in which unifying ideas triumph, only gradually to lose their hold on the imagination and to be replaced by factional struggle and particularism.

It is possible that we are on the threshold of a new such cyclical turn.

* * *

At the root of the problem lies the very large and very deep question of human identity. In a sense, the master-idea of Western civilization is the view that the identifying feature of the human being qua [as] human being is the faculty of reason. When the Greek philosophers hit upon this notion of man as the rational animal, they made possible the creation of large political orders on a basis other than that of pure despotism.

Furthermore, as Socrates and his students saw, this conception transcended differences of nationality and race: rational man could not be defined as Athenian or Spartan or even Greek or barbarian. And with this insight, the philosophers ceased to be good citizens of their cities, their *poleis*, at least in the terms of those cities: they became citizens of the rational universe—to use a somewhat later term, cosmopolitans—and they challenged the laws and gods of their fellow citizens....

Periods when [the classical idea of rational man] is in the ascendancy have been the great periods of civilization as we in the West know it. It is during such periods that peace reigns, learning spreads and advances, and the arts flourish. Yet experience shows that this idea does not hold indefinitely.

Perhaps the reason simply has to do with the inherent restlessness of human beings. When it first appears on the scene, the idea of rational man has a demythologizing force; it is an exploder of myth. Socrates' notion of rational man was subversive of the laws, customs, and gods of Athens—which is why he was condemned to death by his fellow citizens. Roman law, too, was subversive of local traditions and local religions; it was the "modern" idea of its era. The Renaissance was anti-traditional in the same sense—introducing ideas from the classics that raised questions about Christian beliefs.

Perhaps human beings have an overriding need for myth, or perhaps the act of demythologization always contains within it the seeds of its own destruction. At any rate, periods of demythologization tend to be followed by periods of remythologization....

Remythologization and reversion to ethnic particularism have tended to go hand in hand. People cease to find satisfactory selfhood in large unities, become alienated from the larger whole, and begin to seek identity in smaller units. Such periods are characterized by diminished will on the part of those who stand for reason to defend reason, by a diminished appeal of reason to the human imagination. Civilization is destroyed by those whose attachment to religious or ethnic identity gives them the zeal which the defenders of reason come to lack. Civilization falls victim to barbarians from without and zealots from within. In such periods, as Yeats famously wrote, "The best lack all conviction, while the worst/ Are full of passionate intensity."

* * *

There are hints of all this in the emerging mood of our own time. The ferocious war in the Balkans is but one manifestation of a reemergent barbarism apparent in many corners of the earth. In the Balkans, the voices of the rational and the tolerant—for example, officials of the secular-minded Bosnian government— have been drowned out by the guns of ethnic fanatics. Efforts to secure democracy on the basis of rational Western principles have been crushed by the bloodthirsty exponents of "ethnic cleansing."

The new barbarians differ fundamentally from the old enemies of liberal democracy in feeling no need to justify themselves before the court of reason. The Communists, too, practiced barbarism, but they harbored a powerful imperative to vindicate themselves on the basis of some general truth: hence their elaborate ideology. Paradoxically, it was to prove they had the truth that they fashioned huge tissues of lies. Much the same was true of the Nazis, who invented the technique of the Big Lie.

The new tyrants—such characters as Slobodan Milosevic, Radovan Karadzic [both are Serbs], or for that matter Saddam Hussein—feel no such pressures. They offer as justification for their actions the thinnest pretexts. Their explanations are less an appeal to reason than a pure gesture of defiance.

Precisely because these tyrants lack intellectual seriousness, we are likely to discount them. But we forget that the great ideological struggle that characterized most of our century was the exception rather than the rule in history. Usually the enemies of civilization have not been so intellectually well-armed as the Communists (and even, in their way, the Nazis) were; but despite this they have often succeeded in prevailing. The once-mighty Romans, after all, were finally defeated by forces culturally, intellectually, and technologically inferior to them....

Nor is this problem merely one of foreign policy or regional conflict. The very idea of rational man—the cardinal concept of our civilization—is, as we have already seen, under explicit attack in our own universities. Our students are today being taught that such categories as "African-American," "female," or "person of color" are in effect more fundamental than the category of American, let alone of rational man, the human being qua [as] human being.

While the motives and consequences may be vastly different in the two cases, the multiculturalist doctrine that is fragmenting our universities as well as our intellectual life, and the "ethnic cleansing" of the Serbs, belong to the same troubling cultural and historical moment.

It is especially disturbing that this should be happening here, for America has always been the most rationally constituted of nations. It is the heir and perfecter of the great Roman idea of the *civis*, a country where nationality has nothing to do with ethnicity, a nation which has fought, through civil war and great domestic turmoil, to realize, however imperfectly, the principle of universality and tolerance.

We are now in an age that will move either toward ever greater fragmentation and violence or toward the ever wider spread of the tolerance and rationality by which we in the West have learned to live and prosper. As was true for most of this century, it is American leadership that will determine the path that history finally takes.

NO

Francis Fukuyama

AGAINST THE NEW PESSIMISM

The end of the cold war has brought about a remarkable consensus between former hawks and doves—at least those professionally involved in some fashion with international affairs, whether they be journalists, academics, or politicians—to the effect that the world has become a much worse place since the demise of the Soviet Union. The pessimistic analysis runs roughly as follows:

In 1989, with the fall of the Berlin Wall, everyone was filled with euphoria over the collapse of Communism and believed that the entire world was turning to democracy. But this expectation proved extraordinarily naive: the collapse of Communism led not to democracy but to the unleashing of virulent nationalism and/or religious passion. Now, about four years later, we see that the world is not progressing toward the "global village" but retreating into atavistic tribalism, whose ugliest expression is the "ethnic cleansing" witnessed in Bosnia.

Nor, according to the pessimistic account, is the former Yugoslavia an isolated case. Rather, Yugoslavia demonstrates that modernity is a very thin veneer indeed; what has happened there portends the resurgence of ethnic passions throughout Eastern Europe and the former USSR. And not just in that region. Even among the apparently stable democracies of Western Europe, attacks on foreign residents and immigrants are just the tip of a larger racist iceberg.

Our international institutions, by this same account, are woefully inadequate to the job of maintaining global order. The United Nations, which many people hoped would become far more effective after the cold war than it was in the days of the Soviet veto, has gotten overextended and is now presiding over policy failures in Bosnia, Somalia, and Haiti. The fecklessness of the European Community (EC) and NATO in failing to stop the slaughter in Bosnia shows how laughable was George Bush's concept of a "new world order." Instead of order we have a world far more dangerous and insecure than that of the cold war. Just as in 1914—so the pessimists conclude—the Balkans in our own day may serve as the tinderbox for a larger European conflict.

This litany, promoted by media and academic pundits around the world, makes the present situation sound very, very bad indeed. But I would argue that it misses the deeper reality of the contemporary situation, and vastly exaggerates the problems we face.

One reason it does so is that the pessimistic outlook is held primarily by Europeans or by Americans focused on European affairs, and represents a highly Eurocentric view. For a "return to tribalism" is not a helpful formula for understanding much of the rest of the world.

* * *

Let us begin at home. After having come through a bruising recession, the United States now leads the industrialized world in economic growth, hitting a rate of close to 4 percent in the fourth quarter of 1993. This latest recession performed the positive function of all recessions: it forced corporations to trim fat and focus on productivity, leaving American companies leaner and more competitive than they have ever been (albeit at a cost in certain jobs). Many of the productivity-enhancing innovations introduced in the 1980's, mostly related to information and communications technology, are now finally showing up on corporate bottom lines, particularly in the service sector. Who today would trade the American semiconductor, computer, aerospace, banking, or biotech industries for their Japanese counterparts? Or, for that matter, the American automobile industry for the German one?

As Henry S. Rowen of Stanford has pointed out, the new reality of the 21st century is that many poor people around the world are going to get rich. This is nowhere more true than in Asia, a region

that is hardly descending into tribal violence. Its problems are, rather, ones of adjustment to newfound prosperity. China, the world's largest country, grew an astonishing 13 percent in 1993, and every other country in the region (with the exception of Japan) forged ahead at comparable rates despite the recessions in other parts of the world.

Just as the proponents of modernization theory predicted in the 1950's, democracy has been following in the wake of economic development: the election of Kim Young Sam in South Korea last year represents a final break with that country's authoritarian past, while Taiwan will hold its first completely free elections in the near future. The most remarkable development is occurring in Japan. Despite Karel Van Wolferen's protestations that nothing ever changes in Japan, the Japanese political system is slowly moving away from the corrupt machine politics of the past couple of generations toward a more genuinely pluralistic democracy.

There are, it is true, serious security problems in Asia, the most important being North Korea's nuclear program. Further, the whole region will have to adjust to a very large and dynamic China, which in a decade may have an impact on regional politics comparable to the emergence of a unified Germany after 1871. But the likelihood seems low that in ten years China will still be a unitary, purposeful, authoritarian superpower with external ambitions, given the massive and rapid socioeconomic transformation it is now undergoing. A fragmenting or unstable China would also cause serious problems for the region, but not a balance-of-power threat.

In general, the character of internal relations in East Asia is remarkably different from that of Europe: security concerns have for some time now taken a back seat to economic issues as the chief preoccupation of the region's best minds. This perhaps explains why the countries most directly threatened by North Korean nuclear weapons—South Korea and Japan, as well as China— are decidedly more relaxed about the problem than is the distant United States. They believe that North Korea is one of the world's weakest states, economically and politically, and they maintain that its erratic behavior is the product of weakness rather than strength. Since time is working against the Kim Il Sung regime, it is in their view better dealt with through patience.

Finally, Latin America's prospects look brighter than at any time since the first decades of the century. Despite recent setbacks in Haiti and Venezuela, three of the region's large economies—those of Chile, Mexico, and Argentina—have liberalized substantially over the past decade, and have experienced low inflation and high growth. The code to economic development—a liberal one— has been cracked (or, more properly, relearned after decades of Marxist and Keynesian confusion), and those countries that have mustered the political will to follow its dictates are being rewarded.

Indeed, one of the great slanders of last fall's debate on the North American Free Trade Agreement (NAFTA) was Ross Perot's assertion that Mexicans were desperately poor people who could not afford to buy anything. In the next generation, Americans will have to get used to thinking about Mexico not as a political and economic basket case, but as an avid consumer and increasingly aggressive competitor. Even Peru, by most measures one of the world's most troubled countries, has seen a flood of new investment and positive economic growth since the Fujimori government's arrest of Abimael Guzman, the leader of the Shining Path guerrilla movement. With the passage of NAFTA and the successful conclusion of the Uruguay round of the General Agreement on Tariffs and Trade (GATT), the foundations have been laid for another generation of economic growth in Latin America.

* * *

Now let us turn to Europe. There, it is clear, nationalism and ethnic violence *have* been worse than anyone expected four years ago. Civil or interstate wars have been raging in Georgia, Azerbaijan, and Tajikistan, with many other potential conflicts just beneath the surface. But the chief indictment of the new world order centers, of course, on Bosnia, a horror the like of which has not been seen in Europe since the Holocaust.

The Bosnian conflict has four possible implications for the broader security of Europe. The first is that the war there could spread and involve other Balkan countries, and then the great powers of Europe. The second is that Yugoslavia will set an encouraging precedent for new conflicts among other intertwined ethnic groups in the former Communist world —Hungarians and Romanians, Poles and Lithuanians, Russians and Ukrainians. The third is that ethnic cleansing will legitimate racial and ethnic intolerance even in the apparently stable democracies of Western Europe, undermining their political fabric at a particularly delicate moment. And lastly, the ineffectiveness of international organizations like the EC, NATO, and the UN in dealing with the Yugoslav crisis will damage their credibility and encourage further aggression.

These fears are real, and should not be dismissed lightly. On the other hand, each one can and has been greatly overstated.

Take the question of escalation. The scenarios by which the Yugoslav civil war could lead to a larger conflagration tend to be rather nebulous. Other Balkan countries could indeed get involved if conflict spreads to the Serbian province of Kosovo, or to Macedonia. But of the interested outside powers, Albania—Europe's poorest and most backward country—wields virtually no power, while Greece would likely side with Serbia in crushing Macedonian independence.

Far more important than local Balkan considerations, however, is the absence of a larger great-power rivalry in Europe. In 1914, Europe was divided between two hostile alliances, and if war had not broken out over the Balkans, it could just as well have been sparked by Tangier or the Baghdad Railway. Today, the great powers of Europe are, if anything, struggling to avoid messy foreign entanglements as they try to deal with pressing domestic economic problems. Regional conflicts were of concern during the cold war because the superpower competition left open the constant possibility of superpower intervention and ultimately escalation. But the absence today of larger great-power rivalries means that sectional strife will remain regionalized in its impact, however horrendous the consequences may be for local populations. The ironic result is that even as the world is being united through communications technology, it is being regionalized and *dis*connected politically by the absence of a global great-power rivalry.

The second fear, that the Yugoslav example will be replicated among other ethnic groups, has already been realized in many places. But most of these conflicts, such as those in Transcaucasia and Central Asia, can and have been safely ignored by the outside world. (The only one that will pose direct security concerns for Europe is between Russia and Ukraine, an issue that will be dealt with below.)

The truth is that the mutual hatred of Yugoslavia's constituent groups is in many respects an extreme and atypical situation, and other parts of Eastern Europe look much less bleak. Economically, recent news is encouraging. Virtually all East European countries that have engaged in shock therapy or some variant of radical market reform have seen their inflation rates come down and their production bottom out and then rebound. Poland's GNP stopped falling in the second half of 1992 and is now rapidly on the way up. While recent elections in Poland brought back to power a left-wing coalition including the former Communists, this does not represent a rejection of reform so much as a desire to modulate its pace. Hungary, the Czech Republic, Slovakia, Slovenia, Lithuania, and Latvia are similarly poised for economic turnarounds, much like Western Europe in the early 1950's.

* * *

The third fear—that Bosnia will undermine tolerance and democracy in Western Europe—is supported by the wave of anti-immigrant violence in Germany, Italy, France, and most recently Austria. Nevertheless, the embourgeoisement of West Europeans has gone very far, and their situation is quite different from that of the rural Serbs and Croats driving the current struggle in Yugoslavia. If one scratches the typical Italian, German, or Frenchman of today, one is unlikely to find a vicious nationalist itching to come out. Such individuals certainly exist in Western Europe, but they have thus far been segregated at the margins of their societies. With any degree of sensible leadership, and in the absence of new discontinuities like war or depression, there is no reason to think they will not remain there.

The fourth and final fear concerns the weakness of international institutions in dealing with the war in Yugoslavia. The international community's single most important failure was actually an error of commission rather than omission—that is, the placing of a UN arms embargo on all the combatants in the civil war, and the subsequent failure to lift it so as to give the Bosnian Muslims a chance to defend themselves. An early ending of the embargo was the only policy option that had a chance of stopping Serb aggression at a reasonable cost to the outside world, and the fact that it was so bitterly opposed by the Europeans and so weakly advocated by the United States is both a moral failure and a political mystery.

On the other hand, the failure of various international organizations to intervene actively to promote order in the ways suggested by some does not reflect impotence so much as prudence. It is not self-evident that multinational, or even single-country organizations can intervene effectively and at reasonable cost in many conflicts that are primarily ethnic and/or civil in nature. Those, like Anthony Lewis of the *New York Times*, who argue that appeasement of Serbia encouraged the nationalists in Russia to vote for Vladimir Zhirinovsky in last December's parliamentary election should consider what lessons would have been drawn from a *failed* Western intervention.

The UN cannot function as a serious security organization except when it acts as a cover for unilateral American intervention, as in Korea or the Gulf. It has gotten into trouble in Somalia and Haiti because it did indeed outrun its mandate. As for NATO, it is an effective security organization, but primarily in those canonical big-war scenarios for which it was originally designed. Those who want to extend NATO's functions to include ethnic peacekeeping and the like seriously risk involving it in contingencies for which it is not particularly well suited, thereby unintentionally subverting its ability to execute tasks it is better able to perform. It is true that the world community does not have an effective instrument to promote order and security in regions like Eastern Europe today; but if the chance of escalation is low, this lack will not be critical.

* * *

The gloomy Europeanist assessment of the implications of ethnic conflict would be more cogent if there were an ongoing great-power rivalry. And in fact, many do postulate that one exists, latently if not overtly. Thus, a view is currently coalescing that Russia is well under way toward restoring the old union, using the cause of ethnic Russians stranded in the "near abroad" by the breakup of the Soviet Union to bully and threaten the other Soviet successor states. Some, like Zbigniew Brzezinski, believe it is almost inevitable that President Boris Yeltsin will fall and that Moscow will go back to its authoritarian, expansionist ways. Others, like Henry Kissinger, believe that Yeltsin himself harbors great-power yearnings, while analysts like William Odom argue that Yeltsin has already sold his soul to the Russian military in return for its support in his showdown with parliament....

Ultimately, those who take a jaundiced view of Russian intentions have already written off Yeltsin's democratic experiment. They argue—with much plausibility—that the political situation in Russia is unlikely to stabilize, or the economy to turn around, or democratic institutions to start putting down roots any time soon. Yet the policy question the United States faces is whether *we* want to be the ones to turn out the lights, especially when the new constitution adopted last December at least clears the way for a hyper-presidential regime that has some chance of promoting economic reform and a moderate foreign policy.

* * *

At any given historical moment there are always ominous clouds on the horizon. The current nightmares of specialists in international relations—nationalism or fundamentalism run amok; immigration; a growing gap between rich and poor countries; uncontrolled nuclear proliferation; and the like—many not be as dangerous as they are portrayed. Others less discussed may be more urgent....

* * *

It would be very surprising if the collapse of the largest empire in the world had not caused enormous instability and confusion. We are obviously in the midst of a prolonged transition period as political, economic, and interstate systems transform themselves into something else. But it is vital not to take transitional turbulence for a permanent state of affairs, or to ignore the elements of order that exist while focusing on extreme cases of disorder in relatively unimportant parts of the world.

To be sure, it is primarily specialists in international affairs who are pessimistic; others, like investment bankers, who have to put money on the line behind their views of world order, tend to be much more sanguine. But among people professionally involved with international affairs, the liberals tend to be unhappy with the idea that the West won the ideological struggle of the cold war outright, and are eager to assert that the vindication of capitalism and liberal democracy is only apparent. Many conservatives, for their part, remain wedded to a dour view both of human nature and human institutions.

And then there is a simple matter of prudence: who, liberal or conservative, would not find it safer to be remembered as a Cassandra than as a Pollyanna? A Cassandra proved wrong (and there are many of them populating our TV talk shows and newspaper columns) is never held accountable; indeed, such people retain an aura of moral seriousness for their tragic sense of human history. Naive Pollyannas, by contrast, are routinely held up to ridicule. In the stock market, those who are unduly bearish are punished over the long run. The "market" for views on international affairs is, unfortunately, not quite so self-correcting.

POSTSCRIPT

Has the World Become a More Dangerous Place Since the End of the Cold War?

The international system is undergoing a significant shift. The debate among political scientists of the impact of such shifts on stability is extensive and can be reviewed, in part, by consulting Manus I. Midlarsky, "Polarity and International Stability: Comment," and Ted Hopf, "Polarity and International Stability: Reply," *American Political Science Review* (March 1993).

Is the world more dangerous in the post–cold war era? That depends on your assessment of various threats. Surely, there is more local instability in many regions, as the events in Bosnia, Rwanda, and elsewhere attest. Even the peaceful dismemberment of countries is unsettling to some. For an overview of how the system operates in a "lawless" environment, read Hedley Bull, *The Anarchical Society* (Columbia University Press, 1995) and James N. Rosenau, *Turbulence in World Politics: A Theory of Change and Continuity* (Princeton University Press, 1992). Turning to the future, the view that a new, more orderly world order is not in the offing is the theme of Hans-Henrik Hold and Gerog Sorenson, eds., *Whose World Order: Uneven Globalization and the End of the Cold War* (Westview Press, 1995).

Also certain, at least for now, is that the threat of a potentially civilization-ending nuclear exchange between the United States and its allies and the former Soviet Union and its allies has declined considerably. It is also possible to argue that democracy and other positive approaches to governance are spreading, albeit slowly and unevenly, around the world. For this view, see Tony Smith, *America's Mission: The United States and the World Wide Struggle for Democracy in the Twentieth Century* (Princeton University Press, 1995).

A related and important question is whether the future will be dark or bright. That depends. It depends in part on individuals and in part on whole populations of people. Many of the issues that need to be addressed to promote a hopeful future involve two main questions: How active internationally should each country be, and what role should each country take (unilaterally or collectively in association with the United Nations) to maintain or restore stability? Related issues involve how much monetary aid to give to help promote stability, the future desirability of nuclear weapons, and others. There is a great deal of uncertainty in the world; whether it will be more or less dangerous than what we experienced during the cold war depends in significant part on what we do to promote or allow instability, on the one hand, or to secure the peace, on the other.

ISSUE 2

Is It Wise to Admit East European Countries into NATO?

YES: Zbigniew Brzezinski, from "A Plan for Europe," *Foreign Affairs* (January/February 1995)

NO: Michael E. Brown, from "The Flawed Logic of NATO Expansion," *Survival: The IISS Quarterly* (Spring 1995)

ISSUE SUMMARY

YES: Zbigniew Brzezinski, a professor of foreign policy, argues that U.S. support of an expanded NATO will allow it to help shape a peaceful Europe in the future.

NO: Michael E. Brown, a fellow of the Center for Science and International Affairs at Harvard University, contends that the risks and costs associated with expanding NATO in the immediate future outweigh any possible advantages that could be gained.

The North Atlantic Treaty Organization (NATO) is a military alliance that was established in 1949. The alliance consists of the United States, Canada, 13 Western European countries, and Turkey. The initial purpose of NATO was to counter the threat that many in the West thought that the Soviet Union posed.

When President Harry S. Truman was attempting to persuade the U.S. Senate to ratify the NATO treaty, the administration told Congress that U.S. troops would not be stationed in Europe. Truman agreed to language in the treaty that even if a NATO member were attacked, the other countries would decide what to do in accordance with their respective "constitutional provisions." This, Congress was assured, meant that the White House would have to get legislative approval before committing Americans to war in Europe. These assurances soon went by the board. The alarm about possible communist aggression set off by North Korea's invasion of South Korea in 1950 soon led to the dispatch of over 100,000 U.S. troops to Europe. With Americans stationed on the front line, any attack by the Soviet Union and its Warsaw Pact allies on NATO would have inevitably brought the United States into the war.

The threat posed by the Soviet Union is no more. Indeed, the Soviet Union, the Warsaw Pact, and the cold war are no more. One indication of the reduced sense of danger held by President Bill Clinton is his call during the 1992 presidential campaign to reduce U.S. forces assigned to NATO by about two-thirds. Clearly, the significant changes in the international climate have raised the question of NATO's future.

Many people support a strong and even an expanded NATO. They see its purpose as evolving to become part of the growing emphasis on collective security that is evident in the expansion of UN peacekeeping missions and other international efforts to keep or restore the peace. This evolution has taken two paths.

The first path is the expansion of NATO's mission to include peacekeeping, perhaps even peacemaking. NATO never fired a shot in anger during the cold war. Indeed, NATO's first foray into combat was not against Soviet-led communist forces but against the Bosnian Serbs. In support of UN operations in the former Yugoslavia, NATO forces played an increasingly assertive role in the Balkan conflict. Warplanes attached to NATO sometimes bombed Serb positions, and after UN peacekeepers were taken hostage by the Serbs, NATO dispatched units from some of its European members to serve as a more potent force to protect the UN and, by extension, the Bosnian Muslims. The peace accord signed in November 1995 by the Bosnian Muslims, the Serbs, and the Croats rested in part on the dispatch of 40,000 to 50,000 NATO troops to Bosnia to supervise the peace. Advocates of this role for NATO insist that it is not one of altruism. Instead, they point out that World War I was ignited in 1914 by events that began in Sarajevo, Bosnia, when Serb assassins killed Archduke Franz Ferdinand of Austria-Hungary. It may be, NATO proponents contend, that preventing or limiting conflict in Bosnia and in other parts of Europe in the 1990s and beyond will prevent the kind of conflagrations that consumed Europe in 1914 and that dragged much of the rest of the world, including the United States, into the fighting.

The second path in the proposed future of NATO is the expansion of the alliance's membership to include countries to the east, including many former enemies. A preliminary step came in 1993 with a proposal to create associated membership, styled the "Partnership for Peace" program, for some Eastern European countries. This would encourage defense consultation and planning, but not the obligations of an alliance. Several countries accepted the idea, and after an initial negative response, Russia agreed in mid-1994 to join the loose association. A more significant proposal came when President Clinton proposed in December 1994 to bring Poland and some other Eastern European countries into full NATO membership. That set off a bitter Russian reaction. Moscow sees the move as an attempt to isolate Russia and to bring a powerful alliance closer to Russia's western border.

There the matter rests for the moment. In the following selections, both Zbigniew Brzezinski and Michael E. Brown indicate that they support NATO. They very much disagree, however, on the issue of whether or not NATO membership should be expanded.

YES

Zbigniew Brzezinski

A PLAN FOR EUROPE

HOW TO EXPAND NATO

The Clinton administration today confronts three important and interrelated questions generated by the end of the Cold War: First, what should be the scope of the Euro-Atlantic Alliance? Second, what should be the role of Germany within post–Cold War Europe? And third, what should be Europe and NATO's relationship with Russia?

It is essential to answer all three if America's prolonged commitment to Europe is to be crowned with historic success. The failure to respond decisively to the first question could create uncertainties regarding the second and automatically conjures up troubling prospects regarding the third. Hence, the response must be comprehensive.

It is axiomatic that the security of America and Europe are linked. The Europeans almost unanimously want to preserve the Euro-Atlantic alliance. But that means both sides must define what today constitutes "Europe" and what is the security perimeter of the Euro-Atlantic alliance. It also calls for shaping a closer relationship between Europe and Russia—one that facilitates the consolidation of a truly democratic and benign Russia.

This agenda is as daunting in its sweep as the one that America faced in the late 1940s. And it is pertinent to recall that the formation of NATO was not just a response to the Soviet threat; it was also motivated by the recognition that an enduring Euro-Atlantic security framework was needed for the assimilation of a recovering Germany into the European system. Today, in the wake of the reunification of Germany and the liberation of Central Europe, the ongoing expansion of Europe—favored by a powerful Germany—necessitates addressing head-on the issue of expanding NATO. That expansion in some cases should precede the enlargement of Europe; in others, it might have to follow it.

As the European Union reaches out for new members, so will Europe's security organ, the Western European Union. The WEU has already created a special category of associated partners, comprised of several Central European states. Their formal membership in the EU will create additional economic bonds and shared political interests inseparable from the security dimension. With most of the European Union's members also participating in NATO, neutrality by the alliance in the face of an attack on a WEU member will become inconceivable. As a practical matter, the issue of formally widening the alliance can thus no longer be avoided.

Failure to address this issue will compound the disintegrative trends in the Euro-Atlantic alliance that the Bosnian tragedy has made so evident. The disgraceful indecisiveness of the policies of both the Bush and Clinton administrations has helped create divisive coalitions within NATO, pitting Britain and France, backed from the outside by Russia, against America and Germany. Bosnia as a regional conflict thus represents an immediate challenge to the political cohesion of the alliance. The absence of a longer-range design for Europe can deprive the alliance of its historical *raison d'être*.

AN UNCLEAR POLICY

It is not carping criticism to point out that, so far, the Clinton administration has projected neither a strategic vision nor a clear sense of direction on a matter of such salience to Europe's future as enlarging NATO. To be sure, the president has stated (and his spokesmen have been repeating it like a sacred mantra) that the issue is no longer "whether" NATO will be expanded "but when and how." The task of presidential leadership, however, is not just to define questions but also to provide answers. "When and how" is precisely what begs for answers.

The ambiguity in U.S. policy was intensified by the conflicting emphases of the president's principal advisers.

President Clinton himself stated that NATO expansion "will not depend upon the appearance of a new threat in Europe." In contrast, his deputy secretary of state publicly affirmed, "Another factor, of course, that will determine the expansion of NATO is the overall security environment in Europe." His vice president has gone the furthest in assuring the Central Europeans that "the security of the states that lie between Western Europe and Russia affects the security of America." The chairman of the Joint Chiefs of Staff was even blunter, stating that "any threat to the East European countries... would be considered a threat to the United States." The vice president also indicated that NATO will be expanded in stages, arguing that this "will be of benefit even to those countries who are not in the first group to join," but the deputy secretary of state argued that Russia's and Poland's prospects of being admitted to NATO are the same.

There has been particularly widespread confusion [in the Clinton administration] regarding the role of NATO's Partnership for Peace—an ambiguous voluntary association of participating states—in an enlarging alliance. The president's own comments have contributed to that confusion: "Twenty-one nations have now joined that partnership since we began it, and they are already moving to fulfill the dream of a unified and peaceful Europe." Is that to mean that Kazakhstan or Kyrgyzstan are in the same category as the Czech Republic or Hungary? Is the partnership meant to provide equal security to all? Is it a promise of NATO membership to all or to none? If all are eligible, then, as a practical matter, none are admissible.

A German commentator on this issue aptly quoted Frederick the Great's axiom: "He who wants to defend everything defends nothing, and he who wants to be everyone's friend has no friends in the end." Senator Richard Lugar was undoubtedly right when he noted that "the Partnership for Peace must begin with the honest *premise of strategic differentiation*. All countries are *not* equal in the West's strategic calculus" (italics in original). Such strategic differentiation has been slow in coming and the State Department has even actively lobbied against congressional efforts to provide it.

Fortunately, by late 1994, the Clinton administration had begun to fashion a more consistent and forward-looking policy on NATO expansion. Its proposal to initiate an alliance-wide debate regarding the "when and how" of NATO expansion was a positive step, one that could over time generate the needed comprehensive approach. It came none too soon, since failure to resolve the persisting ambiguity in current U.S. policy was intensifying Central European anxieties and causing divisive debates within key allied governments, notably Germany....

Continued U.S. waffling could also consolidate Russian opposition to any expansion of NATO so that any eventual move to widen the alliance will unavoidably be seen as conveying a hostile message to Moscow. In the meantime, because of that ambiguity, Russian leaders with whom a clear-headed Western plan for NATO's expansion could be constructively discussed are being locked into an increasingly negative posture by the rising crescendo of highly vocal Russian opposition. There is little to be gained and a great deal to be risked by more delay in explicitly answering the question of "when and how."

GERMANY AND RUSSIA

The need for such an answer is dictated, above all, by the changing circumstances of both Germany and Russia. NATO was formed in large measure as a response to the challenges posed to a stable European order by the disproportionate power of these two states. Over the last 40 years, NATO created a secure framework for both a constructive role for Germany in a unifying Europe and the protection of Western Europe from the Soviet Union. Today the challenge is to find a formula that consolidates Germany in a wider Europe and facilitates a cooperative relationship with the new Russia—while eliminating any potentially disruptive geopolitical vacuum between the wider Europe and the new Russia.

It must be recognized that both Germany and Russia are in the midst of sensitive and complex national redefinitions. It is no reflection on Germany—a model citizen of the democratic European community—to note that a reunited Germany has the choice of either continuing to become an increasingly European Germany or seeking a German Europe. The former is much likelier within the framework of an expanded European Union and especially a more rapidly expanding NATO, with America deeply engaged in the shaping of that expansion. The latter is more likely if NATO atrophies while an insecure Central Europe, left to its own devices, again becomes a hunting ground for its powerful western and eastern neighbors.

That is why the next phase in the construction of Europe will have to involve the deliberate promotion of close German-Polish political cooperation. Today's Western Europe would not be a reality without prior German-French reconciliation. The post–Cold War Europe will not become a real "Europe" without a deep and wide-ranging reconciliation between Germany and Poland. Security must be a major aspect of any real cooperation between them. It will make a decisive difference to Europe's future whether such security cooperation —already pursued by them within the WEU—is undertaken within or without the Euro-Atlantic alliance (that is, with or without America's involvement).

The ongoing redefinition of Russia poses potentially starker choices. Germany's democracy is not at issue, but Russia's democracy is tenuous at best. Moreover, Germany's commitment to the West is enduring; the only issue is how integrated or unilateral Germany's role within the new Europe will be. Russia's relationship to the West—indeed, its very inclination to define itself as part of the West—is uncertain. Fundamentally, the political struggle within Russia is over whether Russia will be a national and increasingly European state or a distinctively Eurasian and once again an imperial state.

That debate is sharpening. The void left by communist ideology has not yet been filled. Among the several contending schools of political thought, the "Westernists" or "Europeanists" are certainly not gaining ground. Some, like Foreign Minister Andrei Kozyrev, who used to lead this camp, seem to be defecting. Increasingly, the most articulate and politically appealing leaders seem to be those who argue that Russia is destined to exercise geopolitical sway over Eurasia, that it is the embodiment of a distinctive Eurasian identity, and that its special political status must be asserted directly in Eurasia and indirectly in Central Europe. The Russian debate and the growing appeal of the "Eurasianists" signal the historical urgency of defining more precisely a stable political and territorial relationship between Europe, including its Euro-Atlantic security system, and post-Soviet Russia.

The requisite definition need not now address—let alone reject—the question of whether Russia eventually might become an integral part of NATO. [Volker] Rühe, the German defense minister, is probably correct in stating that Russia's participation would so dilute the alliance as to render it meaningless—but there is no current need to dot the i's and cross the t's on this sensitive issue. It is not even clear whether the Russians wish to be part of NATO. But if excluded and rejected, they will be resentful, and their own political self-definition will become more anti-European and anti-Western.

Prudence therefore dictates that the issue of Russia's association be kept open, depending on how fast, deep, and wide the expansion of the European Union will be and whether the Euro-Atlantic security system matches that expansion. The question of Russia's participation will have to be faced only when a wider NATO has actually reached the frontiers of Russia—and only if by then Russia satisfies the basic criteria for membership. Neither is likely soon.

In the meantime, the United States should take the lead in what will doubtless be a prolonged discussion in the alliance regarding the criteria that any new members must satisfy; the timing and stages of any expansion, its special modalities, the most constructive way to respond to legitimate Russian concerns, and the best ways to address some unavoidable complications resulting from expansion. In doing so, President Clinton will also have to take into account the growing domestic and foreign interest in this issue and the manifest need for American leadership.

A PROGRAM FOR ACTION

The criteria for NATO membership should be generic: they should define the essential political standards any new member must satisfy to qualify for the alliance's security umbrella. The alliance is, after all, a community of like-minded democratic states that share a common political culture, are contiguous to one another by land and sea, and are convinced that a threat to the security of one would adversely affect the security of the others. French Defense Minister François Léotard put it well: "The possibility that the new democracies will join the Atlantic alliance must not be viewed on the basis of solely military considerations, but should also be viewed globally, combining the various political, military, economic, and even cultural dimensions of their integration with the West."

Some opponents of NATO expansion have lately taken refuge in defining capricious preconditions for entry, demanding, for example, that the armed forces of any would-be member first be fully upgraded to NATO standards. Since no Central European nation could afford this, the demand is an obvious exclusionary tactic. In any case, a distinction should be made between political criteria that qualify a state for admission into an allied community and operational and logistical standards for effective military integration once within the community. The former need to be satisfied before admission; the latter can be pursued over a number of years both before and after admission.

There appears to be a broad consensus that the basic criteria for membership include a stable democratic system based on a functioning market economy; the absence of entangling territorial or ethnic disputes; an evident respect for the rights of national minorities; preferably, geographical contiguity to the alliance; constitutionally grounded civilian control over the military; and transparency in defense budgets and policy. As a practical matter, interoperability in logistics, communications, command and control, and weaponry would be desirable, but these could be pursued after formal admission.

The explicit articulation of such basic criteria for NATO expansion would prejudge neither the timing nor the scope of the alliance's future expansion. It would, however, clarify the existing situation, making it more obvious which states might qualify and roughly by when. The criteria would also serve as a spur for desirable internal reforms among would-be members. These criteria would strengthen the emerging consensus that in the foreseeable future only four Central European countries—the Czech Republic, Poland, Hungary, and Slovakia—are likely to be considered seriously. It would leave open the possibility for others, including theoretically Russia itself.

The first step, which should be taken at the earliest opportunity this year, would be for the alliance to declare formally its criteria for expansion and to indicate which countries at this stage appear to meet them. This would terminate the counterproductive debates with Moscow over whether NATO should or should not expand. The longer this is delayed, the more vociferous Moscow's objections are likely to be.

This step would not be tantamount to admission, but it would set the formal process of admission in motion. During that process, some further differentiation may become necessary: instead of four Central European countries, the first cut might include only Poland and the Czech Republic. Slovakia, for internal reasons, may qualify later, and that could have the effect (for geographical reasons) of somewhat complicating Hungary's admission, unless NATO is willing to leapfrog spatially. An unintended benefit of a step-by-step expansion would be the implicit message that NATO does not intend to be an exclusive club with slightly increased but closed membership, that a new line is not being drawn after the first admissions, but that the alliance's expansion is a staged and long-term process of enlarging the democratic community. Others can aspire to it and thus have an incentive to meet its standards.

Even the initially limited expansion of NATO would take several years. Unanimity on expansion in the alliance will not be easy to achieve. Negotiations between allies—even with strong American leadership and energetic German support—are likely to be tedious, with some states blackmailing the alliance on this issue to obtain satisfaction for their parochial concerns (the example of Greece on Macedonia springs to mind). The new members will also have to satisfy the alliance that they will address over time a large number of post-admission issues pertaining to logistics, operations, command and control, as well as weapons standardization—all of which will take time and money to resolve.

Nonetheless, it is certainly possible, given effective and focused leadership, to complete the political phase of the admissions process by the years 1996–98, at least for Poland and the Czech Republic and perhaps for Hungary and Slovakia as well—and in any case for all four by the end of the decade.

MEETING RUSSIA'S CONCERNS

In expanding NATO, one should note that neither the alliance nor its prospective new members are facing any imminent threat. Talk of a "new Yalta" or of a Russian military threat is not justified, either by actual circumstances or even by worst-case scenarios for the near future. The expansion of NATO should, therefore, not be driven by whipping up anti-Russian hysteria that could eventually become a self-fulfilling prophecy. NATO's expansion should not be seen as directed against any particular state, but as part of a historically constructive process of shaping a secure, stable, and more truly European Europe.

Since any foreseeable expansion of the alliance is likely to be pacific, the specific military dispositions arising from enlarged membership need not involve the forward deployment of NATO troops—especially American and German forces —on the territory of the new Central European members. Periodic joint maneuvers, coordinated planning, prepositioning of equipment, and joint command exercises would be sufficient to give substance to the guarantees inherent in NATO's Article Five, while the formula of "no forward deployment" of NATO forces in Central Europe would underline the nonantagonistic character of the expansion. This should mitigate some of Russia's legitimate concerns.

There are other steps that should be taken to reassure Russia, to propitiate its sense of status, and—most important—to engage it in a transoceanic and transcontinental security system. However, not all of Russia's concerns are legitimate—and the alliance should not shrink from making that known.

... The present circumstances call for a ... display of constructive firmness. The Kremlin must be made to understand that bluster and threats will be neither productive nor effective and may even accelerate the process of expansion. Russia has the right neither to veto NATO expansion nor to impose limited sovereignty on the Central European states.

At the same time, Russia should be approached on a two-track basis: the independent decision of the alliance to enlarge its membership should be accompanied by a simultaneous invitation to Russia to help create a new transcontinental system of collective security, one that goes beyond the expansion of NATO proper. Such a two-track strategy for enhancing European peace in the post–Cold War era would satisfy, both substantively and symbolically, the common Russian insistence on a wider all-European security system....

The two-track strategy—combining the expansion of NATO with new transcontinental security architecture embracing Russia—would represent a productive response to Russia's concerns. In fact, some Russian leaders have privately indicated that they would not be averse to the proposed arrangement—though their freedom of choice is narrowing as Russian nationalists, feeding on continued American ambiguity, become more vocal. It is a felicitous coincidence that the plan outlined here would constructively exploit some earlier Russian ideas—notably President Boris Yeltsin's late 1993 suggestion of a special relationship between Russia and NATO. A Russia whose goal is neither to render NATO impotent nor again to dominate Central Europe would have good reason to favor this approach.

* * *

Admittedly, the expansion of NATO, even if accompanied by a positive resolution of Russia's [current] concerns, will create new problems.

... The Russian obsession with big-power status, the growing desire to reconstitute a bloc of at least satellite states within the territory of the former Soviet Union, and the effort to limit the sovereignty of the Central European states could produce a crisis with the West. In such a case, an enlarged NATO would have no choice but to become again a defensive alliance against an external threat.

The resulting disruption in the construction of a wider transcontinental security system would be damaging, especially to Russia itself. Several decades ago, the Soviet Union spurned participation in the Marshall Plan and chose instead to go it alone—until it collapsed from historical fatigue. Threatened by the new Muslim states to the south and facing a possible future conflict in the east, today's Russia is in no position to engage also in a conflict with the West. Moscow can perhaps delay somewhat the enlargement of NATO, but it can neither halt Europe's growth nor prevent the concomitant extension of the Euro-Atlantic security umbrella over the wider Europe. It can merely isolate itself again. The Kremlin leaders should realize this. The two-track plan outlined here could help them avoid the basic error made by their Soviet predecessors.

BEYOND CHARLEMAGNE

American public opinion, especially given the Republican landslide in the November 1994 congressional elections, would support such a program. Despite the ill-considered negative lobbying by the powerful officials [at] the State Department, the Congress, even prior to the recent elections, approved the so-called Brown amendment.... This law stipulates that henceforth four Central European states are to benefit from the special cooperative privileges in logistics and weapons acquisition otherwise reserved for NATO members. Earlier in 1994, the Senate overwhelmingly approved a resolution favoring the eventual inclusion in the alliance of several Central European states. The 1994 elections reinforced congressional support for early NATO expansion.

The expansion of NATO will bring new responsibilities, and some will argue against it. The proposed expansion is a serious step that should be undertaken with a full appreciation of its additional burdens and even risks. But America's crucial relationship with the larger Europe must be addressed. The Partnership for Peace has already enlarged the scope of the alliance's obligations by stating that each "active participant" in the partnership would be entitled to consultations with NATO if it felt threatened. Partnership for Peace members are thus de facto covered by Article Four, which provides for consultations regarding out-of-area threats. Under Article Five, formal membership in the alliance would guarantee protection against an attack, entailing a major new obligation to which some will doubtless object.

Critics will probably evoke the worst-case scenario in arguing against any

new obligations—namely, the risk of U.S. entanglement in a conflict in Central Europe. Although the probability of any such conflict is low, it is fair to counter: could NATO really remain passive if some new form of aggression occurred? Would America and Europe not feel threatened by an invasion of Central Europe? Would there not be massive pressures for a strong reaction? Last but not least, would any such attack be more or less likely if it was known in advance that NATO would be obligated to respond? Paradoxically, the worst-case scenario raises questions that actually reinforce the case for NATO expansion as a form of deterrence—even though the approach advocated here should be pursued not as a hostile initiative but as a part of a larger architectural effort designed eventually to span Eurasia.

At the other extreme, exploiting the... 50th anniversary of [the] Yalta [Conference between Great Britain, the Soviet Union, and the United States in February 1995], some will argue that the failure to expand the alliance foreshadows Yalta II —a de facto recognition of a special Russian sphere of power within the territory of the former Soviet Union and Central Europe. Continued hesitation and ambiguity regarding America's longer-range vision of Europe's security will fuel these charges. Even though, given the current state of Russia and the new realities in Central Europe, a new Yalta is not even possible, nothing less than a display of presidential leadership will rebuff the growing temptation to engage in demagogy on the sensitive issues of relations with Russia and Europe's future.

A number of European states would support forthwith such an American initiative. Others will hesitate or initially oppose it altogether. Germany will be sympathetic, and that is critical. France has been ambivalent, but its desire to retain a commanding position in the EU is enhancing its stake in expanding the current Franco-German liaison into a wider Franco-German-Polish axis, thereby widening the scope of European security cooperation. Britain has its own special reasons for favoring a wider, rather than a deeper, Europe—and it is simply a fact of life that a wider Europe cannot be two-thirds safe and one-third insecure. It will take time and effort to translate these inchoate European attitudes into affirmative unanimity. It can happen over the next several years—but only if America leads.

U.S. leadership, to be resonant, must also provide a longer-range vision of Europe's future, thereby defining the American-European connection by tomorrow's shared goals, not yesterday's fears. In scope, today's "Europe" still evokes Charlemagne's: essentially a Western Europe. That Europe had to be an American protectorate, with European unity forged beneath NATO's umbrella by France and a truncated Germany. But in the post–Cold War era, the territorial reach of the emerging Europe is more reminiscent of the Petrine Europe of the Holy Roman Empire. By 2010, that Europe may also include some southern European states (such as Romania, Bulgaria, and others), which will doubtless insist on admission in the footsteps of their Central European neighbors. Most important, a united and powerful Germany can be more firmly anchored within this larger Europe if the European security system fully coincides with America's.

The progression from Charlemagne's Europe of 1990 through the Petrine Europe of 2010 will set the stage—perhaps by 2020—for seeking Charles de Gaulle's vision of a Europe stretching "to the Urals." At this time, no one can say what precise shape such a Europe might take. Nor can one define what America's relationship with it might be. But one way or another, both America and Russia will have to be engaged in truly cooperative relationships with the European Union to make a Europe to the Urals feasible. The evocation of such a vision—of a plan for Europe—is a powerful incentive to shape a future that will truly benefit the current as well as the next generation of Americans and Europeans.

NO

Michael E. Brown

THE FLAWED LOGIC OF NATO EXPANSION

There is a strong consensus in the American foreign-policy establishment and, to a lesser extent, in Western Europe that at least one or two Central European states should become full members of the North Atlantic Treaty Organisation (NATO) in the near future. US President Bill Clinton stated after the January 1994 NATO summit that, 'the question is no longer whether NATO will take on new members, but when and how'. Clinton reaffirmed his commitment to NATO expansion during his trip to Europe in July. Some German leaders, Defence Minister Volker Rühe in particular, have been outspoken in their support of NATO expansion. The communiqué issued at the end of the ministerial meeting of the North Atlantic Council (NAC) in December 1994 stated that NATO enlargement was expected and that it would be welcomed. Prominent former policy-makers—including Henry Kissinger, Zbigniew Brzezinski, Harold Brown and James Baker—support NATO expansion, as does the Republican leadership of the new US Congress. Many experts on both sides of the Atlantic also support this broad position.

Although many Western policy-makers and analysts believe that NATO should expand, there is a debate over when and how this should take place. There are three main schools of thought. First, some believe that NATO should proceed slowly and bring one or two new states into the Alliance at a time. Poland and the Czech Republic are generally seen as being at the front of the queue, with Hungary and, perhaps, Slovakia leading subsequent waves. This school believes that starting the accession process in three to five years and proceeding incrementally will minimise the possibility of a hostile Russian response. Second, some believe that NATO should move quickly to extend membership to Poland, the Czech Republic, Hungary and Slovakia (the Visegrad four). Those who advocate this course of action believe that Russian expansionism is either already under way, or inevitable. Third, some believe that NATO expansion should be closely coordinated with expansion of the European Union (EU). This, it is said, would minimise the risk of NATO enlargement being seen as threatening to Russia and help prevent the

From Michael E. Brown, "The Flawed Logic of NATO Expansion," *Survival: The IISS Quarterly*, vol. 37, no. 1 (Spring 1995). Copyright © 1995 by The International Institute for Strategic Studies. Reprinted by permission. Notes omitted.

Alliance and the EU's military arm, the Western European Union (WEU), from having conflicting security commitments.

Current US and NATO policy embraces a gradualist approach to enlargement, at least as far as timing is concerned. At the December 1994 NAC meeting, Alliance leaders decided that there would be a study of the issue in 1995 and that the results of these deliberations would be presented to interested parties before the end of the year. American policy-makers hope (although they cannot yet say so publicly) that accession discussions will begin in 1996 and that the Alliance's membership will begin to expand in 1996, 1997 or 1998.

This article argues that all three schools of thought are misguided because they all proceed from the premise that NATO expansion should, without question, take place. Its contention is that all of the arguments most commonly put forward in support of NATO expansion are flawed and that enlargement is unnecessary given the current strategic and political situation in Europe. Moreover, NATO expansion could spark a backlash in Russia that could damage European and American security.

NATO expansion should not be a mechanistic process or tied to a rigid timetable as many of its supporters suggest. Rather, it should be linked to strategic circumstances: if Russia begins to threaten Eastern and Central Europe militarily, then NATO should offer membership and security guarantees to the Visegrad four and perhaps other states as well. NATO should declare that it will expand if necessary, but that it will not expand until strategic circumstances demand it.

Adopting this approach would give NATO a nuanced strategy that would maximise the Alliance's chances of developing a stable, peaceful security order in Europe while guarding against the possibility of Russian aggression. Russian leaders interested in cooperation with the West would be in a better position to keep expansionist elements under control and have a powerful incentive to pursue benign policies towards their neighbours in Eastern and Central Europe. American and Western European leaders should nurture this relationship while laying the political and military groundwork for extending new security commitments should NATO expansion become necessary.

There are risks associated with adopting this approach. NATO leaders would have to decide which Russian actions would prompt expansion and would have to sustain a consensus on enlargement under difficult geopolitical circumstances.

The risks and potential costs associated with other approaches, however, are greater. Prompt expansion of NATO—bringing the Visegrad four into the fold quickly—would probably lead to Russian actions in Eastern Europe and in the area of arms control that would weaken, not enhance, European and American security. A new East–West confrontation would probably develop, with much of the responsibility lying with NATO members. Adopting a gradualist approach would reduce, but not eliminate, these risks.

Deciding among these approaches is, therefore, not clear cut. In the end, however, one should have more faith in NATO's ability to act decisively when vital interests are threatened than in

Russia's ability to accept provocation without retaliation.

NATO EXPANSION IS NOT NEEDED

Advocates of NATO expansion put forward six main strategic and political arguments for widening the Alliance.

First, it is said that NATO enlargement is needed to deter Russian aggression in Eastern and Central Europe. Some commentators are concerned that, because Russia has strengthened its position in Central Asia and the Caucasus over the past year or two and because Moscow has long considered Eastern and Central Europe to be part of its sphere of influence, Russia will try to dominate this region again. Former US National Security Adviser Zbigniew Brzezinski is concerned that Russia's 'imperial impulse remains strong and even appears to be strengthening'. Another former US official, Peter Rodman, maintains that Russia is getting back on its feet and that 'the lengthening shadow of Russian strength' poses a threat to Central European security. 'Russia is a force of nature', he says, and Russian imperialism is 'inevitable'.

NATO is a collective defence organisation designed to deter and, if necessary, defend against direct military threats to member-states. Russia does not at present pose a military threat to Central and Eastern Europe and is not strengthening its conventional military capabilities. The Conventional Forces in Europe (CFE) Treaty obligates Russia to keep much of its firepower east of the Urals. According to authoritative sources, no Russian combat formations currently operate at more than 75% of their authorised manpower levels and roughly 70% of all divisions operate at less than 50% of authorised levels. Moreover, Russia's military lead-

ership is in disarray at both the ministerial and operational levels. The inability of the Russian military to quash a small number of lightly armed insurrectionists in Chechnya testifies to its current operational capabilities. Western defence and intelligence experts believe that the Russian military is incapable of launching a conventional offensive against the West and that it would take Moscow at least a year to field such a capability. Indeed, Brzezinski concedes that 'neither the alliance nor its prospective new members are facing any imminent threat'. Talk of a Russian military threat, he notes, 'is not justified, either by actual circumstances or even by worst-case scenarios for the near future'. NATO leaders will, therefore, have plenty of time to extend membership and security guarantees to states in Central and Eastern Europe if Russia begins to build up its offensive conventional capabilities.

If the Russian military threat were real, or even slight but growing, one would expect states in Eastern and Central Europe to be building up their military forces. This, however, is not the case. Poland, which has powerful historical reasons for fearing Russia, is reducing military conscription from 18 to 12 months. In the past year, the Polish Army disbanded one of its 11 mechanised divisions and converted another into an armoured cavalry division. Hungary is reducing conscription from 12 to ten months. The Czech Army has converted one of its three mechanised divisions into a mechanised brigade and disbanded its infantry division. None of these armies acquired much new equipment in the past year. These are not the actions of states concerned about military threats.

Second, advocates of NATO expansion maintain that, even if there is no Russian military threat, membership should be offered to Central Europe because this would 'project stability' into the region. Michael Mandelbaum argues that NATO expansion would extend the Alliance's 'zone of stability' eastwards, while Volker Rühe insists that 'if we do not export stability, we will import instability'. This is one of the most prominent arguments in favour of NATO expansion.

It is certainly true that there is instability in the eastern half of Europe: there are ethnic problems in Estonia and Latvia; Ukraine has ethnic difficulties in Crimea and severe economic problems; Russian involvement in Moldova has galvanised a secessionist split that also engages Romania; and war rages in the Balkans, which may spread to Macedonia, Albania and Bulgaria.

No one, however, is suggesting that NATO should extend membership to any of these countries in the near future. Those countries at the front of the NATO queue—Poland, the Czech Republic and Hungary—are in fact quite stable. They have few ethnic minorities and ethnic violence is virtually non-existent. The Czech–Slovak divorce stands out as a model of peaceful conflict resolution. Violent border disputes are unlikely and inter-state conflict in general is highly remote.

The case for 'projecting stability' into this part of Central Europe is therefore specious. If one looks at specific cases, instead of treating Eastern Europe as an analytically indistinguishable whole, one finds that these countries and the region they encompass are already quite stable.

This stability is reinforced by the desire Poland, the Czech Republic and Hungary have to join the EU. Because these states are determined to join, and because their chances of doing so are quite good, they have a powerful incentive to treat ethnic minorities well, respect international borders and international norms of behaviour, and conduct their internal and external affairs peacefully.

Even if intra-state or inter-state tensions appear in the region, NATO membership would not be the solution. The Alliance does not have the means to address the political and economic problems that are the cause of many ethnic disputes, nor does it have the political and economic levers needed to contain intra-alliance conflicts. NATO is a collective defence organisation, not a collective security organisation. It was unsuccessful in preventing the Turkish invasion of Cyprus in 1974, and there is no reason to think it would be better at preventing or controlling intra-regional disputes in the Visegrad area should Central European states join the Alliance. The EU is better positioned to address the root causes of ethnic conflict and better equipped to deal with violence when it breaks out because of its leverage over countries anxious to join the Union.

Third, advocates of NATO expansion maintain that, because it will take many years for former Warsaw Pact states to meet the economic and political standards of the European Union, the West must do something to reassure these states about their prospects of being fully integrated into the West. Since EU membership will not be attained for many years, it is said, NATO membership should be extended to bridge the gap. This will allow the Visegrad states, in particular, to join Europe's most important security organisation while waiting to join its most important economic institution. According to Ronald Asmus, Richard Kugler and Stephen Larrabee, NATO must 'provide a political and security anchor to tie these countries to the West'.

This is another specious argument. Although there are good reasons for being unsure about Russia's geopolitical orientation in the future—its interest in 'Westernising' has ebbed and flowed since the time of Peter the Great—there is no doubt about Polish, Czech and Hungarian inclinations. These countries are historically, politically, culturally, socially and economically linked with Western Europe. Although these countries would like to become NATO members and will be disappointed if it is not forthcoming, this will not lead them to turn away from Western Europe. As Vaclav Havel, the President of the Czech Republic and a leading enthusiast of NATO expansion, observed, 'we have always belonged to the Western sphere of European civilisation'.

Fourth, advocates of NATO expansion claim that taking steps to bring Visegrad states into the Alliance would help to dampen aggressive nationalism and promote democracy in the region. Robert Zoellick argues that taking firm steps towards expansion would 'strengthen the hands of democratic reformers in these nations'. Asmus, Kugler and Larrabee maintain that the lack of a Western security commitment to the region 'threatens to undercut democracy and the reform process in these fragile democracies and to rekindle nationalism' in the region.

While extending NATO membership would help to reinforce democratic reforms in the Visegrad area, it will not have a decisive impact on domestic political developments in these countries. Aggressive nationalism is unlikely to develop in this region because there are few ethnic problems. In addition, the prospect of joining the EU is the key to outside in-

fluence over domestic political developments in Central Europe. Governments in Central Europe are instituting minority rights safeguards and embracing democracy in part because they want to do so, but also because they must do so if they are to become members of the European Union. They will continue to implement such policies if NATO membership is not forthcoming—even if it is specifically denied—as long as they have a realistic chance of joining the EU. Central Europe might not be happy with the slow pace with which the EU is moving towards accession, but it is highly unlikely that they will deviate from the democratic path as long as membership is a possibility. NATO membership will play a secondary and non-essential role in reinforcing democratic trends in Central Europe as long as these countries are moving towards membership of the EU. Holding back on NATO membership will, therefore, not 'undercut democracy' or 'rekindle nationalism' in the region.

Fifth, advocates of NATO expansion argue that it is needed to address German concerns about Russia and, more specifically, about the fate of the states to its immediate east. If Russia adopts aggressive policies and if NATO fails to extend security commitments to the Visegrad area, the 'security vacuum' in Central and Eastern Europe could lead Germany to establish bilateral security ties with its Eastern neighbours. This, it is said, could lead to a German–Russian confrontation in Central and Eastern Europe, NATO's demise and the return of balance-of-power politics to Europe. Henry Kissinger has argued that, 'if things turn out badly in Russia, it would lead to a no-man's land between Germany and Russia, a condition that has caused many European wars'. Delaying

NATO expansion, he maintains, 'invites Germany and Russia to fill the vacuum between them either unilaterally or bilaterally—a contingency everyone in Europe, Germany above all, seeks to avoid'.

There is no doubt that a German–Russian security competition in Central and Eastern Europe must be avoided and that German security concerns must be addressed. It does not follow, however, that NATO should now make a commitment to extend membership to states in this region. Russia does not pose a military threat to Central and Eastern Europe at the present time. If Russia becomes more aggressive towards this region in the future, NATO will have sufficient time to respond before Moscow poses a military danger to its Western neighbours. A German–Russian security competition need not ensue.

Germany is naturally and rightly concerned about the possibility of Russian aggression and instability in Poland and the Czech Republic. Significantly, however, the German government is not pushing for the rapid expansion of NATO. In the run-up to the December 1994 ministerial meeting of the North Atlantic Council, Germany played a leading role in modifying an American proposal for a six-to-eight-month study of enlargement. Germany, along with France, argued successfully in favour of a longer study. Germany's main concern was that moving quickly to expand NATO would trigger a backlash in Russia that would endanger European security. As German Foreign Minister Klaus Kinkel argued: 'We cannot risk reviving East–West strategic rivalry. It would be tragic if, in reassuring some countries, we alarmed others'. If Germany were worried about Russian aggression or the dangers posed

by a security vacuum to its east, it would be urging the United States to move faster—not slower—towards NATO expansion.

Given that Russia does not now pose a military threat to Eastern and Central Europe and that Germany is urging caution on enlargement, it is hard to argue that there is a looming security vacuum in Central Europe or that NATO foot-dragging is pushing Germany to renationalise its security policy.

A sixth and final argument made by advocates of NATO expansion is that it is important for all members of the WEU to join NATO as well. Although all current WEU members belong to NATO, this may not be so in the future if the European Union takes on new members, some or all of whom might join the WEU as well. Should this happen, Finland or Poland, for example, might have security guarantees from Germany and France through the WEU, but not through NATO. This, it is said, could 'destroy the Atlantic Alliance' and, through 'backdoor' security commitments, 'draw the United States into a conflict over which it had little if any control'.

This is a danger only if Russia poses a military threat to its Western neighbours and only if the expansion of the Alliance is tied to a mechanistic timetable or to the attainment of a high level of inter-operability between NATO and Central European military forces, as some suggest. The danger is that WEU security commitments could be extended to non-NATO states that are exposed to Russian aggression. This could indeed strain the Atlantic Alliance and draw the United States into a conflict it was not formally obligated to fight.

This problem disappears, however, if NATO membership is tied to strategic circumstances—the emergence of a Russian military threat. In the absence of such a threat, it makes little difference if some states have only WEU security commitments: intra-regional disputes involving WEU members are unlikely to escalate enough for either the United States to be drawn in or for NATO to be thrown into particular disrepute. If there is a Russian military threat, NATO membership should be extended to all WEU, and perhaps several non-WEU, members.

NATO EXPANSION WOULD BE COUNTER-PRODUCTIVE

In addition to serving no compelling strategic or political purpose, extending NATO membership and security guarantees to states in Central and Eastern Europe could have profound and unfortunate consequences for European and American security. It would undoubtedly have reverberations in Russian domestic politics and could lead Moscow to adopt foreign and defence policies that would diminish, not enhance, European and American security.

Diminished security for the West is probable if the four Visegrad states are rapidly incorporated into NATO. This is also likely even if NATO adopts a gradualist approach to expansion, moving slowly to bring in one or two states at a time, perhaps in conjunction with moves to expand the European Union and the WEU.

NATO expansion has three potentially harmful consequences for European and American security.

First, expansion would strengthen the hands of radical nationalists and political opportunists, who will use NATO's action to discredit the current leadership and its pro-Western line. This would im-prove the opposition's chances of seizing power, either through the electoral process or through unconstitutional means. Many of Russia's leading nationalist figures and some of its military leaders do not have a deep and abiding commitment to democratic rule. A return to authoritarianism would consequently be more likely.

The prospects for the democratic reform process in Russia are uncertain at best. Given Russia's long history of authoritarian rule, it would not be wise to assume that democracy will take hold. There is a chance, however, that it will succeed. The fate of the reform process will, of course, be determined largely by domestic developments, but external actions could play a role as well. NATO expansion, which would be characterised by radical nationalists and opportunists as a devastating blow to Russian national security and yet another humiliation of a once-great power, could play an important role in the struggle for power in Moscow. In the absence of a military threat, it would be foolhardy for NATO to take steps that will hurt democracy's chances in Russia.

Second, NATO expansion will probably lead Russia to adopt a more aggressive policy in Eastern Europe. If President Boris Yeltsin or another reformer is still in office, he will have to adopt a tougher line to maintain his hold on power. Most Russian policy-makers, even those supporting democratic and economic reform, have strong nationalist inclinations; they would not have to be pushed hard to adopt more assertive foreign and defence policies. If NATO enlargement brings radical nationalists to power, they will by definition adopt a more confrontational stance towards the West.

In either case, Russian leaders would characterise NATO expansion as an attempt to shift the European balance of power in the West's favour and as a delineation of spheres of influence in Central and Eastern Europe. The West, they would conclude, had unilaterally defined its sphere of influence; Russia, they would argue, should take steps to secure a buffer of its own and establish greater control over non-NATO areas. Extending NATO membership to some states in Central and Eastern Europe would draw a line in the region between areas protected by the Alliance and areas over which Russia would probably seek to exert greater control.

In current discussions about NATO expansion, only four states—Poland, Hungary, the Czech Republic and Slovakia —are mentioned as near-term candidates for admission. If NATO brings these four states into the fold, twice that number—Estonia, Latvia, Lithuania, Belarus, Ukraine, Moldova, Romania and Bulgaria—might find themselves subjected to mounting Russian pressure. Belarus, Ukraine and Moldova, for example, might be pressured to join the Russian Federation or participate in the transformation of the Commonwealth of Independent States (CIS) into a federal entity. Many, perhaps most, of the states left out of NATO will be drawn into Russia's orbit in ways that might otherwise be avoidable.

It is, thus, entirely possible that Russian aggression in Eastern Europe will be encouraged, not discouraged, by NATO expansion. The threat that NATO deployments were meant to address could be triggered by NATO actions, once again dividing Europe into two blocs. European security as a whole—Central and Eastern European security in particular —would be diminished, not enhanced.

Third, if the foregoing analysis of Russian domestic politics is correct, policymakers in Moscow—reformers and radical nationalists—will characterise NATO expansion as a change in the balance of power. Military leaders will see NATO enlargement as both a strategic threat and a bureaucratic opportunity: it will allow them to make a politically powerful case for reviving Russia's moribund military forces.

NATO expansion could, for example, lead Russia to pull out of the conventional and nuclear arms-control agreements that currently structure Moscow's military relations with the West. Even now, Moscow feels that the flank limitations of the CFE Treaty unfairly impinge on Russian national security. NATO expansion would undoubtedly lead many in Russia's political and military circles to argue that the Treaty as a whole should be abandoned. Similarly, many in Moscow object to some of the provisions of the second Strategic Arms Reduction Talks Treaty (START II). NATO enlargement would probably lead Moscow to push harder for the renegotiation of these provisions. Moscow's interest in additional nuclear arms-reduction agreements—which radical nationalists would characterise as disarmament in the face of aggression—would undoubtedly be dampened. Moscow's willingness to allow Western inspectors to monitor its denuclearisation efforts—which radical nationalists would characterise as espionage—would probably diminish. Russian withdrawal from the cooperative denuclearisation process now under way could not be ruled out.

Unfortunately, it is not entirely implausible that NATO expansion would drive the Russian leadership to call for a military build-up designed to strengthen Russia's military and international position. This would undoubtedly appeal to many Russian politicians, military leaders and citizens. It is certainly true that Russia does not have the economic wherewithal to begin a rapid military build-up, but it does have a military-industrial base, however withered, on which to build. It would take time for Russia to rebuild its conventional arsenal and restore the offensive conventional capabilities it once had, but its ability to do so should not be doubted. Although Russia's economy and military are currently weak, the same was true of Germany's in January 1933.

Bringing all four Visegrad states into the Alliance quickly would push Russian reformers to adopt a tougher foreign policy and strengthen the hands of Russian politicians opposed to cooperation with the West. Whether radical nationalists would be able to use this as a springboard to power is impossible to say, but there is no denying that rapid NATO expansion involves significant risks. The Alliance should pursue this course only if its leaders believe that Russian aggression in Central and Eastern Europe is inevitable and if NATO is only interested in or capable of protecting Poland, Hungary, the Czech Republic and, perhaps, Slovakia.

Advocates of NATO enlargement have proposed three main ways of minimising these risks. First, some argue that NATO should extend membership to all four Visegrad states, but with two caveats: that these states would not join NATO's integrated military command structure; and, more importantly, that Alliance forces would not be deployed on their territory. Henry Kissinger has argued

that this kind of 'qualified' NATO membership would extend defensive guarantees without exacerbating Russian security concerns.

There are two problems with this argument. First, many if not most Russian leaders will nonetheless view NATO expansion as an aggressive act. No matter how NATO expansion is packaged, it will involve American nuclear and military guarantees to states in Central Europe. It will be seen in Moscow as a change in the balance of power and an extension of Washington's—and Bonn's—sphere of influence. Many Russian leaders will argue that direct action must be taken to safeguard the country's national security interests. Second, extending qualified membership would not sidestep the problems created by drawing a new line in Eastern Europe. Extending qualified NATO membership to some states in the region will probably lead Moscow to adopt more aggressive policies towards others. Many in Russia will see NATO expansion in any form as the delineation of Central and Eastern Europe into two spheres of influence.

Many advocates of NATO expansion propose a second course to minimise such risks: moving slowly and extending membership to only one or two new states at a time. This, it is said, would give Western leaders time to convince Russian leaders that NATO's intentions were benign. Bringing in only one or two states at a time would reinforce this impression.

This approach faces the same basic problems as the first. Russian leaders will see any form of NATO expansion, even if it is incremental, as a change in the balance of power and an extension of Washington's and Bonn's sphere of influence. NATO efforts at 'spin control' will fail in the face of these overriding geostrategic concerns. In addition, this approach will not sidestep the problem of drawing a new line in Eastern Europe: it will simply draw a bad line. Only one or two states would be brought into NATO and a very large number would be left out, perhaps to face a resurgent or strident Russia.

Some advocates of NATO expansion therefore propose a third course of action: extending membership to new states only as they are brought into the European Union and the WEU. This, it is said, will minimise the risk of NATO enlargement being perceived by Moscow as threatening and help keep Alliance and WEU security commitments from going in different directions.

The main problem with this approach is that many Russian leaders will challenge the contention that this is not an aggressive act. They will agree that expansion of the European Union is for economic and political reasons and that expansion of the WEU is to 'project stability' into the region, but they will have difficulty viewing NATO expansion, American security commitments and American nuclear guarantees in the same benign terms. Because NATO is first and foremost a collective defence organisation, Russian leaders will quite rightly see its enlargement as having an anti-Russian dimension—regardless of how it is presented or packaged.

A second problem with this option is the linking of NATO expansion to European Union and WEU enlargement. There are instances in which the two should not be linked. For example, if Russia embarked on an expansionist course, it would not be wise to wait until Poland was ready to join the EU before bringing it into NATO. Conversely, Finland is set to join the European Union at the end of 1995; its highly capable military makes it a suitable candidate for membership of the WEU, but it is far from clear that NATO membership should follow. The EU and NATO have distinct, but complementary roles to play in European affairs.

Proposals for minimising the risks associated with NATO expansion cannot eliminate them completely. Given the nationalist inclinations of most Russian policy-makers, the hypersensitivity in Russia to national security issues and Moscow's treatment in international affairs, the strong showing of radical nationalists in recent elections and the volatile state of Russian domestic politics, it is hard to anticipate Russian reactions to NATO actions. Although the development of a kinder, gentler Russia is far from certain, it is not in the interests of the United States or Europe to take steps that would make Russian authoritarianism or belligerence more likely.

NATO EXPANSION AND EUROPEAN SECURITY

To keep great-power conflict from breaking out in Central and Eastern Europe, two interrelated security problems need to be addressed. First, Russian aggression in Eastern and Central Europe must be discouraged. Second, instability in Eastern and Central Europe must be kept to a minimum. In each area, NATO and the EU have indispensable, complementary roles to play. Western strategy for dealing with these security problems should be based on an understanding of this complementarity and the development of this partnership for peace.

Western Strategy and Russia

The West must not be sanguine about Russia's imperialistic past, its aggressive policies in parts of the former Soviet Union or the prospects for democracy and market reform in Russia. It is entirely possible that Moscow will embark on an expansionist course in Eastern Europe in the future.

Over the past year or two, Russian leaders have pursued a more assertive policy towards other former members of the Soviet Union. Moscow has reestablished control over parts of Central Asia and the Caucasus and put considerable political and economic pressure on Ukraine. If Russia were to regain control of Ukraine, it might try to re-establish a sphere of influence in Central and Eastern Europe.

NATO leaders should state in clear and unequivocal terms that it will extend Alliance membership and full security guarantees to Central and Eastern European states if Russian actions merit this response. NATO leaders should state, furthermore, that one of the purposes of the Partnership for Peace programme is the development of closer military ties with the states of Central and Eastern Europe and preparing the military foundation for expansion and new defence arrangements in the region should Russian behaviour call for such steps.

Russian actions that should trigger NATO expansion into Central and Eastern Europe fall into four broad categories. First, NATO should expand if Russia builds up its conventional military forces near neighbouring states in the West in violation of the CFE Treaty. This would constitute a direct military threat to Central and Eastern Europe. Second, NATO should expand if Moscow violates its pledges to respect international borders in general and Ukrainian sovereignty in particular. This would indicate that Russia's expansionist impulses had prevailed over its public commitments to honour the international status quo. Third, NATO should expand if Moscow absorbs Ukraine or Belarus into the Russian Federation or transforms the CIS into a federal entity. This would represent a change in the European balance of power and would indicate that Russia was once again pursuing an imperialist agenda. Fourth, NATO should expand if Moscow withdraws from either of the strategic arms reduction treaties (START I and II) or discontinues the denuclearisation process to which it has committed itself. This would indicate that Russian military policy was moving in a more confrontational direction.

NATO leaders should make it clear, however, that although the Alliance will expand if it is needed, expansion will not take place until it is needed. This would give Moscow's leaders a powerful incentive to live up to the international commitments they have made. NATO would position itself to deter and defend against Russian aggression in Eastern and Central Europe, but it would not stimulate Russia's nationalistic impulses.

The European Union also has a role to play in discouraging and protecting Eastern and Central Europe from Russian aggression. If Moscow tries to re-establish a sphere of influence in Eastern and Central Europe, it is quite possible, and perhaps probable, that Russia will rely on economic and political instruments of leverage: blatant military aggression would ruin its relations with the West and precipitate the same sort of military confrontation that drove it into bankruptcy during the Cold War. NATO membership will not insulate Central and Eastern European states from Russian economic and political machinations. Should Russia embark on this course, the key to safeguarding these states will be integrating them into the Western European economic system and the EU: this would reduce their economic and political vulnerability. This should be done as a preventive measure, and it can be done without provoking a hostile Russian reaction.

At the same time, the West should make a concerted effort to develop a stable, peaceful relationship with Moscow and to bolster Russia's democratic and economic reforms. Washington should continue to treat Moscow as a valued and respected partner. NATO, as Zbigniew Brzezinski has suggested, should propose signing a formal treaty with Russia that would reassure Moscow about the Alliance's benign intentions, reinforce Russia's non-aggression pledges and strengthen the consultative and planning mechanisms embodied in the North Atlantic Cooperation Council (NACC) and the Partnership for Peace programme. This would also reassure Russia about its role and stature in international affairs.

The European Union, for its part, should develop closer political and economic ties with Moscow. Lowering trade barriers would be a particularly constructive step in the near term. This would bolster Russia's democratic and market reforms, which have experienced initial problems. In the long term, the goal should be the development of a Russia that would be fully integrated politically and economically into European affairs and would, therefore, be eligible for membership of the EU. This is decades away and, indeed, may never happen, but is nonetheless a worthwhile long-term objective.

Western Strategy and Central and Eastern Europe

Russian expansionism and the renationalisation of Western European defence policies can best be prevented by minimising turmoil and conflict in Central and Eastern Europe. Instability in the region will present Moscow with geostrategic opportunities that, if history is any guide, it will find hard to resist. Instability in this region is of special concern for Germany because of its proximity. If problems here are not addressed by the European Union or NATO, Germany will be inclined to undertake initiatives of its own. Problems in Central and Eastern Europe could trigger a German–Russian security competition and the renationalisation of Western European foreign and defence policies that Europe would do well to avoid.

It does not follow, however, that extending NATO membership to states in Central and Eastern Europe will address the problems that this region faces. Once again, both NATO and the EU have essential roles to play.

NATO is a collective defence organisation, not a collective security organisation. Its contribution to Central and Eastern European security should be the extension of full membership and security commitments if Russia takes steps that merit these actions. The Alliance should continue, through bilateral partnerships and multilateral exercises, to develop closer security relationships with Central and Eastern European states and to make the military forces of NATO and non-NATO Europe more interoperable. If Russia embarks on an aggressive or expansionist course, NATO must be ready to extend full membership and defence commitments quickly.

The EU has an essential role to play in Central and Eastern Europe. It, more than NATO, is the key to dampening intra-state and intra-regional conflicts that do not involve Russia. NATO cannot address the political and economic roots of ethnic conflicts, nor does it have the political and economic levers to contain intra-regional conflicts. The EU is better positioned in both respects. By lowering trade barriers and extending more economic assistance, the EU could stimulate economic development, thereby dampening ethnic tensions in Eastern Europe. By outlining a course for bringing Central and Eastern European states into the fold, the European Union would give potential members powerful incentives to protect minority rights, embrace democracy and meet international norms of behaviour. This would maximise the EU's leverage in the short run and the prospects for stability in Central and Eastern Europe in the long run.

NATO is the ultimate guarantor of Central and Eastern European security against external threats—for example, Russian aggression. The European Union is the key to promoting stability within the region. NATO should expand if circumstances demand, but the EU should expand as quickly as it can.

The United States has to accept that NATO and the EU have complementary roles to play in European security. There are countless references to this complementarity in official communiqués, but it is only in the past year or two that there has been an acceptance of this principle in American thinking. The Clinton administration deserves credit for its enthusiastic, seemingly genuine, endorsement of a European security and defence identity and the development of a common European foreign and security policy. It is possible that the EU's role in security policy will grow, especially in Central and Eastern Europe. This does not necessarily mean, however, that NATO is being eclipsed or that American involvement in European security is no longer needed. This is not a zero-sum game, in which one organisation's gain is necessarily another's loss. Developing a better appreciation of this at an official level and communicating it effectively to the American people will be one of the challenges that Washington will have to face.

WEIGHING RISKS

The strategy outlined above can be criticised on three main grounds. First, critics will say that President Yeltsin is simply trying to use the West's fear of radical Russian nationalists to prevent NATO expansion. It would be a mistake, they will argue, to allow Yeltsin's gambit to succeed. There is no doubt that Yeltsin is indeed playing the 'nationalist card' in his negotiations with the West over NATO expansion. However, the West should not worry about radical Russian nationalists because Yeltsin says they are dangerous; the West should worry about Russian nationalism because its analysis of Russian domestic politics suggests that it has the potential to be dangerous.

Second, critics will point out that it will be difficult to identify the Russian actions that will trigger NATO expansion. There is no doubt that this is a challenging problem; the criteria for expansion outlined in this article constitute only a first effort. Nevertheless, some Russian actions —building up military forces in the west in violation of the CFE Treaty—would clearly constitute grounds for NATO enlargement. Expanding and refining this list of criteria should be within the capabilities of the Western strategic studies community.

Third, critics will argue that NATO should expand now, when there is only a minor threat from Moscow and when most of Europe is peaceful. If NATO waits until Moscow becomes more aggressive, they will say, the Alliance will fail to act because Russian actions might not constitute clear threats to European security, NATO leaders might disagree about what to do or Alliance leaders might worry that expansion will lead to a further deterioration in relations with Moscow. The Alliance will lack either the clarity, consensus or will to act decisively at the crucial moment. As a result, states that could have been brought under NATO's umbrella will be lost.

This argument cannot be dismissed lightly. But the difficulty in deciding whether to expand in the face of Russian aggression can be minimised if concrete steps are taken to develop and sustain a consensus within the Alliance while relations with Moscow are on a constructive footing. The key will be agreeing that Russian actions that change the balance of power or have military implications demand a military response from the West—expansion of the NATO Alliance.

Alliance support for NATO expansion will be hard to mobilise because the current strategic case for enlargement is weak: why should NATO members bear the costs and run the risks associated with expansion when Russia does not pose a military threat to Central Europe? Alliance support for NATO expansion will be easier to mobilise if and when Russia poses a clear and present danger to Central and Western European security. Critics of the strategy outlined in this article underestimate the problems associated with expansion in a low-threat environment and overestimate the problems associated with expansion in a high-threat environment.

In addition to laying the political groundwork for expansion, the Alliance will have to lay the military groundwork for possible enlargement. Fortunately, this process is already under way both multilaterally (through NACC consultations) and bilaterally (through the Partnership for Peace programme). The latter, launched in January 1994, involves Central and Eastern European states (and others) in joint planning activities and joint training exercises. The expectation is that over time these partnerships will close the gap that currently exists between NATO and non-NATO forces in virtually every aspect of military policy, including doctrine, forces, organisation and training. In many cases, close working relationships will develop and a foundation for joint military operations will be created. Military obstacles to NATO expansion will gradually disappear. These cooperative efforts must be continued.

There are risks and costs associated with all of the positions on NATO expansion discussed in this article. Prompt enlargement of NATO—bringing the Visegrad four into the Alliance quickly—will, in all probability, cause a backlash in Russian domestic politics that will weaken whatever chances the democratic reform movement has. This could easily lead to actions in Europe and arms-control policy that will have a significant, adverse impact on European and American security. An East–West confrontation could well ensue. If those who favour this course of action are wrong about Russia's imperialistic impulses, NATO members will have only themselves to blame for bringing about this sorry state of affairs.

Those who favour gradualist approaches can reduce, but not eliminate these risks. Given the volatile and unpredictable state of Russian domestic politics, one should be wary of confidently predicting that Russia will quietly accept NATO expansion in Central and Eastern Europe. It seems far more likely that Russian leaders will seize on NATO enlargement—which will involve an American military commitment and nuclear guarantee—to push an expansionist agenda of their own.

On balance, the risks and costs associated with near-term expansion of the NATO Alliance are greater than those associated with linking expansion to strategic circumstances.

POSTSCRIPT

Is It Wise to Admit East European Countries into NATO?

The issue of NATO and its membership is part of a larger series of questions that are related to current changes in the world system. With the cold war over and with much of Europe becoming increasingly integrated within the structure of the European Union, the future security arrangements for the continent are subject to a great deal of debate. There are a number of articles that address this issue in Alexander Moens and Christopher Anstis, eds., *Disconcerted Europe: The Search for New Security Architecture* (Westview Press, 1994). For a broader perspective on the future of European cooperation in many areas, read Dominique Moïsi and Michael Mertes, "Europe's Map, Compass, and Horizon," *Foreign Affairs* (January/February 1995).

Americans must consider the question of what the future U.S. relationship with NATO, as well as with the world, should be. The need for Americans to rethink their security arrangements is taken up by John D. Steinbruner in "Reluctant Strategic Realignment," *The Brookings Review* (Winter 1995). Some Americans believe that, with the cold war over, the job of NATO is done and the United States should move back toward its traditional aversion to permanent involvement in European affairs. Most Americans reject that stand, with only a minority (25 percent) in favor of reducing or ending the U.S. commitment to NATO, according to a 1994 survey.

This does not mean, however, that Americans do not have their qualms about the responsibilities of NATO membership. Accepting Poland and other Eastern European countries into NATO would mean that the United States would be forced to defend them against attacks by Russia or any other antagonist. For a discussion by a Russian of Moscow's relations with the West, read Yuri N. Afanasyev, "Seems Like Old Times? Russia's Place in the World," *Current History* (October 1994). Furthermore, if Russia were also brought into NATO, as some people propose, then it is conceivable that U.S. soldiers and other Western alliance troops might someday have to defend Siberia from encroaching Chinese armies. No one foresees that in the near future, but China does have great military potential. All these possibilities and more make many Americans leery. A 1994 poll found that only 42 percent of the American public supported the idea of extending NATO membership to Poland, Hungary, and the Czech Republic. And only 32 percent of Americans were willing to support sending U.S. troops to defend Poland if it were invaded by Russia. Indeed, only a narrow majority (54 percent) of Americans were willing to respond "yes" to the statement "I favor the use of U.S. troops if Russia invaded Western Europe."

Many Americans are also averse to sending U.S. troops to the Balkans, whether they are part of a UN or NATO peacekeeping mission or not. Polls in late 1995 revealed that a substantial majority of Americans are opposed to President Bill Clinton's proposal to send approximately 20,000 U.S. troops to Bosnia as part of the NATO peacekeeping force. But after Clinton's address to the nation in late 1995, a thin plurality of Americans (46 percent in favor, 40 percent opposed, 14 percent undecided) indicated a willingness to support sending troops to Bosnia.

Yet for all the uncomfortable possibilities of Americans becoming involved in the kind of turmoil that has characterized the Balkans in the 1990s or even some future, greater military confrontation, the alternative of ignoring the world in the hope that the ocean boundaries of the United States will insulate the country from the world's troubles is not realistic. That did not happen in 1914; it did not happen in 1941; it is unlikely to happen in any general war of the future. Perhaps, then, the old advice that "an ounce of prevention is worth a pound of cure" is worth remembering, even heeding.

ISSUE 3

Should the United States Abandon Its Superpower Role?

YES: Doug Bandow, from "Keeping the Troops and the Money at Home," *Current History* (January 1994)

NO: Anthony Lake, from "The Price of Leadership: The New Isolationists," *Vital Speeches of the Day* (June 1, 1995)

ISSUE SUMMARY

YES: Doug Bandow, a senior fellow at the Cato Institute and a former special assistant to President Ronald Reagan, argues that while the United States should remain engaged globally in many ways, it should bring its military home and curtail expensive foreign aid programs.

NO: Anthony Lake, special assistant for national security affairs for the Clinton administration, maintains that calls from the ideological left and right to stay at home rather than being engaged abroad are ill-considered and that U.S. national interests make full international engagement imperative.

Isolationism was one of the earliest and most persistent characteristics of U.S. foreign policy. In his 1796 Farewell Address, President George Washington counseled, "Our detached and distant situation invites and enables us ... to steer clear of permanent alliance with any portion of the world, ... taking care always to keep ourselves ... in a respectable defensive posture."

Washington's view played a strong role in U.S. foreign policy making until World War II. It is not true that the country was isolationist until that point and then became internationalist. It is more accurate to say that there has always been among Americans a tension or an ambiguity about isolationism and internationalism. Even during the 1700s and 1800s the world could not be ignored, as U.S. foreign trade, sporadic clashes with other countries, and other factors occasioned U.S. international involvement. In the late 1800s and increasingly in this century, U.S. global interaction intensified as trade grew in volume and importance; as U.S. military and economic power gave the country world-class strength; and as the speed of communications, transportation, and military movement shrank the world operationally.

Still, isolationism remained both a strong and respectable policy through the 1930s. World War II brought an end to that. The emergence of the United States from that conflict as the world's richest and most militarily powerful country combined with the perceived global threat from communism—

backed by Soviet military strength—combined to thrust the United States into virtually unchallenged internationalism. The very term *isolationism* became discredited.

Isolationism did not altogether disappear, however. Although distinctly a minority view, surveys throughout the cold war period showed that public support for isolationism existed among Americans. Gallup polls from 1945 through 1986 indicate that the percentage of Americans surveyed who said the United States should "stay out" of world affairs averaged 27 percent. There was a slight uptrend over the years, rising from an average of 23 percent during the first 10 years of the survey to 32 percent during the last decade of the period covered to 1986. Over the years, an average of 7 percent had no opinion; 66 percent favored the United States playing an "active part" in world affairs.

Now the isolationist–internationalist debate has resurfaced. Three factors have been the main causes for this renewed debate. First, the cold war and the perceived threat from the Soviet Union have ended. Therefore, one of the main thrusts behind U.S. internationalism, the containment doctrine that countered the communist and Soviet military threat, has become irrelevant. Second, U.S. economic power has declined, at least relative to the rest of the world, and the country is experiencing troubling economic conditions. Americans now want to concentrate on the home front. A poll taken in 1995 found that 73 percent of all Americans thought that their country should reduce further its involvement in world affairs in order to concentrate on domestic problems. Another recent survey indicated that 83 percent of Americans believe that protecting the jobs of American workers from foreign competition should be an important U.S. foreign policy goal. Third, the upsurge in global instability in Bosnia and elsewhere seems to many Americans to threaten to draw their country's human and financial resources into a never-ending series of expensive, frustrating engagements that seem unrelated to the safety and prosperity of the United States. Because of these and other factors, many Americans are convinced that huge defense budgets, gaping trade imbalances, increasing foreign ownership of U.S. economic assets, and other symptoms demonstrate that internationalism has become too expensive a policy to pursue. In particular, they are unwilling for the United States to continue to bear the cost of being a hegemon, a dominant superpower.

Doug Bandow is among those who would have the United States step back from superpower status. He argues that the United States should calculate military interventions and foreign aid on a strict cost/benefit basis, and that if Americans do so they will see that it is wiser most often to keep their troops and money at home. Anthony Lake, in contrast, contends that the prosperity and safety of the United States are inextricably bound up with the economic health and stability of the world and that Americans must maintain its leadership of the world.

YES

Doug Bandow

KEEPING THE TROOPS
AND THE MONEY AT HOME

We are living in exciting times. Who would have believed when George Bush was elected president that a year later the Berlin Wall would fall? That non-Communist governments would take power throughout Eastern Europe, Germany would reunite, and the Soviet Union would disintegrate? That the menace of aggressive Soviet communism would disappear? That the chairman of the Joint Chiefs of Staff Colin Powell would admit, "I'm running out of villains. I'm down to Castro and Kim Il Sung."?

In this dramatically changed world the interventionist stance that has dominated United States foreign policy for nearly five decades must be reexamined. The United States will be a global power, but what kind of power? Should it continue to seek global hegemony, or should it go back to being, in former ambassador to the UN Jeane Kirkpatrick's words, a "normal country"?

THE INTERVENTIONIST'S OUTLOOK

Today the American military is spread around the globe. President Bill Clinton says that 100,000 United States troops in Europe is the minimum required, despite the disappearance of any credible threat to the West and the ability of the prosperous European Community—which includes two nuclear powers, Britain and France—to deter a resurgent Russia in the future. Indeed, George Bush went so far as to state that he did not foresee that "utopian day" when all America's soldiers might come home arriving for perhaps another hundred years.

The Clinton administration, following the lead of its predecessor, also seems committed to retaining at least 100,000 troops in East Asia. Japan is the world's second-ranking economic power and faces no serious military threats; nevertheless, Tokyo apparently is slated to continue as an American defense dependent indefinitely. South Korea has 12 times the GNP [gross national product] and twice the population of Communist North Korea, yet Clinton suggests that United States forces will remain so long as Seoul wants them, which could be forever.

From Doug Bandow, "Keeping the Troops and the Money at Home," *Current History* (January 1994). First appeared in *Orbis: A Journal of World Affairs* (Fall 1992). Copyright © 1992 by The Foreign Policy Research Institute. Reprinted by permission of JAI Press.

And many would like to further expand America's role as global policeman. Three years after the mercifully short war against Iraq in the Persian Gulf, the United States remains entangled in Kuwait, Saudi Arabia, and the affairs of Iraq's Kurdish minority, risking a long-term presence in one of the world's most volatile regions. Bulgaria, the Czech Republic, Hungary, and Poland all want United States defense guarantees, preferably through formal membership in NATO [North Atlantic Treaty Organization]. America is enmeshed in Somalia and has threatened to intervene in the Balkans. Some press for involvement in Liberia's three-sided civil war, to bring peace, or against Haiti's military regime, to bring back democracy. Others write of America's obligation to guarantee Taiwan's security, prevent North Korea, Iran, and others from building weapons of mass destruction, and wage low-intensity conflicts around the world —in Latin America, Asia, the Middle East, and Africa. And columnist Ben Wattenberg wants the United States to go on making weapons simply to stay "Number One."

Given the expansiveness of the United States role abroad, it is time to ask: Is there anything the American people are not forced to pay for? Is there anything young Americans are not expected to die for?

THE IMPORTANCE OF JUSTIFYING POLICY

To answer these questions, one must first decide on the purpose of the national government. But rarely, alas, is this issue even addressed. The current administration speaks of a foreign policy of "enlargement"; hyper-internationalists cite the alleged need to spread democracy and enforce peace; and unreformed cold warriors warn of new enemies and threats requiring a military as large as that which successfully contained the Soviet Union. None consider whether their grand designs are consistent with America's organization of government, however.

Among the primary duties of the United States government, the first is to safeguard the country's security in order to protect citizens' lives and property. (The federal government also has some obligation to attempt to protect American citizens traveling abroad, but ultimately those who do business outside the United States must voluntarily incur the risks of doing so. Thus the formal justification for the entry of the United States into World War I—to uphold the right of Americans to travel on armed belligerent merchantmen carrying munitions through declared submarine zones—was patently absurd.) The government's second primary duty is to preserve the constitutional system and liberties that make America unique and worth living in. Every foreign policy action should be consistent with these two functions, and the president, legislators, and other officials can have no higher goals.

This is not, of course, to say that there are no other important ideals in life. For instance, the apostle John wrote in his first epistle, "This is how we know what love is: Jesus Christ laid down his life for us. And we ought to lay down our lives for our brothers." But the moral duties that individuals acknowledge are very different from duties established by the civil institutions that govern all. John did not suggest that we should force our neighbors—indeed, everyone in our entire country—to lay down their lives for others.

Yet many people no longer perceive any moral dimension to taxing and drafting citizens to implement government policies. Joshua Muravchik of the American Enterprise Institute, for example, sees no problem in promoting "common purposes" so long as such actions "don't involve curtailing the rights of our own citizens, but involve only taxing them." Yet taxation, and conscription, the policy used for years to obtain the needed personnel for Washington's extensive overseas commitments, certainly "involve curtailing the rights of our own citizens." An activist foreign and military policy should, therefore, require a justification that warrants circumscribing—often severely—people's freedom.

A FOREIGN POLICY OF HIGHER PRINCIPLES?

Advocates of an interventionist foreign policy have, of course, advanced many lofty justifications: To promote democracy. To ensure stability. To protect human rights. To stop aggression. To enforce international law and order. To create a new world order. And on and on. Such appeals to higher principles and values are very seductive; suggesting that foreign policy should be based on the promotion of the national interest sounds decidedly cold and selfish in comparison.

The moral goals articulated by many interventionists are important, but citizens should have no illusions about the ability of the United States government to promote, let alone impose, them. Furthermore, recourse to such principles is often simply a rationalization for pursuing strategic or political ends. A cursory survey of activist foreign policy decisions ostensibly taken in the name of higher moral principles reveals ample evidence of both naïveté and sophistry.

For instance, in 1990 policymakers in Washington proclaimed their love of democracy and the free market, but years later there is still little sign of reform in Kuwait City, which was "liberated" during the Gulf War; American troops fought to make the Middle East safe for a monarchy that has largely evaded fulfilling its promises of greater domestic freedom. Despite its professed ideals, the United States used its armed forces to prop up authoritarian regimes in Korea and Vietnam. In two world wars it cultivated grand alliances with, respectively, an authoritarian Russia (although by the time the United States officially declared war, the czar had been overthrown) and a totalitarian Soviet Union. It viewed its bases in and defense treaty with the Philippines as equally important during the presidencies of autocrat Ferdinand Marcos and democrat Corazon Aquino.

Not only has American intervention often been motivated by factors other than disinterested selflessness, but Washington has equally often bungled the job. Financial assistance to a host of third world autocracies has strengthened the enemies of freedom and democracy. Aid and support tied the United States to failing dictatorships in Iran and Nicaragua; the two regimes' collapses resulted in neither democracy nor allies. America's entry into World War I to promote a utopian world order had perhaps the most disastrous consequences of any international meddling by any state ever; by allowing the allies to dictate an unequal and unstable peace, it sowed the seeds of the planet's worst conflagration, which bloomed just two decades later.

Even more important than the question of Washington's sincerity and realism in promoting higher principles in its foreign policy is the question of cost. How much money—and how many lives—should be sacrificed to bring American principles to other countries? Restoring Kuwait's sovereignty proved surprisingly cheap, but there were no guarantees United States and coalition casualties would be so light. How many American lives did policymakers think Kuwait's liberation would be worth? Five thousand? Fifty thousand? And even if Iraq was the aggressor, the deaths of estimated tens and possibly even hundreds of thousands of Iraqis, many of them either civilians or military conscripts, must also be recognized as a very real cost of United States intervention.

How many body bags per foreign life saved would make intervention elsewhere worthwhile? Why did Iraq's earlier brutal assaults on its Kurdish minority not warrant war? What about Syria's depredations in Lebanon? China's swallowing of Tibet? The war between India and Pakistan? Or Pol Pot's mass murder in Cambodia?

If young American males—and now females—are born to give their lives overseas to forestall aggression, protect human rights, and uphold a new world order, should not the United States have gone to war to unseat the two dictators who (unlike, say, Ho Chi Minh, Iraq's Saddam Hussein, or Serbia's Slobodan Milosevic) truly *were* the moral equivalent of Hitler—Stalin and Mao? Why was protecting human rights in these instances not worth war? If the answer is that the cost would have been too great, then those who attempt a moral explanation for sacrificing 58,000 Americans for Vietnam but refusing to offer up some unspecified larger number to free more than 1 billion Chinese need to elucidate their methodology—unless, of course, they believe the United States should have ignited World War III in the name of some more just world order.

In fact, the United States did not intervene to liberate the two largest Communist states because doing so was not perceived to be in America's interest, owing to the catastrophic costs that such actions surely would have entailed. For all the idealism embodied in the moral explanations for United States behavior, American intervention is generally animated by a spirit of realpolitik [politics based on practical factors]....

As unsatisfactory as an emphasis on the national interest may be to some, it is the only proper basis for American policy. Such an approach reflects the purpose of the United States government —to protect the security, liberty, and property of the American people— in a way the international pursuit of utopian ideals does not. Reasons of national interest and security are the only legitimate justification for United States intervention abroad.

WEIGHING COSTS

It is not enough, however, to decide that the United States has one or more interests at stake in some foreign matter, because interests are not of unlimited value. The benefits of gaining desired objectives have to be balanced against the cost of intervention.

Perhaps the most obvious expense is financial. NATO accounts for roughly half the entire United States military budget; the defense of the Pacific runs to about $40 billion. Operation Desert Shield cost

$60 billion or more (though that bill was largely covered by coalition states). Foreign aid adds another $12 billion annually to the deficit. All told, roughly 70 percent of America's military outlays goes to prepare for conventional wars abroad. As General Wallace Nutting, former commander in chief of the United States Readiness Command, has observed, "We today do not have a single soldier, airman, or sailor solely dedicated to the security mission within the United States."

American domestic freedoms also suffer as a result. World Wars I and II resulted in massive assaults on civil liberties, including the suppression of dissent and free speech, and culminated in the incarceration of more than 100,000 Japanese Americans. Much more modest, but still unsettling, was the anti-Arab Sentiment unleashed during the short war against Iraq. Moreover, a panoply of security restrictions that grew out of the cold war continues to limit Americans' freedom.

Both wars also vastly expanded the government's economic powers. Federal spending in 1916 was just $713 million; it shot up to $18.5 billion in 1919, eventually settling back to the $3-billion level throughout the 1920s, more than quadruple its prewar level. Similarly, federal outlays in 1940 were $9.5 billion. Spending increase nearly tenfold, to $92.7 billion, fell to $29.8 billion in 1948—triple prewar figures—and then began its inexorable climb. Burton Yale Pines of the National Center for Public Policy Research argues that "today's mammoth federal government is the product not so much of the New Deal but of the massive power assembled in Washington to wage Wold War II and the Cold War." Some of the government's regulations have never been reversed: New York City, for instance, still suffers from the destructive effects of rent control, a supposedly temporary wartime measure.

Similarly, America's interventionist foreign policy has malformed the domestic constitutional system. We have seen both a centralization of power in the federal government and the aggrandizement of the presidency. How far we have come is reflected by the fact that serious thinkers who purport to believe in jurisprudential interpretation based on the original intent of the framers argue that the president can launch a war against another sovereign state without congressional approval. And although United States participation in formal UN forces is rather limited, it represents an even greater abrogation of congressional authority, since the act allowing participation dispenses with the need for a declaration of war when such troops are involved.

Further, intervention has a great human cost. Woodrow Wilson's fantasies of a new world order drove him to take the country into the mindless European slugfest of World War I, which left 116,000 Americans dead and led to the outbreak within one generation of an even worse war, which killed another 407,000 (mostly young) Americans. Since the end of the second world war, more than 112,000 American citizens have died in undeclared conflicts. It is one thing to ask Americans to die for the United States Republic. It is quite another to expect them to sacrifice their lives in the interest of power-projection politics more characteristic of an empire.

Finally, intervention could one day threaten the very national survival of the United States. Biological, chemical, and nuclear weapons are spreading and ballistic missiles [are] increasingly available. Terrorism has become a fixture of international life. With the growing ability of even small political movements and countries to kill United States citizens and to threaten mass destruction, the risks of foreign entanglements increase. No longer are the high costs limited to soldiers in the field. In coming years the United States could conceivably lose one or more large cities to demented or irrational retaliation for American intervention. A modest Strategic Defense Initiative program would reduce these risks, but it would never be able to provide full protection.

DIFFERENT WAYS AND MEANS

How, then, should the United States formulate a foreign policy? Every action taken abroad should reflect the purpose behind the creation of the government: namely, to serve the interests of American society and the people who live in it. Washington's role is not to conduct glorious utopian crusades around the globe. It is not to provide a pot of cash for the secretary of state to pass out to friendly regimes to increase United States influence abroad. It is not to sacrifice the lives of Americans to minimize other peoples' sufferings. In short, the money and lives of the American people are not there for policymakers, or even the president, to expend for purposes other than defending the American community.

Of course, some analysts argue that promoting moral values, particularly democracy and human rights, advances American national interests by making conflict—or at least war—less likely. The link is tenuous, however. Indeed, in the Middle East, North Africa, and some other states, true democracy is as likely to unleash destabilizing as stabilizing forces, particularly Islamic fundamental-

ism. The end of the totalitarian rule that kept simmering ethnic tensions in eastern Europe under control has already resulted in violent conflict in the Balkans: it was "democratic" decisions to secede from Yugoslavia after free elections in Slovenia and Croatia that sparked war. The best we can say is that democracies generally do not attack their neighbors.

Further, America's ability to advance democratic values is inconsistent at best. There is little the United States can do to make Haiti a free country, for example; sustaining in power a demagogue like Jean-Bertrand Aristide, even an elected one, certainly will not. And Washington's policies often throw United States commitment to democracy into question. Foreign aid, in particular, has assisted authoritarian rulers more often than liberal forces all over the third world. In the absence of any direct link between important United States objectives and the imperative to advance democracy in a particular country, American resources should not be used in this way.

Furthermore, to decide that a specific intervention is consistent with the purpose of the United States government is not enough to justify it. Decisionmakers also need to assess whether there are alternative means of achieving the goal. A free Europe is certainly important to the United States, but keeping 100,000 troops there is not necessary. The Soviet threat has disappeared, while Europe's ability to defend itself has expanded. A sharply reduced potential Russian threat may remain in coming years as Moscow struggles with daunting economic, ethnic, and political problems, but civil war is far more likely than aggression against the West. Indeed, according to the International Institute for Strategic Studies, Russia now spends less than Germany alone on the military. Thus there is no reason the Europeans, with three times the economic strength of a decaying Russia (and a larger gross national product than America) and a new buffer in the former Warsaw Pact states, cannot create their own security system to deter any potential threat.

Indeed, those who should be most concerned about a Russian revival—the Germans—aren't. Last year Chancellor Helmut Kohl announced his nation was going to cut troop levels 40 percent through 1995. If Bonn sees no need to maintain a large military for its protection, there is certainly no cause for America to maintain troops in Germany. Washington is increasingly begging the Europeans for the right to defend them.

Similarly, South Korea is vastly stronger than North Korea by every measure except current military strength. Seoul's growing edge has become increasingly obvious as South Korea has stripped away all of the north's allies, particularly Russia and China. The south is fully capable of eliminating the military imbalance on the peninsula. South Korean officials do not deny their country's ability to sharply increase its defense efforts; instead, they tend to complain about having to bear the added expense. This is hardly a justification for an American presence. Seoul could gradually increase its military spending—which would be unnecessary if the north enters into meaningful arms control negotiations—as United States forces were phased out. The potential North Korean acquisition of a nuclear weapon is serious, but the continued presence of American ground forces will do nothing to stop nuclear proliferation; rather, the troops would simply serve as nuclear hostages....

It might be difficult to fashion alternative solutions that do not involve direct United States intervention, and Washington might not always be fully satisfied with the outcome. But it is unrealistic to expect the United States to assume the responsibility for maintaining global order. Instead, Washington should seek to promote cost-effective policies that yield results most consistent with the government's duty to protect Americans' security and constitutional freedoms.

Even if there appear to be no alternatives to a United States commitment, the United States must weigh benefits against costs before it intervenes, and avoid or extricate itself from tragic but ultimately irrelevant conflicts. For example, more people died in 1993 in Angola than in Bosnia. Starvation stalks Liberia and Sudan, both victims of vicious civil wars. Yet there has been no groundswell for intervention in Angola, and no UN relief mission for the latter two. The Trans-Caucasus is suffering from seven separate conflicts. All are human catastrophes, but none affects a single vital American interest or warrants the death of even one United States soldier. The point is not that American lives are worth more than others', but that the primary duty of the United States government is to safeguard the lives of its own citizens—servicemen included—not sacrifice them for even seemingly worthy causes.

What if United States policymakers concluded that South Korea would not defend itself if Washington pulled out its troops? In fact, Seoul would probably be the last American ally to give up, but what if it decided to do so? A northern takeover of the south would be a tragedy for the latter, but it would have little impact on the United States, whose security would remain largely unchanged and whose economy would suffer only marginally from the loss of a midsize trading partner. The threat to go to war should be reserved for cases involving vital American interests. Korea is a peripheral, rather than a substantial, interest of the United States, and does not justify spending billions of dollars and risking tens of thousands of lives every year, especially if the peninsula goes nuclear.

A similar analysis could have been conducted for the Gulf. Even if the other regional powers had not taken steps to contain Iraq, the likelihood of Saddam Hussein striking Saudi Arabia was overplayed, since this would have left him dangerously overextended. (In fact, United States intelligence knew at the time he was withdrawing his best units to Iraq after seizing Kuwait.)

The consequences even of a highly unlikely conquest of the entire Gulf were overstated. In this fantastic worst-case scenario, Saddam would have controlled about one-fifth of international petroleum production; enough to nudge prices up, to be sure, but not enough to control them or wreck the international economy. Nor did Saddam's invasion of Kuwait threaten America's ally Israel. On the contrary, Iraq only attacked Israel in a desperate attempt to split the coalition; absent the United States presence, Baghdad would surely not have attacked Israel since it was fully capable and willing to retaliate.

THE LUXURY OF UNINVOLVEMENT

The United States enjoys many advantages that provide it with the luxury of remaining aloof from geopolitical conflicts that engulf other countries. American benefits from relative geographic isolation, for example. (This does not insulate it from nuclear attack, of course, which is why it should try to develop some form of missile defense.) The United States is also the world's largest single economic market, which reduces the impact of the loss of one or more trading partners. (Germany and Japan, for example, would suffer far more if the American market was denied them.) Moreover, the United States has a constitutional system and political philosophy that have endured for more than 200 years and have proved to be popular around the world.

This unique status allows America to balance the costs and benefits of intervention differently from most other states. Alliances make a lot more sense among European states threatened by a Soviet Union, for instance, or between Saudi Arabia and its neighbors when they are threatened by Iraq. Observes political commentator and former presidential candidate Patrick Buchanan, "Blessed by Providence with pacific neighbors, north and south, and vast oceans, east and west, to protect us, why seek permanent entanglements in other people's quarrels?"

For this reason, the United States is rarely open to charges of appeasement, such as are sometimes rightly leveled at other countries, for intervention is seldom required to protect its vital interests. For example, had France and Britain accurately perceived the potential threat posed by Nazi Germany, they should have blocked the remilitarization of the Rhineland and they certainly should not have helped dismember Czechoslovakia (through active intervention, it should be noted). Washington's failure to leave its expeditionary force in Europe in 1919 or to raise a new one in 1933, however, did not constitute appeasement. Similarly, it would not be appeasement for the United States to decline to defend a populous and prosperous South Korea; for Seoul to choose not to augment its forces once United States troops were gone, however, would be.

In fact, there is nothing wrong in principle with appeasement, if this means only diplomatic accommodation and avoidance of war. In the late nineteenth and early twentieth centuries, Austria-Hungary, Britain, France, Germany, and Russia all resolved potentially violent disagreements without conflict by making concessions to one another that could be termed "appeasement." The case of Nazi Germany was different, because Hitler wanted far more than could be given to him, and because the allies materially weakened themselves—for example, by eviscerating Czechoslovakia—in attempting to satisfy him.

The end of the cold war has resulted in a new world order, whether or not the United States defines or polices it. The Russian military remains a potent force, of course, but it is far less capable than that possessed by the Soviet Union, and Moscow's will to use it in an aggressive fashion appears to have dissipated. Moreover, the ability of American allies —a Japan that is the second-ranking economic power in the world, a reunited Germany that dominates Europe, and so on—to contain Russia has grown. These two changes alone give the United States an opportunity to refashion its foreign policy.

A new, noninterventionist policy should rest on the following bedrock principles:

- The security of the United States and its constitutional system should remain the United States government's highest goal. Individuals may decide to selflessly risk their lives to help others abroad; policymakers, however, have no authority to risk their citizens' lives, freedom, and wealth in similar pursuits.

- Foreign intervention is usually expensive and risky, and often counterproductive. Many smaller nations may still need to forge preemptive alliances to respond to potentially aggressive regional powers. Because of America's relative geographic isolation and other advantages, however, intervention is rarely necessary to protect our security and free institutions. This is especially true today, with the disappearance of a threatening hegemonic power.

- America's most powerful assets for influencing the rest of the world are its philosophy and free institutions, the ideas of limited government and free enterprise that are now sweeping the globe, and its economic prowess as the world's most productive nation. These factors ensure the nation's influence irrespective of the size of its military and where its soldiers are stationed. The United States can best affect others through private means— commerce, culture, literature, travel, and the like.

- The world will continue to suffer from injustice, terror, murder, and aggression. But it is simply not Washington's role to try to right every wrong —a hopeless task in any event. The American people are entitled to enjoy their freedom and prosperity rather than having their future held hostage to unpredictable events abroad. Their lives and treasure should not be sacrificed in quixotic crusades unrelated to their basic interests.

The world is changing faster today than it has at any time since the end of World War II. As a result, the United States has no choice but to refashion its foreign policy. While Washington should remain engaged throughout the world culturally, economically, and politically, it should bring its military home and curtail expensive foreign aid programs. After bearing the primary burden of fighting the cold war, Americans deserve to enjoy the benefits of peace through a policy of benign detachment. War may still be forced upon them, of course. But as John Quincy Adams observed shortly after the nation's founding, America should not go abroad "in search of monsters to destroy."

NO

Anthony Lake

THE PRICE OF LEADERSHIP:
THE NEW ISOLATIONISTS

Delivered at The National Press Club, Washington, D.C.,
April 27, 1995

Let me begin with a simple but alarming fact: The United States could be on the brink of unilateral disarmament. Did that get your attention? I hope so, because it is true. No, we are not about to junk our jets or scuttle our ships. Our military is strong and ready—and there is a strong bipartisan consensus to keep it so. But we are on the verge of throwing away—or at least damaging—many of the other tools America has used for 50 years to maintain our leadership in the world. Aid to emerging markets, economic support for peace, international peacekeeping, programs to fight terrorism and drug trafficking, foreign assistance: Together with a strong military, these have been key instruments of our foreign policy.

Presidents since Harry Truman have used these tools to promote American interests—to preserve our security, to expand our prosperity and to advance democracy. Their efforts were supported by Democrats and Republicans—and the broad majority of the American people. Congress consistently provided the needed resources for these tasks. Because of this resolve, coupled with our military might, we prevailed over the long haul in the Cold War, strengthened our security and won unparalleled prosperity for our people.

Now, I deeply believe our success is in danger. It is under attack by new isolationists from both left and right who would deny our nation those resources. Our policy of engagement in world affairs is under siege—and American leadership is in peril.

A few of the new isolationists act out of conviction. They argue that the end of the Soviet menace means the serious threats are gone—that we should withdraw behind our borders and stick to concerns at home. Fortress America, they say, can shut out new dangers even though some of the new threats facing us—like nuclear proliferation, terrorism, rapid population growth and environmental degradation—know no boundaries.

But most of the new isolationists do not argue such a position or even answer to the name isolationist. They say they are part of the postwar bipartisan consensus... that their goals are its goals—democracy, security, peace and prosperity. But they won't back up their words with deeds.

These self-proclaimed devotees of democracy would deny aid to struggling democracies. They laud American leadership, but oppose American leadership of coalitions, advocating only unilateral action instead.

Yes they praise peace. But then they cut our help to those who take risks for peace. They demand greater prosperity. But they shy away from the hard work of opening markets for American workers and businesses. Under the cover of budget-cutting, they threaten to cut the legs out from under America's leadership.

These are the back-door isolationists—and they are much more numerous and influential than those who argue openly for American retreat. They can read the polls, and they know that the American people want the U.S. to be engaged in the world. Support for American leadership in the world is about as strong as ever—a Chicago Council on Foreign Relations survey [published in *Foreign Policy* (1995)] shows two-thirds or more want us to remain deeply engaged. So these back-door isolationists and unilateralists cast themselves as the true guardians of American power. But through their actions, they could become the agents of an America's retreat. They champion American leadership, but they want it the one way you can't have it: and that is on the cheap.

They want America to turn its back on 50 years of success. They are working—whether they know it or not—to destroy part of the foundation for our peace and prosperity, the great legacy of our post-war leaders: Vandenberg, Truman, Marshall, Acheson. These men faced their own challenge from isolationists. But they saw the cost of our earlier withdrawal after Versailles was terribly, terribly damaged—saw it in the wreckage of Europe and Asia after World War II and the casualties America suffered liberating those continents. And they understood that investing in a vigorous foreign policy was the only way to prevent another catastrophe.

They knew the price of leadership. They spent what was necessary to maintain America's security. And they went further, creating the United Nations and the Bretton Woods institutions [such as the International Monetary Fund] and covering those bills, pouring Marshall aid into Western Europe to save it from despair and communism, and they and their successors in later Administrations developed the new tool of technical assistance—so that democracy and prosperity got a better chance around the world.

Look at the results: the map is almost covered with democracies, many of them strong allies. Markets that fulfill needs and dreams are expanding. A global economy supports American jobs and prosperity. These are the returns on 50 years of American political and economic investment abroad—the benefits of 50 years of bipartisan engagement.

But these achievements are not cut in stone. We will not go on reaping these benefits automatically. Back-door isolationism threatens to propel us in the wrong direction at a real moment of hope —when our engagement can still make a dramatic difference, by securing rather than frittering away our victory in the Cold War.

We could forfeit that victory because in many places, democracy still needs nurturing. Some market economies have not sunk deep roots. And the post-Cold War world has brought into new focus real and powerful dangers that threaten what we have worked for: aggression by rogue states, international terrorism, economic dislocation. These are new forms of an old conflict—the conflict between freedom and oppression, the conflict between the defenders of the open society and its enemies.

There is no expiration date on these lessons from five decades: Defeating these threats requires persistent engagement and hands-on policies. Defeating them demands resources. Throwing money at problems won't make them go away—but we also cannot solve problems without money. The measure of American leadership is not only the strength and attraction of our values, but what we bring to the table to solve the hard issues before us. That is why President Clinton has said that he will not let the new isolationism prevail.

Make no mistake. The American people want their nation to lead. Americans know the world is growing closer; they know our security and prosperity depend on our involvement abroad. And they agree with President [Clinton], who has said before and since he took office: "For America to be strong at home, it must be strong abroad."

Plenty of Americans also say they want us to spend less abroad—until they know the real numbers. Most think that we spend 15 percent or more of the federal budget on foreign aid. They think 5 percent would be about right.

They would be shocked to know that little more than 1 percent—$21 billion out of a $1.6 trillion dollar budget—goes for foreign policy spending, and less than $16 billion to foreign assistance. That's a lot of money, but not the budget-buster that neo-isolationists pretend. And that is 21 percent less in real terms than spent in FY 1986. They would also be surprised to learn that others recognize the reality of necessary resources far better than we. The richest, most powerful nation on Earth—the United States—ranks dead last among 25 industrialized nations in the percentage of GNP devoted to aid.

These are facts that should be better known. And more of our citizens should know that our foreign policy resources are devoted towards goals that the American people support.

- $6.6 billion a year promotes peace—including our efforts in the Middle East, the help we give U.S. allies to defend themselves, and our contribution to UN peacekeeping missions around the world, such as those on the Golan Heights, the Iraq-Kuwait border and in Cambodia.
- $2.4 billion builds democracy and promotes prosperity—helping South Africa, for example, hold free elections and transform itself peacefully.
- $5 billion promotes development—that includes jobs programs in Haiti to increase employment, improve infrastructure and help that nation get back on its feet.
- $1.7 billion provides humanitarian assistance—like caring for refugee children in the former Yugoslavia—because Americans have always wanted their country to alleviate suffering in areas of the most compelling need.
- And the remainder is for the State Department and other agencies that work every day to advance America's interests abroad.

This is the price of American leadership—and the backdoor isolationists don't want us to pay it. But imagine how the world would look if we did not. Take what I call the George Bailey Test. You remember George—he is the character played by Jimmy Stewart in the Christmas classic "It's a Wonderful Life." In that film, the angel Clarence shows George how Bedford Falls would have fallen apart without him.

Allow me to play Clarence briefly and take you through a world without American leadership. Imagine:

- If Ukraine, Belarus and Kazakhstan joined the club of declared nuclear weapons states because we couldn't do the deals to denuclearize them.
- If Russian missiles were still pointed at our cities, because we couldn't push to de-target them.
- If thousands of migrants were still trying to sail to our borders, because we had not helped restore democracy in Haiti.
- If nearly 1 million American jobs had not been created over the last three years alone—because we had not promoted U.S. exports.
- If we had to fight a war on the Korean peninsula—the implication of what some critics urged—because we did not confront the threat of a North Korea with nuclear weapons.
- If another quarter of a million people had died in Rwanda because we had not deployed our military and they had not done such a fine job in the refugee camps.
- Or, if we had paid tens of billions of dollars more and suffered more casualties because we insisted on fighting Operation Desert Storm against Iraq by ourselves.

Imagine that. Each of these efforts cost money and the hard work of building international coalitions. But you and I are safer, better off and enjoy more freedom because America made these investments. If the backdoor isolationists have their way, much of what we have worked for over two generations could be undone.

Speaker [Newt] Gingrich recently described what the world might look like if America retreats. He described "a dark and bloody planet... in our absence you end up in Bosnia and Rwanda and Chechnya." He added, "They are the harbingers of a much worse 21st century than anything we've seen in the half century of American leadership."

It does not have to be that way. If we continue to invest in democracy, in arms control, in stability in the developing world, in the new markets that bring prosperity, we can assure another half century of American leadership.

But already, because of decisions in the last few years, we sometimes cannot make even modest contributions to efforts that deserve our support. America is a great nation—but we cannot now find the small sum needed to help support peacekeepers in Liberia, where a million people are at risk of renewed civil war. Or the money to fund adequately UN human rights monitors in Rwanda. We can barely meet our obligations in maintaining sanctions on Serbia. This is no way to follow the heroic achievements of the Cold War. And I can't imagine that this fits any American's vision of world leadership. It doesn't fit mine.

Nickel and dime policies cost more in the end. Prevention is cheap—and doesn't attract cameras. When the all-seeing eye of television finds real suffering abroad, Americans will want their government to act—and rightly so. Funding a large humanitarian effort after a tragedy or sending in our forces abroad to assist will cost many times the investment in prevention.

Some costs of shortsighted policies must be paid in our neighborhoods: In 1993, Congress cut by almost one-third our very lean request for funding to combat the flow of narcotics into our country—and that funding has been declining in real terms ever since. As a result, we are scaling back programs to wipe out production of drugs and block their importation, as well as training programs for police, prosecutors and judges in foreign countries. America pays a far higher cost in crime and ruined lives.

These are some of the constraints we have lived with in the past few years. And now, however, American leadership faces a still more clear and present danger. Budget legislation being prepared in Congress could reduce foreign affairs spending by nearly a quarter—or $4.6 billion. That would mean drastic cuts or the elimination of aid to some states of the former Soviet Union, and into the security assistance programs that help U.S. allies and friends provide for their own defense. It would sharply reduce or eliminate our contributions to international peace operations. It would lame the agencies—like... the [Export-Import] Bank—that have played a key role in expanding U.S. exports. It would threaten our non-proliferation efforts and the Arms Control and Disarmament Agency. It could eliminate assistance for some programs that save children's lives.

These cuts would cripple our legacy of leadership. The strength to lead does not fall from heaven. It demands effort. It demands resources.

A neo-isolationist budget could undercut our strategic interest in democracy in Russia and the former Warsaw Pact. And it would directly affect America's security: We must continue to fund the farsighted programs begun by Senator [Sam] Nunn and [Richard] Lugar to reduce nuclear arsenals in the former Soviet Union. The $350 million in Nunn-Lugar funds made it possible for Ukraine to dismantle its arsenal and accede to the Non-Proliferation Treaty. That made it easier for us to pull back from the Cold War nuclear precipice—and save some $20 billion a year on strategic nuclear forces. That is just one of the more dramatic examples of how our foreign spending literally pays off.

A neo-isolationist budget could harm our efforts to prevent rogue states and terrorists from building nuclear weapons. We are spending $35 million over three years to employ thousands of weapons scientists in the former Soviet Union on civilian research projects. That helps keep them off the nuclear labor market—and from selling their skills to an Iraq or Iran.

A neo-isolationist budget could nearly end our involvement in UN peace operations around the world—operations that serve our interests. Presidents since Harry Truman have supported them as a matter of common sense. President [George] Bush in particular saw their value: last year nearly 60 percent of our UN peacekeeping bill went to operations begun with his Administration's support. His Secretary of State, James Baker, made a strong defense for these operations when he remarked that "We spent trillions to win the Cold War and we should be willing to spend millions of dollars to secure the peace."

This is burdensharing at its best. UN peace operations:

- Save us from deploying U.S. troops in areas of great importance—for example, Cyprus or the Indian subcontinent.
- They help pick up where our troops left off—for example, along the border of Iraq and Kuwait. In Haiti, UN troops are saving us resources by replacing most of our own withdrawing troops.
- They are building democracy in Namibia, Mozambique and Cambodia —all missions we helped design. In Cambodia, the UN negotiated the withdrawal of Vietnamese forces and then held the country's first democratic election. After the years of the Killing Fields, 90 percent of the electorate turned out to vote—while UN peacekeepers protected them from the Khmer Rouge.

We would pay much more if we performed even a small number of these missions unilaterally. Instead, the price we pay now in manpower and money is reasonable: Of the 61,000 UN peacekeepers deployed around the world, only some 3,300 are American. We pay the equivalent of half of one percent of our total defense spending for UN peace operations —less than a third of the total UN cost and less than the Europeans pay in proportion to their defense spending. We participate in these operations only after careful consideration of the command arrangements and costs—but we gain immense influence through our ability to lead multinational efforts.

And a neo-isolationist budget would severely undercut our work for peace. The President has said that "America stands by those who take risks for peace." This is true in Northern Ireland, in South Africa, the Middle East and around the world.

For the Middle East peace process to continue—and for negotiations in other regions to succeed—we must have the resources to support the risk-takers. We cannot convince the holdouts from the peace process that we will stand behind a just and lasting settlement if we back away from our current commitments. That means maintaining aid to Israel, Egypt and the Palestinians and fulfilling our pledge of debt relief to Jordan. In the Middle East, our vital security and economic interests are on the line. We must not fold our hands—and leave the game to the opponents of peace—just when we are so close to the verge of winning.

A neo-isolationist budget could throw away decades of investment in democracy. In the last 15 years, the number of democracies in the world has almost doubled—and USAID provided assistance to most of the newcomers. For example, in Mozambique, a nation emerging from years of strife, AID assistance helped register 6 million out of a possible 8 million voters and turn the polling there into a success. Now, when these societies are most fragile, is not the time to cut this lifeline for democracy.

And a neo-isolationist budget would directly damage our own livelihoods. Our economy depends on new markets for U.S. goods and high-paying jobs for American workers. That is why President Clinton led efforts to expand free trade with the landmark GATT agreement, NAFTA, and the free trade agreements in the Asia-Pacific region and in the Americas. And this Administration has worked harder, I believe, than any other to promote American exports. Imagine, for example, where we would be without the Commerce Department's efforts on this score. Secretary [Ron] Brown's staff worked with other agencies last year on export deals that support 300,000 U.S. jobs.

In many cases, we were in a position to close deals because America had been engaged in those countries for years. Consider two statistics: AID programs in some countries have helped increase life expectancy by a decade. And every year, AID's immunization program saves 3 million lives. These are statistics not only of humanitarian hope. They are part of efforts to help create stable societies of consumers who want to buy our goods—not masses of victims in need of relief.

In addition, our support of the multilateral development banks also helps nations grow and their economies prosper. We contribute $1.8 billion while other nations contribute $7 billion—and that capital leverages more than $40 billion in lending. If we stopped our contributions, we would lose our influence. And others might also follow our lead, and that would cripple these important institutions.

The backdoor isolationists who claim they are saving America's money cannot see beyond the green of their own eyeshades: Our assistance has repaid itself hundreds and hundreds of times over. That was true when Marshall aid resuscitated European markets after the war. And in South Korea, which now imports annually U.S. goods worth three time as much as the assistance we provided in nearly 30 years.

And while we preserve our tradition of assistance, we are reforming its practice. AID has become a laboratory for Vice President [Al] Gore's efforts to reinvent government—it is eliminating 27 overseas missions and cut its workforce by 1200.

Now, with the "New Partnership Initiative," we will improve our assistance programs even more—by focusing on the local level. This will enhance the efforts of non-governmental organizations and raise the percentage of our aid that is channeled to them to 40 percent—because these organizations are on the ground and more responsive than distant national governments. This puts our resources to better use, helping nations so they can become self-sufficient.

Every one of us in this room knows that winning support for an activist foreign policy has never been easy in America.

Throughout the history of our Republic, we have never lived in literal isolation. In a world of instant communication and capital flows, we cannot do so now. That is not the issue. Literal isolationism is not an option.

What is at issue is whether we will have the policies and resources that can shape and support our involvement in ways that benefit our people in their daily lives—whether by opening markets or by preventing conflicts that could embroil us. It is at those times that our government failed to engage in such efforts that our people have paid the greatest price—as in World War II, following a period of irresponsible American retreat.

The genius of our postwar leaders was to see that technology and American power had changed the world and that we must never again remain aloof. But they had a hard time winning support even with the memories of war still fresh.

As he put his case forward, President Truman had an uphill struggle. But a foreigner saw that it was America's moment to lead—and told us so. [British Prime

Minister] Winston Churchill stirred the nation with his appeal for an engaged foreign policy. Today, we remember his address as the Iron Curtain speech, but Churchill called it "The Sinews of Peace." The phrase plays on a saying of the Romans: "Money is the sinews of war." Churchill's message was that preserving peace—like waging war—demands resources.

Today, that message rings as true as ever. This is a moment of extraordinary hope for democracy and free markets. But nothing is inevitable. We must remain engaged. We must reach out, not retreat. American leadership in the world is not a luxury: it is a necessity. The price is worth paying. It is the price of keeping the tide of history running our way.

POSTSCRIPT

Should the United States Abandon Its Superpower Role?

The past five years have radically altered the previous four decades of world politics and the accompanying assumptions about U.S. foreign policy. Not only did the bipolar era and the cold war end, so did the Soviet Union. These changes obviated a significant part of the popular rationale for the extended U.S. presence in the world. The anticommunist foreign policy consensus has been replaced with discord. What role should the United States play in the world? What are the country's vital interests, and how much internationalism can Americans afford?

It would be incorrect to assume that most Americans are isolationists. In 1994, 65 percent of the public thought that it would be best for the United States to take an "active part" in world affairs. Americans also support the United Nations, with 65 percent of the respondents to a 1995 survey saying they agreed that "the United States should cooperate fully with the United Nations." A good, recent survey of American attitudes can be found in John E. Rielly, "The Public Mood at Mid-Decade," *Foreign Policy* (Spring 1995).

Yet, as pointed out in the introduction to this debate, the public also wants first to safeguard American wealth and energy at home, and it is wary about overseas, especially military, involvement.

The term *globocop* has been commonly used to disparage the idea that the United States should try to act like the world's police officer. Instead, as one quip goes, many Americans now lean toward the role of "globoGarbo," a reference to actress Greta Garbo's famous phrase, "I want to be alone." Those who favor the internationalist position are apt to characterize this viewpoint as isolationist. President Bill Clinton, for one, warns that "domestic renewal is an overdue tonic ... [but that] isolationism and protectionism are still poison." Others disagree. Robert Zoellick, undersecretary of state for the Bush administration, says that Americans now practice "show-me internationalism" and "want each case demonstrated on its own terms why the U.S. should engage." As far as American emphasis on domestic-oriented foreign policy goals, such as protecting jobs and stopping the inflow of drugs, Zoellick maintains, "That's a pretty good common-sense position."

The current U.S. debate goes beyond simple internationalism versus isolationism. Also important are the views of *unilateralists,* who argue that the United States should usually act independently to pursue its self-interested foreign policy goals, and *multilateralists,* who maintain that the country should try to act in concert with other countries and with international organizations to achieve common goals. This debate is played out in the Summer 1995 edition of *Foreign Policy*, with Secretary of State Warren Christopher taking the multilateralist side in "America's Leadership, America's Opportunity," and Senate majority leader Bob Dole (R-Kansas) arguing the unilateralist point of view in "Shaping America's Global Future." Christopher maintains that Americans should "galvanize the support of allies, friends, and international institutions in achieving common objectives" and avoid the unfortunate choice of either acting alone or doing nothing during humanitarian and political crises. Dole replies that "international organizations... will not protect American interests. Only America can do that." Dole objects to relying on a multilateralist approach because international organizations will "at best, practice policymaking at the lowest common denominator, finding a course that is the least objectionable to the most members."

Labels such as "internationalist" and "isolationist" or "multilateralist" and "unilateralist" are helpful in classifying foreign policy views. But they go only so far. To determine your position and to evaluate the positions of others, the next step is to identify specifically what U.S. interests are and what Americans are or should be willing to do to maintain them.

ISSUE 4

Is Islamic Fundamentalism a Threat to Political Stability?

YES: Daniel Pipes, from "Same Difference," *National Review* (November 7, 1994)

NO: John L. Esposito, from "Political Islam: Beyond the Green Menace," *Current History* (January 1994)

ISSUE SUMMARY

YES: Daniel Pipes, editor of *Middle East Quarterly*, argues that just as those who considered the Soviet threat a myth were naive, so are those who dismiss the threat from Islamic fundamentalists naive.

NO: John L. Esposito, a professor of religion and international affairs, holds that it is wrong to view Islam as a monolith whose adherents are mostly dangerous fanatics.

Several Islamic political concepts are important to this issue. Some tend to bring Muslims together; others work to divide Muslims.

One of the forces that serve to promote Muslim unity is the idea of the *ummah*, the spiritual, cultural, and political community of Muslims. In part, this means that Muslims are less likely than people from the Western cultural tradition to draw distinct lines between the state, religion, and the individual. Belief in the *ummah* also implies that the adherents to Islam should join spiritually and politically in one great Muslim community. A related unifying element of Islam is that Muslims distinguish between Muslim-held lands ("the house of Islam") and non-Muslim lands ("the house of unbelief").

A sense of common history is another factor that works to bring Muslims together. After a triumphant and powerful beginning, including the spread of Islam and its culture into Europe and elsewhere from its Middle Eastern origins, the political fortunes of the Muslims declined slowly after about the year 1500. Part of this decline was due to losses to predominately Christian European powers. By the 1920s almost all Muslim lands were under the direct or indirect control of colonial powers, which were mostly European and Christian.

There are also strong forces that tend to divide Muslims. One of these is the frequent rivalry between the majority Sunni sect and the minority Shi'ite sect. A second factor that divides Muslims is the degree to which they believe in the strict adherence to the *shari'ah*—the law of the Koran, which is composed of God's (Allah's) teachings—to govern both religious and civil conduct. Muslim traditionalists (fundamentalists, according to common usage) want to establish legal systems based on the *shari'ah* and to reinstitute many practices, such as banning alcohol and having women cover their faces, that declined under the influence of Western culture. Other Muslims, who are often called secularists, believe that religious and civil law should be kept relatively separate and that Koranic law is flexible enough to allow changes in tradition. There is considerable strife occurring in Algeria, Egypt, and several other Muslim countries based on the traditionalist-secularist struggle.

Nationalism (primary political loyalty to a national state) is a third factor that divides Muslims. Individual Muslim countries are fiercely nationalistic. Achieving full Muslim political unity would necessarily entail giving up patriotism and other manifestations of nationalism. A fourth factor, and one that further solidifies nationalism, is the major ethnic and sectarian differences within Islam. Indonesians, Iranians, Kazakhs, Pakistanis, and many other Muslim peoples are not ethnic Arabs and do not speak Arabic.

What has made all these forces of unity and division among Muslims of global concern begins with the Muslim world's change of fortune since its nadir after World War I. There are now many more independent Muslim countries. Moreover, Muslim countries are becoming increasingly more dependent, among other things, on the wealth that petroleum has brought them. By extension, Muslims everywhere have begun to reclaim their heritage in what might be called a "Muslim pride" movement.

The Muslim revival has many interrelated parts. One involves rejecting direct interference by outside powers. Rejection of outside domination entails reaction against the European–North American West, which Muslims closely identify with the Christians and imperial powers that long beset the house of Islam. There is also an intensifying of the efforts of many Muslims to "get back to their roots." That has strengthened the appeal of traditionalism, and there is a struggle in many Islamic countries between the secularists (usually in power) and the traditionalists for control of the government.

The resurgence of Muslim countries and pride has numerous impacts, current and potential, on world politics. First, the secularist-traditionalist struggle within countries will, depending on the outcome, influence their foreign policies. Second, intra-Islamic strife has in part already led to international conflict, such as the Iran-Iraq war. Muslims have also tended to unite, be that in support of Afghans, Palestinians, or others who in the Muslims' view are being oppressed. Some Muslims have also reverted to terrorism; some Muslim countries have supported this tactic.

The issue is whether or not resurgent Islam, especially its traditionalist/fundamentalist aspects, represents a threat to political stability. In the following selections, Daniel Pipes argues that the traditionalists are indeed fundamentally antithetical to stability. John L. Esposito, in disagreement, argues that the traditionalists are not inherently dangerous and should be viewed within their cultural context.

YES

Daniel Pipes

SAME DIFFERENCE

The Western confrontation with fundamentalist Islam has in some ways come to resemble the great ideological battle of the twentieth century, that between Marxism–Leninism and liberal democracy. Not only do Americans frame the discussion about Iran and Algeria much as they did the earlier one about the Soviet Union and China, but they also differ among themselves on the question of fundamentalist Islam roughly along the same lines as they did on the Cold War. Liberals say: Co-opt the radicals. Conservatives say: Confront them. As usual, the conservatives are right.

At first glance, how to deal with fundamentalist Islam appears to be a discussion unrelated to anything that has come before. Islam is a religion, not an ideology, so how can the U.S. Government formulate a policy toward it? A closer look reveals that while Islam is indeed a faith, its fundamentalist variant is a form of political ideology. Fundamentalists may be defined, most simply, as those Muslims who agree with the slogan: "Islam is the solution." When it comes to politics, they say that Islam has all the answers. The Malaysian leader Anwar Ibrahim spoke for fundamentalist Muslims everywhere when he asserted some years ago that "we are not socialist, we are not capitalist, we are Islamic." For the fundamentalists, Islam is primarily an "ism," a belief system about ordering power and wealth.

Much distinguishes fundamentalism from Islam as it was traditionally practiced, including its emphasis on public life (rather than faith and personal piety); its leadership by schoolteachers and engineers (rather than religious scholars); and its Westernized quality (e.g., whereas Muslims traditionally did not consider Friday a Sabbath, fundamentalists have turned it into precisely that, imitating the Jewish Saturday and Christian Sunday). In brief, fundamentalism represents a thoroughly modern effort to come to terms with the challenges of modernization.

The great majority of Muslims disagree with the premises of fundamentalist Islam, and a small number do so vocally. A few... have acquired global reputations, but most toil more obscurely. When a newly elected deputy to the Jordanian parliament last fall called fundamentalist Islam "one of the greatest dangers facing our society" and compared it to "a cancer" that "has to be surgically removed," she spoke for many Muslims.

Americans can in good conscience join them in criticizing fundamentalism. As an ideology, fundamentalist Islam can claim none of the sanctity that Islam the religion enjoys.

BATTLE LINES

In responding to fundamentalist Islam, Americans tend, as I have suggested, to divide along familiar liberal and conservative lines. More striking yet, the same people hold roughly the same positions they held vis-à-vis that other quasi-religious ideology, Marxism–Leninism. A left-wing Democrat like George McGovern advocates a soft line, now as then. A right-wing Republican like Jesse Helms argues for a tough line, now as then. Consider the following parallels:

Causes. The Left, in keeping with its materialist outlook, sees Communist or fundamentalist Islamic ideology as a cover for some other motivation, probably an economic one. The Russian Revolution expressed deep-seated class grievances; fundamentalist violence in Algeria, the State Department tells us, expresses "frustration arising from political exclusion and economic misery." In contrast, the Right sees radical utopian ideology as a powerful force in itself, not just as an expression of socio-economic woes. Ideas and ambitions count at least as much as the price of wheat; visions of a new order go far toward accounting for the revolutions of 1917 and 1979.

Solutions. If misery causes radicalism, as the Left argues, then the antidote lies in economic growth and social equity. The West can help in these areas through aid, trade, and open lines of communication. But if, as the Right believes, ambitious intellectuals are the problem, then they must be battled and defeated. In both cases, liberals look to cooperation, conservatives to confrontation.

The West's responsibility. The Left sees Western hostility as a leading reason why things have gone wrong. According to one journalist, the West "made its own sizable contribution" to the current crisis in Algeria. It's the old "blame America first" attitude: just as Americans were responsible for every Soviet trespass from the Gulag to the arms race, so they are now answerable for the appearance [in Iran] of the Ayatollah Khomeini (due to U.S. support for the Shah) and for the many Arab fundamentalist movements (due to U.S. support for Israel). The Right adamantly denies Western culpability in both cases, for that would absolve tyrants of their crimes. We made mistakes, to be sure, but that's because we find it hard to contend with racial utopian movements. Along these lines, [one analyst] argues that "we are at the beginning of what promises to be a long war in which new moral complexities... will present themselves as once they did in the days of Soviet Communism."

A single source. When the State Department disclaims "monolithic international control being exercised over the various Islamic movements," it uses almost the same words it once used to speak of Marxism–Leninism. For decades, American "progressives" insisted that Communist organizations around the world had indigenous sources and did not owe anything to Moscow (a claim easier to make so long as Moscow's archives remained closed). To which conservatives typically replied: Of course there's no "monolithic international control," but there is an awful lot of funding and influence. Teheran administers a network akin to an Islamic Comintern, making its role today not that different from Moscow's then.

The antis. For many decades, the Left saw those Russians, Chinese, and Cubans whose firsthand experience turned them into anti-Communists as marginal elements. In similar fashion, the Left today looks at anti-fundamentalist Muslims as inauthentic. Churches are among the worst offenders here. For example, in one recent analysis, a German priest presented the extremist element as the Muslim community per se. The Right wholeheartedly celebrates the new antis, like the old, as brave individuals bringing advance word of the terrors that result from efforts radically to remake society.

Do moderates exist? The Left distinguishes between those ideologues willing to work within the system (deemed acceptable) and those who rely on violence and sabotage (deemed unacceptable). The Right acknowledges differences in tactics but perceives no major difference in goals. Accordingly, it tends to lump most Communists or fundamentalists together.

Motives. When the other side strikes out aggressively, the Left often excuses its acts by explaining how they are defensive. Invasions by Napoleon and Hitler explain the Soviet presence in Angola; a legacy of colonial oppression accounts for the depths of fundamentalist rage. The Right concludes from events like the downing of a Korean Airlines flight or the World Trade Center bombing that the other side has offensive intentions, and it listens to no excuses.

Fighting words. The two sides draw contrary conclusions from aggressive speech. Liberals dismiss the barrage of threats against the West (Muslim prisoner in a French court: "We Muslims should kill every last one of you [Westerners]") as mere rhetoric. Conservatives listen carefully and conclude that the West needs to protect itself (French Interior Minister Charles Pasqua: fundamentalist groups "represent a threat to us").

Threat to the West. If they are approached with respect, says the Left, Marxist–Leninists and fundamentalist Muslims will leave us alone. Don't treat them as enemies and they won't hurt us. The Right disagrees, holding that all revolutionaries, no matter what their particular outlook (Communist, Fascist, fundamentalist), are deeply anti-Western and invariably target the West. Their weaponry ranges from ICBMs to truck bombs, but their purpose is the same: to challenge the predominance of modern, Western civilization.

And if truck bombs are less threatening than missiles, it should be noted that fundamentalists challenge the West more profoundly than Communists did and do. The latter disagree with our politics but not with our whole view of the world (how could they, as they pay homage to Dead White Males like Marx and Engels?). In contrast, fundamentalist Muslims despise our whole way of life, including the way we dress, mate, and pray. They admire little more than our military and medical technologies. To appease Communists means changing the political and economic spheres; to appease fundamentalists would mean forcing women to wear the veil, scuttling nearly every form of diversion, and overhauling the judicial system.

Future prospects. In the 1950s, the Left portrayed Marxism–Leninism as the wave of the future; today, it ascribes the same brilliant prospect to fundamentalist Islam. In other words, these radical ideologies are an unstoppable force; stand in their way, and you'll not only get run over, you might even spur them on. But conservatives see utopianism enjoying only a temporary surge. The effort to remake mankind, they say, cannot work; like Communism, fundamentalism has to end up in the dustbin of history.

CONCILIATION OR CONTAINMENT?

Summing up, the Left is more sanguine than the Right about both Communism and fundamentalist Islam. It's hard to imagine a conservative calling the Ayatollah Khomeini "some kind of saint," as did Jimmy Carter's ambassador to the United Nations, Andrew Young. It's about as uncommon to hear a liberal warning, along with France's Defense Minister François Léotard, that "Islamic nationalism in its terrorist version is as dangerous today as National Socialism was in the past." On the scholarly level, a liberal Democrat like John Esposito publishes a book titled *The Islamic Threat: Myth or Reality?*, in which he concludes that the threat is but a myth. In sharp contrast, Walter McDougall, the Pulitzer Prize–winning historian and sometime assistant to Richard Nixon, sees Russia helping the West in "holding the frontier

of Christendom against its common enemy," the Muslim world.

These contrary analyses lead, naturally, to very different prescriptions for U.S. policy. The Left believes that dialogue with the other side, whether Communists or fundamentalist Muslims, has several advantages: it helps us understand their legitimate concerns, signals that we mean them no harm, and reduces mutual hostility. Beyond dialogue, the West can show good will by reducing or even eliminating our military capabilities. Roughly speaking, this is the Clinton Administration's position. In Algeria, for instance, the Administration hopes to defuse a potential explosion by urging the regime to bring in fundamentalist leaders who reject terrorism, thereby isolating the violent extremists.

The Right has little use for dialogue and unilateral disarmament. Communists and fundamentalists being invariably hostile to us, we should show not empathy but resolve, not good will but will power. And what better way to display these intentions than with armed strength? Now as then, conservatives think in terms of containment and rollback. For conservatives, Algeria's regime fits into the tradition of friendly tyrants —states where the rulers treat their own population badly but help the United States fend off a radical ideology. It makes sense to stand by Algiers (or Cairo), just as it earlier made sense to stick by Ky in Saigon or Pinochet in Chile.

Of course, the schemas presented here do not align perfectly. The Reagan Administration searched for "moderates" in Iran (an effort led by none other than Oliver North), and the Bush Administration enunciated a soft policy toward fundamentalism. The Clinton Administration, in contrast, has pursued a quite resolute policy toward Iran.

Interests sometimes count for more than ideology. Circumstance on occasion compels the U.S. Government to aid one enemy against another; thus, we have recently helped fundamentalist Afghans against Communist ones, and Communist Palestinians against fundamentalist ones. The liberal Clinton Administration speaks out against a crackdown on fundamentalists in Algeria, where the stakes are low for Americans, but accepts tough measures in Egypt, where the United States has substantial interests. The conservative French government bemoans the crackdown in Egypt (not so important for it) but encourages tough measures in Algeria (very important).

Still, the basic pattern is clear. And as the lines of debate sort themselves out, the two sides are likely to stick more consistently to their characteristic positions. This suggests that while Marxism–Leninism and fundamentalist Islam are very different phenomena, Westerners respond in similar ways to ideological challenges.

They do so because of a profound divide in outlook. American liberals believe that mankind is by nature peaceful and cooperative; when confronted with aggression and violence, they tend to assume it is motivated by a just cause, such as socio-economic deprivation or exploitation by foreigners. Anger cannot be false, especially if accompanied by high-minded goals. Less naïvely, conservatives know the evil that lurks in men's hearts. They understand the important roles of fanaticism and hatred. Just because an ideology has utopian aims does not mean that its adherents have lofty motives or generous ambitions.

The Left's soft approach to fundamentalist Islam predominates in Washington, and in the universities, the churches, and the media. Indeed, to recall one of the Left's favorite phrases, it has become the hegemonic discourse in the United States. On the other side stand nothing but a handful of scholars, some commentators and politicians, and the great common sense of the American people. Americans know an opponent when they see him, and they are not fooled by the Left's fancy arguments. That common sense prevailed in the Cold War and no doubt will suffice yet again to overcome the follies of the New Class.

NO

John L. Esposito

POLITICAL ISLAM:
BEYOND THE GREEN MENACE

From Ayatollah Khomeini to Sheik Omar Abdel Rahman, from Iran to the World Trade Center, government leaders and opinion makers in the West and in the Middle East have warned of the dangers of militant Islam. If the 1980s were dominated by images of embassies under siege, American hostages, and hijackings, the 1990s bring prophecies of insurgent movements wielding nuclear weapons and employing urban terrorism. Headlines announce the possibility of a worldwide Islamic uprising and a clash of civilizations in which Islam may overwhelm the West. Television viewers see the bodies of Coptic Christians and tourists killed by Egyptian extremists and take in reports of Algerian militants' pitched battles with police. All fuel alarmist concerns reflected in publications and conferences with titles like "Roots of Muslim Rage," "Islam: Deadly Duel with Zealots," and "Awaiting God's Wrath: Islamic Fundamentalism and the West."

For more than four decades governments formulated policy in the midst of a superpower rivalry that defined the globe and the future in terms of the visible ideological and military threat posed by the Soviet Union. In the aftermath of the cold war, the fall of the Soviet Union and the discrediting of communism have created a "threat vacuum" that has given rise to a search for new enemies. For some Americans the enemy is the economic challenge the Japanese or the European Community represent. For others it is an Islamic world whose 1 billion Muslims form a majority in more the 48 countries and a rapidly growing minority in Europe and America. Some view Islam as the only ideological alternative to the West that can cut across national boundaries, and perceiving it as politically and culturally at odds with Western society, fear it; others consider it a more basic demographic threat.

The 1990s, however, reveal the diversity and complexity of political Islam and point to a twenty-first century that will shake the assumptions of many. While some Islamic organizations engage in terrorism, seeking to topple governments, others spread their message through preaching and social services and demand the right to gain legitimate power with ballots rather than bullets. But what of militant Islam? Is there an international Islamic threat? Will humanity witness the rise of a "new Comintern" led by "religious Stalinists" poised to challenge the free world and impose Iranian-style Islamic republics through violence, or through an electoral process that enables Islamic movements to "hijack democracy"?

FAITH, FUNDAMENTALISM, AND FACT

Muslims vary as much in their interpretations of Islam as followers of other faiths with theirs. For the vast majority of believers, Islam, like other world religions, is a faith of peace and social justice, moving its adherents to worship God, obey His laws, and be socially responsible.

Indiscriminate use of the term "Islamic fundamentalism" and its identification with governments and movements have contributed to the sense of a monolithic menace when in actuality political Islam is far more diverse. Saudi Arabia, Libya, Pakistan, and Iran have been called fundamentalist states, but this tells us nothing about their nature: Saudi Arabia is a conservative monarchy, Libya a populist socialist state headed by a military dictator. Moreover, the label says nothing about the state's Islamic character or orientation. Pakistan under General Muhammad Zia ul-Haq embodied a conservative Islam, and Saudi Arabia still does; Islam in Libya is radical and revisionist; clerics dominate in Iran. Finally, although fundamentalism is popularly equated with anti-Americanism and extremism, and Libya and Iran have indeed often denounced America, Saudi Arabia and Pakistan have been close allies of the United States and the mujahideen that resisted the Soviet occupation of Afghanistan received support from Washington for years.

The Iranian revolution of 1978–1979 called attention to a reassertion of Islam in Muslim personal and public life that subsequently came to be referred to by many names: Islamic resurgence, Islamic revivalism, political Islam, and more commonly, Islamic fundamentalism. The totally unexpected ousting of the shah of Iran by an Islamic revolution led by the charismatic Ayatollah Ruhollah Khomeini and the creation of an Islamic republic under the mullahs stunned the world. Fear that Iran would export Islamic revolution to other countries of the Middle East became the lens through which events in the Muslim world were viewed. When Khomeini spoke, the world listened—supporters with admiration, detractors with disdain and disgust or, often, anxiety.

The 1979 takeover of the United States embassy in Teheran and Khomeini's expansionist designs, Libyan leader Muammar Qaddafi's posturing and promotion of a third world revolution, and Egyptian President Anwar Sadat's 1981 assassination by Muslim extremists supported the projection of a militant Islamic fundamentalism. Hostage-taking, hijackings, and attacks on foreign and government installations by groups such as the Islamic Liberation Organization, Jihad, and Takfir wal Hijra (Excommunication and Flight) in Egypt and by the Iranian-funded Hezbollah and Islamic Jihad in Lebanon received enormous publicity. In the late 1970s and throughout the 1980s the prevailing picture of the Islamic world in the West was of militants bent on undermining countries' stability, overthrowing governments, and imposing their version of an Islamic state. The result was the facile equation: Islam = fundamentalism = terrorism and extremism.

THE ROOTS OF RESURGENCE

The reality is that Islamic revivalism was not the product of the Iranian revolution but of a global reassertion of Islam that had already been under way and that extended from Libya to Malaysia.

The causes of the resurgence are many and differ from country to country, but common catalysts and concerns are identifiable. Secular nationalism (whether in the form of liberal nationalism, Arab nationalism, or socialism) has not provided a sense of national identity or produced strong and prosperous societies. The governments in Muslim countries —mostly nonelected, authoritarian, and dependent on security forces—have been unable to establish their political legitimacy. They have been blamed for the failure to achieve economic self-sufficiency, to stem the widening gap between rich and poor, to halt widespread corruption, to liberate Palestine, to resist Western political and cultural hegemony. Both the political and the religious establishments have come under criticism, the former as a westernized, secular elite overly concerned with power and privilege, and the latter (in Sunni Muslim nations) as leaders of the faithful who have been co-opted by governments that often control mosques and religious universities and other institutions....

Islamic revivalism is in many ways the successor to failed nationalist programs. The founders of many Islamic movements were formerly participants in nationalist movements: Hasan al-Banna of the Muslim Brotherhood in Egypt, Rashid Ghannoushi of Tunisia's Renaissance party, and Abbasi Madani of the Islamic Salvation Front in Algeria. Islamic movements have offered an Islamic alternative or solution, a third way distinct from capitalism and communism. Islamists argue that secularism, a modern bias toward the West, and dependence on Western models of development have proved politically inadequate and socially corrosive, undermining the identity and moral fabric of Muslim societies. Asserting that Islam is not just a collection of beliefs and ritual actions but a comprehensive ideology embracing public as well as personal life, they call for the implementation of Sharia, or Islamic law, as a social blueprint. While the majority within the Muslim world seek to work within the system, a small but significant minority believes that the rulers in their countries are anti-Islamic and that they have a divine mandate to unseat them and impose their vision.

In general, the movements are urban-based, drawing heavily from the lower middle and middle classes. They have gained particular support among recent university graduates and young professionals, male and female. The movements recruit from the mosques and on campuses where, contrary to popular assumptions, their strength is not so much in the religious faculties and the humanities as in science, engineering, education, law, and medicine....

In many Muslim countries an alternative elite exists, its members with modern educations but self-consciously oriented toward Islam and committed to social and political activism as a means of bringing about a more Islamic society or system of government. This phenomenon is reflected in the presence—and often dominance—of Islamists in professional associations of lawyers, engineers, professors, and physicians. Where permitted to participate in society, Islamists are found in all sectors, including government and even the military.

FROM PERIPHERY TO CENTER

Demonization of Islam proceeded throughout the 1980s, but by late in the decade a more nuanced, broad-based, diverse Islamic world was increasingly evident. Beneath the radical façade, apart from the small, marginalized extremist groups, a quiet revolution had taken place. While a rejectionist minority had sought to impose change from above through holy wars, many others reaffirmed their faith and pursued a bottom-up approach, seeking a gradual Islamization of society through words, preaching, and social and political activity. In many Muslim countries Islamic organizations had become energetic in social reform, establishing much-needed schools, hospitals, clinics, legal societies, family assistance programs, Islamic banks and insurance companies, and publishing houses. These Islamically oriented groups offered social welfare services cheaply and constituted an implicit critique of the failure of the regimes in the countries to provide adequate services.

Along with social activism went increased political participation. In the late 1980s economic failures led to mass demonstrations and food riots in Egypt, Tunisia, Algeria, and Jordan. Moreover, the demand for democratization that accompanied the fall of the Soviet Union and the liberation of Eastern Europe touched the Middle East as well. Throughout the decade many governments in the Muslim world charged that the Islamic activists were merely violent revolutionaries whose lack of popular support would be evident if elections were held, but few governments showed themselves willing to put this claim to the test. When political systems were opened up and Islamic organiza-

tions were able to participate in elections, the results stunned many in the Muslim world and in the West. Although Islamists were not allowed to organize separate official political parties, in Egypt and Tunisia they emerged as the leading opposition. In the November 1989 elections in Jordan they captured 32 of 80 seats in the lower house of parliament and held five cabinet-level positions and the office of speaker of the lower house. Algeria, however, was the turning point.

Algeria had been dominated for decades by a one-party dictatorship under the National Liberation Front (FLN). Because FLN was socialist and had a strong secular elite and feminist movement, few took the Islamic movement seriously; moreover, the movement had been among the least well known of the country's groups outside its borders, even among Islamists. The stunning victory of the Islamic Salvation Front (FIS), an umbrella group, in 1990 municipal elections sent a shock wave around the globe.

Despite the arrest of front leaders Abbasi Madani and Ali Belhadj; the cut-off of state funds to municipalities, often crippling FIS officials' ability to provide services; and gerrymandering to create districts more favorable to itself, the ruling party failed to prevent an even more stunning sweep by the FIS in parliamentary elections held in December 1991. As Islamists at home and across the Muslim world celebrated, the military intervened, forcing the resignation of Algeria's president, arresting FIS leaders, imprisoning more than 10,000 people in desert camps, and outlawing the front, and seizing its assets.

In the face of the repression much of the world stood silent. The conventional wisdom had been blind-sided. While most feared and were on their guard against "other Irans," the Islamic Salvation Front's victory in Algeria raised the specter of an Islamic movement coming to power through democratic elections and ballots worried many world leaders even more than bullets. The justification for accepting the Algerian military's seizure of power was the charge that the FIS really only believed in "One man, one vote, one time." The perceived threat from revolutionary Islam was intensified by the fear that it would capture power from within the political system by democratic means.

THE TRIPLE THREAT

In contrast to other parts of the world, calls for greater political participation and democratization in the Middle East have been met by empty rhetoric and repression at home and by ambivalence or silence in the West. Middle Eastern governments have used the danger posed by Islamic fundamentalism as the excuse for increasing authoritarianism and violations of human rights and the indiscriminate suppression of Islamic opposition, as well as for the West's silence about these actions.

Fear of fundamentalism, like fear of communism, has made strange bedfellows. Tunisia, Algeria, and Egypt join Israel in warning of a regional and international Islamic threat in their bids to win Western aid and justify their repression of Islamists.... Israeli Prime Minister Yitzhak Rabin justified the expulsion of 415 Palestinians in December 1992 by saying that "Our struggle against murderous Islamic terror is also meant to awaken the world, which is lying in slumber ... We call on all nations, all peoples to devote their attention to the greater danger inherent in Islamic fundamentalism[, which] threatens world peace in future years ... [W]e stand on the line of fire against the danger of fundamentalist Islam."

Israel and its Arab neighbors have warned that a resurgent Iran is exporting revolution throughout much of the Muslim world, including Sudan, the West Bank and Gaza Strip, Algeria, and Central Asia, as well as to Europe and America; indeed, Egyptian President Hosni Mubarak has urged the formation of a "global alliance" against this menace.

Islam is often portrayed as a triple threat: political, civilizational, and demographic. The fear in the 1980s that Iran would export its revolution has been superseded by the larger fear of an international pan-Islamic movement with Iran and Sudan at its heart. In this decade, despite Iran's relative failure in fomenting revolution abroad, visions of global Islamic threat have proliferated, combining fear of violent revolution and of Algerian-style electoral victories. French writer Raymond Aron's warning of an Islamic revolutionary wave generated by the fanaticism of the Prophet and Secretary of State Cyrus Vance's concern over the possibility of an Islamic-Western war have been succeeded by columnist Charles Krauthammer's assertion of a global Islamic threat of "fundamentalist Koran-waving Khomeiniism" led by Iran.

The Ayatollah Khomeini's condemning of novelist Salman Rushdie to death for blasphemy for his *Satanic Verses*, combined with Iraqi President Saddam Hussein's call for a holy war against the West during the 1991 Persian Gulf War, reinforce fears of a political and cultural confrontation. This is magnified by some who, like Krauthammer, reduce contemporary realities to the playing out of ancient rivalries: "It should now be clear that we are facing a mood and a movement far transcending the level of issues and policies and the governments that pursue them. This is no less than a clash of civilizations—a perhaps irrational but surely historic reaction of an ancient rival against our Judaeo-Christian heritage, our secular present, and the worldwide expansion of both."

Muslim-Western relations are placed in the context of a confrontation in which Islam is again pitted against the West—"our Judaeo-Christian and secular West"—rather than specific political and socioeconomic grievances. Thus the assault on the West is seen as "irrational," mounted by peoples peculiarly driven by their passions and hatred; how can Western countries really respond to this?

The politics of the Middle East refutes theories of a monolithic threat. Despite a common "Islamic" orientation, the governments of the region reveal little unity of purpose in interstate or international relations because of conflicting national interests and priorities. Qaddafi was a bitter enemy of Anwar Sadat and Sudanese leader Gaafar Nimeiry at the very time that all were projecting their "Islamic images." Khomeini's Islamic republic consistently called for the overthrow of Saudi Arabia's Islamic state on Islamic grounds. Islamically identified governments also differ in their stance toward the West. Libya's and Iran's relationships with the West, and the United States in particular, were often confrontational; at the same time, the United States has had strong allies in Saudi Arabia, Egypt, Kuwait, Pakistan, and Bahrain. National interest and regional politics rather than ideology or religion remain the major determinants in the formulation of foreign policy.

The World Trade Center bombing last year gave impetus to a third current, the portrayal of Islam as a demographic threat. The growth of Muslim populations in Europe and the United States has made Islam the second-largest religion in Germany and France and the third-largest in Britain and America. Disputes over Muslim minority rights, demonstrations and clashes during the Salman Rushdie affair, and the Trade Center bombing have been exploited by strident voices of the right—politicians such as France's Jean-Marie LePen, neo-Nazi youth in Germany, and right-wing political commentators in the United States.

NO DEMOCRACY WITHOUT RISKS

For Western leaders, democracy in the Middle East raises the prospect of old and reliable friends or client states transformed into more independent and less predictable nations, which generates worries that Western access to oil could become less secure. Thus stability in the Middle East has often been defined in terms of preserving the status quo.

Lack of enthusiasm for political liberalization in the region has been rationalized by the assertion that Arab culture and Islam are antidemocratic (an issue never raised to a comparable degree with regard to the former Soviet Union, Eastern Europe, or Africa). The proof offered is the lack of a democratic tradition, and more specifically, the glaring absence of democracies in the Muslim world.

The history of that world has not been conducive to the development of democratic traditions and institutions. European colonial rule and postindependence governments headed by military officers, ex-military men, and monarchs have contributed to a legacy in which political participation and the building of strong democratic institutions are of little concern. National unity and stability as well as the political legitimacy of governments have been undermined by the artificial nature of modern states whose national boundaries were often determined by colonial powers and whose rulers were either put in place by Europe or simply seized power. Weak economies, illiteracy, and high unemployment, especially among the younger generation, aggravate the situation, undermining confidence in governments and increasing the appeal of "Islamic fundamentalism."

Experts and policymakers who question whether Islamic movements will use electoral politics to "hijack democracy" often do not appear equally disturbed that few rulers in the region have been democratically elected and that many who speak of democracy believe only in the risk-free variety: political liberalization so long as there is no danger of a strong opposition (secular or religious) and loss of power. Failure to appreciate that the issue of hijacking democracy is a two-way street was reflected in the West's responses to the Algerian military's intervention and cancellation of the election results.

Perception of a global Islamic threat can contribute to support for repressive governments in the Muslim world, and thus to the creation of a self-fulfilling prophecy. Thwarting participatory politics by canceling elections or repressing populist Islamic movements fosters radicalization. Many of the Islamists harassed, imprisoned, or tortured by the regime, will conclude that seeking democracy is a dead end and become convinced that force is their only recourse. Official silence or economic and political backing for regimes by the United

States and other Western powers is read as complicity and a sign that there is a double standard for the implementation of democracy. This can create the conditions that lead to political violence that seemingly validates contentions that Islamic movements are inherently violent, antidemocratic, and a threat to national and regional stability.

More constructive and democratic strategies are possible. The strength of Islamic organizations and parties is also due to the fact that they constitute the only viable voice and vehicle for opposition in relatively closed political systems. The strength at the polls of Tunisia's Renaissance party, the Islamic Salvation Front, and Jordan's Muslim Brotherhood derived not only from a hard core of dedicated followers who backed the groups' Islamic agendas but from the many who wished simply to cast their vote against the government. Opening up the political system could foster competing opposition groups and thus weaken the monopoly Islamic parties have on opposition voters. (It must be remembered that the membership of Islamic organizations does not generally constitute a majority of the population.) Finally, the realities of a more open political marketplace—having to compete for votes, and once gaining power having to govern amid diverse interests—could force Islamic groups to adapt or broaden their ideology and programs.

The United States should not in principle object to the involvement of Islamic activists in government if they have been duly elected. Islamically oriented politicians and groups should be evaluated by the same criteria as any other potential leaders or opposition parties. While some are rejectionists, most will be critical and selective in their relations with the United States, generally operating on the basis of national interests and showing a flexibility that reflects understanding of the globally interdependent world. The United States should demonstrate by word and action its belief that the right to self-determination and representative government extends to an Islamically oriented state and society, if these reflect the popular will and do not directly threaten United States interests. American policy should accept the ideological differences between the West and Islam to the greatest extent possible, or at least tolerate them.

All should bear in mind that democratization in the Muslim world proceeds by experimentation, and necessarily involves both success and failure. The transformation of Western feudal monarchies to democratic nation states took time, and trial and error, and was accompanied by political as well as intellectual revolutions that rocked state and church. It was a long, drawn-out *process* among contending factions with competing interests and visions.

Today we are witnessing a historic transformation in the Muslim world. Risks exist, for there can be no risk-free democracy. Those who fear the unknown, wondering how specific Islamic movements will act once in power, have legitimate reasons to do so. However, if one worries that these movements might suppress opposition, lack tolerance, deny pluralism, and violate human rights, the same concern must apply equally to the plight of those Islamists who have shown a willingness to participate in the political process in Tunisia, Egypt, and Algeria.

Governments in the Muslim world that espouse political liberalization and democracy are challenged to promote the development of civil society—the institutions, values, and culture that are the foundation of true participatory government. Islamic movements, for their part, are challenged to move beyond slogans to programs. They must become more self-critical, and speak out not only against local government abuses but against those of Islamic regimes in Iran and Sudan, for example, as well as acts of terrorism by extremists. They are urged to present an Islamic rationale and policy that extend to their opposition and to minorities the principles of pluralism and political participation they demand for themselves. The extent to which the growth of Islamic revivalism has been accompanied in some countries by attempts to restrict women's rights and public roles; the record of discrimination against the Bahai in Iran, the Ahmadi in Pakistan, and Christians in Sudan; and sectarian conflict between Muslims and Christians in Egypt, Sudan, and Nigeria pose serious questions about religious pluralism, respect for human rights, and tolerance in general.

Islamic revivalism has run counter to many of the presuppositions of Western liberal secularism and development theory, among them the belief that modernization means the inexorable or progressive secularization and Westernization of society. Too often analysis and policy-making have been shaped by a liberal secularism that fails to recognize it too represents a world view, not the paradigm for modern society, and can easily degenerate into a "secularist fundamentalism" that treats alternative views as irrational, extremist, and deviant.

A focus on "Islamic fundamentalism" as a global threat has reinforced the tendency to equate violence with Islam, to fail to distinguish between illegitimate use of religion by individuals and the faith and practice of the majority of the world's Muslims who, like adherents of other religious traditions, wish to live in peace. To equate Islam and Islamic fundamentalism uncritically with extremism is to judge Islam only by those who wreak havoc—a standard not applied to Judaism and Christianity. The danger is that heinous actions may be attributed to Islam rather than to a twisted or distorted interpretation of Islam. Thus despite the track record of Christianity and Western countries when it comes to making war, developing weapons of mass destruction, and imposing their imperialist designs, Islam and Muslim culture are portrayed as somehow peculiarly and inherently expansionist and prone to violence and warfare.

There are lessons to be learned from a past in which fear of a monolithic Soviet threat often blinded the United States to the Soviet bloc's diversity, led to uncritical support for (anti-Communist) dictatorships, and enabled the "free world" to tolerate the suppression of legitimate dissent and massive human rights violations by governments that labeled the opposition "Communist" or "socialist." The risk today is that exaggerated fears will lead to a double standard in the promotion of democracy and human rights in the Muslim world as can be witnessed by the Western concern about and action to support democracy in the former Soviet Union and Eastern Europe but the muted or ineffective response to the promotion of democracy in the Middle East and the defense of Muslims in Bosnia and Herzegovina. Support for democracy and human rights is more effective if it is consistent around the world. Treating Islamic experiences as exceptional is an invitation to long-term conflict.

POSTSCRIPT

Is Islamic Fundamentalism a Threat to Political Stability?

There are nearly 1 billion Muslims in the world, constituting a majority among the Arabs as well as in several non-Arab countries, including Algeria, Indonesia, Iran, Morocco, Pakistan, Sudan, Turkey, and several former Soviet republics. There are other countries, such as Nigeria and the Philippines, in which Muslims constitute an important political force. Indeed, only about one of every four Muslims lives in the Middle East. The history and beliefs of Muslims are complex and rich; finding out more about them is rewarding, and it helps to curtail the tendency to stereotype those about whom we may know little. To learn more about Islamic history and Islam's relations with Europe, read *Islam and the West* by Bernard Lewis (Oxford University Press, 1993). A somewhat more negative view can be found in Oliver Roy, *The Failure of Political Islam* (Harvard University Press, 1994). A view that the Islamic era may just be dawning can be found in Judith Miller, "Faces of Fundamentalism," *Foreign Affairs* (November/December 1994).

There can be little doubt that the interplay between Islam and politics remains an important issue in world affairs. Fundamentalism remains strong. A civil war in Yemen in mid-1994 between the traditionalist north and the secular (even somewhat leftist) south was won handily by the fundamentalists.

From a Western point of view, the images are mixed and the future ramifications are uncertain. Muslim countries, like most less developed countries, face many difficulties in preserving their traditional values while adopting so-called modern practices, which are mostly those promoted by the dominant European–North American powers. Indeed, the rush of technological advancement associated with modernity, the loss of cultural identity, and other aspects of a rate of change unparalleled in world history are troubling for many people in many countries around the world. As Hamad Alturki, a professor of political science at King Saud University in Riyadh, Saudi Arabia, puts it, "People are tackling previously unheard questions like: How do we deal with concepts of the state and region? How should we cope with the age we live in? And what should our relationship be with the 'other,' be that other persons, other creeds, other states, or other thoughts?" It is important to note that the traditionalist movement in Muslim countries is part of a larger effort of people to find belonging and meaning in a rapidly changing world dominated by huge, impersonalized governments, businesses, and other organizations. It is possible to argue that some of the causes of Islamic fundamentalism are the same factors that have strengthened the so-called

Christian right in the United States, Hindu fundamentalists in India, and even the politicization of some elements of ultra-Orthodox Judaism in Israel.

Amid the turmoil, there are many signs that Muslim countries are adjusting to what is arguably a spreading homogenization of global culture. As elsewhere, democracy has taken hold in some Muslim countries and struggles to survive or begin in others. Algeria, for example, held elections in November 1995 despite threats of violence by the Front for Islamic Salvation. There are many secular trends in Muslim countries; some aspects of Muslim culture, such as the low status of women, that bother many Westerners are also beginning to change. One symbol of that change is the increasing political roles of Muslim women. Benazir Bhutto, the first woman to head the government of a predominantly Muslim country, is currently the prime minister of Pakistan. And Tansu Ciller, a Muslim woman who holds a Ph.D. in economics from the University of Connecticut, became Turkey's first female prime minister in 1993. The growing moderation of Muslim policy toward Israel is another encouraging development. Limited Palestinian autonomy has been established in Gaza and parts of the West Bank. Some believe that this will lead to peace and help defuse Muslim anger. Two worthwhile readings on these matters are S. V. R. Nasr, "Democracy and Islamic Revivalism," *Political Science Quarterly* (Summer 1995) and Rex Brynen, Bahgat Korany, and Paul Noble, eds., *Political Liberalization and Democratization in the Arab World: Theoretical Perspectives* (Lynne Rienner Press, 1995).

There are other indications, however, of the powerful appeal of religion-based politics. Prime Minister Ciller's hold on power was shaken by Turkey's parliamentary elections in December 1995, in which the Islamic fundamentalist party won the most votes. Other aspects of Muslim politics are disturbing. There is a strong element of violence, for example. Muslim countries (Iraq, Iran, Libya, Sudan, Syria) make up a majority of those designated by the U.S. State Department as officially supporting terrorism (state terrorism). The anger and terrorist tactics of traditionalists were brought home to Americans in 1993 when Muslims with connections to an Egyptian cleric residing in the United States exploded a bomb in the World Trade Center in New York City. Groups such as Hamas that promote violence continue to have a strong following. Violence between secularist governments and fundamentalist dissidents continues in Algeria, Egypt, and elsewhere. And there is an ongoing civil war between the fundamentalist Muslim government of Sudan and Christian rebels in the southern part of the country.

ISSUE 5

Will the Israelis and Palestinians Be Able to Achieve Lasting Peace?

YES: Robert Satloff, from "The Path to Peace," *Foreign Policy* (Fall 1995)

NO: Clovis Maksoud, from "Peace Process or Puppet Show?" *Foreign Policy* (Fall 1995)

ISSUE SUMMARY

YES: Robert Satloff, executive director of the Washington Institute for Near East Policy, maintains that peace between the Israelis and Palestinians can be achieved despite what will be a difficult process.

NO: Clovis Maksoud, director of the Center for the Study of the Global South, depicts the current peace efforts as flawed and predicts that they will lead to disillusionment and strife.

The essence of the problem in the Middle East was well put by Prime Minister Yitzhak Rabin of Israel when he first came to power in 1992. Speaking beyond his immediate audience in the Knesset, Israel's parliament, to the Palestinians, Rabin noted that "we have been fated to live together on the same patch of land. We lead our lives with you, beside you, and against you." "With you" and "beside you" are immutable realities for Israelis and Palestinians. The core of this debate is whether or not recent Israeli-Palestinian peace efforts will make "against you" a thing of the past.

The history of Israel/Palestine dates to biblical times when there were both Hebrew and Arab (Canaanite) kingdoms in the area. In later centuries, the area was conquered by many others; from 640 to 1917 it was almost continually controlled by Muslim rulers. In 1917 the British captured the area, Palestine, from Turkey.

Concurrently, a Zionist movement for a Jewish homeland arose. In 1917 the (British foreign secretary Arthur) Balfour Declaration promised increased Jewish immigration to Palestine. The Jewish population in the region began to increase slowly, then it expanded dramatically because of refugees from the Holocaust. Soon after World War II, the Jewish population in Palestine stood at 650,000; the Arab population was 1,350,000. Zionists increasingly agitated for an independent Jewish state. Conflict increased, and London turned to the UN for a solution. The UN plan to divide the area into Jewish and Palestinian Arab homelands never went into effect. Instead, when the British withdrew in 1947, war immediately broke out between Jewish forces and the region's

Arabs. The Jews won, establishing Israel in 1948 and doubling their territory. Most Palestinian Arabs fled (or were driven) from Israel to refugee camps in Gaza and the West Bank (of the Jordan River), two areas that had been part of Palestine but were captured in the war by Egypt and Jordan, respectively.

As a result of the 1967 Six Day War between Israel and Egypt, Jordan, and Syria, the Israelis again expanded their territory by capturing several areas, including the Sinai Peninsula, Gaza, the Golan Heights, and the West Bank. In its search for peace, the UN passed Resolution 242, calling on the Arabs to respect Israel's existence within secure borders in exchange for Israel's withdrawal from the occupied territories. Also in this period the Palestine Liberation Organization (PLO) became the major representative of Palestinian Arabs. Resolution 242 remained only a goal, however, because the PLO and the Arab states would not recognize Israel's legitimacy and because Israel refused to give up some of the captured territory.

Then attitudes began to change. After yet another war in 1973, the once-again defeated Arabs became more willing to accept Israel in exchange for peace. Similarly, war-exhausted Israelis became more willing to compromise with the Arabs to achieve peace. The first major effort resulted in a peace treaty in 1979 between Egypt and Israel that resulted in the return of the Sinai Peninsula to Egypt.

Since 1979 events have moved slowly in the Middle East, and there has been much violence. Yet progress has also occurred. Public talks held in Madrid, Spain, began among the protagonists in 1991. Israeli elections brought the Rabin government to power in 1992, and it was willing to compromise with the Arabs more than its more conservative predecessor had been. Bilateral secret peace talks between the Israelis and Palestinians in Norway soon commenced and led to an agreement in 1993. Among the agreement's terms are provisions to increase over time both the level of Palestinian autonomy in Gaza and the West Bank and the amount of territory that the Palestinians will control. Then, in 1994, Israel and Jordan signed a peace treaty, bringing peace another step closer, and leaving only Syria in a technical state of war with Israel. Peace is closer, but it is by no means at hand. The 1993 peace accord provided only a framework for the future, and there are many details to be worked out before successive steps are possible. The future of Jerusalem, the eastern half of which is technically part of the West Bank, is especially difficult because it is so emotionally central to all parties. The Palestinian areas are impoverished, and the PLO, which has become close to a de facto government of these areas, faces monumental challenges. Moreover, some Arabs and Israelis oppose the peace efforts as selling out to the enemy and giving up the land that each considers his or her birthright.

Will the Israeli-Palestinian agreement of 1993 lead to a permanent peace? Robert Satloff argues that it will if both sides act with courage and persistence. Clovis Maksoud disagrees, contending that the agreement is flawed and will ultimately fail.

YES

Robert Satloff

THE PATH TO PEACE

In October 1991, in a royal palace in Madrid, a dour, monosyllabic Israeli prime minister sat across a great, rectangular table from second-tier representatives of the Palestinian people, whose own organizational leadership was banished from the proceedings because of its reliance on terrorism as policy. Today, the two principals, Israel and the Palestine Liberation Organization (PLO), are formally bound by a contractual agreement witnessed by the United States and Russia to settle all disputes peacefully and to negotiate the end of their century-old conflict by determining the "final status" of the West Bank and Gaza and other critical issues.

Seated near the Palestinian representative in Madrid was the foreign minister of the Hashemite Kingdom of Jordan, whose soldiers—then (and perhaps still) the finest in the Arab world—were the first to cross the Jordan River on May 15, 1948, to take up arms against the fledgling Jewish state. Today, Israel and Jordan are at peace, having negotiated a remarkably creative treaty that not only ends 46 years of war but sketches a blueprint for a warm web of political, economic, and human relationships.

Also at that table was the foreign minister of Syria, a country that earned its spot on the U.S. government's list of terror-supporting states both for its direct role in terrorism and for its sponsorship and sufferance of Palestinian, Lebanese, Armenian, Turkish, and other terrorist groups. Though miffed that lesser Arab brethren brokered their own separate agreements with Israel, Syrian representatives—including the chief of staff of the Syrian armed forces, a lofty position in a military dictatorship—are today quietly negotiating with their Israeli counterparts on aspects of a peace treaty that is hailed by supporters (and detractors) as a potential "peace to end all wars" in the Middle East.

Overall, the diplomatic record since Madrid is resoundingly positive. For that, the Bush and Clinton administrations, which have been the principal sponsors of the peace process, deserve wide acclaim. The speed of change has been so rapid . . . that the novel has become ho-hum. That, however, does not make the change any less significant.

In historical terms, the greatest achievement of the Madrid process is to have bolstered a dynamic change in Arab-Israeli relations from conflict to negotiation to, in some hopeful areas, recognition of mutual interests. For most observers, the operative issue today is not the imminence of Arab-Israeli war but the battle being waged on many fronts between the region's moderate forces—Arab, Israeli, and Turkish—and their reactionary, atavistic nemeses, both secular and religious. After a half century of simmering intercommunal conflict in what was once Mandatory Palestine and a quarter century of interstate conflict that spanned a far wider arena, the last two decades have witnessed a slow but consistent process of peacemaking, both within societies and between states and peoples. In this process, most Arab leaders (and, to an alarmingly lesser degree, their peoples) have come to terms with Israel's strength, resilience, and permanence; Palestinians have gained recognition of nationhood from everyone that matters (most importantly, Israel); and Israelis, now able to flit about the region from Marrakech to Manama, feel more secure to do business in Milan and Manila. Through it all, the win-win process of peacemaking has come to supplant the zero-sum process of warfare, which the Arabs clearly lost but from which Israel could not gain.

Against this litany of good news stand two unhappy realities. First, as the fate of the 1983 peace accord between Israel and Lebanon shows, the peace process is neither irreversible nor irrevocable. The post–Gulf war successes of [the peace process] were made possible by the historic confluence of American dominance, Soviet irrelevance, Israeli strength, Palestinian disillusionment, and a general sense of realism and pragmatism that took hold in the Arab world. As those ingredients shift, the process changes, and the ability of those achievements to survive future tests, such as succession crises, will change, too.

Second, because the Arab-Israeli conflict has been a systemic phenomenon, in which the ideological, economic, social, cultural, political, and military energies of states, nations, and peoples were committed... to "the struggle," ending the conflict will require decades of effort and perhaps even generational change. It is important to recall that on just the diplomatic level, nearly 10 years were needed —from the [beginning of] talks in 1973 to the final Israeli withdrawal from the Sinai in 1982—to create peace between Egypt and Israel; Syria and Israel began a negotiating process at about the same time, but they remain far from signing, let alone implementing, a peace accord. To the dismay of diplomats, the end of the Arab-Israeli conflict is not just one shuttle mission, one secret negotiation, or one signing ceremony away. In fact, Uday Hussein, the son of the leader of the Arab state most recently to attack Israel, could still in June 1995 editorialize in his Baghdad newspaper *Babil* that the Arabs need to improve upon Egyptian leader Gamal Abdel Nasser's exhortation to throw the Jews into the sea because some of them might still swim to safety.

AMERICAN INTERESTS

For the United States, helping to achieve Arab-Israeli peace remains a vital national security policy, even though the region is no longer a setting for potential superpower confrontation—a main reason for Washington's devotion to peacemaking in the 1960s, 1970s, and 1980s. In the late 1990s, Arab-Israeli peace is a key element in maintaining America's two overriding interests in the Middle East: the safety and survival of Israel and secure, unhindered access to the region's oil and gas at reasonable prices.

For the former U.S. interest, the relevance is obvious; for the latter, the impact of peace is more complicated but no less direct. Domestically, peace would permit America's friends to devote a greater share of their nations' resources to solving economic and social problems, denying radicals fertile ground for propagandizing and proselytizing at home. Regionally, peace would deprive troublemakers like Saddam Hussein the "wedge issue" of Palestine to make mischief in the region and would permit Arabs, Israelis, and Westerners to focus their energies on the two challenges to regional stability that threaten them—the secular radicalism of Iraq and the religious militancy of Iran. What makes the potential payoff of peace so great for the United States is that it would affirm a strategic consensus between America and all of its regional allies.

Recognizing the two unhappy realities of the peace process—that past achievements are not necessarily irreversible and that future successes may take considerable time—the Clinton administration faces steep challenges between now and November 1996. The Israel-PLO accord of September 1993, a breakthrough of seismic proportions, risks succumbing to popular disenchantment on both sides owing to a sinister cycle of terrorism, retribution, deprivation, disillusion, and more terrorism. The Jordan-Israel peace treaty of October 1994, another signal achievement, risks settling into an unfulfilling "peace of the elites," because the Jordanian man-in-the-street (or soldier-in-the-barracks) has yet to benefit from

its trickle-down effects. The Egypt-Israel peace of March 1979, foundation for the peace process, risks eroding as an array of issues—from Egypt's criticism of Israel's nuclear policy to competition for dwindling U.S. aid dollars—divides these pioneers in peacemaking. The multilateral peace process, a little-known but innovative series of experts' discussions on transnational issues (e.g., water resources, environment, economic development, refugees, arms control, and regional security), risks atrophying without the political commitment of the region's leaders. The process of Israel's political and economic integration into the Middle East, heralded by diplomatic openings throughout North Africa (except Libya) and the Arab Gulf, risks slowing without having achieved an end to the Arab boycott of Israel.

On top of all this, the Clinton administration has made the achievement of an Israel-Syria peace agreement one of its highest priorities. This reflects both the wish of the Israeli government, whose relations with the United States are at a historic high after the quarrels of the George Bush–[then–Israeli prime minister] Yitzhak Shamir years, and the predilection of Bill Clinton, Secretary of State Warren Christopher, and the latter's "peace team." The reason for this situation is simple: Peace with Syria, it is argued, would have implications far beyond a straightforward bilateral agreement. Reconciliation between "the beating heart of Arab nationalism" on the one hand and the "Zionist entity" on the other would constitute the keystone to what is termed "comprehensive peace." Comprehensive peace means ending the Arab conflict on Israel's borders, committing Damascus to cut off Hizbollah and other terrorist groups, giving the "green light" for an Israeli-Lebanon peace agreement, and removing all obstacles to Israel's normalization with the wider Arab world. For the United States and Israel, the attainment of a comprehensive peace would confirm the wisdom of strategic cooperation in the peace process and would usher in a truly "new Middle East."

With so much at stake, neither Washington nor Jerusalem has been shy about pursuing peace with Syria. Israel, for example, has put aside its preference for direct talks, accepting what Israel's chief negotiator has termed "trilateral negotiation" (with Washington as the third party), and it has not required Syria to end its support for anti-Israel (e.g., Hizbollah) terrorism as a precondition of formal bargaining. On the American side, its interest in an Israel-Syria peace is such that Christopher has visited Syria 19 times on 12 trips to the Middle East in just 30 months. (By contrast, he has visited America's troubled neighbor Mexico only once.) These exertions notwithstanding, Israel-Syria negotiations move at a glacial pace. After more than three and one-half years of talks, the two sides are only now beginning serious bargaining on the core issue of security. Even this tentative step forward first required agreement to postpone talks on three other critical items—the extent of Israel's territorial withdrawal, the parameters of normalization, and the timetable for implementing a peace accord. Should the Syrians be truly committed to an agreement, finalizing it will take time, even if its contours appear clear.

STEPS TOWARD PEACE

Both Americans and Israelis go to the polls in 1996, and sometime in the first half of that year electoral politics will intrude on the peace process, making progress less likely. With so much in the peace process uncertain, there is much to do and little time. For the United States, this needs to be a period of shoring up past achievements and working toward new ones. To meet that challenge, U.S. diplomats should return to first principles that have been honed from nearly 30 years of peacemaking efforts. *First, secure an environment in which Arabs and Israelis can settle their disputes through negotiation.* In practical terms, this approach involves proactive, ongoing efforts to insulate the peace process from its enemies—Iraq, Iran, and transnational terrorism. Madrid happened because of U.S. leadership in the Gulf war; without that leadership, and without the continued deterrence of the region's radical forces, the chances for further progress toward Arab-Israeli peace are slim.

Second, reduce the risks of peacemaking for those who contemplate compromise and support the courage of those who opt for it. Four simultaneous efforts are necessary to the realization of this principle:

- Continue to work in partnership with Israel. The strength of the U.S.–Israeli relationship is critical to helping Israelis persevere with the peace process in the face of suicide car bombs and *katyusha* rocket attacks, demands to cede strategic territory in exchange for promises of peace, and harangues over Israel's strategic deterrent.

- Redouble efforts to promote international aid and investment in the West Bank and Gaza Strip as a way to bolster popular support for the pro-Oslo Palestinian leadership while taking a firm stand against backsliding, mismanagement of aid funds, and sufferance of terrorism. Although the Israel-PLO negotiations are largely a bilateral affair, the United States must try to ensure that the Palestinian Authority (PA) does not wither on the vine (as many Arab parties seem willing to permit) while at the same time insisting that the PA not receive a "free pass" when it comes to meeting its contractual commitments.

- Remove the issue of Jordanian debt relief from White House–congressional feuding and find low-cost ways (such as excess defense articles, corporate trade missions, and increased funding for International Military Education and Training (IMET)) to help Jordanians realize the benefits of peace. Failing to find some support for Jordan's peacemaking efforts would be not only penny-wise and pound-foolish as far as the Jordanians are concerned, but it would send negative signals to Damascus and elsewhere about America's resolve in support of peacemakers.

- Broaden ongoing dialogue with Egypt to ensure that the special U.S.–Egyptian relationship remains on firm footing as Egyptians contemplate a Middle East in which they are no longer the only state at peace with Israel. A stable Egypt is the linchpin of a stable Middle East. It is especially important to talk early, seriously, and creatively with Egypt about ways to bolster U.S.–Egyptian strategic ties and the future of the U.S. economic assistance package.

Third, with Syria, be prepared. Having engineered direct negotiations at a high level—the two sides' chiefs of staff—the United States should let the negotiations take their course, injecting itself into the process only when both needed and asked by the two sides. This means that the United States should be prepared at the highest level to act as an honest broker should Israel and Syria together seek U.S. mediation; to serve in a limited role as monitor should they together seek U.S. help in implementing terms of a future agreement; and to press U.S. demands on Syria regarding terrorism, proliferation, narcotics, counterfeiting, Lebanon, and human rights lest they be lost in the festivities accompanying an Israel-Syria breakthrough. (A "mechanism" established by Presidents Clinton and [Syrian president] Hafez al-Assad in January 1994 to address these concerns died an early death.) Striking the proper pose between advancing U.S. interests in Israeli-Syrian peace and protecting U.S. concerns about the troubled U.S.–Syrian relationship is a difficult balance, only somewhat eased by Syria's own desire for improved ties with Washington.

Finally, maintain perspective, composure, and momentum. Like the stock market, the peace process is on a historically upward slope, but that does not mean it is immune from great shocks. From outside the process, terrorism . . . , assassination plots* and coup attempts . . . can all be expected. Inside the process, progress toward "final status" arrangements will itself produce intense and divisive disputes over sensitive issues, not least of which is Jerusalem. Through it all, America's role is to help its friends and partners work toward agreements that promote stability, satisfy their basic re-

*[Satloff here seems to foreshadow the death of Israel's prime minister Yitzhak Rabin, who was assassinated in November 1995, shortly after this article was published.—Ed.]

quirements, and terminate sources of future conflict.

Burdened with daunting challenges to safeguarding past achievements and substantial obstacles to finding future breakthroughs, the Arab-Israeli peace process faces a difficult time ahead. For the Clinton administration, which has invested so much to see still so much left undone, solace should come in knowing that this will not be the first, the only, or the most troubled period in a historic process that is still unfolding.

NO

Clovis Maksoud

PEACE PROCESS OR PUPPET SHOW?

From the outset, the Declaration of Principles between Israel and the Palestine Liberation Organization (PLO) has been flawed. The choreographed ceremony at the White House on September 13, 1993, and the ensuing euphoria rendered any objective analysis superfluous. Those who objected, questioned, or dissented were drummed out and summarily dismissed as "rejectionist," "enemies of peace," and "unrealistic." The excitement of the United States and Western sponsors betrayed a sense of relief at ending a conflict the resolution of which had eluded the international community for nearly 50 years. Genuine political grievances were pushed aside by a plethora of promises of economic aid. Quickly, however, the unfulfilled promises became a new cause for disillusionment. And the repressive measures of the Palestinian Authority (PA) against opposition elements led to suspicion that it was more an instrument for Israeli security than a precursor to an independent Palestinian state. Skepticism about the agreement was thus reinforced. The consequences of the agreement for the Palestinians can become even more serious if national unity is ruptured—a prospect that is coming too close to realization.

Treated as parasitical and intrusive, dissenting views were never allowed to be factored into the "peace process." The United States, eager for a speedy diplomatic achievement, sought to impress on all parties that the peace process, as envisaged by the terms of the Declaration, was irreversible. When concerns were expressed, the instant response by the American foreign policy establishment—official and think tank alike—was that "this is the only game in town." This patronizing attitude of the principal sponsor of the peace process foreclosed exposure to views and ideas that would have encouraged a more profound understanding of the flaws of the agreement and of the pain, anxieties, and repressed feelings of Palestinians and Arabs, intellectuals, and many political leaders. Shunned by the United States, these constituencies became increasingly alienated from the American-led effort and more responsive to the growing radical opposition to the Declaration and the peace process.

Railroading this Oslo agreement between Israel and the PLO through to completion and proclaiming an ultimate diplomatic success were opportunities too tempting for the United States and its allies to pass up; but this approach only deepened the frustration and humiliation permeating large segments of the Palestinian and Arab constituencies. More recently, the United States further demonstrated total obliviousness to legitimate Palestinian rights and sensitivities when it vetoed in the United Nations Security Council a mild resolution condemning Israel's planned confiscation of Palestinian land in Jerusalem. The fact that Israel subsequently postponed plans to carry out the confiscation has not allayed Palestinian and Arab fears.

Many ask why the Palestinians should be frustrated and angry. Why should the Declaration, which recognizes the PLO as the representative of the Palestinian people and promises to improve their quality of life and provide them an opportunity for self-government, be denounced by large segments—perhaps the majority—of the Palestinian people inside and outside the occupied territories? Many also wonder what would be the alternative. When these questions are put forward by the U.S. Middle East policy establishment —logical as the questions may be—they are asked with a patronizing arrogance and cynical style that belies the logic of the rhetoric.

Let me, therefore, take this opportunity to spell out some of the answers in the hope and expectation that a long-awaited reassessment—even a revision—of U.S. policy will soon take place. There is still a need to respond to the increasingly nagging question of what went wrong. Unanswered, this question will come to haunt those who are responsible for and involved in Middle East affairs. What are the flaws that block achieving a just settlement of the Palestinian-Israeli conflict, and what can be done to restore confidence in a peace process, the purpose of which is to secure a durable and comprehensive peace?

THE DECLARATION'S FAILURES

To begin, the Declaration and the derivative Cairo accords undermine the legal foundations for a Palestinian national patrimony and therefore the rights of the Palestinian people to eventual self-determination. By failing to extract Israel's recognition that it is an *occupying power* in the occupied Palestinian territories—including East Jerusalem—these agreements put in jeopardy any sovereign prerogatives to which the Palestinian people are entitled. All the extensive and cumulative jurisprudence of U.N. resolutions on this issue are rendered irrelevant if not obsolete. In addition, by glossing over the issue of the legal status of the Palestinian territories as *occupied* and by refusing to comply with the articles of the Fourth Geneva Convention, the Declaration gives Israel license to continue violating the human, civil, national, and political rights of the Palestinians. Israel was in effect absolved of responsibility for its brutal and illegal practices in the occupied territories from June 1967 forward. The Oslo Agreement confirmed, albeit unintentionally, the validity if not the legality of the Israeli settlements. Moreover, while even Prime Minister Yitzhak Rabin has admitted that some of the settlements are costly, they continue to be used by Israel as a pretext to ensure its security and the security of individual Israelis while at the same time undercutting the emergence—at any time—of a territorially coherent Palestinian national patrimony that could serve as the foundation for an eventual Palestinian state. The Israeli settlements were deemed "illegal" by the Carter administration, they were labeled "obstacles to peace" by the Reagan and Bush administrations, and Clinton administration spokespersons recently called them "not helpful." But they have acquired a material presence and a life of their own of which the United States is increasingly accepting. Such an American attitude encourages Israeli policy and discourages both Palestinians' aspirations and a sense of justice.

The interim period envisaged by the peace process gives Israel a free hand to more heavily populate and expand the settlements and their infrastructure. Israel will be able to "cantonize" the West Bank and Gaza Strip and preclude the emergence of a Palestinian state or even a viable national Palestinian entity in the occupied territories. The postponement of key issues, such as the status of Jerusalem and the settlements, will enable Israel's Labor-led government to persist in its practice of selective and creeping annexation—as distinct from total annexation, advocated by most members of the Likud party—with uninterrupted regularity and to present facts on the ground as an irreversible fait accompli. In this respect, the ongoing expansion of municipal Jerusalem into "Greater Jerusalem" in effect incorporates much of the West Bank into Israel's self-proclaimed capital.

The Declaration's failure to refer to Israel as an occupier constitutes a serious blunder on the part of the PLO: It allows Israel to be a claimant to the land it has always sought rather than the occupier that it is. Hence while the PLO discusses issues with Israel on the assumption that it is now the occupying authority, Israel deals with the questions of Palestinian empowerment more as an internal civil issue, without reference to political sovereignty. For this reason, many delays and misunderstandings have taken place. This situation will persist as long as the terms of reference remain vague and the stronger party (Israel) imposes its own interpretation.

The Oslo agreement postponed a third crucial issue in addition to Jerusalem and the settlements—namely, the future of Palestinian refugees. The refugees perceive the Oslo and Cairo agreements as detrimental to their legal, national, and human rights. Postponing consideration of this problem might have been tolerable if an outcome had been envisaged and spelled out. But the absence of any reference to a possible solution to this problem reinforced their sense of dispossession and disenfranchisement, increasing their fears about their destiny. It also escalated tensions with the peoples of the host countries. In Lebanon in particular, this lapse is more acute as social peace there remains fragile and the political balance among contending religious groups precarious.

That major issues such as the ultimate status of refugees, Jerusalem, and the settlements were shelved summarily without even the outlines of a possible outcome underlines a perplexing insensitivity to the overall Palestinian condition on the part of all the parties—especially the PLO leadership. The rush by PLO chairman Yasir Arafat to gain *access* to the United States and to achieve recognition by its government made Israel the broker for the PLO's entry into the White House. The price exacted by Israel was the PLO's acquiescence to Israel's political agenda. The national disenfranchisement of the Palestinian people—now ironically continuing with the participation of the PLO —remains central to U.S. policy. Adding insult to injury, the United States took measures both to assure Israel's superior strategic edge in security and to end the Arab economic boycott. Nudging its friends in the Arab world to normalize relations with Israel before Israel withdrew from the occupied territories was a very heavy price for the recognition granted to the PLO. This action inevitably led to a widespread perception that the PLO-Israel agreements are undermining the sense of community not only among the Palestinians but also among the Arabs and are reinforcing Israel's hegemony in the region. Throughout the Arab world there is a strong feeling that breaking the common Arab political stand and forcing the Arab states and the PLO into dealing separately with a stronger Israel will ensure Israel's hegemony and U.S. tutelage for regional development and stability. If this impression continues to gain currency, and peace becomes a humbling and a humiliating experience for Palestinians and Arabs, then the present arrangements with the Palestinians as well as the other Arab parties will increasingly be questioned and will render the peace process vulnerable.

Recently, the Syrian talks and the Jordanian peace treaty with Israel have produced progress, despite the continuing core problem in Israeli-Arab relations —namely the issue of Palestinian national rights. At the same time, many in the Arab world are convinced that Palestinian empowerment in municipal and administrative matters is intended to foreclose any acceptable outcome in the long term. Besides, the PLO-Israel talks cannot be described as negotiations. Negotiation presumes agreement on an outcome—or at least the broad parameters of an outcome. In the Declaration there is no mention of a feasible and mutually acceptable result from the peace pro-

cess. In other words, real negotiation is not an exploration of whether Palestinians have or do not have the right to self-determination in the same sense that it is not an exploration of Israel's right to exist or be secure. Negotiation is the mechanism to spell out the modalities, the timetable, and the phases to give shape to what should have been agreed upon as the final outcome—namely an independent and secure Palestine and a secure Israel within the borders determined by U.N. Security Council Resolution 242.

The fact that this internationally recognized right has been omitted from the Declaration exacerbates the sense of futility among a large majority of the Palestinian people. Palestinians are also concerned that they are being used as a stepping stone in Israel's effort to normalize its relations with Arab states before Palestinian national rights are recognized and realized and before Israel withdraws from occupied Arab lands in Syria and Lebanon. U.S. pressure in this endeavor—such as ending the Arab boycott, proposing joint projects such as a Middle East Development Fund, and so forth—only strengthens the Palestinians' conviction that the United States is tied to Israel's agenda. It also shields from condemnation and sanctions Israel's violations of U.N. resolutions and international law.

The United States is rightly considered the Mideast's pivotal superpower and, at the same time, the major strategic partner and sponsor of Israel. However, Palestinians feel that this U.S. role enables Israel to deal with them as a defeated adversary rather than as an equal partner in search of a historic reconciliation. The American role, given the transparency of its bias, is at best to render the terms of surrender benevolent and internationally marketable. This explains the growing anger and disappointment of both Palestinians and other Arabs at Arafat's leadership and the self-rule authority over which he presides.

U.S. policymakers succeeded in brokering separate peace agreements between Israel and Egypt (1979) and between Israel and Jordan (1994) and have made painstaking efforts to do so between Israel and Syria. Lacking such a U.S. effort on behalf of Palestinians and Israel, the chances for the emergence of a Palestinian state in the foreseeable future are dim at best. Every separate peace treaty that was and is being made between an Arab party and Israel has weakened the negotiating position of the other Arab parties. True, this approach achieved short-term U.S. and Israeli objectives, especially in light of upcoming elections in both countries. The Arab parties directly involved in the peace process were persuaded that responding to U.S. pressure and a U.S. timetable would help avert another Likud victory and thus ensure a relatively better deal. With the United States committed to a militarily superior Israel—it is the only nuclear power in the region—and with the Arab front fragmenting, Israeli hegemony has been assured.

Yet, despite these apparent achievements, U.S. policy in the Middle East is shortsighted. It plants the seeds of an unraveling of present arrangements. It transforms opposition into anger. Its intervention—however well intentioned—is perceived as aggressive and unmindful of other options. Current U.S. policy has accepted Israel's characterization of minor acts of compliance with international law and U.N. resolutions—e.g., troop redeployment, talks of a partial withdrawal from the Golan Heights, and so on—

as major concessions. American acceptance of such Israeli terms has led the United States to marginalize and subsequently remove the U.N. from any legitimate role in the Arab-Israeli conflict. Amidst their disarray, the Arab parties become, to varying degrees, negotiating dependencies on the American mediating, though still partisan, role. The long-term sustainability of such agreements is thus in doubt; for even if this situation is satisfactory to the United States, Israel, and some of the Arab regimes, it is not so for the majority of Arabs. The depth of popular frustration with and alienation from the terms of the peace process will inevitably result in popular opposition to current Arab regimes. These sentiments mean that future political upheavals or movements for democratic change may run counter to what most Arabs currently see as a flawed and humiliating peace.

CORRECTIVE ACTIONS

What can the PLO do, at this late stage in the peace process, to ensure both the inalienable rights of the Palestinian people and the internationally recognized rights of all the states in the region as prescribed by U.N. Security Council Resolution 242? I believe that the PLO should return to its intended role: providing a framework for Palestinian peoplehood and for national unity between those under occupation and those in the refugee camps and in the diaspora. Arafat needs to reengage the national institutions, e.g., the Palestine National Council and the PLO Executive Committee, reinvigorate them, and resume leadership of the whole Palestinian people. Accordingly, he should not be headquartered in territory that is still occupied and under de facto Israeli rule. He should thus appoint a local Palestinian administration for the autonomous areas and make the PLO its empowering authority rather than have the PA, over which he presides, be empowered by Israel. This administration would be clearly transitional pending a negotiated outcome that would restore internationally recognized Palestinian political rights.

Such a development would rescue the PLO and the Palestinian people from the confused juridical limbo the Oslo Accords have placed them in—a legitimacy derived from the occupier. If this change takes place, then the PLO will be extricated from the quagmire of municipal functions, from the stigma of being Israel's enforcer, and from the constraints of its equivocal legal status. It will regain legitimacy in the eyes of the vast majority of the Palestinian people inside and outside the territories. It will also regain the freedom to act in the name of the Palestinians as a whole as well as the ability to expedite consideration of critical issues that have been postponed, such as the future of Jerusalem, the settlements, the refugees, and, most significantly, Palestinian sovereignty. It will thus be in a position to negotiate these issues with Israel on a more equal footing. This and only this will retrieve the PLO'S credibility and legitimacy among its Palestinian constituency. Restoring the PLO to the Palestinian mainstream will in turn legitimize and salvage the peace process from the growing misgivings of official and public Arab opinion. Mainstream Palestinian and Arab opinion strongly favors a negotiated, just peace with Israel. It opposes an imposed and humiliating peace of the sort that the current flawed process and assumptions are seen to be constructing.

As we reflect on this second anniversary of the Declaration of Principles agreement, it is not too late to examine what has gone wrong. That kind of reexamination can help avoid a repetition of what happened when Lebanon abrogated the May 17, 1983, peace agreement—brokered by the United States under the duress of Israeli occupation. The starting point for erecting a structure of durable peace in the whole Middle East is for Israel and the United States to recognize unequivocally that the Palestinians are a people with the inalienable right to self-determination. Accordingly, Israel must negotiate in good faith and straightforwardly with the PLO over nothing less than the terms of its withdrawal from the occupied territories and the modalities of Palestinian sovereignty. Equitable resolutions to the issues of Jerusalem, the refugees, and the settlements would then be not difficult to achieve. America's role would then no longer be at odds, as it is now, with the overall international consensus on the Palestine question, and the United States could truly serve as an honest broker. Failing that, the current peace process may be sowing the seeds for the dramatic future unraveling of a flawed peace.

POSTSCRIPT

Will the Israelis and Palestinians Be Able to Achieve Lasting Peace?

The Middle East's torment is one of the most intractable problems facing the world. In addition to the ancient territorial claims of Jews and Palestinian Arabs, complexities include long-standing rivalries among various religious and ethnic groups and countries in the region. There are also great tensions within the two principal groups, the Palestinians and the Jews. Arab fundamentalist groups such as Hamas oppose the peace efforts of PLO chairman Yasser Arafat. There were numerous predictions that Arafat would be assassinated by extremists for supposedly betraying the Palestinians, just as Egypt's president Anwar Sadat had been killed in 1981 after signing the peace accord with Israel. As it turned out, it was Prime Minister Yitzhak Rabin who was assassinated. In November 1995 a Jewish fundamentalist, 27-year-old Yigal Amir, shot Rabin to death as he was leaving a peace rally in Jerusalem attended by 100,000 Israelis. Amir told a court that his goal was to keep all of the West Bank as part of a greater Israel, and he expressed disbelief that "an entire people never noticed [Rabin] setting up a Palestinian state with an army of terrorists... [that Israelis soon] will have to fight." When asked if he had acted alone, the assassin replied, "It was God." The event occasioned massive press coverage of the event, the background of the peace process, and the prospects for the future. A good source is the *New York Times*, especially the November 5, 6, and 7, 1995, editions.

It may be that Amir's effort to slay the peace process served to strengthen it. Israel's right wing was discredited, and the resolve of those favoring compromise with the Arabs was redoubled. Arabs also reached out. King Hussein of Jordan called the fallen Jewish leader "a brother and... a friend." Security considerations prevented Arafat from attending the funeral, but he pronounced himself "very sad and shocked at this awful and terrible crime against one of the brave leaders of Israel and one of the peacemakers." For an earlier and somewhat pessimistic view of the Middle East peace process, read Leon Hadar, "The Middle East Peace Process," *USA Today* (November 1994).

Yet there were others who were not grief stricken. One Jewish fundamentalist characterized Rabin's death as "divine justice and divine retribution" on the grounds that "there is a law that if a fellow Jew hands over or is about to hand over a Jewish community to a non-Jewish enemy or a non-Jewish government, such as under the Roman Empire, then that Jew is considered a traitor who should be handed over unto death." Other Jews, who deplored the act, said that they could "understand the frustration the young man who killed Rabin must have been feeling." Similar sentiments could be found among Arabs. One Palestinian living in the West Bank said, "I don't feel sorry for what happened to Rabin. Our people remember him as the man behind breaking Palestinian bones, demolishing houses, and deporting people." The Libyan government news agency described Rabin as a "terrorist" whose "hands were covered with the blood of martyrs."

Even if one puts aside such strident views, the death of Rabin bodes ill for the future. Many Israelis trusted Rabin to maintain their security amid compromises with the Palestinians because of his stature as a former general who had, at times, dealt severely with both Israel's foreign enemies and its domestic Arab opponents. Shimon Peres, Rabin's successor, may not enjoy the same level of confidence. The issue of the West Bank is especially troubling for Israelis. There are still 140,000 Israelis living in the West Bank and removing them will be traumatic for Israel. The issue is also a matter of grave security concern. The Jews have suffered mightily throughout history; repeated Arab terrorism represents the latest of their travails. It is arguable that the Jews can be secure only in their own country and that a West Bank (which cuts Israel almost in two) is crucial to Israeli security. If the end result of the 1993 peace accord is, as many suspect it will be, an independent Palestine centered in the West Bank, that would create a defense nightmare, especially if new hostilities with the Palestinians were to occur.

ISSUE 6

Will China Become an Asian Superpower?

YES: Denny Roy, from "Hegemon on the Horizon? China's Threat to East Asian Security," *International Security* (Summer 1994)

NO: Michael G. Gallagher, from "China's Illusory Threat to the South China Sea," *International Security* (Summer 1994)

ISSUE SUMMARY

YES: Denny Roy, a professor of political science at the National University of Singapore, argues that a burgeoning China poses a long-term threat to Asia-Pacific security.

NO: Michael G. Gallagher, who has taught international studies in both China and the United States, suggests that the benefits that China can gain from peaceful economic development and the growing military strength of China's Asian neighbors make it likely that concerns about China trying to dominate the Asia-Pacific region are overwrought.

China is one of the oldest, most sophisticated, and most powerful countries (and empires) in the world. Through 14 Chinese dynasties (from the Hsia, 1994–1523 B.C., to the Manchu, A.D. 1644–1911), China built a civilization marked by great culture, engineering feats, and other advances. China also established wide political dominion, exercising sway over a wide regional area.

Eventually China's political fortunes declined. The last truly Chinese dynasty (the Ming) was overthrown by the Manchus from the north in 1644. By the 1800s outside powers came to dominate a decaying China. The British seized Hong Kong and leased it until 1997; huge tracts of Chinese territory were seized by the Russians; the island of Formosa (Taiwan, Nationalist China) was taken by Japan in 1895, and various European countries and Japan came close to making China a colony by dividing it up into zones of interest that they dominated.

By 1926 a struggle for power among various factions led to the establishment of a central government under Nationalist Chinese leader Chiang Kai-shek. Although Chiang's government proved corrupt and ineffective in many ways, it did largely consolidate power and moved to edge foreign influences out of China. That trend became even stronger in 1949 when Chiang's government fell to the communists led by Mao Zedong.

For two decades many in the West were caught up in the psychology of the cold war and perceived China to be part of the communist monolith headed by the Soviet Union. That was never true; and in any case, by the late 1960s China had gained enough strength and showed enough independence (including sharply clashing with the USSR over border areas) that even the coldest warrior had to see that China was a rising power in its own right. An important symbol of that shift was President Richard M. Nixon's visit to China in 1972. Relations improved even more after Chairman Mao Zedong died in 1976 and Deng Xiaoping came to power. The waning of the cold war further persuaded both powers to seek better relations.

Other changes have occurred within China. After some turmoil following the death of Mao, Deng moved to moderate the impact of communist ideology on China's economic policy. Greater economic ties with the industrialized West were sought. China moved slowly to establish limited capitalism to improve economic performance. China's economy is now rapidly expanding and is one of the largest in the world.

By many standards, China is already a major power. Geographically, it is large and strategically located; its 1.2 billion people constitute the world's largest population; and its more than $600 billion gross domestic product is the world's eighth largest and growing at the astounding rate (1992–1994) of 13 percent annually. China reports defense spending (1993) of only $7.3 billion, but many analysts believe that the real figure could be two or three times higher. With 3,000,000 personnel in uniform, China has the globe's largest military. Its conventional forces still lack Western levels of technological sophistication, but the country does possess strategic-range nuclear weapons. China is also a permanent member of the UN Security Council, thus possessing a veto in that organization.

Moreover, China has begun to assert itself slowly on the international stage. It has clashed with the United States, India, the Soviet Union, and Vietnam over border areas during the years since Mao took power. China will retake control of Hong Kong in 1997 and will reincorporate the Portuguese holding of Macao in 1999. The government in Beijing further claims that Taiwan is a legal part of China. China has also sent military forces to occupy some of the Spratly Islands, which Beijing claims. The island group lies in the South China Sea in the middle of one of the world's busiest shipping lanes.

The issue debated here focuses on what the future of China will be. Denny Roy contends that China will become a regional superpower. Michael G. Gallagher examines China's many problems: the infighting for power that may occur when the aged Deng dies, China's need for peace to develop economically, and the growing strength of China's neighbors. He concludes that these factors will restrain China from making any aggressive attempt to become a superpower.

YES

Denny Roy

HEGEMON ON THE HORIZON? CHINA'S THREAT TO EAST ASIAN SECURITY

Northeast Asia has been relatively peaceful for the past forty years. The post–Cold War era, however, will bring new security challenges to the Asia-Pacific region. Perhaps the most serious of these challenges involved China's expected emergence as a major economic power in the near future. While a developed, prosperous Chinese economy offers the region many potential benefits, it would also give China the capability to challenge Japan for domination of East Asia.

China's recent economic growth signals a change in East Asia's distribution of power and draws renewed attention to Chinese foreign policy. What are the consequences of Chinese economic growth for regional security?

I argue that a burgeoning China poses a long-term danger to Asia-Pacific security for two reasons. First, despite Japan's present economic strength, a future Chinese hegemony in East Asia is a strong possibility. China is just beginning to realize its vast economic potential, while Japan's inherent weaknesses create doubts about the ability of the Japanese to increase or sustain their present level of economic power. China also faces less resistance than Japan to building a superpower-sized military. Second, a stronger China is likely to undermine peace in the region. Economic development will make China more assertive and less cooperative with its neighbors; China's domestic characteristics make it comparatively likely to use force to achieve its political goals; and an economically powerful China may provoke a military buildup by Japan, plunging Asia into a new cold war.

ASIA'S FUTURE: CHINA OR JAPAN AS NUMBER ONE?

With the United States apparently committed to a drawdown of its global military forces, the Asia-Pacific region seems to have a vacancy for a successor hegemon. Many analysts expect Japan to inherit this mantle on the basis of its impressive economic strength and influence. Nevertheless, two formidable obstacles stand between Japan and hegemony: the instability of Japanese economic strength and the weakness of Japan's armed forces.

From Denny Roy, "Hegemon on the Horizon? China's Threat to East Asian Security," *International Security* (Summer 1994). Copyright © 1994 by the President and Fellows of Harvard College and The Massachusetts Institute of Technology. Reprinted by permission. Notes omitted.

Japan's inherent economic vulnerabilities amply justify [the] term "fragile superpower." The fragilities include Japan's lack of natural resources and consequent dependence on foreign supplies of raw materials; an aging workforce... a labor shortage... a declining savings rate; and a dangerously unfavorable corporate capital-to-debt ratio. Like the United States, Japan has begun to move production to developing countries with lower labor costs, which threatens to erode its economic base and to increase unemployment. These characteristics and developments may undermine the long-term stability of Japanese economic power.... Finally, the political environment of the post-Cold War era, with its increased interest in trade blocs and "managed trade," is likely to prove less favorable to Japanese economic growth. The massive trade surplus that has become Japan's "staff of life" is in jeopardy, and Japan's relatively small, stingy home market could not compensate for the opportunities lost due to protectionism that now looms in the bigger overseas markets....

Japan's military weakness is the other principal obstacle to Japanese hegemony. Rather than an "economic superpower," Japan is really an incomplete major power. As long as the Japanese choose not to expand their capacity to project military power, they will lack the abilities to protect their economic interests abroad and to exert decisive global political influence.

Tokyo also faces strong disincentives against attempting to deploy military forces commensurate with its economic strength. Consequently, the Japanese government is unlikely to undertake heavy rearmament in the absence of a serious new threat (such as a stronger China, discussed below). One problem with increased military spending is that it would erode some of Japan's economic strength. Japan would begin to suffer the financial drain that it largely avoided during the Cold War by relying on U.S. protection.

More serious are the political disincentives. The great majority of Japanese still oppose an increase in either the size or the role of their armed forces....

Significantly, this [view] appears to be based more on circumstances than on principle. The Japanese know that a military resurgence in their country would provoke other Asian-Pacific countries to form an anti-Tokyo coalition that might eventually strangle Japan. While balancing is sometimes inefficient, prompt and efficient anti-hegemonic balancing against Japan is virtually assured by the lingering legacy of fascist Japan's Asia policy in the 1930s and early 1940s.

Present circumstances—a relatively weak China and Russia, an engaged but non-threatening United States, and the region's historical fear of Japanese military power—thus rule out an unprovoked Japanese military buildup, leaving Japan dependent on others for protection and unable to qualify as a hegemonic candidate. A change in these circumstances, however, could spark a *reactive* Japanese rearmament, discussed below.

If Japan is an overachiever that has to a large degree transcended its handicaps, China has long been a perennial underachiever. Despite its large territory and population, substantial natural resources, and the economic vigor demonstrated by Chinese everywhere except inside the People's Republic, China's various economic development strategies have posted disappointing results since the intrusion of the West during the Qing

Dynasty heralded the end of the ancient order [in 1911].

But with the economic reforms implemented by [now retired leader] Deng Xiaoping and his protegés, China now shows signs that it is beginning to realize its economic potential. China's economy grew by 12.8 percent in 1992, helped greatly by $11 billion in foreign investment, and by another 13 percent in 1993.... The International Monetary Fund recently reported that based on "purchasing power parity" statistics, China has the world's third largest economy. Even at a more modest annual growth rate of 8 to 9 percent, the target declared by China's economic czar Zhu Rongji, China's economy will double in size within nine years....

China's sudden economic surge raises the possibility that early in the next century, China will be a more powerful country than Japan. To the "Japan As Number One" argument that Japan will soon replace the United States as the world's strongest economic power, others reply that "Japan will never become number one.... China is growing so much faster that it will overtake Japan before Japan has a chance to overtake the United States."

Taken as a whole, China is still profoundly poor, and probably faces many setbacks en route to prosperity. Several problems threaten to prevent China's growth into an economic superpower. The most serious is the possibility of fractionalization—the breakup of the Chinese empire into several autonomous states—a tendency that has been accelerated by China's recent economic success. Another hurdle is continued state ownership of much of China's economy. Employing about one-third of the urban Chinese work-force, these state-owned industries are largely unprofitable.... Other difficulties include a chronically high population growth rate, which exacerbates unemployment and siphons capital investment away from industry and into less productive sectors such as housing and environmental protection; inflation, the "running dog" of rapid economic growth; and widespread official corruption and profiteering.

Nevertheless, China holds several important economic and political advantages that may make Beijing's long-term prospects for an Asia-Pacific hegemony better than Japan's.

In the economic sphere, China combines its high growth rate with a large territorial and population base.... This gives China a huge potential domestic market—over a billion customers within its own borders. In contrast, Japan lacks a large domestic market and is thus vulnerable to protectionism. China's natural resource endowments are [excellent.] The Chinese are self-sufficient in food production and supply most of their own energy needs....

Another possible Chinese economic advantage is... [the] network of ethnic Chinese with proven entrepreneurial prowess throughout the region. Chinese minorities in Southeast Asia, most of whom still speak the dialects of their ancestral home provinces in the PRC [People's Republic of China], own disproportionately large shares of their adopted states' capital. In Indonesia, for example, where Chinese account for only 5 percent of the population, they control 75 percent of the country's wealth.... [T]he overseas Chinese are likely to prefer customers, suppliers, and investors with whom they share language, culture, and ancestry. The overseas Chinese network gives China a significant long-term edge in the competition to establish an economic empire in East Asia.

China also has an important political advantage over Japan. To dominate the region, either Japan or China would need much larger military forces. China's edge is that the region would be more accommodating to a buildup of Chinese military power than to a Japanese buildup. The reason is historical. Although the foreign policy of the PRC has hardly been pacific, China's record of aggression pales in comparison with that of Japan in this century. . . .

[Also,] the Chinese government has sought to assure the region that "China does not seek hegemony now, nor will it do so in the future, even when it is economically developed." Beijing and its apologists have steadily counter-attacked the "China threat" argument as an attempt by anti-China Westerners "to sow discord between China and its neighboring countries and to destroy China's plans of reunification and economic development." There is substantial sympathy for China's position within the region. For example, Singapore Senior Minister Lee Kuan Yew, the dean of southeast Asian statesmen, said after Beijing lost its bid to host the 2000 Olympic Games, "America and Britain succeeded in cutting China down to size. . . . The apparent reason was 'human rights.' The real reason was political, to show Western political clout." . . .

This is not to deny that East Asians are concerned about China's recent military upgrading program. They clearly are. But the predominant sentiment throughout the region is appeasement. There is no serious support for any response stronger than trying to get the Chinese "incorporated into a multilateral security framework." . . .

The region [therefore] appears prepared to tolerate a Chinese buildup, and would probably not form a balancing alliance unless China's external behavior became significantly more threatening than it is now. China thus faces far weaker political constraints against building a superpower-sized military capability—an important prerequisite of hegemony—than Japan.

If China can avoid disintegration, its inherent long-term economic and political advantages justify the expectation that during the first decade of the next century the "Middle Kingdom" is likely to become the most powerful country in East Asia.

THE IMPACT OF A STRONG CHINA ON REGIONAL SECURITY

The prospect of Chinese dominance has important ramifications for peace in the region. A stronger China would endanger East Asian security in two ways. First, China would be tempted to establish a regional hegemony, possibly by force. Second, the rise of Chinese power might trigger a response from Japan, bringing East Asia under the shadow of a new bipolar conflict.

Economic Development and Chinese Foreign Policy

While some scholars argue that ancient China established a track record of benevolent hegemony, two patterns in the foreign policy of the PRC suggest that neighboring countries might find life with a powerful China unpleasant. First, China has from time to time behaved in ways offensive to the rest of the world, seemingly undaunted by the possible consequences of negative global opinion. Second, China has shown its willingness to use force to settle disputes, even when its own territory is not under attack.

If a relatively weak and developing China has established such patterns, would a stronger, developed China abandon them? The question of whether economic development will make Chinese foreign policy more pacific or more assertive divides commentators roughly into two theoretical camps. The liberal position holds that prosperity will make China behave more peacefully, while realists argue that greater economic strength would embolden a unified China to expand its political influence in the region, perhaps to the grief of its neighbors. An evaluation of the primary arguments for both these positions suggests that the realists have the stronger case.

Two arguments are commonly advanced in support of the liberals' prosperity-causes-peace proposition. The first is that economic development leads to political liberalization, and with it greater government accountability to the demands of the mass public. ...

Unfortunately, ... [t]he establishment of a liberal democracy in China is extremely unlikely in the foreseeable future. The obstacles are daunting, and since crushing the student rebellion in Tiananmen Square [1989], Beijing has shown little interest in further political liberalization. Even if China does eventually begin to respond to pressures for liberalization, many observers ... see "soft authoritarianism," in which the state allows considerable economic freedom but retains tight control over politics, as a more likely model for the Chinese than Western-style democracy. In any case, prosperity will not automatically result in meaningful mass public input into China's foreign policy decisions. Without democratiza-

tion within, there is no basis for expecting more pacific behavior without.

A second argument for the pacifying effects of Chinese prosperity is the interdependence argument. According to this view, China is aware that its economic development depends on maintaining financial, trade, and diplomatic ties with other countries. Dependence on the outside world will therefore, it is argued, deter Beijing from contemplating any acts that might offend foreign governments or jeopardize China's access to international capital, technology, and markets. ...

Problems with the interdependence argument, however, weaken its persuasiveness. First, economic interdependence may heighten rather than defuse political tensions. The threat or practice of economic coercion has sometimes driven states to war. If used against China, this strategy might backfire, pushing Beijing to try to establish direct control over the foreign resources and markets the Chinese consider vital to their well-being.

A second weakness of the interdependence argument is that in China's case, the deterrence value of interdependence is severely limited. In the past, the liberal capitalist countries have proven greatly reluctant to pressure Beijing, and this pressure, when applied, has produced poor results. Western governments easily succumb to the ageless warning against "isolating" China. ... For their part, the Chinese leaders have learned from past experience that the threat of collective international punitive action against them is largely a paper tiger. In the most recent confirmation of their view, the perpetrators of the Tiananmen massacre were first runners-up in the competition for the right to host the 2000 Olympic Games.

Finally, interdependence may be doomed by its own success. Throughout its modern history, China has been an economically backward country trying to catch up with the earlier-industrializing West and Japan.... An "open door" to the international economy, with heavy dependence on imports of capital and technology and exports of low-to-middle-end manufactures, is China's most successful strategy to date. But dependence means vulnerability. Like all national governments, the Chinese leaders are naturally inclined to "control what they depend on (from abroad] or to lessen the extent of their dependency." Dependence is a necessary evil, part of the price that capital-poor, developing economies must pay to achieve rapid modernization. The security threat of vulnerability to economic coercion is compensated for by the security benefit of a growing economy, the basis of future military and political strength.... But as a developing country becomes strong and wealthy relative to the other states in the system, both the benefits it realizes from interdependence and the costs of establishing its own sphere of influence decrease. Today's weak China has to suffer the vulnerabilities of interdependence, but tomorrow's strong China will not. The more powerful China grows, the less it needs the aid and approval of the other major powers to get what it needs. Over the long term, interdependence cannot offer other countries much hope of reining in a burgeoning China.

Realists would not in any case expect prosperity to make China more pacific. If the international behavior of states is strongly influenced by threats and opportunities governments perceive in the international system, as realists assume, then China's growth from a weak, developing state to a stronger, more prosperous state should result in a more assertive foreign policy.... As China fulfills its economic potential, it will conform to [this] pattern. An economically stronger China will begin to act like a major power: bolder, more demanding, and less inclined to cooperate with the other major powers in the region.

The realist argument has powerful historical support. A stronger China will be subject to the same pressures and temptations to which other economically and militarily powerful countries of recent history succumbed, including Britain, Nazi Germany, the Soviet Union, and the United States. Each sought to dominate the part of the globe within its reach (although the particular character of each hegemony varied, from relatively benign to malign).

China is Prone to Using Force

... [There are] several reasons [why] a strong China [may well] use force in pursuit of its goals in the region....

First,... the Chinese government is a typical Third World regime: authoritarian and unstable.... [T]hese latter characteristics create war-proneness.... [S]ince Third World governments are not democratic, their accountability to the mass public is limited, which increases the possibility that ruling elites will go to war for their own purposes against the wishes of the majority. An authoritarian regime may even embark on hostile overseas adventures against its country's interest if the regime expects this will help it maintain its own political power. Militarism and hyper-nationalism, partly facilitated by state control of the media, are more prevalent in the Third World, making their populations more supportive of adventurism. Finally, the leaders of Third World states are more likely to undertake aggressive action abroad to divert the public's attention from domestic political problems.

China is subject to all of these factors. Both its state and society are unstable. A single party monopolizes power, suppressing serious dissent, and authority is located in persons rather than institutions. Presiding over a sprawling, largely destitute, populous empire, the central government lives in constant fear of insurrection. To the familiar problems of poverty are now added the new problems of rapid, uneven economic growth, including massive corruption and a growing disparity between the rich and the poor....

A second reason why China... [may] use force... is that China is a dissatisfied power.... [China] is still trying to recover territory and prestige lost to the West during the *bainiande ciru* ("century of shame"). China's irredentist claims have brought sharp disagreements with Britain, Taiwan, Vietnam, Japan, India, and Malaysia, among others. Its fear of exploitation and conquest by foreigners remains strong. The Chinese leadership perceives the international environment as primarily hostile, and their own place within it insecure. The Soviet Union is gone, but the Chinese believe the United States "has never abandoned its ambition to rule the world, and its military interventionism is becoming more open." Beijing is deeply resentful of attempts by the United States and others to foment "peaceful evolution," which Chinese leaders fear will result in social and political chaos and the destruction of their plans for China's economic development. Although they have submitted out of necessity, the Chinese remain highly averse to interdependence, and to subjection to international norms and regimes.

Accordingly, ... the Chinese government sees the use of force as a serious policy option. Indeed, Chinese leaders speak much more belligerently at home than abroad. Even in official public statements, China continues to renew its threat to attack Taiwan if the island declares itself independent of the mainland, and refuses to rule out the use of force to settle the South China Sea islands dispute.

Finally, China is... able to mobilize its population for war....

The multi-million-member People's Liberation Army [PLA] has obediently carried out a variety of unsavory orders from Beijing, including the attacks by PLA "volunteers" on American and South Korean troops in Korea, the occupation of Tibet, the punitive incursion into Vietnam, and the slaughter of unarmed demonstrators in Tiananmen Square. It could be counted on to enforce China's hegemonic imperatives as well.

If China is prone to using force, Chinese economic development carries with it the problem of making more force available for Beijing to use....

CONCLUSIONS

China represents [the greatest] long-term threat to East Asian security.... If behavior reflects capabilities, China's potential to build a larger economy also makes it... assertive and uncooperative. China is [apt to use] force... and will likely remain so after its economy has grown, because the Chinese government is authoritarian, unstable, wants to redress the status quo, and can mobilize large military forces with comparative ease. China is also [hard] to deter... because it is less vulnerable to economic coercion, and will be even less dependent on outside suppliers as its economy continues to develop.

Furthermore, past experience gives Beijing good reason not to take the threat of economic sanctions seriously.

How should the United States and the other major Asia-Pacific powers prepare for the Chinese challenge? Three general strategies are possible. The first would be to suppress China's economic growth and thereby preempt its development into a superpower. This might be attempted through a cutoff of economic contact with China, similar to U.S. policies toward North Korea, Cuba and, until recently, Vietnam.

This option, however, stands little chance of success. An economic embargo is politically impossible in the case of China. Even if the governments in Asia, Western Europe, and North America could be persuaded that such a strategy was strategically sound, their fears of missed economic opportunities and cheating by coalition partners would remain major barriers. Furthermore, economic suppression of China, while perhaps precluding one form of security threat from China, would likely create others, including massive outflows of Chinese economic refugees, Chinese vulnerability to territorial challenges by bordering states, and the breakdown of centralized control over China's nuclear weapons arsenal. An economically retarded, chaotic China is scarcely more desirable than a highly prosperous, united China.

A second policy option would also aim at undercutting China's potential strength, but by another means: strategic economic engagement designed to increase regionalism within China's borders. The current trend in China is toward a decline in control by the central government in Beijing and greater leeway for regional authorities to run their own economic and political affairs. The United States and other capitalist countries could attempt to foster this tendency by providing information and incentives to encourage their nationals who do business in China to target the regions most committed to free market reforms and least responsive to Beijing's control. China's capitalist business partners could also push for arrangements that would promote greater regional autonomy, undermining the central government's control over local prices, profits, and wages. The goal would be to strengthen the linkages between individual Chinese provinces and foreign states, and to weaken the links between the provinces and Beijing, making regional governors less likely to cooperate with attempts by the central government to marshal resources for campaigns of overseas conquest or coercion.

However, an open attempt by the United States and other foreign governments to foment fractionalization in China would also be counterproductive. This policy would convince the Chinese their worst fears of Western neo-imperialism were correct. Chinese nationalism would increase, and links between Beijing and the provinces would likely grow stronger rather than weaker as more Chinese saw the need to work together against the apparent attempt by foreigners to divide and conquer. Such a policy would also alienate America's Asia-Pacific allies, who would wonder why the more distant and powerful United States was taking such an aggressive approach when so many of them are prepared to accommodate a strong China. Without their cooperation, U.S. efforts to shape Chinese development could not succeed.

In short, openly attempting to thwart China's economic growth by imposing an embargo or encouraging national disintegration would probably not work, and would likely backfire by increasing Beijing's insecurity and hostility toward the West.

A third possible strategy for the major powers would be to continue their participation in China's economic development, encouraging positive behavior when feasible (e.g., Most Favored Nation trade status as a reward for progress in human rights), and organizing an anti-China coalition only if and when threatening behavior occurs. While the free flow of capital and goods may be providing nourishment for a future hegemon, it also helps promote regional autonomy, political liberalization, and cross-cutting linkages between various parts of China and the outside world. From a political standpoint, it is far better to rely on the free market than initiatives by foreign governments to achieve these goals. Nevertheless, this strategy requires the other major powers and the ASEAN [Association of Southeast Asian Nations] states to be prepared to react swiftly to undue assertiveness by the stronger China of the near future. A powerful China provides another reason for a continuing U.S. military presence in the region. It may also breathe new life into the shaky U.S.-Japan alliance. In the meantime, multilateral security regimes might focus on persuading China to limit its power-projection weapons systems and to agree to shared or divided ownership of the South China Sea Islands.

In the absence of an ideal solution, continuing to abet China's growth, while hoping defensive balancing will not be necessary, is the least problematic option for the outside world. Continued and unrestrained economic engagement conveys implicit acquiescence to the possibility of an economically and militarily powerful China, with all its attendant risks. But this approach has its positive points as well: it is the least threatening from China's perspective, and it allows for the possibility that unrestrained trade and investment will continue to weaken the central government's control over the provinces, reducing Beijing's potential for foreign aggression. This strategy also recognizes the limits on the ability of outside countries, even powerful ones, to manipulate China. . . . It may well be inescapable that China's destiny remains in its own hands.

From the point of view of the rest of the world, the ideal China, perhaps, would be a medium-sized China, with an economy and military forces about the size of present-day Japan's. While continuing to export goods of increasing quality, this more prosperous China could also provide surplus capital for investment abroad and a vast market for foreign imports, finally fulfilling the dream of nineteenth-century Western traders. The Chinese might also maintain qualitatively improved but numerically smaller military forces structured for rapid deployment to China's borders and coastal waters, but not far beyond. This mid-size China would be a prominent economic and political player in the region, engaging in diplomatic give-and-take with the other major powers, but not a hegemon.

Unfortunately, current developments foretell an economically gigantic China with a historic fear of foreigners, a distaste for cooperation, and an interest in developing a blue-water navy and long-range air combat capabilities. These may be the first signs of what will develop into the greatest threat to the region's stability since the Pacific War.

NO

Michael G. Gallagher

CHINA'S ILLUSORY THREAT
TO THE SOUTH CHINA SEA

The rebirth of Chinese power after five hundred years of decline is one of the major events of this decade: "The rise of China, if it continues, may be the most important trend in the world for the next century." And indeed, on the economic side of the ledger China has turned in a stunningly impressive performance over the last fifteen years. Economic growth has averaged 9 percent since 1978. China's 1993 growth rate was 13 percent. In 1994, industrial output is expected to top 15 percent. Fast-paced economic growth has made mainland China a favorite of foreign investors. In the first nine months of 1993, $15 billion (U.S.) was spent by overseas investors in the China market.

China's leadership has apparently decided to invest a portion of that new wealth in a major upgrading of the combat power of the People's Liberation Army (PLA). Special attention is being paid to the buildup of air and seapower. This combination of rapid economic growth and increasing military strength has many, in Asia and elsewhere, wondering exactly what the Chinese intend to do with their newly acquired power: "China has increasing weight to throw about. But its neighbors still question whether this weight will be thrown behind efforts to build a more secure and stable Asia."

One focus of this concern over Chinese intentions is the Spratly Islands. At the far end of the South China Sea from the Chinese mainland, this collection of stony outcroppings and islets is perhaps the main source of international tension in Southeast Asia with the end of the Cold War. In a world of shrinking natural resources, the mainland Chinese have clearly stated what flag they think should fly over the potentially oil-rich island group: "these islands and reefs are within Chinese territory and other countries are definitely not allowed to invade and occupy them." Ominous statements of that sort have driven people to worry that China's growing economic and military strength may tempt it to expand at the expense of its neighbors in Southeast Asia. "Beijing's buildup on Hainan and Woody Island [the largest island in the Paracels group], signal[s] an inclination to dominate the South China Sea by force rather than negotiate shared control with the other claimants to the Spratlys."

From Michael G. Gallagher, "China's Illusory Threat to the South China Sea," *International Security* (Summer 1994). Copyright © 1994 by the President and Fellows of Harvard College and The Massachusetts Institute of Technology. Reprinted by permission. Notes omitted.

The head of the Malaysia Institute of Maritime Affairs, Hamzah Ahmad, feels that China is seeking to replace the United States and Russia as the region's main military power. "China should not attempt to revive the Middle Kingdom mentality and expect tribute from Southeast Asia," he declared in October 1993.

But fears of a looming conflict over the Spratly Islands may be premature. China's huge size and tremendous numbers may no longer be a decisive advantage in the competition for the control of the Spratly Islands. The growing wealth of its maritime rivals, and their willingness to invest in high-technology weaponry, combined with serious political constraints, both international and domestic, on overseas adventures, have diminished any military advantages China might at one time have enjoyed over its neighbors.

This paper is divided into four sections. The first discusses the basis for the dispute over the Spratly Islands.... The next section analyzes the military balance between China and some of its smaller neighbors.... The section that follows it describes some of the international political and economic constraints on aggressive action in the South China Sea. The concluding section discusses the domestic problems now facing China and how they might affect Chinese behavior with regards to the South China Sea.

BACKGROUND OF THE DISPUTE

To a casual observer, it might seem strange that the Spratly Islands could be the flashpoint for a major international confrontation. Of the 230 islands that make up the Spratly group, only seven are more than 0.1 square kilometers in area. Thity is the largest island in the group; claimed by the Philippines, it is less than one mile long and just 625 yards wide. Many of these so-called islands are merely rocky outcroppings that are underwater at high tide.

These minuscule islands, however, possess significance well beyond their actual size. The islands sit astride sea routes through which twenty-five percent of the world's shipping passes, including the supertankers carrying the petroleum that fuels the economies of Japan, Taiwan, and South Korea. Large quantities of oil may also lie beneath the islands as well:... [perhaps] from 1 billion to 105 billion barrels of oil. In addition, the area is a rich fishery: 2.5 million tons of fish were harvested from the waters around the islands in 1980.

.... The Chinese assert that their claim to the Spratly Islands dates back 1700 years to the time of the Han Dynasty. But the only independent confirmation of Chinese claims to the Spratlys dates from 1867, when a British survey ship discovered a group of fishermen from Hainan working the area's rich fishing grounds. Despite the sparseness of historical evidence to support their claims to the islands, the Chinese have been forthright about their intention to claim those resources. In February 1992, China's National People's Congress passed a declaration stating that the Spratlys Islands were an integral part of Chinese territory. China's claims to the Spratlys are easier to understand when one realizes that the Chinese regard control of the ocean's resources as vital to their nation's continued existence.

Claims to the resources of the South China Sea have been backed by China's willingness to use force to compel recognition of its rights. In January 1974

Chinese forces drove South Vietnamese naval forces out of the Paracel Islands after a sharp clash in which one South Vietnamese corvette was sunk and two destroyers were damaged. Chinese and Vietnamese forces skirmished a second time in the South China Sea in March 1988. This time the two navies fought over the disputed Johnson Reef in the Spratly islands, far to the south of the 1974 Paracels clash. Chinese forces sank three Vietnamese supply ships, killed seventy-two Vietnamese, and captured nine. By the end of 1988 the Chinese had occupied six atolls in the Spratly Islands. China continued its expansionist activities in the Spratlys when it occupied Da Lac reef in July 1992. ...

Along with the use of force, China has throughout the 1970s and 1980s used fishing fleets, the dispatch of "oceanographic" vessels carrying high-ranking naval and civilian personnel on cruises through the disputed areas, and the construction of airfields, blockhouses, and other facilities in both the Paracels and Spratly Islands to make China, if not first claimant on the scene, at least the party on the spot with the most muscular presence. China may be practicing Cold War "salami tactics," absorbing the South China Sea in small bits so as to avoid a violent response from potential adversaries.

During the 1970s, Vietnam was China's only competitor in the Paracels. In contrast, presently China must share the Spratly Islands with other nations. China has garrisoned seven atolls, but Vietnam has occupied twenty-one atolls, the Philippines has placed troops on eight, and the Malaysian flag flies over two atolls. Although outside confirmation for Chinese claims to the Spratly Islands date from the 1860s, other countries can marshal evidence to support their claims as well. Vietnamese claims to the islands date from 1862 and 1865, when cartographic surveys of the South China Sea showed the islands as part of Vietnam. The Philippines' claims date from 1938, when Manila tried to interest Japan in a joint occupation. In 1971, Philippine President Ferdinand Marcos fairly summed up the non-Chinese view of the Spratly dispute when he declared the islands "derelict and disputed."

Apart from the declared parties to the Spratly dispute, any reasonable examination of the situation in the South China Sea must consider the attitudes of both the wealthiest and the largest of the Association of Southeast Asian Nations (ASEAN) states, Singapore and Indonesia. Among the nations of Southeast Asia the tiny city state of Singapore is by far the most prosperous and technologically advanced, but its government is acutely aware of its dependence on the unimpeded flow of shipping through the Malacca Straits and the open waters of the South China Sea beyond [and thus is wary of China.] ...

Indonesia... [also has] every reason to be wary of China's intrusion into the South China Sea. Nervousness over Chinese expansionism certainly pushed along Indonesia's February 1993 stopgap purchase of thirty-nine vessels from the former East German navy and the follow-on plans to construct twenty-one modern frigates in local shipyards. ...

THE MILITARY EQUATION

Table 1 suggests that China would be capable of bringing vastly superior military strength to bear in any armed confrontation over the Spratly Islands. Overwhelming numbers would support

Table 1

Naval and Air Forces Available to China, Selected ASEAN Countries, and Vietnam.

	Combat Aircraft		Large Warships	Patrol Craft (SSM)		Submarines
China	5000		54	860	(207)	46 + 5 SSN
Malaysia	69 + 6 armed helos		4 frigates	37	(8)	0
Singapore	192 + 6 armed helos		6 corvettes	24	(6)	0
Indonesia	81		17 frigates	48	(4)	2
Vietnam	185 + 20 armed helos		7 frigates	55	(8)	0

Notes: Aircraft totals include naval air forces; patrol craft include gun and torpedo boats; SSM = Surface-to-Surface Missiles, SSN = attack submarines.

Source: Compiled from International Institute of Strategic Studies, *The Military Balance 1993–94* (London: Brassey's, 1993), pp. 145–165.

China's leaders if they one day decided to expel rival claimants from the disputed islands.

The bulk of China's modern weaponry has been purchased at garage-sale prices from the increasingly decrepit military of the Russian Republic....

However, China's rivals for control of the Spratly Islands have not been standing idly by while the PRC [People's Republic of China] stockpiles weaponry. In July 1993, Malaysia announced its decision to buy eighteen MiG-29s and eight McDonnell Douglas F-18s as part of its military modernization program.... In June 1992, GEC-Marconi of the United Kingdom agreed to build for the Royal Malaysian Navy two modern frigates [equipped with anti-aircraft and anti-ship missiles] for approximately $425 million.... [T]hese up-to-date vessels, operating in conjunction with the new MiGs and F-18s and the missile-armed patrol craft already in Malaysia's possession, would provide a credible defense of Malaysia's claims in the South China Sea....

Singapore is [also]... in the process of building a military force to match the growing sophistication of its economy. With 192 aircraft... Singapore's air force is already the most potent in Southeast Asia. The Navy's six *Victory*-class corvettes and six *Sea Wolf* missile patrol craft are armed with U.S. *Harpoon* and Israeli *Gabriel* anti-shipping missiles....

Economically, Indonesia is still lagging behind star performers like Malaysia and Singapore, but its military does have its modern components. Alone among ASEAN states, Indonesia operates its own submarine force.... The Indonesian air force also flies twelve F-16s, while the navy's frigates and patrol craft are armed with *Exocet* and *Harpoon* anti-shipping missiles.

By the year 2000, moreover, the island nation's poverty may be a receding memory for many of its citizens.... [Thus] Indonesia is likely to have the money available for continued military modernization.... [And its] rulers are committed to a strong modernization effort....

GEOGRAPHY

Geography is another difficulty the Chinese must cope with in the event of an armed confrontation over the Spratly Islands. The main Chinese naval bases in the South China Sea, Yulin on Hainan Island and Zhanjiang, the headquarters of China's South Seas Fleet on the mainland, are much farther from the disputed islands than are the bases of potential enemies. Chinese surface forces facing serious opposition in the waters surrounding the Spratly Islands would require effective air cover in order to survive. Currently, the People's Liberation Army Air Force (PLAAF) lacks modern aircraft with the range, speed, and maneuverability necessary to protect a large Chinese naval force operating in the Spratly group....

Even with the... [addition of warplanes purchased from Russia and] Chinese-produced fighter aircraft ... the Chinese could still face serious difficulties in providing effective air cover over the Spratly Islands....

Since it is likely that Chinese naval forces would have to operate in the vicinity of the Spratly Islands with only limited air support, they would often be forced to fend for themselves in the event of air attack. Here Chinese prospects are dismal. Chinese naval vessels are adequately equipped with short-range antiaircraft guns, but ships equipped with modern antiaircraft missile systems are virtually nonexistent. At the start of 1994, in the entire People's Liberation Army Navy (PLAN) there were only four ships... equipped with surface-to-air missile (SAM) systems....

With the demise of the Soviet Union, China now has the world's second largest submarine fleet, after the United States. But all of the PLAN's diesel-powered boats are based on 1950s Soviet designs. Only forty-six of the fleet's one hundred boats are on active duty. As

for the five Chinese-built *Han*-class nuclear attack boats in PLAN service, only two boats are believed to be fit for duty due to maintenance and technical problems. Additionally, the twin afflictions of obsolescence and poor maintenance may make Chinese submarines excessively noisy when submerged, making China's submarine fleet vulnerable to modern anti-submarine warfare technology.... Limited funding makes it unlikely that China would be able to purchase more than a few... modern [Russian submarines], and the establishment of a shipyard to construct the submarines on Chinese soil is unlikely before the late 1990s at the earliest. If tensions over the Spratly Islands erupt into a crisis over the next several years, China could find itself in the unenviable position of being able to field only a relatively small amount of mostly foreign-manufactured modern weaponry, operating far from any safe haven, against potential adversaries armed with increasingly up-to-date equipment, much of it manufactured locally.

MILITARY MODERNIZATION

China's lack of SAM-equipped warships and its creaky submarine fleet only serve to highlight a fact that is often left out of any discussion about China's ability to threaten its neighbors militarily: the PLA is very large, but is deficient when it comes to the sinews of warfare in the 1990s.

Chinese military technology is still as much as twenty years behind the West. One major obstacle is lack of money....

China's military industry has a well-documented history of problems with reverse engineering.... One reason for these failures may be that the PLA has the tendency to rush a new weapon into service without a thorough debugging. Lack of extensive automation or computerized quality control also hamper the PLA's efforts to close the technology gap with the outside world.

Modern Chinese-produced weaponry has often proved itself ineffective. Towards the end of the 1991 Gulf War, Iraqi shore batteries fired two of China's much-publicized Silkworm missiles at the battleship USS *Wisconsin* and its escorting destroyer, HMS *Gloucester*. One missile disintegrated and fell into the sea. The second missile was shot down by a *Sea Dart* missile fired by the *Gloucester*.

... Unless the PRC can overcome its inability to successfully develop and, especially, to mass-produce modern military equipment, the PLA faces the high probability of merely being locked into a higher level of technological obsolescence than is now the case.

INTERNATIONAL CONSTRAINTS ON CHINESE BEHAVIOR

Great powers are often viewed by their smaller neighbors with deep suspicion, and the fear that one nation will become overwhelmingly powerful tends to drive that country's rivals into each other's arms.

Starting in the early 1970s, the Five Power Defense Arrangement (FPDA) has provided an embryonic network for military cooperation among ASEAN and outside powers. Including Singapore, Malaysia, Britain, Australia, and New Zealand, the FPDA has over the last twenty years sponsored joint air exercises at the Payar Lebar airport in Singapore, including 1992 exercises that involved aircraft from Malaysia, Singapore, and Australia. In July 1992 Vice Admiral

Soedibyo Rahardjo, the chief of staff of Indonesia's armed forces, and Brigadier General Lee Hsien Yang of Singapore, the armed forces chief of staff and son of Singapore's former prime minister Lee Kuan Yew, signed an agreement to establish joint anti-piracy patrols. ...

While the 1992 anti-piracy agreement and the joint air exercises hardly represent military cooperation on the scale of the NATO Cold War alliance, they have laid down a foundation on which future cooperation could be built. ...

From the standpoint of international public opinion, the ASEAN states are in a much better position *vis-à-vis* China than Vietnam was in the 1970s and 1980s. Chinese moves against Vietnam during that period were based on a unique set of circumstances: China's 1974 gains in the Paracels were acquired at the expense of the soon-to-be-extinct government of South Vietnam, which had been judged a pariah in the court of international public opinion. ...

In 1988, a communist-ruled Vietnam was again an international outcast due to its 1978 invasion of Cambodia. Two hundred thousand Vietnamese troops were mired in a protracted guerrilla war against the Khmer Rouge. ... The Chinese had astutely judged the international situation to be favorable to them before they drove the Vietnamese Navy away from Jones Reef in the Spratly Islands. ...

Since the 1979 Chinese invasion, Vietnam has pulled out of Cambodia and opened its economy to foreign investment. With the lifting of the U.S. trade embargo in early 1994, this new cloak of international acceptance may give Vietnam greater protection against Chinese aggression, despite a 50 percent reduction in its armed forces, than at any time since the immediate aftermath of the 1979

Sino-Vietnamese War, when Hanoi enjoyed both military superiority over the PLA and the benefit of a security treaty with the now defunct Soviet Union.

Vietnam's ASEAN neighbors may also be able to draw upon international respectability. With the exception of the Philippines, all the ASEAN states are enjoying rising levels of prosperity.... While none of these governments is fully democratic, they present a more pleasant face to the world than China's present regime. Any major Chinese military action to clear its rivals out of the Spratly Islands is likely to cause a level of international protest second only to that which followed the Iraqi seizure of Kuwait. More importantly, given the island groups' strategic position astride main shipping routes, large-scale violence over the Spratly Islands has a good chance of bringing larger powers onto the scene.

Worried about potential for violence in post–Cold War Asia, the governments of Singapore, Thailand, and Malaysia have offered port facilities to the United States. Even Indonesia, usually among the most reluctant of ASEAN members when it comes to inviting outsiders to assist in the region's troubles, signed an agreement in the fall of 1992 allowing the United States Navy the use of the... dockyard in Surabaya. With Thailand, the United States carries out forty mostly small-scale joint exercises every year.

Depending on the magnitude of the problem, the United States might simply decide to increase its arms sales to the countries that felt most anxious about Chinese intentions. This policy has been followed for many years with regards to Taiwan.... All the ASEAN states already use at least some American equipment, so a policy of containing China by building

up the militaries of its rivals would be relatively easy to implement.

Apart from military and diplomatic maneuvers to block any threat from China, the ASEAN states are trying to deter any aggressive moves in their direction by fostering economic ties with the Chinese. Singapore has sought to broaden economic ties with the PRC....

The ASEAN states' growing economic ties with China raise the following question. Given the economic carrot the Chinese can dangle in front of the business people of Southeast Asia, wouldn't it be easier for the ASEAN countries to go along with China's claims in the South China Sea rather than put an increasingly profitable relationship at risk?

However, the Spratly Islands sit astride vital sea lanes and possess important natural resources. A nation, if it has the means, will usually seek to prevent a hostile power from gaining control of important lines of communication and natural resources. For example, for centuries it was standard British policy to prevent enemy nations from gaining control of the Low Countries, which would have threatened London's control of the North Sea and the English Channel. And as noted above, the ASEAN states possess ever more capable military forces. Given the obvious technological defects of Chinese naval and air forces, there is no real reason for China's neighbors in Southeast Asia to submit to Chinese bullying. In fact, if a confrontation does take place in the South China Sea over the next several years, China's opponents, aware of the low technological level of China's sea and air forces, may simply decide that China is bluffing.

... Beijing [must also] consider its own trade and investment interests when deciding what action to take over the

Spratly Islands. By the fall of 1993, $83 billion (U.S.) in direct investment had been pledged to the China market by foreign investors.... Thus China must seek out overseas investors. Two Chinese firms, the Harbin Group and Shanghai United, have signed technology transfer agreements with Westinghouse. Another Chinese firm, the Dongfang group, is hoping for joint venture agreements with Siemens, Hitachi, and General Electric.

A stable international environment is usually viewed as beneficial to trade and foreign investment. Given both economic and military risks, Chinese leaders would have to ask themselves if islands that are barely noticeable on the map are really worth the risk of even a temporary disruption of the impressive flow of foreign investment into their country.

DOMESTIC CONSTRAINTS ON CHINESE BEHAVIOR

In addition to economic enticements, rivals with growing arsenals, and diplomatic difficulties, problems within China itself may place additional limits on Chinese actions beyond the borders of the PRC. Indonesian and Malaysian strategists have pointed out that China's defense spending has grown by 20 percent over the last two years, but what they have failed to discover (or to mention) is where the new money is going within the PLA's sprawling infrastructure. Public statements concerning the PLA's post–Cold War strategy constantly say that China needs to form a well-equipped rapid reaction force designed to be deployed quickly to trouble spots on China's frontiers. But of the 3 million PLA soldiers now on active duty, less than one-fourth are in units scheduled to be modernized. With the gov-

ernment paying only a portion of their operating expenses, these units are being forced to go in to sideline business activities. The newly modernized units are reportedly to be stationed across China, but there is to be an especially heavy concentration of modernized units in Northeast China to defend Beijing. These units are also receiving much of the modern equipment that is reaching the PLA. Chinese strategists say that the three armies are deployed to defend China's capital from any possible threat from the increasingly run-down Russian Far Eastern Command. But with such a large part of the PLA left out of the modernization effort, the primary mission of the three armies may be to protect the Chinese leadership from any future internal unrest.

Chinese society has developed a web of hairline cracks from the frenetic pace of the transition from a command to a free-market economy. China's fast-growing economy has sparked an urban inflation rate of 20–26 percent annually. A similar burst of inflation in 1988 helped set the stage for the uprising in Tiananmen Square in 1989. With private enterprise comprising an ever-growing share of China's GDP, power is flowing out of Beijing into the provinces and the hands of individuals....

People in China are no longer dependent for their livelihoods on the *Danwei*, the state-controlled work units that formerly dominated every aspect of a worker's life. Many state employees nowadays just stop by their workplaces to pick up their paychecks, which merely supplement the income from the jobs they hold in the bustling private sector. In a society where housing and medical care were once virtually free, enterprises are prodding their employees to buy their own housing, and doctors and nurses are now demanding bribes for treatment.

Entire villages of illegal migrants from the countryside have grown up on the fringes of most large Chinese cities. Since these places do not have Communist Party–run street committees, it has become very difficult for Chinese Public Security to control the transients' comings and goings. China may have up to 100 million people drifting across the country in search of work. Moreover, ten percent of the urban population may be underemployed. China's long history is dotted with great rebellions whose basic material was the jobless and the homeless. The Chinese government's disquiet over the situation was reflected in the Shanghai newspaper *Wenhuibao:* "The floating population, which exists without the normal controls, is fertile soil for the growth of secret societies. If they get together and form organizations, then the large group of people without a steady income will be a great threat to stability. If they join with the millions of unemployed in the cities, then the results will be even more unimaginable."

The people left behind in the villages of China's vast countryside are also feeling the effects of their nation's rapid economic development. Widening economic opportunities have led to rampant official corruption, much of it in the countryside. Local officials extort money from the peasants under the guise of special "taxes," including fees levied on old radios and televisions, and forced "loans" from peasants to local bureaucrats in return for dubious IOUs. In some parts of the countryside, refusal to give in to this extortion can lead to jail, with one's family forced to pay in return for one's release. Hong Kong newspapers reported 200 incidents of peasant unrest

in 1992 alone.... The destruction of the old social contract, the epidemic of petty corruption, and the creation of a huge class of undocumented and possibly uncontrollable transients are trends, that, if they continue over the next few years, are likely to divert the attention of China's leadership far away from the reefs and islets of the Spratly Islands.

It could be argued that a short, sharp war in the South China Sea might be just what China's leaders need to divert the Chinese people's attention away from problems at home. History is filled with such instances: for example in 1982, Argentina's military junta thought an easy victory over the tiny British garrison in the Falklands would shore up its shaky position at home. But the wars that China has fought since 1949 indicate a different pattern. Chinese leaders seem to like having their domestic house in order before they tackle foreign enemies. When China entered the Korean War in November 1950, communist control of the mainland was unchallenged. Chiang Kai-shek and the remnants of the Nationalist armies had fled to Taiwan in disarray; although ragtag groups of Nationalist soldiers were still loose in the remote jungles of Southwest China, they posed no threat to the Communists' domination of mainland China. China intervened in Korea strictly for reasons of international prestige and national security. Mao Zedong felt that China could not tolerate the destruction of a fellow communist government in North Korea by the U.S.-led United Nations forces. More importantly, with the Americans driving towards the Yalu River, the Chinese government was anxious about the potential threat to Manchuria, China's main industrial region.

China's last war, the 1979 invasion of Vietnam, was also fought against a background of foreign threats and domestic peace. In December 1978, Vietnam had invaded Cambodia and toppled from power Beijing's Khmer Rouge allies. Vietnam's principal ally and China's main adversary, the Soviet Union, had taken over the former U.S. Navy base at Cam Ranh Bay. China's leaders, fearing Russian encirclement and disturbed by what they believed to be a steep decline in U.S. ability to fend off Soviet expansionism after the fall of South Vietnam, felt they had to go to war to demonstrate to their enemies that China could deal with challenges to its security without outside assistance.

Within China itself, however, the political situation was calm. Deng Xiaoping and his fellow economic reformers had swept most of the remaining Maoists from power and had tightened their control over the government. In 1978, Deng Xiaoping had started the program of economic reforms that was to make China one of the great economic success stories of the 1990s.

China's quiet intervention in the Vietnam War during the 1960s was the only occasion when Beijing has intervened militarily beyond its frontiers during a time of domestic crisis. The Cultural Revolution, Mao's last great effort to ideologically purify China and eliminate his political enemies, riddled China with factional feuds from one end of the country to the other.... Despite the turmoil, the Chinese dispatched 50,000 engineering and air defense troops to North Vietnam. The reasons for that deployment were the same ones that led to the Korean War intervention: defense of an ally and worries over the security of Chinese territory from foreign attack. China's relations with the United States had been in a deep-freeze since Korea. With the U.S. Air Force bombing Hanoi and the Americans sending 500,000 troops to South Vietnam, China's leaders decided not to take any risks with their nation's security....

What the examples of Korea and the two wars involving Vietnam show is that Chinese leaders carefully balance China's domestic situation against the nature of any external threats. In both the Korean War and the 1979 invasion of Vietnam, domestic stability in China allowed Beijing a free hand overseas. Only in the case of the 1965–68 intervention in Vietnam did Chinese leaders decide to involve themselves on foreign soil while their country suffered from domestic conflict. Even then, the Chinese dispatch of troops to North Vietnam had limited defensive goals, was carried out quietly, and was quickly terminated once the danger of a U.S. attack on China had died away. This suggests that Beijing will behave cautiously if faced with the combination of internal unrest and the threat of foreign war.

CONCLUSION

Today, the PLA's largest source of relatively modern military technology is the military-industrial complex left behind by the former Soviet Union. The generals of the PLA should not forget the uselessness of Soviet armor during the Gulf War. Geography also argues against easy Chinese success in any military operations against the Spratly Islands. Even if all the reported sales of Russian military equipment are consummated, China, due to the distance of the Spratly Islands from major Chinese bases, would find it difficult to maintain a continuous air umbrella with a large force of aircraft over the ships of its South Sea Fleet. Considering the

PLAN's lack of SAM-equipped warships, the absence of effective air cover might place the PLAN in the same fatal situation as the *Prince of Wales* and *Repulse* were fifty years ago when Japanese warplanes sent them to the bottom of the South China Sea. Even if the PLAN had many SAM-equipped vessels on hand, they might not help Chinese forces operating in the vicinity of the Spratly Islands. Much of China's weaponry, as we have already seen, is simply not very good. Results for the Chinese could be disastrous if they came up against a force armed with even a small number of "smart" weapons. Such a situation is almost certainly unavoidable since China's regional rivals are growing in both wealth and technological prowess. During the 1982 Falklands War, fewer than half a dozen Argentine aircraft armed with *Exocet* missiles sank the modern British destroyer *Sheffield* and several other vessels. A few more hits, particularly on one of the all-important aircraft carriers, could have cost Britain the war. China is so poorly equipped for the type of short, destructive high-tech fighting that was the hallmark of the naval warfare around the Falklands that one analyst recently declared: "An expansionist maritime policy is not an option given the current state of the (Chinese] fleet's equipment and training."

The ASEAN states are slowly moving in the direction of increased military cooperation, with China being the only possible target of such efforts. The fast-paced economic growth of most ASEAN states has made them very popular with foreign investors, particularly those from Japan and Taiwan. Their economic star status, in tandem with the Spratly Islands' location along important sea lanes, almost certainly guarantees a ma-jor international outcry and open-handed assistance for these states in the event of aggressive action by China. China could face the same type of diplomatic isolation and drop-off in foreign investment that it suffered in the wake of the massacre in Tiananmen Square. Even Vietnam, with its new openness to foreign investment, would no longer be the isolated target of opportunity it once was. Violent Chinese action in the Spratly Islands would make other nations believe that China was an East Asian version of Saddam Hussein's Iraq, shattering China's carefully crafted public relations image as a poor nation lifting itself up by its own efforts to join the ranks of the advanced nations.

The force of domestic pressures may set another obstacle in the path of China's maritime ambitions. Much of the PLA's re-equipment program and troop deployment patterns may be at least partially dictated by the need to guard against new outbreaks of internal disorder. Eleven Chinese provinces suffered from peasant unrest in 1992. Brought on by the most spectacular economic transformation since Japan finished its modernization at the beginning of this century, the shredding of China's social fabric is likely to continue. In the last few years of the twentieth century, the PLA and its political masters may have little time for foreign adventures.

If the mainland Chinese want to acquire a larger slice of the resources of the South China Sea, they are probably going to have to negotiate for it. Perhaps in recognition of this situation, the Chinese in August 1993 opened talks with Vietnam aimed at sorting out the two sides' territorial claims in the South China Sea. China's ASEAN neighbors, along with efforts to widen economic ties with China, are engaged in diplomatic efforts of their own to head off any potential crisis. Over the last eighteen months, Singapore, Malaysia, and Indonesia have pushed for exchange visits of defense officials and officers with China in the hope of reducing chances for any misunderstandings.

Broadening opportunities for trade, continued negotiations, and the deterrents to Chinese action already discussed make it unlikely that a major military confrontation over the Spratly Islands will erupt in the near future. The situation should be monitored carefully, however. Since its creation in 1949, the People's Republic of China has often displayed great astuteness in the conduct of its foreign policy. The opening of relations with the United States in the 1970s and China's use of the 1990–91 Gulf Crisis to pull itself out of the public relations quick-sand of Tiananmen are proof. But the Chinese retain the very human capacity for self-delusion. China's last war, the 1979 invasion to "punish" Vietnam, cost the PLA heavily. A month of heavy fighting bought the Chinese 20,000 casualties and little else. The Chinese were forced to withdraw behind their borders without the satisfaction of having inflicted serious damage on the battle-hardened Vietnamese army. But considering the rewards of continued peace, outsiders can hope that Chinese decision makers will avoid past mistakes and what could be a major tragedy not only for China, but for the prosperity and stability of East Asia as well. A war over the dribs and drabs of land that make up the Spratly Islands would be a sorry way indeed to start off the Pacific Century.

POSTSCRIPT

Will China Become an
Asian Superpower?

Richard Nixon, in his posthumously published book *Beyond Peace* (Random House, 1994), wrote, "China has emerged as the world's third strongest military and economic power.... We should not underestimate China's ability to disrupt our interests around the world if our relationship become belligerent rather than cooperative." Regardless of whether or not Nixon's ranking of China is correct, there can be no doubt that China is powerful and growing more so yearly. One indication of that strength was the 1994 decision by President Bill Clinton to abandon his campaign pledge to withdraw China's most-favored-nation trade status with the United States unless Beijing adopted significant human rights reforms.

The next few years are apt to be pivotal for China. One relevant issue is, Who will take charge after Deng Xiaoping, born in 1904, dies or becomes so infirm that his behind-the-scenes control ends? One view of China's foreign policy in the coming post-Deng era can be found in Allan S. Whiting, "Chinese Nationalism and Foreign Policy After Deng," *China Quarterly* (June 1995).

There are also important questions over how assertive China is likely to be in making claims to regain lost territory from Russia and others, reincorporating Taiwan, or securing a regional sphere of influence. During 1995 China reacted very strongly to the unofficial visit of Taiwan's president Lee Teng-hui to the United States. Adamant that Taiwan should in no way be considered independent, China held military exercises along their coast across the Taiwan Straight and in reputed tests fired several missiles that landed in the sea near Taiwan. China also continued to press its claim to the Spratly Islands during 1995. Furthermore, China has shown strong interest in developing military capabilities that would allow it to project its conventional, and perhaps tactical nuclear, forces far beyond its borders and immediate coastal region. Whether all this portends aggressive behavior or is merely symptomatic of China assuming more of the regional and global role warranted by its power can be explored further in Gerald Segal, "China's Changing Shape," *Foreign Affairs* (May/June 1994). It is important to note that China's Southeast Asian neighbors are not waiting passively to see what China will do. The Association of Southeast Asian Nations (ASEAN), which was established as a trade group, has begun to deal with political issues and with security and could become a de facto alliance to balance Chinese power in the region. This possibility is discussed in Kusuma Snitwongse, "Securing ASEAN's Future: An Overview of Security in Southeast Asia," *Harvard International Review* (Spring 1994).

ISSUE 7

Should the U.S. Economic Embargo Against Cuba Be Lifted?

YES: William Ratliff, from "The Case for Lifting the Embargo," *The World & I* (March 1994)

NO: Michael G. Wilson, from "Hastening Castro's Fall," *The World & I* (March 1994)

ISSUE SUMMARY

YES: William Ratliff, a senior research fellow at the Hoover Institution, Stanford University, contends that continuing the long-standing U.S. economic embargo against Cuba reduces the likelihood of a peaceful transition to democracy in Cuba. He concludes that the embargo should therefore be lifted.

NO: Michael G. Wilson, a senior analyst for inter-American affairs and trade policy at the Heritage Foundation, argues that the United States should maintain its economic embargo against Cuba in order to hasten the downfall of the government of Fidel Castro.

The intimate interaction between the politics of Cuba and those of the United States goes back to the origins of the Monroe Doctrine of 1823. President James Monroe declared that year that the Western Hemisphere was not subject to "further colonization" and that any attempt by an outside power aimed at "oppressing ... or controlling by any other manner" part of the so-called New World would be viewed "as the manifestation of an unfriendly disposition toward the United States." Implicit in these words was the principle of *no transfer*, the ideal that the then-existing colonies could not be transferred from one country to another. This very much involved Cuba, which rumors at the time suggested might be given to Great Britain by Spain. Even at this early date, the Americans saw Cuba, which lies 90 miles to the south of Florida, as having a particular attachment to the United States.

The Monroe Doctrine created in American minds the notion that they exercised some special, legitimate authority over the hemisphere, especially Central America and the Caribbean. Cuba was a particularly central focus of that paternal instinct. American interest in annexing Cuba eventually subsided, but it never vanished. In 1848 President James K. Polk considered trying to purchase Cuba from Spain for $100 million.

The Civil War precluded any attempt to annex Cuba, but the island remained an issue. The outbreak of an independence movement in Cuba in 1870 spurred more American interest. Americans sympathized with the Cuban revolutionaries. The growth of imperialist sentiment among Americans also played a role as they began to covet many territories in the Caribbean and the Pacific. All this culminated in part in the Spanish-American War of 1898, which was ignited when the U.S. battleship *Maine* blew up and sank in Havana's harbor. As a result of the one-sided U.S. victory, Cuba and Puerto Rico in the Caribbean, as well as the Philippines and Guam in the Pacific, came under either direct or indirect U.S. control. The 1904 (Theodore) Roosevelt Corollary to the Monroe Doctrine asserted that the United States had the right to intervene in the affairs of other nations of the Western Hemisphere to stop actions unacceptable to the United States. The corollary justified for Americans repeated interventions in the region, including the occupation of Cuba (1898–1922).

Like many other countries in the hemisphere, Cuba was frequently controlled by dictators, who were supported or tolerated by Washington. This situation changed in Cuba when rebels led by Fidel Castro toppled right-wing dictator Fulgencio Batista in 1959. Americans were alarmed by Castro's leftist sentiments, and escalating United States–Cuba tension saw Castro align his country with the Soviet Union. President John F. Kennedy's attempt to overthrow Castro in 1961 failed dismally at the Bay of Pigs. Cuba became a point of superpower conflict in 1962 when the Soviets deployed intermediate-range, nuclear-warhead missiles on the island. The Cuban missile crisis and ultimate withdrawal of the Soviet missiles resecured the Western Hemisphere for American interests. But it also secured Castro because the United States pledged to Moscow that if it withdrew its nuclear weapons from Cuba, Washington would never again invade the island.

Unable to topple Castro by force, the United States has continued a policy of stringent economic sanctions against Cuba since the early 1960s. There have also been times when U.S. policymakers held Cuba out as a threat to U.S. interests. President Ronald Reagan, for example, ordered a U.S. invasion of the Caribbean country of Grenada in 1983 in part because he was alarmed by growing Cuban influence and the Cuban-assisted construction of a major airfield there. The administration also blamed Cuba for supporting leftist movements in the hemisphere. As Secretary of State Alexander M. Haig, Jr., put it, such support constituted "a textbook case of indirect armed aggression by a Communist power [the USSR] through Cuba."

The USSR, the cold war, and—some would argue—the reasons for isolating Cuba and trying to topple the Castro government have ended. Few dispute the fact that Castro's government is not democratic and is sometimes brutal. But William Ratliff, in the following selection, contends that ending the sanctions on Cuba will help produce a peaceful transition to a democratic, post-Castro government. Michael G. Wilson, in disagreement, urges that the sanctions be continued to hasten Castro's downfall.

YES

William Ratliff

THE CASE FOR LIFTING THE EMBARGO

For the first time in more than three decades, there is serious talk about making fundamental changes in U.S. policy toward Cuba. But the talk has not yet led to constructive change in Washington, where inertia and domestic politics often spawn foreign-policy neglect and disaster.

U.S. diplomatic and economic pressures on Cuba made sense in the past as a response to Fidel Castro's active support for the Soviet bloc and international policies that were contrary to [U.S.] national interests. For decades, those interests coincided with objectives of the majority of Cuban exiles in the United States. Thus, the U.S. government and Cuban-Americans cooperated in a variety of programs intended to hobble or topple the "maximum leader."

Then the Cold War ended, and Castro, one of the few survivors on the communist side, became a relic marginalized by the history he had said would absolve him. All of the original national-security grounds for imposing the embargo against Cuba disappeared. When this happened, the interests of Americans as a whole diverged from those of the most militant members of the Cuban American community and their supporters.

THE CUBAN DEMOCRACY ACT

In late 1992 Congress passed the Cuban Democracy Act (CDA), legislation spearheaded by Rep. Robert Torricelli (D-New Jersey) with strong support from the Cuban American National Foundation (CANF). The CDA increases pressure on Cuba and allows Bill Clinton less flexibility with respect to Cuba than any president has had in decades. But if Clinton is in a box, it is one of his own making. President Bush at first wisely opposed the CDA's embargo tightening, just as President Reagan had rejected the idea in the early 1980s. But when candidate Clinton decided to support the legislation, Bush caved in and did so too. In the scramble for votes, the Torricelli Bill became law.

In a speech at Washington's Center for Strategic and International Studies (CSIS) just after Clinton's inauguration, Torricelli summarized the essence of U.S. policy enshrined in the law: "We [the United States] will increase the

From William Ratliff, "The Case for Lifting the Embargo," *The World & I* (March 1994). Copyright © 1994 by *The World & I*. Reprinted by permission.

pressure. We have drawn the line. We await only for Cuban patriots to bring about an end of the dictatorship."

The CDA expands the existing U.S. embargo, which had long prohibited trade and investment in Cuba, to include sanctions against U.S. subsidiaries in Third World countries (and even foreign ships) doing business with the island, as well as against any country that gives assistance to Cuba. It states that because the United States cooperated with allies during transitions in Europe, "it is appropriate for those allies to cooperate with United States policy" toward Cuba. The act encourages some humanitarian assistance, improved telecommunications, and greater information flow across the Straits of Florida.

In the end, the objective of U.S. policy is to make life in Cuba so miserable that the people will rise up and depose Castro. The Clinton administration's top Latin American official, Alexander Watson, assistant secretary of state for inter-American affairs, testified last November that without vigorous enforcement of the provisions of the CDA, "our leverage to promote peaceful change would dissipate overnight."

The first objective of U.S. policy toward Cuba, according to the CDA, is, as it should be, "to seek a peaceful transition to democracy" in Cuba. But an increasing number of people with long records of opposition to, noting current conditions in Cuba and that the original national-security reasons for the embargo are gone, have concluded that the tougher U.S. policy makes a peaceful transition less rather than more likely.

Former Reagan NSC [National Security Council] Latin Americanist Roger Fontaine and I made that argument in a *Washington Post* op-ed piece last year.

Many others whose anti-Castro credentials cannot honestly be challenged also urge a change....

Indeed, throughout Latin America and the world, people of all ideological persuasions who dislike Castro, as well as those few who still admire him, all think the CDA approach is wrong. There is not the remotest chance of other governments joining in what they see as a petty U.S. vendetta against an enfeebled dinosaur left over from the Cold War.

FACING THE FACTS

The assumption of the Torricelli law is that the United States and Cuba will be better off when Castro and his closest allies are gone. The question we must try to answer is whether our present policy will contribute to the most peaceful possible removal of Castro by the Cubans themselves.

To find the answer we must look objectively into several other matters. Will our current policy significantly increase the ranks of those willing to stick their necks out to replace Castro? Or will it stiffen the backs of Fidel's committed supporters and rally a substantial number of other Cubans behind the "maximum leader" as the lesser of several perceived evils?

Most anti-Castro critics of current U.S. policy believe that the latter prospect is more likely. This scenario would greatly increase prospects for a more violent denouement, perhaps even a civil war. As Castro's forces get stronger, the opposition may become all the more dependent on outside support for its very survival, never mind victory, when the showdown begins.

Thus, even as pressures for U.S. intervention increase, the price of involvement goes up; our action itself would seem to confirm the dictator's warnings about Washington's wanting to set up a puppet government in Havana and drive more of the fearful into line behind Castro.

And we should realize that if the United States intervenes in Cuba, U.S. casualties will be hundreds of times higher than they were in Panama in 1989.

WHY CHANGE NOW AND HOW?

The United States needs to change its policy for several reasons: to avoid creating a crisis that is likely to precipitate U.S. intervention; to kill Castro's scapegoat—the "evil and omnipotent" United States—and stick him with responsibility for Cuba's current condition; and to reduce tensions among Cubans now and in the future. By doing so, we would lessen the chance of bloodshed or defeat of the opposition during the showdown and discourage hostilities that would hamper Cuba's peaceful development under a new government.

An essential first step toward an up-to-date foreign policy is separating U.S. policy-making from all private Cuban American organizations. The reasonable ties of earlier decades have become a barrier to objective consideration of what policy would best serve the national interests of Americans and, I believe, of Cubans as well. In 1992, former Assistant Secretary of State Elliott Abrams remarked on this linkage: "Some distancing [from CANF] is now needed," he said, "to avoid verifying Castro's propaganda that Cuban-American millionaires and Washington are in collusion." Bush's about-face on the CDA because of direct and indirect pressures by Cuban Americans confirmed the existence of the influence and the fact that politicians give in to it.

As Ernesto Betancourt put it in the *New York Times*, "We must free our Cuba policy from the stranglehold of Florida politics."

And we must absolutely reject the argument advanced by some Miami Cubans—like the one interviewed in *Insight* magazine [in June 1994]—who argue that "too many people have suffered and died for us to compromise." It may be indelicate but not irrelevant to ask who "us" is and to note that there is no evidence whatsoever that Cubans who still live with their families in Cuba, even when they want Castro out, go along with this relentlessly belligerent sentiment.

It is no sign of moral strength or principled consistency for the United States to impose intense suffering on the Cuban people to force them to rise up in desperation to overthrow their dictator, or, alternatively, to make them live in increasing misery in apparent punishment for their failure to take up arms against a ruthless tyrant.

AN INVASION FROM THE STATES?

One of the main reasons very few Cubans challenge Castro's strong repressive apparatus is that they see no acceptable alternative to Castro at home or abroad. Gen. Arnaldo Ochoa, who might have been one, was executed on trumped-up drug charges in 1989 so he could not rally opposition. In 1989–90, the Interior Ministry was purged of its minister and hundreds of high officials who were fed up with Fidel.

Castro constantly drums out the warning that after him comes the deluge of Miami millionaires, the "worms" of the Batistiano [dictator Fulgencio Batista, who was toppled by Castro on January 1, 1959] past, who with Washington's support will impose reforms like those that have made such chaos in Russia and much of eastern Europe. In that "new" Cuba, Castro warns, old scores will be settled by throwing hundreds of thousands out of their houses and jobs, perhaps into prison. The masses will lose their social security, however limited it may be, and wind up sleeping and starving in the streets.

The CDA itself gives credence to Castro's charge that Washington intends to dictate the policies of a post-Castro government. Section 1708A lists a series of changes that must be made by *any* Cuban government—even a post-Castro government—before the United States will renew trade and other relations; the changes include giving evidence that the country is "moving toward establishing a free-market economic system." Even the most ardent free marketer can see that if a post-Castro government is to be independent, it must be free to decide for itself, in its wisdom or foolishness, what kind of economic system it wants. Washington has no right to demand one system or another. As Andres Oppenheimer notes in *Castro's Final Hour*, this reminds many Cubans of "the worst days of U.S. meddling in the island's internal affairs."

KILL THE MYTH IN CUBA

What the United States *should* do is unilaterally drop the embargo and show in as many ways as possible that the U.S. government will not try to dictate Cuba's future leaders or policies. This course of action would accomplish many things, especially if done in one dramatic stroke, which due to inertia and domestic politics is, alas, unlikely to happen.

Such a policy would be a major step toward what former Cuban Interior Ministry official Juan Antonio Rodríguez Menier has called "killing Castro while he is still alive." Castro is, above all else, a myth. His carefully cultivated image is that of a selfless socialist who strives to promote the interests of the Cuban people and the downtrodden of the earth despite constant battering from the enemy of mankind, U.S. imperialism.

On the surface, this hoary Cold War nonsense seems to hold water. The "maximum leader" and his dwindling chorus abroad can point to many examples of U.S. skullduggery, ranging from sending Castro loaded [poisoned] cigars [in the early 1960s] to the CDA's Section 1708A. These facts are accompanied, of course, by relentless lies about how the United States pushed Castro into the Soviet camp.

The truth is that Castro deliberately chose the domestic and international policies and alignments that brought destitution to the Cuban people and conflict with the United States and other countries. Today, the embargo remains Castro's chief and invaluable scapegoat, something he and his lackeys drag out routinely to excuse the decades of his disastrous domestic and international choices. Even a research report by Radio Martí recently noted that "Cuban officials clearly state that the lifting of the embargo could create a high-risk political situation for which they are not prepared."

Dropping the embargo means getting off Castro's back, not giving him a free ride. We should not negotiate diplomatic relations because we should not negotiate with him at all. We should not give him or any unfriendly successor aid or buy Cuban sugar or other products that would come at the expense of other Caribbean nations. We should pull out of the naval base at Guantánamo, which we do not need, only when there is a democratically elected government and the Russians have evacuated the surveillance facility in Lourdes.

KILL THE MYTH ABROAD

By lifting the embargo unilaterally and not negotiating with Castro, we would demonstrate that he has become irrelevant: His economic model is totally discredited, and he has stopped supporting revolutionary movements because he no longer has military and economic aid to prop up his own economy or fund foreign involvement. What is more, military intervention is out of fashion today, and, given the appalling condition of Cuba's economy, Castro cannot afford to offend the international community.

But though his form of revolution—violence to establish a dictatorial regime—is on the outs today, and antigringo sentiment is at its lowest point in decades in Latin America, this may not be so several years from now; as recent incidents from Argentina to Mexico suggest. The tragic probability is that many free-market reforms being tried around the hemisphere today will fail, in varying degrees, and that frustration with "U.S. imperialism," which supposedly imposed the reforms, will increase.

If "U.S. imperialism" is still strangling Castro when this reversal comes, or if Washington has already crushed him as a martyr, he will be as much a hero as he was in the past, the only Latin who stood up to the gringo tyrants until the end. If the United States has backed off, however; and Castro has had to take at least some responsibility for his past

policies and failure to reform, his image and example will be less poignant.

ECONOMIC CONSEQUENCES OF CHANGE

Dropping the embargo is not likely to make a major difference in U.S. investment or trade with Cuba; it will simply remove the barrier to free trade for firms that want to consider business in Cuba. Cuban trade with Latin America declined last year, from an already low level, because Cuba has neither goods to sell nor dollars with which to buy from other countries. That situation will not change until Cuba has reformed substantially As long as Castro rules arbitrarily and forcefully dominates a miserable and impoverished people, instability and uncertainty must remain primary concerns for potential investors in a world with much more inviting markets. Finally, some potential investors may be concerned that if the Miami Cubans go back, they will follow through on the threat some have made to confiscate investments made during the Castro years, a threat Torricelli seemed to endorse in his CSIS speech. This is precisely the kind of comment that seems to demonstrate "collusion" between Cuban American millionaires and Washington.

AN ATTACK FROM CUBA?

Cuba still has an imposing military force, the third-largest in Latin America. It is possible that when Castro can no longer deny the inevitability of his fall, he will try to seal his anti-imperialist image by going out with an attack on the United States, perhaps by bombing a nuclear facility in Florida.

How can we prevent such a kamikaze attack? The best thing we can do is defang the Cuban military by removing its incentive to commit suicide on Castro's behalf. That is, once again, we must convince Cubans that the United States will not support reprisals against everyone who served in the government or military or who has benefited in some way from the regime. Then fewer Cuban pilots would consider taking off to attack the United States. Indeed, if assured that the United States will not press for reprisals, the military is more likely to move against Castro and promote a transition to a more representative government that can live at peace with Washington and other neighbors.

WHAT WILL WE DO?

I must agree with the unnamed U.S. official quoted in the *Wall Street Journal* ... who said, "What we are doing is waiting for a disaster to happen so we can react." The president and our legislators figure they have enough to worry about with health care, Bosnia, and the like. For them, Cuba simply isn't important enough to make it worth taking on the noisy and wealthy voters who gave us the Cuban Democracy Act. They are inclined to try to forget Cuba in the futile hope that it will go away.

Thus, the most we can probably expect from Washington is grudging and gradual reform, perhaps eventually going beyond support for more contact between Americans and Cubans to a depoliticized advisory board at [the U.S.-operated, anti-Castro] Radio Martí and an end to the useless TV Martí. President Clinton, who has foolishly recommitted himself to the CDA since the election, should go farther and push for some of the changes Donald Schulz suggested in his article in the Summer 1993 issue of *Journal of InterAmerican Studies*, such as taking full advantage of loopholes in Torricelli's legislation to gradually undermine it.

But here is the rub. Gradualism is precisely the wrong way to go because it fails to send the right signal decisively to Cuba and the world. What we really need is to reject the pressures of the past, suddenly and with a barrage of publicity showing we have done so and why. This is how we can dramatically kill the scapegoat and at the very least seriously wound Castro while he is still alive.

The United States is trying to move beyond the Cold War in its policies toward many regions of the world, even in some respects in Latin America. We are seriously considering dropping the embargo on Vietnam and selling communications satellites to Beijing. Would that the president and Congress had the wisdom and courage to do the same in our relations with Cuba.

NO

Michael G. Wilson

HASTENING CASTRO'S FALL

Cuban dictator Fidel Castro recently marked the 35th anniversary of the revolution that brought him to power with a defiant call for a defense of the socialist policies that have ruined the Cuban economy and isolated his country. Speaking on January 1 [1994] in the eastern city of Santiago de Cuba, Castro asserted that the revolution had successfully defended itself against what he labeled the "imperial power"—the United States—and would continue to do so. By rejecting any meaningful political or economic reforms, Castro has guaranteed the downfall of his regime.

SEVEN SCENARIOS

A close analysis of the Cuban situation clearly indicates that the communist regime's days are numbered. The reasons are many: Castro's stubborn defense of socialism and authoritarian rule; a shortage of hard-currency reserves, with only between $10 and $15 million left in the coffers; an economy that has shrunk by at least 75 percent over the last two years; new tensions within the military; and a populace that strives for freedom and entrepreneurship. The Clinton administration must begin to prepare for the inevitable transformation of Cuban society.

Regardless of how Castro's government falls, the United States must be ready to respond. Several scenarios are possible. They are listed here with a probability rating of 1 (low) to 5 (high).

Scenario 1: Cuban military or intelligence forces launch a coup (probability 4 to 5).

Beneath the top layer of Castro loyalists, there are many younger and better-educated technocrats increasingly eager to open Cuba to the outside world. This growing segment of Cuban society poses the most serious threat to Castro's power. Moreover, morale in the armed forces has reached an all-time low. Defecting pilots often complain that military officers are excluded from the newly legal dollar economy and other perks that are dispensed to Communist Party officials, thereby turning integral members of the island's elite into second-class citizens.

Ousting Castro and his inner circle would enable officers in the Cuban military or intelligence services to distance themselves from the regime's crimes and blunders. Such a coup, however, would have to be a sudden action carried out by a small group, rather than an elaborately organized conspiracy. The reason: Castro's extensive counterintelligence capabilities likely would detect the coup early on. Nevertheless, Cuba's isolation, the fall of international communism, and growing anti-Castro sentiment in Cuba would give this scenario a high probability rating of between 4 and 5.

Scenario 2: Food riots, demonstrations, and strikes lead to a spontaneous anti-Castro revolt (probability 4).

Cuba's loss of foreign support, combined with the democratic and free-market wave that has swept the Americas, has emboldened the Cuban people. This makes revolt against Castro's rule more likely Moreover, the collapsing economy, severe food shortages, and increased prodemocracy information from the United States have fueled a steadily growing mood of public discontent. As the economy continues to implode and the effects from the cutoff of Russian aid become more severe, Cubans may take to the streets as the Romanians did in 1989. Because democracy and free markets are infectious, this scenario warrants a fairly high probability rating of 4.

Scenario 3: Castro is assassinated (probability 3 to 4).

Castro's personal-security precautions, combined with his impressive counterintelligence capabilities, make this a risky choice for his opponents. Recent purges in Cuba, including the July 1989 purge against war hero Maj. Gen. Arnaldo

Ochoa and other possible Castro opponents, have made an assassination attempt less likely. The execution or imprisonment of Castro's political enemies will likely deter other would-be plotters. Castro nevertheless continues to make enemies both at home and abroad—thus the probability rating of between 3 and 4.

Scenario 4: Castro prolongs the decline (probability 3).

Castro routinely shifts the blame for Cuba's economic troubles onto the U.S. economic embargo and his former allies in the Soviet bloc, while trying to increase agricultural output to compensate for the decline in outside aid and trade subsidies. He also is seeking new trading partners in Canada, Europe, Latin America, and Asia to replace the former ones in the Soviet Union and Eastern Europe. Finally, he is hoping that an influx of tourists and new investment film abroad, combined with his halfhearted reform program, will generate enough hard currency so his regime can survive. These desperate efforts could enable Castro to hang on for several more years—thus the middle-range probability of 3.

Scenario 5: Castro transfers power to another leader (probability 2).

Castro could transfer power to another individual but still control the regime from behind the scenes. This might be done if Castro's health falters, or if he continues to promote false political reforms. The most talked about political successors to the Cuban dictator are his brother, Defense Minister Raúl Castro, and Foreign Minister Roberto Robaina. If Castro were to turn over power to another leader, he could go into exile in Mexico or Spain. Castro's determination to "perfect socialism" in Cuba, however, makes this scenario unlikely—thus the probability rating of 2.

Scenario 6: Castro initiates Cuban-style perestroika and glasnost (probability 1).

This is often referred to as the "Nicaragua solution," because the communist Sandinistas in Nicaragua attempted unsuccessfully to retain power in 1990 by reforming the system and holding elections. Although they continue to call many of the shots in Managua, it is unlikely that Castro would be unwilling to voluntarily surrender power or "rule from below" as the Ortega brothers are trying to do. The Cuban dictator sees himself as "maximum leader" and would have great difficulty accepting any role other than that of Cuba's ultimate authority—thus the low probability rating of 1.

Scenario 7: The United States or a multinational coalition ousts Castro with military force (probability 1).

Although Castro constantly warns the Cuban people of an imminent U.S. invasion, there is little chance that the Clinton administration or a U.S.-led multinational force would intervene in Cuba to protect human rights, to stop the outflow of Cuban refugees, or establish democracy. The White House understands that the Castro regime will collapse under the weight of its failed policies, the U.S. embargo, and the frustrations of the Cuban people. The only chance that the United States would intercede in Cuba would be if massive and prolonged bloodshed broke out during a transition to a new government, or if a massive wave of Cuban boat people tried to reach the Florida coast during a period of turmoil—thus the low probability rating of 1.

PREPARING FOR THE INEVITABLE

Most of the responsibility for bringing democracy and a free-market system to Cuba rests on the shoulders of the Cuban people at home and the Cuban exile community abroad, but the Clinton administration should maintain U.S. efforts to hasten Castro's downfall. Washington must continue to make it clear that it is unwilling to lift the embargo until Castro and his government are out of power. Clinton also must refrain from entering into any form of political dialogue with the regime.

Although it is difficult to determine which form of change will come to Cuba, it is certain that the Castro regime, in its current form, cannot last much longer. In a recent CIA report on Cuba, experts warn that the Clinton administration could face a crisis in Cuba that could launch a massive wave of political refugees and create demands for U.S. armed intervention. The CIA report adds that Castro can be expected to use force to hold on to power, "even at the risk of a bloodbath." If he is overthrown, it cautions, the new era in Cuba will initially be marred by violence.

Washington, therefore, should seek to assure that the transition from dictatorship to democracy in Cuba occurs as peacefully as possible. To be fully prepared for each scenario, the Clinton administration must develop a range of contingency plans to provide guidelines for reacting to political change and violence in Cuba. If the United States fails to take these precautions now, hastily designed strategies, such as our policies in Somalia and Haiti, could lead to a larger loss of life and lost opportunities in Cuba.

POSTSCRIPT

Should the U.S. Economic Embargo Against Cuba Be Lifted?

Since the end of the cold war, U.S. policy toward Cuba has wavered back and forth. To read about the rich expanse of Cuban history, consult Geoff Simons, *Cuba: From Conquistador to Castro* (St. Martin's Press, 1995). The Clinton administration has made tentative moves toward easing, perhaps eliminating, U.S. economic sanctions against Cuba. Among other factors, the United States is virtually alone in its restrictions on financial dealings with Cuba. Most other countries consider the U.S. position anachronistic, and there has been pressure in the United Nations and the Organization of American States for Washington to end its sanctions on Cuba. Many U.S. business leaders are also pressing the White House to ease the sanctions. Castro has made it increasingly possible for outsiders to set businesses in Cuba and earn profits. As a result, companies from Europe and elsewhere are beginning to invest in Cuba. American business leaders do not necessarily support Castro, but they are afraid that unless they are also allowed to invest (which Havana will permit but Washington will not), they will be shut out of the Cuban market. A discussion of the Cuban political economy is available in Susan Eva Eckstein's *Back from the Future: Cuba Under Castro* (Princeton University Press, 1994).

A great deal of U.S. policy has become enmeshed in U.S. domestic and especially presidential politics. Florida has the fourth largest number of electoral votes for the office of president and, thus, is a key state in the 1996 election. The ideology and electoral hopes of the Republicans have persuaded them to back strong sanctions against Cuba. Democratic president Bill Clinton is caught in a dilemma: keeping tight sanctions weakens Castro, but it also tends to prompt Cubans fleeing poverty to try illegal entry into the United States. Cuban American voters in Florida like the sanctions; many other voters in Florida are opposed to a new influx of refugees. Both political parties are advocating policy toward Cuba based on "a straightforward political calculation" aimed at winning Florida in the 1996 election.

The United States has said that the fundamental requirement to end the sanctions is for Castro to allow free elections and restore democracy. On this issue, see Carollee Bengelsdorf, *The Problem of Democracy in Cuba* (Oxford University Press, 1994). The president of Cuba's National Assembly, Ricardo Alarcon, expressed his government's view of the Clinton proposal by stating that Cuba could not agree to any conditions if they were imposed by "the very same nation that refused to accept our independence. Cuba is simply not a U.S. colony."

PART 2

Economics and International Affairs

International economic and trade issues have an immediate and personal effect on individuals in ways that few other international issues do. They influence the jobs we hold and the prices of the products we buy—in short, our lifestyles. In the worldwide competition for resources and markets, tensions arise between allies and adversaries alike. This section examines some of the prevailing economic tensions.

- Is the New General Agreement on Tariffs and Trade Beneficial?

- Should the Developed North Increase Aid to the Less Developed South?

- Is There a Global Environmental Crisis?

ISSUE 8

Is the New General Agreement on Tariffs and Trade Beneficial?

YES: Michael Kantor, from Statement Before the Committee on Finance, U.S. Senate (March 1994)

NO: Ralph Nader, from Statement Before the Committee on Finance, U.S. Senate (March 1994)

ISSUE SUMMARY

YES: Michael Kantor, U.S. special trade representative for the Clinton administration, argues that the new General Agreement on Tariffs and Trade (GATT) will provide a major boost to the global economy, from which the United States will benefit a great deal.

NO: Ralph Nader, a longtime consumer advocate, maintains that the new system of international governance found in the GATT will lead countries in the wrong direction because it will adversely affect democracy and sovereignty.

One of the important political and economic changes during the twentieth century has been the rapid growth of economic interdependence between countries. The impact of international economics on domestic societies has expanded rapidly as world industrial and financial structures have become increasingly intertwined. Foreign trade wins and loses jobs; we depend on petroleum and other imported resources to fuel our cars, homes, and industries; inexpensive imports help keep inflation down and our standard of living up; the very shirts on our backs and the televisions we watch were probably made in a foreign country. Global exports grew from $53 billion in 1948 to $3.5 trillion in 1993.

During the twentieth century, the United States moved to a position of international economic and political prominence that, at times, approached dominance. Americans have successfully used their leadership position to promote a great degree of global trade, investment, and monetary relations. After World War I, the world economy quickly slipped into a protectionist pattern. In the United States this trend was epitomized by the Smoot-Hawley Act of 1931, which dramatically increased tariffs. Other countries erected similar barriers, and the world economy deteriorated into increased competition for market access and eventually into open conflict.

The push to reduce trade barriers that occurred during and after World War II was designed to prevent a recurrence of the global economic collapse of the 1930s and the war of the 1940s. Policymakers believed that protectionism had caused the Great Depression; that the ensuing human desperation had provided fertile ground for the rise of dictators who promised national salvation and who sought out political scapegoats within their societies to blame for what had occurred; and that the spawning of fascism had set off the horror of World War II. In sum, policymakers thought that protectionism caused economic depression, which caused dictators, which caused war. Beyond this political rationale, there were a series of economic theories that also supported the idea of free trade. As early as 1776, for example, Adam Smith argued in *The Wealth of Nations* that all nations would prosper if each produced what it could most efficiently and cheaply make and then traded those commodities to other countries for the goods that they, in turn, produced most efficiently and cheaply.

Based on these political and economic theories, American policymakers took the lead in establishing a new international economic system beginning with the 1944 Bretton Woods (New Hampshire) Conference, attended by 44 countries. The conference and its ensuing efforts worked to provide greater opportunities for the capitalist nations to prosper in the post-war world by creating, among other things, the International Monetary Fund (IMF), the World Bank, and the 1947 General Agreement on Tariffs and Trade (GATT). The acronym GATT designated both the treaty and the organization established as the principal institution to open market access around the world.

During the years following its creation, GATT was successful. Tariff and nontariff barriers (NTBs, such as quotas) to trade dropped substantially. A series of discussions (called "rounds") to strengthen the treaty resulted in revisions that lowered tariffs and NTBs and expanded GATT's coverage from just merchandise trade to service trade (such as banking) and other areas of economic interchange. The latest GATT revision talks (the Uruguay Round, so named for the country wherein the negotiations were first convened) were completed and signed by 124 countries, including the United States, in April 1994. The Uruguay Round made important changes. Among these was the establishment of a new coordinating body, the World Trade Organization (WTO). The WTO has the power to monitor free trade and assess penalties on countries violating the GATT, thus giving more power than ever before to an international trade organization.

This sets the stage for the debate that follows. The Clinton administration presented the revised GATT to Congress for its approval. The first selection is drawn from the congressional testimony of the president's chief trade negotiator, Michael Kantor, in support of GATT. Kantor argues that approving GATT will benefit the United States in many ways. Taking the opposite view, longtime consumer advocate Ralph Nader testifies that free trade is imperiling the welfare of many Americans and that the WTO is a threat to U.S. sovereignty.

YES

Michael Kantor

STATEMENT OF MICHAEL KANTOR

INTRODUCTION

I appreciate the chance to be here today to discuss with you the Uruguay Round agreement, reached by 117 countries on December 15 [1994]. As this committee well knows, the agreement marked the completion of more than seven years of negotiations.

The Uruguay Round agreement will reduce barriers blocking exports to world markets... and will create a more fair, more comprehensive, more effective, and more enforceable set of world trade rules. In order to assure the efficient and balanced implementation of the agreements reached, they also created a new World Trade Organization (WTO).

The [Clinton] Administration believes that the Uruguay Round agreement will justify the years of hard work and frequent disappointment that has marked the negotiating process. It will provide a major boost to the global economy in the coming years and into the next century, from which the United States will benefit a great deal. This agreement sets the stage for the U.S. to become a more competitive, productive and prosperous nation in the years to come....

The Uruguay Round trade agreement is the largest, most comprehensive trade agreement in history. The existing GATT [General Agreement on Tariffs and Trade] system was incomplete; it was not completely reliable; and it was not serving U.S. interests well. The new agreements open up major areas of trade and provide a dispute settlement system which will allow the U.S. to ensure that other countries play by the new rules they have just agreed to.

The successful conclusion of the Uruguay Round negotiations was an important part of the President's strategy for strengthening the domestic economy....

The economy was stagnant. Unemployment was high, and confidence was down. In just one year, we have turned a corner. Our economy is growing and millions of jobs have been created. People are getting back to work.

But these are just the first steps in preparing our nation for the 21st century....

From U.S. Senate. Committee on Finance. *Results of the Uruguay Round Trade Negotiations.* Hearings, March 9, 16, and 23, 1994. Washington, DC: Government Printing Office, 1994.

An essential element in this strategy is to expand and open foreign markets. Expanding trade is critical to our ability to compete in the global economy and create high-wage jobs. That is why the President spent so much time in 1993—with not only the Uruguay Round but also the North American Free Trade Agreement, the establishment of the Japan Framework, the Asia Pacific Economic Cooperation conference to facilitate trade in that region. That is why we vigorously enforced our trade laws which resulted in opening the markets for heavy electrical equipment in Europe, telecommunications in Korea, construction in Japan, and enhanced protection for copyrighted and patented products in a number of nations, led by Taiwan and Thailand.

The U.S. economy is now woven into the global economy. Over a quarter of the U.S. economy is dependent on trade. Where we once bought, sold and produced mostly at home, we now participate in the global marketplace. American workers compete with their foreign counterparts every day, sometimes within the same company. By expanding our sales abroad, we create new jobs at home and we expand our own economy.

The global economy presents rewards not risks. Our greatest risk is in failing to understand the challenge. Jobs related to trade earn, on average, 17 percent more than jobs not related to trade. Prosperity is the partner to change and American workers are at their best when facing the challenges of a new era.

The benefits of trade ripple through our economy. Trade benefits not only the company that exports, but also the company which produces parts incorporated in exported products, the insurance agency which insures exporters, and the grocery store near the exporter's factory. At the same time, increased access to foreign markets and increased competition at home benefit consumers. Lower trade barriers reduce prices, improve the quality, and widen the choice of consumer good. This benefits both families and companies looking for good bargains and good quality.

U.S. workers and companies are poised to take advantage of the dynamics of the global economy, if they have access to foreign markets and can be ensured they are competing on fair terms with their foreign counterparts. Fast growing economies in Latin America and Asia are hungry for American goods. Countries around the globe are embracing market economies and are in need of everything from hospital equipment to consumer goods.

"Made in the USA" still represents a standard of excellence, especially for products that will become more important in the coming century. America leads the world because of our imagination and creativity.

The United States, then, is positioned economically, culturally and geographically to reap the benefits of the global economy.

Economically, because our workers are the most productive in the world, and our economy is increasingly geared towards trade.

Culturally, because of our tradition of diversity, freedom and tolerance will continue to attract the best and the brightest from around the world ensuring that we will never stagnate as a people.

Geographically, because we are at the center of a nexus between our historic trading partners in Europe and Japan, and the new dynamic economies in Latin America and Asia.

Our trade policy is guided by a simple credo. We want to expand opportunities for the global economy, but insist on a similar responsibility from other countries.

Trade is a two way street. After World War II, when the American economy dominated the world, we opened ourselves up, to help other countries rebuild. It was one of the wisest steps this country ever took, but now we cannot have a one way trade policy. The American people won't support it and the Administration won't stand for it.

For other nations to enjoy the great opportunities here in the U.S. market, they must accept the responsibility of opening their own market to U.S. products and services. Ultimately, it is in their own self interest to do so, because trade fosters economic growth and create jobs in all countries involved. If a country closes itself to U.S. goods and services, they should expect the same from us.

The Uruguay Round ensures American workers are trading on a two-way street, that they benefit from this new globalized economy; that they can sell their products and services abroad; and that they can compete on a level playing field.

President Clinton led the effort to reinvigorate the Uruguay Round and to break the gridlock, which had stalled the negotiations despite seven years of preparation and another seven years of negotiations.

We did not accomplish everything we wanted to in the Uruguay Round. In the services area, we wanted to go further than the world was ready to go. The transition periods for patent and copyright protection are longer than we wanted. We were bitterly disappointed by the European Union's intransigence with respect to national treatment and market access for our entertainment industries.

But the final result is very good for U.S. workers and companies. It helps us to bolster the competitiveness of key U.S. industries, to create jobs, to foster economic growth, to raise our standard of living and to combat unfair foreign trade practices. The agreement will give the global economy a major boost, as the reductions in trade barriers create new export opportunities, and as the new rules give businesses greater confidence that export markets will remain open and that competition in foreign markets will be fair.

More importantly, the final Uruguay Round agreement plays to the strengths of the U.S. economy, opening world markets where we are most competitive. From agriculture to high-tech electronics, to pharmaceuticals and computer software, to business services, the United States is uniquely positioned to benefit from the strengthened rules of a Uruguay Round agreement that will apply to all of our trading partners.

THE URUGUAY ROUND

The Uruguay Round is the right agreement at the right time for the United States. It will create hundreds of thousands of high-wage, high-skill jobs here at home. Economists estimate that the increased trade will pump between $100 and $200 billion into the U.S. economy every year after the Round is fully implemented.

This historic agreement will:

- cut foreign tariffs on manufactured products by over one third, the largest reduction in history;

- protect the intellectual property of U.S. entrepreneurs in industries such as pharmaceuticals, entertainment and software from piracy in world markets;
- ensure open foreign markets for U.S. exporters of services such as accounting, advertising, computer services, tourism, engineering and construction;
- greatly expand export opportunities for U.S. agricultural products by reducing use of export subsidies and by limiting the ability of foreign governments to block exports through tariffs, quotas, subsidies, and a variety of other domestic policies and regulations;
- assure that developing countries live by the same trade rules as developed countries and that there will be no free riders;
- create an effective set of rules for the prompt settlement of disputes, thus eliminating shortcomings in the current system which allowed countries to drag out the process and to block judgments they did not like; and
- open a dialogue on trade and environment.

This agreement will *not:*

- impair the effective enforcement of U.S. laws;
- limit the ability of the United States to set its own environmental or health standards; or
- erode the sovereignty of the United States to pass its own laws.

The Uruguay Round agreement will create a new organization—the World Trade Organization—that will support a fair global trading system into the next century and replace the ... GATT. ...

While the world has benefitted enormously from the reduction of trade barriers and expansion of trade made possible by the GATT, the GATT rules were increasingly out of step with the real world. They did not cover many areas of trade such as intellectual property and services; they did not provide meaningful rules for important aspects of trade such as agriculture; and they did not bring about the prompt settlement of disputes. The old GATT rules also created unequal obligations among different countries, despite the fact that many of the countries that were allowed to keep their markets relatively closed were among the greatest beneficiaries of the system.

The WTO will require that all members take part in all major agreements of the Round, eliminating the free-rider problem. From agreements on import licensing to antidumping, all members of the WTO, will belong to all of the major international agreements.

The WTO will also require developing countries—an increasingly important area of U.S. trade—to follow the same rules as everyone else after a transition period. They will no longer enjoy the fruits of trade, without accepting responsibility and opening their own markets. The WTO will have a strengthened dispute settlement system, but will allow us to maintain our trade laws and sovereignty.

The WTO plays to the strengths of our economy. For example:

Market Access. The WTO will reduce industrial tariffs by over one third. On exports from the U.S. and the European Community, the reduction is over 50 percent. In an economy increasingly reliant on trade opening markets abroad is absolutely essential to our ability to create jobs and foster economic growth here at home. Our nation's workers are the most productive in the world and reduced tariffs will enable these workers to compete on a more level playing field.

Agriculture. U.S. farmers are the envy of the world, but too often they were not able to sell the products of their hard labor abroad, because the old GATT rules did not effectively limit agricultural trade barriers. Many countries have kept our farmers out of global markets by limiting imports and subsidizing exports. These same policies have raised prices for consumers around the world.

The Uruguay Round agreements will reform policies that distort the world agricultural market and international trade in farm products. By curbing policies that distort trade, in particular export subsidies, the World Trade Organization will open up new trade opportunities for efficient and competitive agricultural producers like the United States.

Services. The WTO will extend fair trade to a sector that encompasses 60% of our economy and 70% of our jobs: services. Uruguay Round participants agreed to new rules affecting around eighty areas of the economy such as advertising and accounting, information and computer services, environmental services, engineering and tourism. When a company makes a product, it needs financing, advertising, insurance, computer software, and so forth. Competition for these services is now global. We lead the world in this sector with nearly $180 billion in exports annually. The WTO will implement new rules on trade in services, which will ensure our companies and workers can compete fairly in the global market. While in certain key areas, such as telecommunications and financial services, the U.S. did not obtain the kind of mar-

ket access commitments we were seeking, we kept our leverage by refusing to grant MFN treatment to our trading partners, and continued negotiations.

Intellectual Property. Creativity and innovation is one of America's greatest strengths. American films, music, software and medical advances are prized around the globe. The jobs of thousands of workers here in this country are dependent on the ability to sell these products abroad. Royalties from patents, copyrights and trademarks are a growing source of foreign earnings to the U.S. economy.

The World Trade Organization will administer international rules to protect Americans from the global counterfeiting of their creations and innovations. These are the areas which represent some of the most important U.S. industries of the future. Stemming the tide of counterfeiting works to protect U.S. companies and workers, particularly as U.S. exports of intellectual property goods increase annually.

For example, our semiconductor industry is a driving force for U.S. technology advances and competitiveness. These products affect nearly every aspect of our lives and are incorporated in many of the goods traded internationally.

The TRIPS [Trade-Related Intellectual Property Rights] agreement is the first international agreement that places stringent limits on the grant of patent compulsory licenses for this critical technology. Under TRIPs, this industry's patents and layout designs can not be used for commercial purposes without the permission of the patent or design owner.

In short, the Uruguay Round agreements set the stage for free and fair trade in the world, and global prosperity and partnership at the end of this century and into the next. ...

TECHNICAL BARRIERS TO TRADE

The Agreement on Technical Barriers to Trade [TBT] improves the rules respecting standards and technical regulations. In particular, the agreement provides that standards, technical regulations and conformity assessment procedures (e.g., testing, inspection, certification, quality system registration, and other procedures used to determine conformance to a technical regulation or standard) are not discriminatory or otherwise used by governments to create unnecessary obstacles to trade. The Agreement improves disciplines concerning the acceptance of results of conformity assessment procedures by another country and enhances the ability of a foreign-based laboratory or firm to gain recognition under another country's laboratory accreditation, inspection or quality system registration scheme. The Agreement includes a process for the exchange of information, including the ability to comment on proposed standards-related measures made by other WTO Members and a central point of contact for routine requests for information on existing requirements. Furthermore, unlike the existing TBT Code every country that is a Member of the new WTO will be required to implement the new TBT Agreement.

The new TBT Agreement ensures that each country has the right to establish and maintain standards and technical regulations at its chosen level of protection for human, animal and plant life and health and of the environment, and for prevention against deceptive practices. The Agreement generally encourages the use by governments of international standards, when possible and appropriate. At the same time it provides that each country may determine its appropriate level of protection and ensures that the encouragement to use international standards will not result in downward harmonization.

SANITARY AND PHYTOSANITARY MEASURES

The Agreement on the Application of Sanitary and Phytosanitary ("S&P") Measures will guard against the use of unjustified S&P measures to keep out U.S. agricultural exports. S&P measures are laws, regulations and other measures aimed at protecting human, animal and plant life and health from risks of plant and animal borne pests and diseases, and additives and contaminants in foods and feedstuffs. They include a wide range of measures such as quarantine requirements and procedures for approval of food additives or for the establishment of pesticide tolerances. The S&P agreement is designed to distinguish legitimate S&P measures from trade protectionist measures. For example, S&P measures must be based on scientific principles and not maintained without sufficient scientific evidence and must be based on an assessment of the risk to health, appropriate to the circumstances.

The S&P agreement safeguards U.S. animal and plant health measures and food safety requirements. The agreement clearly recognizes and acknowledges the sovereign right of each government to establish the level of protection of human, animal and plant life and health deemed appropriate by that government. Furthermore, the United States has a long history of basing its S&P measures on scientific principles and risk assessment....

DISPUTE SETTLEMENT

The Dispute Settlement Understanding (DSU) creates new procedures for settlement of disputes arising under any of the Uruguay Round agreements. The new system is a significant improvement on the existing practice. In short, it will work and it will work fast.

The process will be subject to strict time limits for each step. There is a guaranteed right to a panel. Panel reports will be adopted unless there is a consensus to reject the report and a country can request appellate review of the legal aspects of a report. The dispute settlement process can be completed within 16 months from the request for consultations even if there is an appeal. Public access to information about disputes is also increased.

After a panel report is adopted, there will be time limits on when a Member must bring its laws, regulations or practice into conformity with panel rulings and recommendations, and there will be authorization of retaliation in the event that a Member has not brought its laws into conformity with its obligations within that set period of time.

The automatic nature of the new procedures will vastly improve the enforcement of the substantive provisions in each of the agreements. Members will not be able to block the adoption of panel reports. Members will have to implement obligations promptly and the United States will be able to take trade action if Members fail to act or obtain compensation. Trade action can consist of increases in bound tariffs or other actions and increases in tariffs may be authorized even if there is a violation of the TRIPS or Services agreements.

The DSU includes improvements in providing access to information in the dispute settlement process. Parties to a dispute must provide non-confidential summaries of their panel submissions that can be given to the public. In addition, a Member can disclose its submissions and positions to the public at any time that it chooses. panels are also expressly authorized to form expert review groups to provide advice on scientific or other technical issues of act which should improve the quality of decisions.

WORLD TRADE ORGANIZATION

The Agreement Establishing the World Trade Organization (WTO) encompasses the current GATT structure and extends it to new disciplines that have not been adequately covered in the past. The new organization will be more credible and predictable and thus benefit U.S. trade interests.

The WTO will help to resolve the "free rider" problem in the world trading system. The WTO system is available only to countries that are contracting parties to the GATT, agree to adhere to all of the Uruguay Round agreements, and submit schedules of market access commitments for industrial goods, agricultural goods and services. This will eliminate the shortcomings of the current system in which, for example, only a handful of countries have voluntarily adhered to disciplines on subsidies under the 1979 Tokyo Round agreement.

The WTO Agreement establishes a number of institutional rules that will be applied to all of the Uruguay Round agreements. We do not expect that the organization will be different in character from that of the existing GATT and its Secretariat, however, nor is the WTO expected to be a larger, more costly, organization....

ENVIRONMENT

Comprehensive as it is, the Final Act does not cover every several aspect of trade policy of great importance to the United States and to this Administration. Our trading partners recognize that the work of shaping the World Trade Organization to the needs of the 21st century must continue without pause.

In December, the Uruguay Round participants decided to develop a program of work on trade and environment to present to the ministers in Marrakech in April [1999]. We begin with the agreed premise that international trade can and should promote sustainable development, and that the world trading system should be responsive to the need for environmental protection, if necessary through modification of trade rules.

The United States will seek a work program that ensures that the new WTO is responsive to environmental concerns. International trade can contribute to our urgent national and international efforts to protect and enhance environmental quality and conserve and restore natural resources. At the same time, we will continue to advocate trade rules that do not hamper our efforts to carry out vital and effective environmental policies, whether nationally or in cooperation with other countries. We will be working closely with environmental organizations and business groups, as well as the various agencies, and of course this Committee and others in Congress, as we define our trade and environment objectives.

CONCLUSION

... [T]he Uruguay Round [was completed]... at an auspicious time for America. The U.S. economy is expanding; investment is increasing; jobs are being created; and optimism about the prospects for our economy is soaring. This economic expansion reflects the fact that this country is moving in the right direction; and we are doing it together. The policies of the Clinton Administration, starting with our budget plan; the adjustments made over the last several years by our workers and companies—all of our efforts make us as a nation stronger and more competitive.

In setting the negotiating objectives for the Uruguay Round, Congress clearly signalled its belief that strengthening the multilateral rules of the GATT would make America more competitive in world markets. We succeeded. We met those objectives; and I am convinced that the new multilateral rules agreed to in the Uruguay Round will work together with our ongoing efforts to increase regional cooperation. America is uniquely positioned to benefit from expanding trade—in this hemisphere and in the world. The Uruguay Round builds on our strengths. It will benefit us, and the world economy as a whole.

NO

Ralph Nader

STATEMENT OF RALPH NADER

[T]hank you for the opportunity to testify on the Uruguay Round agreements of the General Agreements on Tariffs and Trade (GATT).

Congressional consideration of the agreement will have far-reaching implications [for Americans]. Unfortunately, the limited attention given to the Uruguay Round has focussed on specific problems, including those pertaining to environmental and consumer protection and the agreement's effect on the existing U.S. trade laws.... As important as those issues are, even a cursory reading of the Uruguay Round text demonstrates that the agreement must be viewed as a system of penetrating international governance, not just as a trade agreement.

Few people have considered what adoption of the Uruguay Round agreement would mean to U.S. democracy, sovereignty and legislative prerogatives. As the world prepares to enter the twenty-first century, the proposed GATT system of international governance would lead nations in the wrong direction. The terms of the Uruguay Round would expand the nature of the world trade rules in an autocratic and backwards-looking manner. This system of international governance is chronically secretive, non-participatory and not subject to any independent appeals process. Yet decisions arising from such governance can pull down our higher living standards in key areas or impose trade fines and sanctions until such degradation is accepted.

A major result of this transformation would be to undermine citizen control and chill the ability of domestic democratic bodies to make decisions on a vast array of domestic policies from food safety to communications and foreign investment policies. Most simply, the Uruguay Round's provisions would preset the parameters for domestic policy-making by putting into place comprehensive international rules about what policy objectives a country may pursue and what means a country may use to obtain even GATT-legal objectives, all the while subordinating non-commercial standards, such as health and safety, to the dictates of international trade imperatives.

From U.S. Senate. Committee on Finance. *Results of the Uruguay Round Trade Negotiations.* Hearings, March 9, 16, and 23, 1994. Washington, DC: Government Printing Office, 1994. Notes omitted.

Decision-making power now in the hands of citizens and their elected representatives, including the Congress, would be seriously constrained by a bureaucracy and dispute resolution body located in Geneva, Switzerland that would operate in secret and without the guarantees of due process and citizen participation found in domestic legislative bodies and courts. As well as undermining democratic decision-making the new GATT means an increase in the primacy of the global trade rules over all other policy goals and domestic laws on the federal, state and local levels. This Congress must evaluate the new GATT as a political and legal document, not just as an economic document.

The Uruguay Round agreement would:

- Establish a new global commerce agency, the World Trade Organization (WTO) with increased power, closed procedures and outdated substantive *"trade uber alles"* rules;
- Greatly expand the reach of global trade rules to impose new restraints on many nontariff policies that traditionally have been controlled domestically; and
- Significantly strengthen secretive dispute resolution mechanisms, thus guaranteeing stricter enforcement of the global trade disciplines over every countries' domestic laws and policies.

Taken as a whole, the texts coming out of the Uruguay Round negotiations would strengthen and formalize a world economic government dominated by giant corporations, without a correlative democratic rule of law to hold this economic government accountable. It is bad enough to have the Fortune 200 [largest U.S. corporations], along with European and Japanese corporations,

ruling the Seven Seas of the marketplace which affects workers, the environment and consumers. But, it is a level of magnitude worse for this rule not to have democratic accountabilities to the people.

No one denies the necessity of international trade and commerce. However, societies need to shape their trade policies to suit their economic and social needs —guaranteeing livelihoods for their inhabitants and their children, as well as safe and clean environments. For instance, policies encouraging community-oriented production would result in smaller-scale operations that are more flexible and adaptable to environmentally sustainable production methods and locally rooted firms are more susceptible to democratic controls—they are less likely to threaten to migrate and they may perceive their interests as more overlapping with general community interests. Although the Uruguay Round text has adopted the rhetoric of sustainability, in fact its terms would handicap the very domestic policy approaches that could promote more sustainable economic models.

Some Members of Congress have argued that the Uruguay Round's threats to existing domestic legislation can be limited in implementing legislation. However, the Uruguay Round text makes quite clear that the WTO has the exclusive authority to interpret the terms of the agreement. Thus, any Congressional interpretation or definition in U.S. enabling legislation meant to preserve Congressional prerogatives is irrelevant to the WTO's dispute resolution and other functions.

ESTABLISHMENT OF THE WORLD TRADE ORGANIZATION WOULD SHIFT POWER FROM NATIONS TO AN UNDEMOCRATIC, BACKWARDS-LOOKING INSTITUTION

While USTR [U.S. Trade Representative] Mickey Kantor testified before this committee that the WTO would not be much different than the existing GATT Secretariat, in fact analysis of the WTO text argues otherwise. The Uruguay Round would fundamentally transform the nature of the world trade rules by replacing what has been a contract between countries (GATT) into a new international organization (WTO) with a "legal personality," similar to that of the United Nations.

Establishing a New International Organization

Since its establishment in 1947, GATT has existed as a contract between nations, which have been called "contracting parties." Establishment of the WTO would raise the relative importance and strength of the global trade rules as against non-trade consumer, worker and environmental values by giving them a permanent international organizational structure with an ongoing infrastructure and powers that GATT didn't have, such as self-executing dispute resolution and trade sanctions.... Countries are obliged to ensure that their domestic laws conform with the substantive trade rules of the WTO under an extremely worrisome provision, Article 16–4 of the WTO text:

"Each Member shall ensure the conformity of its laws, regulations and adminis-trative procedures with its obligations as provided in the annexed Agreements."

Strict Obligation of Conformity

This obligation is much more stringent and inflexible than similar provisions in other trade agreements.... Not only would establishment of the WTO add yet another layer of bureaucracy in a vast array of policy areas, but that bureaucracy would be a truly publicly unaccountable, yet highly powerful, one. Moreover, the final text extends the stronger obligation to ensure conformity with the WTO to encompass additional areas of domestic policy: regulations and administrative procedures. Bringing federal and state administrative procedures into conformity with the requirements of all of the WTO agreements could have significant impacts on the openness, citizen participation and due process guarantees available in current domestic administrative procedures.

Control Shifts from Nations to WTO

The Uruguay Round would fundamentally shift control of the international trade rules from each participating country to the new international bureaucracy of the WTO. The WTO rules allow changes to some trade rules by a two-thirds vote of the Members that would then be binding on all Members. Under GATT, such changes could only be taken by consensus. WTO Members also must accept all aspects of the WTO's trade rules, while under GATT, countries who opposed certain provisions or additional agreements would not be bound by them unless that country consented. From a trade perspective, this all-or-nothing rule eliminates the problem of "free riders." From a democracy perspective, this rule forces countries to accept trade in areas that might be undesirable or to forgo some participation in the world trade system. This all-or-nothing approval is unusual in international law because of its sovereignty implications. For instance, the United States and other countries often take "reservations" to certain aspects of treaties, while still approving the overall treaty.

Additionally, the WTO would establish numerous standing committees that could initiate on-going negotiations. Under GATT, additional negotiations could be initiated only by consensus of the parties. Alternatively countries that did not wish to be bound by new negotiations could opt out. After the Uruguay Round, there will be no more "Rounds" of negotiations over which Congress can assert some influence and which Congress must approve.

New Organization Has No Labor or Human Rights, Environment Mandate
The WTO text would establish a powerful new international institution whose mandate looks backwards to an era when environmental and other citizen considerations were not taken into account. The binding provisions setting out the WTO's functions and scope do not incorporate any environmental, health, labor rights or human rights considerations. In fact, the only reference to the environment is in the rhetoric of the WTO's preamble, which does not have the binding legal effect of the agreement. Labor and human rights are not mentioned in the preamble at all. Moreover, there is nothing in the institutional principles of the WTO to inject any procedural safeguards of openness, citizen participation or accountability into the governance of this body or its functions. The WTO does not even have the structural capacity for citizens or non-governmental organizations to have any role in its functions.

ESTABLISHMENT OF THE WORLD TRADE ORGANIZATION GREATLY INCREASES THE IMPACT GLOBAL TRADE RULES WILL HAVE ON COUNTRIES' DOMESTIC LAWS

U.S. membership in the WTO would greatly expand the reach of global trade rules to impose new restraints on many nontariff policies that traditionally have been controlled domestically....

Expansion of Trade Disciplines
... The Uruguay Round would ... put in place more pervasive restrictions in areas such as food standards and "technical standards" such as environmental or safety standards. The expansiveness of the Uruguay Round negotiations means that almost any domestic law that impacts international trade could be considered a "nontariff barrier." Only laws that are more protective of the environment or consumer or worker health and safety are exposed to challenge; extremely weak laws cannot be challenged as providing an unfair subsidy for procedures that fail to meet even minimal international standards in these areas. Thus, the GATT rules envision placing a ceiling on health, safety and environmental protection, but provide no minimal floor beyond which all nations must rise (except against slave labor).

Limitation of Allowable Policy Goals
The WTO's rules would spread such trade disciplines to many issues traditionally controlled by domestic policymakers. Certain goals would be forbidden to all domestic legislatures. For instance, laws with "mixed" purposes,

such as environmental and economic, could easily fall outside of the Uruguay Round's requirement....

The terms of the Uruguay Round would also limit policy goals for which legislatures around the world could strive. One critical issue is the extent to which trade restrictions may be imposed on products based on processing and production methods....

For example, may a country ban imports of shoes made with child labor or prison labor, ban imports of timber that does not come from sustainably managed forests, ban imports of ivory from countries with inadequate elephant conservation programs, ban imports of beef slaughtered in violation of humane standards, ban imports of products produced with ozone-depleting chemicals, ban tuna imports caught in a way that kills too many dolphins, ban fish imports caught with large-scale drift nets, or ban shrimp imports caught without turtle excluder devices?

The United States cannot effectively enforce its own domestic standards if it cannot control its own market to ensure that its domestic producers are not at a competitive disadvantage for merely following U.S. law. However, if a country cannot distinguish goods on the basis of their production methods, it will be unable to provide a level playing field for domestic companies which incur extra labor, safety and environmental compliance costs....

Limitations on Policy Tools

... [D]espite suggestions to the contrary by the USTR, the agreement limits Congress' ability to put in place unilateral trade measures.... The Uruguay Round effectively forbids any country from taking any trade action on any issue covered under the broad expanse of the new trade rules without permission from Geneva. Thus, for instance, once China is admitted to the WTO, Congress will no longer be allowed to condition China's trade status on its human rights record. Under the WTO, China would automatically obtain Most Favored Nation Status and the U.S. would not be allowed to unilaterally deviate from that treatment. As well, many environmental laws, such as dolphin, elephant and other protections enforced through market access limitations, would run afoul of the unilateralism ban. Our laws are in jeopardy even if they are undertaken pursuant to international environmental agreements, since there is no exception to the Uruguay Round's rules for such standards....

Broad-Reaching Implications of "Nontariff Trade Barrier" Concept

Under the WTO, "nontariff trade barrier" would become a code phrase to undermine all sorts of citizen-protection standards and regulations. Corporate interests focus on a safety or health regulation that they don't like, develop a story about why it favors domestic companies over foreign corporations and then demand that the regulation be revoked. As well, the WTO includes two mechanisms for pulling down health, safety and environmental standards—equivalence and harmonization provisions promote the establishment of unified global food, environmental and other standards. The WTO's specific harmonization mechanisms would pull standards down toward international lower common denominators because they require national standards to be based on generally weaker international standards established without citizen input but, with heavy corporate influences. The international standards provide a ceiling but not a floor for such protections.

Under equivalence, the Uruguay Round requires countries to permit imports that do not comply with their own food and other product safety standards where they satisfy different, but "equivalent," standards or processes. This requirement invites wholesale circumvention of U.S. law....

U.S. citizen groups already have enough problems dealing in Washington with corporate lobbyists, legislators and agency officials, without being told that decisions affecting this country's standards will be made in other countries, by other officials, by other lobbies that have no accountability or administrative due process requirements that we have in this country. The problem is exactly the same for citizen organizations in other nations, already struggling against the entrenched monied interests (including foreign subsidiaries) in their own countries.

WORLD TRADE ORGANIZATION DISPUTE RESOLUTION: STRONGER ENFORCEMENT OF BAD RULES

The WTO's dispute resolution power is significantly strengthened compared to that of the GATT, thus guaranteeing stricter enforcement of the global trade disciplines over every countries' domestic laws and policies. This feature of the Uruguay Round must be considered from the perspective of a defendant, not only as a plaintiff which has been the perspective of USTR Kantor....

Secretive Dispute Tribunals
As with the GATT, WTO dispute resolution allows a Member nation to challenge another Member's domestic laws as illegal barriers to trade. Such challenges are decided in secret by panels of three trade experts who are chosen from a preset roster. As a general matter, shifting away "judicial" review to fora that do not have the procedural safeguards of the U.S. federal and state judicial systems is troubling....

Dispute Panels Have No Safeguards to Guarantee Impartiality, Balance or Public Access
The required qualifications for WTO panelists, such as experience in a country's trade delegation or experience as a trade lawyer bringing a trade dispute, will result in panelists with a uniformly pro-trade perspective. In act, with the exception of panelists qualified by merit of academic expertise in trade, the qualifications will result in panelists with a direct professional stake in the existing trade system. Moreover, astonishingly, there are no conflict of interest or other rules to even guarantee that a panelist does not have a direct economic interest in a decision....

There is also no mechanism to guarantee that such panelists even will be exposed to alternative perspectives on environmental or health or labor rights or human rights issues. This is the case because there is no allowance for amicus briefs from interested non-governmental groups or other guaranteed means of access for other viewpoints. In fact, the panel is not required to get technical or scientific help.... Finally, the text specifically forbids identification of which panelists supported which positions and conclusions. This additional layer of secrecy adds to the lack of accountability of the WTO decision-makers with their greatly enhanced vast new powers.

Decisions Are Automatically Approved
... Under the new [WTO] rules, the decisions of the three-person review panels are automatically adopted 60 days after completion, unless there is a consensus among all WTO Members to reject the ruling, or the losing country files an appeal. Thus, within 60 days over 100 countries, including the country that has won the panel decision, must all be persuaded to stop the adoption of the panel report....

Automatic Sanctions If Domestic Laws Are Not Changed
If a country fails to change its law..., the winning country... can request trade sanctions against a country that has refused to change its law. Such a request to authorize sanctions is automatically granted [after] 30 days... unless there is unanimous consensus of all WTO Members to reject the request....

Secretive and Inaccessible Tribunal
The secrecy of GATT dispute resolution is largely perpetuated in WTO dispute resolution. All panel proceedings are conducted in secret. Only representatives of an involved WTO Member, namely the national government of each member country in a dispute, is guaranteed access. If a state law were to be challenged under the WTO, the governor or the state attorney general may only observe the Geneva proceedings, or have access to the case documents at the pleasure of the federal government.... There is no right for public comment or participation, for instance in the form of amicus briefs. This secrecy flies in the face of the U.S. standards of openness and disclosure by which the Congress and courts operate.

A CORPORATE BILL OF RIGHTS: GETTING NATIONAL GOVERNMENTS OUT OF "TRADE" POLICY

While inevitably domestic legislative prerogatives have been somewhat limited by the United States' international obligations, the Uruguay Round represents a revolutionary shift of authority over a vast array of policy areas to an unaccountable, foreign bureaucracy. The result would be expanded control by multinational corporations over the international economy and an increased capacity to undo the most vital health, safety and environmental protections won by citizen movements across the globe, or at the least, to keep future advances at bay. The WTO would give multinational corporations the lever to hold back or weaken central protections of people in the United States by a practical erosion of our domestic sovereignty through an external layer of regulatory bureaucracy that pulls standards, down, but not up. Look at the behavior of U.S. corporations in the United States as compared with their plants in other countries.... The difference can be attributed to what they can get away with by getting away from the rule of law....

It is only recently that corporations developed the notion of using trade agreements to establish autocratic governance over many modestly democratic countries. The world community founded GATT after World War II as an institution to peacefully regulate world trade. At present, more than 100 nations that engage in over four-fifths of world trade belong to it. In its first 40 years of existence, GATT concerned itself primarily with tariffs and related matters; periodically, the GATT signatories would meet and negotiate lower taxes on imported goods, If the Uruguay Round were approved as written, Kraft, General Motors, Merck, Phillip Morris, American Express, Cargill, Dupont, and their foreign allies will have succeeded in turning trade negotiations into power plays against nations retaining a meaningful sovereign right to protect citizens from harm. Global commerce without commensurate global law may be the dream of corporate chief executive officers, but it would be a tragedy for the people of the world with its ratcheting downwards of worker, consumer and environmental standards. The U.S. Congress is one of the only potential barriers to this future of concentrated corporate power backed by "pull down" trade rules.

THE MODERN, GLOBAL "RACE TO THE BOTTOM"

U.S. corporations long ago learned how to pit states against each other in "a race to the bottom"—to provide the most permissive corporate charters, lower wages, pollution standards, and taxes. Often it is the federal government's role to require states to meet higher federal standards. Now, through their campaign for "free trade" particularly via the Uruguay Round, multinational corporations are directing their efforts to the international arena, where desperately poor countries are either pressured or willing to drive conditions downward and backward. There is no overarching "lift up" jurisdiction on the world stage....

Enactment of the Uruguay Round virtually ensures that any local, state or even national effort in the United States to demand that corporations pay their fair share of taxes, provide a decent standard of living to their employees or limit their pollution of the air, water and land will be met with the refrain, "You can't burden us like that. If you do, we won't be able to compete. We'll have to close down and move to a country that offers us a more hospitable business climate." The WTO will accelerate this corporate leverage. This sort of ultimatum is extremely powerful—communities already devastated by plant closures and a declining manufacturing base are desperate not to lose further jobs, and they know all too well from experience that multinational corporations find it easy to exit the United States if they do not get their unfair way....

Worst of all, the corporate-induced race to the bottom is a game that no country or community can win. There is always some place in the world that is a little worse off, where the living conditions are a little bit more wretched. Look at the electronics industry, where dozens of assembly and other factories—in search of ever lower production costs—have migrated from California to Korea to Malaysia. Many of those businesses are now contemplating moving to China, where wages and workplace an environmental standards are still lower. The game of countries bidding against each other causes a downward spiral.

The most important tool countries have to combat serious corporate blackmail is to say, "You are not going to be able to sell in this country if you behave in that manner." Using this logic in the past, the United States has conditioned trade status on labor and human rights for trading partners. Similarly, the United States currently has environmental and conservation laws that forbid sale in our market, for instance, of fish caught with driftnets or using techniques that kill dolphins, and of wild-caught birds. But the Uruguay Round would place at risk the exercise of such national authority to control the domestic market. Under the terms of the WTO, that sort of effort to protect national standards would be considered a "non-tariff trade barrier," and would be proscribed.

THE URUGUAY ROUND: HEADED IN THE WRONG DIRECTION

All over the country there is a bubbling up of citizen activity dealing with the environment and public health....

This percolating-up process for advancing crucial noncommercial values that shape living standards will be stifled by the WTO, with bottom-up democratic impulses replaced by pull-down mercantile dictates. It is inevitable that different policy goals will at times conflict, for instance goals of maximizing trade and goals of public health and environmental protection. However, the decision about which policy goal should take precedence in a particular instance should be decided by those who will live with the results. Under the Uruguay Round, those decisions are largely shifted away from citizen control and domestic democratic institutions to a dispute resolution body located in Geneva, Switzerland which operates in secret and without the guarantees of due process and citizen participation found in domestic legislatures and courts.

Moreover, the substantive trade rules interpreted by the dispute resolution body of the WTO would exercise a supremacy over other policy goals in almost every instance. This grave institutional bias, which subordinates health, safety and other factors to the imperatives of commercial trade is not the way that Congress has legislated over the decades. I strongly urge Congress to reject the Uruguay Round agreement in order to revisit its trade proposals within a democratic structure that protects our domestic federal and state sovereignty, and, to apply President Clinton's words, that "promotes democracy abroad." For it is democracy, not autocracy, that is the strongest and fairest engine for sustainable economic development.

It is the duty of this committee and the Congress to assess the broadest implications of this agreement on the continued viability of democratic institutions here at home and their continued capacity to regulate commerce to suit the needs of their constituents. In two, three or four decades, when historians look back on this period during which so much of the world's system of self-organization is being reconfigured, they will point to the U.S. Congressional debate and consideration of the Uruguay Round as a turning point in the post cold war era. Either they will focus on it as a moment in which Congress resisted the destructive GATT and NAFTA programs designed by society's most powerful forces for their narrow benefit, or they will view it as the moment in which Congress ceded authority to safeguard the interests of this country and its inhabitants to large multinational corporations that would gain excessive power from the Uruguay Round which they were so deeply involved in shaping.

Who among you [in Congress] will be the prophets? Who among you will be the safeguarders? These two roles are different sides of the same coin.

POSTSCRIPT

Is the New General Agreement on Tariffs and Trade Beneficial?

The House of Representatives passed the GATT bill by a vote of 288 to 146; the Senate did so by a vote of 76 to 24. Somewhat unusually, a greater percentage of Republicans than Democrats voted for the measure and thus supported the position of Democratic president Bill Clinton. Speaking for the Republicans, Senate minority leader Bob Dole (R-Kansas) termed the new agreement "far from perfect," but he concluded that, overall, "we're the big beneficiaries, the United States of America, any way you cut it." This view reflects the idea that while free trade creates some loss of jobs and other economic dislocation, protectionism is even more costly. For two books that explore this concern in two of the world's largest trading countries, see Gary Clyde Hufbaurer and Kimberly Ann Elliott, *Measuring the Costs of Protectionism in the United States* (International Institute for Economics, 1994) and Yoko Sazanami, Shujiro Urata, and Hiroki Kawai, *Measuring the Costs of Protectionism in Japan* (International Institute for Economics, 1994).

Whether that attitude persists remains to be seen. Because of its domestic ramifications, trade has also been the subject of considerable political debate. Part of that domestic-international interaction can be seen in Daniel Verdier, *Democracy and International Trade: Britain, France, and the United States, 1860–1990* (Princeton University Press, 1994).

Even though GATT has been approved, the issues surrounding GATT remain relevant because they relate to how far the United States or any other country wants to go in accepting a free trade regime and submitting to the decisions of a supranational organization such as the WTO. Whatever the future of such trade and other areas of economic interchange, there is broad agreement that the outcome will affect the shape of global politics and the strength of individual countries. For more on the international institutions that regulate trade and other aspects of the international political economy, read Miles Kahler, *International Institutions and the Political Economy of Integration* (Brookings Institution, 1995).

In Europe the process of economic integration had gone quite far under the European Union. Recent efforts to create a common currency and to increase political integration have, however, met considerable resistance. For the United States, the free trade movement also includes U.S. membership in the North American Free Trade Agreement (NAFTA) beginning in 1994 and the proposed creation by the year 2005 of the Free Trade Agreement of the Americas (FTAA), which will include virtually all countries in the Western Hemisphere.

ISSUE 9

Should the Developed North Increase Aid to the Less Developed South?

YES: James P. Grant, from "Jumpstarting Development," *Foreign Policy* (Summer 1993)

NO: Editors of *The Economist*, from "The Kindness of Strangers," *The Economist* (May 7, 1994)

ISSUE SUMMARY

YES: James P. Grant, executive director of the United Nations Children's Fund (UNICEF), contends that many world problems stem from the impoverished conditions found throughout much of the world and that one way to jumpstart solutions to these problems is to extend more assistance to the poor countries.

NO: The editors of *The Economist*, a well-known British publication, suggest that the way that aid is typically given and spent makes it a waste of resources and may even have a negative impact on the recipients.

One stark characteristic of the world system is that it is divided into two economic classes of countries. There is the North, which is industrialized and relatively prosperous. Then there is the South, which is mostly nonindustrial and relatively, and sometimes absolutely, impoverished. The countries that comprise the South are also called the less developed countries (LDCs) or the developing countries and were once known in a cold war context as the Third World. By whatever name they are known, however, LDCs have social conditions that are unacceptable. At a macroeconomic level, approximately three-quarters of the world's people live in the LDCs, yet they possess only about one-seventh of the world's wealth (measured in gross national products, or GNPs). On a more personal level, if you compare the lives of the average citizens of Japan and the average citizens of Nigeria, the Nigerians die 27 years earlier, earn an income that is 88 times smaller, are half as likely to be literate, are 53 times more likely to die during childbirth, and will find it 82 times more difficult to find a physician for medical help.

Despite the rhetoric of the North about the LDCs' plight, the countries of the North do relatively little to help. For example, U.S. economic foreign aid in 1994 was approximatley $15 billion, which amounted to only about half of what Americans spent annually in retail liquor stores. Canada's foreign aid, about $2.8 billion, is equivalent to only about a third of what its citizens spent in 1994 on tobacco. Foreign investment in the LDCs is also extremely limited, and what increases there are go to the relatively few countries, such as South Korea, that have been able join the ranks of what are called newly industrializing countries (NICs). Furthermore, loans to the LDCs have declined, and repayment of existing loans is draining much-needed capital away from many less developed countries. Trade earnings are another possible source of development capital, but the raw materials produced and exported by most LDCs earn them little compared to the cost of importing the more expensive finished products manufactured by the North.

There are a number of ways of approaching this issue of greater aid by the North for the South. One approach focuses on morality. Are we morally obligated to help less fortunate humans? A second approach explores more aid as a means of promoting the North's own self-interest; some analysts contend that a fully developed world would mean greater prosperity for everyone and would be more stable politically. A third avenue pursues the causes for the LDCs' poverty and lack of development in order to assess who or what is responsible.

It is possible to divide views on the origins and continuance of the North-South gap into three groups. One believes that the uneven (but unintended) spread of the Industrial Revolution resulted in unequal economic development. From this point of view, the answer to the question "Who is at fault?" is: "Nobody; it just happened." A second group finds the LDCs responsible for much of their continuing poverty. Advocates of this view charge the LDCs with failure to control their populations, with lack of political stability, with poor economic planning, and with a variety of other ill-conceived practices that impede development. This group believes that foreign aid is wasteful and is destructive of the policies needed to spur economic development.

A third group maintains that the North bears much of the responsibility for the South's condition and, therefore, is obligated to help the LDCs. Those who hold this view contend that the colonization of the LDCs, especially during the 1800s, when the Industrial Revolution rapidly took hold in the North, destroyed the indigenous economic, social, and political organizations needed for development. These powers then kept their colonial dependencies underdeveloped in order to ensure a supply of cheap raw materials. Even though virtually all former colonies are now independent, this view persists; the developed countries continue to follow political and economic strategies designed to keep the LDCs underdeveloped and dependent.

In the following selections, James P. Grant takes the position that, notwithstanding the poor media image of the LDCs as a lost cause, there is real momentum for change. He recommends focusing on the children of the LDCs—that if educated, kept healthy, and given other basic advantages, they can be the force for rapid positive change in the LDCs. The editors of *The Economist* argue that aid is ill-managed today and that, even if aid were vastly increased and managed well, it is not certain that the recipient countries would do much better.

YES
James P. Grant

JUMPSTARTING DEVELOPMENT

Anyone who thought, amidst the euphoria of dizzying change starting in 1989, that the end of the Cold War would usher in an age of global harmony and easy solutions has long since been disabused of the notion. Every day we open our newspapers to dark headlines confirming that the world is still a very dangerous place—in some ways more dangerous than before. We are confronted with a host of problems, both old and new, that are reaching crisis proportions. Is there a way of "jumpstarting" solutions to many of those problems? In fact, there is.

To many, it may not seem so. Ethnic conflict, religious hatred, failed states, economic devastation in Eastern Europe and the former Soviet Union, AIDS, and environmental degradation all seem intractable problems. Meanwhile, the number of poor in the world continues to increase at about the same rate as the world's population. The World Bank put their number at 1.1 billion in 1990. A fifth of the world's population is living on less than one dollar a day, and during the 1980s the poor actually lost ground. The 1990s show little evidence that the world economy will return anytime soon to a high growth trajectory.

The negative trends have even begun to afflict the rich. In the last decade, poverty increased in a number of industrialized countries, most notably in the United States and the United Kingdom and, of course, in the former communist countries of Europe. In most of those countries, children bore the brunt of the reversal. In America today, one in five children is poor, the highest level of child poverty in a quarter century in the world's richest country. In both the United Kingdom and the United States, child poverty has nearly doubled in a decade.

Small wonder that the lead article in this journal's spring issue contended that "all the trends" are in the wrong direction and that the world "appears to be at the beginning, not of a new order, but of a new nightmare." Such pessimism, however, can be misplaced. The world is in fact on the threshold of being able to make vastly greater progress on many problems that have long seemed intractable. Rather than merely reacting to situations after they have become critical, as in Somalia, the world has an opportunity in the 1990s

From James P. Grant, "Jumpstarting Development," *Foreign Policy*, no. 91 (Summer 1993). Copyright © 1993 by The Carnegie Endowment for International Peace. Reprinted by permission.

to make an effective—and efficient—social investment to convert despair into hope and go a long way toward preventing future crises and building healthy societies.

The situation today may be analogous to that of Asia in the mid 1960s, when population growth seemed set to outrun the food supply. Many predicted widespread famine, chaos, and instability for the last third of this century. But then, quite suddenly, within four or five years, the Green Revolution took hold in Asia, extending from the Philippines through South Asia to Turkey. In country after country, wheat and rice production increased at annual rates unprecedented in the West. The immediate cause was not so much a scientific breakthrough—strains of the miracle wheats had been around for as many as 15 years—as a political and organizational one. Only by the mid 1960s had fertilizer, pesticides, and controlled irrigation become widely used, thanks in large part to earlier aid programs. At the same time, the combination of Asian drought and increasing awareness of the population explosion created the political will to drastically restructure price levels for grains and agro-inputs, and to mobilize the multiple sectors of society—rural credit, marketing, transport, foreign exchange allocations, media—required for success. U.S. president Lyndon Johnson deserves credit for his leadership contribution to that effort, though his deep personal involvement remains a largely untold story.

We may be in a similar position today, but on a much broader front—poised for advances in primary health care, basic education, water supply and sanitation, family planning, and gender equity, as well as food production—and covering a much wider geographical area, including Africa and Latin America as well as Asia. With an earnest effort from the major powers, the 1990s could witness a second green revolution—extending, this time, beyond agriculture to human development.

Frequent illness, malnutrition, poor growth, illiteracy, high birth rates, and gender bias are among poverty's worst symptoms. They are also some of poverty's most fundamental causes. We could anticipate, therefore, that overcoming some of the worst symptoms and causes of poverty would have far-reaching repercussions on the national and global level. The recent experiences of such diverse societies as China, Costa Rica, the Indian state of Kerala, Sri Lanka, and the Asian newly industrializing countries (NICs) suggest that high population growth rates, which wrap the cycle of poverty ever tighter, can be reduced dramatically. Reducing poverty would give a major boost to the fragile new efforts at democratization that will survive only if they tangibly improve the lives of the bottom half of society. As we know from the experience of Singapore, South Korea, Taiwan, and the other Asian NICs, such progress would in turn accelerate economic growth. By breaking the "inner cycle" of poverty, we would increase the capacity of the development process to assault poverty's many external causes, rooted in such diverse factors as geography, climate, land tenure, debt, business cycles, governance, and unjust economic relations.

We are uniquely positioned to succeed in the 1990s. Recent scientific and technological advances—and the revolutionary new capacity to communicate with and mobilize large numbers of people—have provided us with a host of new tools. The world's leaders can now use them together to produce dramatic, even unprecedented, results.

For example, the universal child immunization effort—the largest peacetime international collaboration in world history—has since the mid 1980s established systems that now reach virtually every hamlet in the developing world and are saving the lives of more than 8,000 children a day—some 3 million a year. Here, too, the technology was not new; vaccines had been available for some 20–30 years. Success has been the result of applying new communication and mobilization techniques to the immunization effort, often led personally by heads of state, making use of television and radio advertisements, and supported by a wide range of local leaders. School teachers, priests, imams, local government officials, nongovernmental organization (NGO) workers, and health personnel all joined the effort. By 1990, more than 80 per cent of the developing world's children were being brought in four or five times for vaccinations even before their first birthdays. As a result, Calcutta, Lagos, and Mexico City today have far higher levels of immunization of children at ages one and two than do New York City, Washington, D.C., or even the United States as a whole.

A similar effort is now being made to spread the use of oral rehydration therapy (ORT) to combat the single greatest historical killer of children, diarrhea, which takes the lives of some 8,000 children every day, down from 11,000 daily a decade ago. ORT was invented in the late 1960s, but only recently have leaders mobilized to use this lifesaver on a national scale. Every year it now saves the lives of more than 1 million children, a figure that could easily more than double by 1995 with increased national and international leadership.

The arsenal is now well stocked with other new technologies and rediscovered practices that can bring tremendous benefits with inspired leadership and only modest funding. Thus, the simple iodization of salt—at a cost of five cents annually per consumer—would prevent the world's single largest cause of mental retardation and of goiter, which affect more than 200 million people today as a result of iodine deficiency. Universal access to vitamin A through low-cost capsules or vegetables would remove the greatest single cause—about 700 cases per day—of blindness while reducing child deaths by up to a third in many parts of the developing world. The scientific rediscovery of the miracles of mother's milk means that more than a million children would not have died last year if only they had been effectively breast-fed for the first months of their lives, instead of being fed on more-costly infant formula. In such diverse countries as Bangladesh, Colombia, Senegal, and Zimbabwe, it has proven possible to get poor children, including girls, through primary education at very little cost. Recent advances have shown how to halve the costs of bringing sanitation and safe water to poor communities, to less than $30 per capita. New varieties of high-yield crops—from cassava to corn—are now ready to be promoted on a national scale in sub-Saharan Africa.

Meanwhile, with such tools in hand, the new capacity to communicate—to inform and motivate—empowers families, communities, and governments to give all children a better chance to lead productive lives. In short, we are now learning to "outsmart" poverty at the outset of each new life by providing a "bubble of protection" around a child's first vulnerable months and years. Strong international leadership and cooperation—facilitated enormously by the end of the Cold War and the expansion of democracy—could leverage that new capacity into wide-ranging social progress.

A CHILDREN'S REVOLUTION

Notwithstanding the media image of the Third World as a lost cause, there is real momentum there for change. In fact, for all the difficulties and setbacks, more progress has been made in developing countries in the last 40 years than was made in the previous 2,000, progress achieved while much of the world freed itself from colonialism and while respect for human and political rights expanded dramatically. Life expectancy has lengthened from 53 in 1960 to 65 today, and continues to increase at a rate of 9.5 hours per day. Thirty years ago, approximately three out of four children born in the developing countries survived to their fifth birthdays; today, some nine out of ten survive.

At the same time, the birth rates in countries as disparate as Brazil, China, Colombia, Cuba, Korea, Mexico, Sri Lanka, Thailand, and Tunisia have been more than halved, dramatically slowing population growth and the inherent strains it places on limited natural resources and social programs. Among the factors that have helped contain population growth, improving children's health is undoubtedly the least well-known and appreciated. As the United Nations Population Division puts it, "Improvements in child survival, which increase the predictability of the family building process, trigger the transition from natural to controlled fertility behavior. This in turn generates the need for family planning." While they are important priorities themselves, reductions in child mortality, basic education of women, and the availability of family planning make a strong synergistic contribution to solving what Yale historian Paul Kennedy calls, in *Preparing for the Twenty-First Century* (1992), the "impending demographic disaster." As population specialist Sharon Camp noted in the Spring 1993 issue of FOREIGN POLICY:

Measures like quality reproductive health care, greater educational and economic opportunities for women, and reductions in infant and child death rates can and will bring about rapid birthrate declines. If all developing countries were to emulate the most effective policies and programs and if donor governments such as the United States were to provide adequate levels of assistance, the population problem could be resolved in the lifetime of today's children.

In fact, a children's revolution is already under way in the developing world, often led by those in power. Developing country leaders took the lead in seeking history's first truly global summit—the 1990 World Summit for Children—with an unprecedented 71 heads of state and government participating. They also pressed for early action on the Convention on the Rights of the Child, which was adopted by the [UN] General Assembly in November 1989 and which has since been signed or ratified in record time by more than 150 countries—with the United States now being the only major exception.

The experience of the past decade showed it possible—even during the darkest days of the Cold War and amid the Third World economic crisis of the 1980s—to mobilize societies and the international community around a package of low-cost interventions and services, building a sustainable momentum of human progress. The United Nations Children's Fund (UNICEF) and NGOs called it the Child Survival and Development Revolution, and as a result more than 20 million children are alive today who would not otherwise be; tens of millions are healthier, stronger, and less of a burden upon their mothers and families; and birth rates are falling.

Leaders are learning that productive things can be done for families and children at relatively low cost, and that it can be good politics for them to do so and bad politics to resist. More than 130 countries have issued or are actively working on National Programmes of Action to implement the goals set by the World Summit for Children, all of which were incorporated into Agenda 21 at the June 1992 Earth Summit in Rio de Janeiro. Those ambitious goals—to be met by the year 2000—include controlling the major childhood diseases; cutting child malnutrition in half; reducing death rates for children under five by one-third; cutting in half maternal mortality rates; providing safe water and sanitation for all communities; and making family planning services and basic education universally available. In 1992, most regions of the developing world took the process a step further by selecting a core of targets for 1995, when the first World Social Summit will review children's progress within the broader development process. For the first time since the dawn of history, humankind is making long-term plans for improving the lives of the young.

In part, that new concern has its roots in the communications revolution that brings daily pictures of large-scale famine or violence into our homes. At the same time, the new communications capacity has permitted deprived populations everywhere to see how much better people can live, firing grassroots movements for reform and democracy. But most of the Third World's suffering remains invisible. Of the 35,000 children under age five who die every day in the developing countries, more than 32,000 succumb to largely preventable hunger and illness. No earthquake, no flood, no war has taken the lives of a quarter million children in a single week; but that is the weekly death toll of the invisible emergencies resulting from poverty and underdevelopment. In 1992, 500,000 children under the age of five died in the kind of dramatic emergencies that attract media attention, but that is a small portion of the nearly 13 million children under five who are killed every year by grinding poverty and gross underdevelopment. The tragic deaths of 1,000 children per day in Somalia last year captured far more public attention than those of the 8,000 children around the world who die every day from the dehydration caused by ordinary diarrhea, which is so easily treated and prevented.

As the international community assumes greater responsibility for proliferating civil strife and other emergencies, it must come to terms with the realities of limited resources. How many operations to rescue failed states like Somalia can the international community afford? It is estimated that the U.S. component of the Somalia operation alone will cost more than $750 million for just four months' involvement, nearly comparable to UNICEF's average annual global budget of recent years, much of which is used to prevent future crises. There are now 48 civil and ethnic conflicts in progress around the globe. The United Nations is involved in 14 peacekeeping operations on five continents. Last year, those operations cost more than $3 billion, about four times higher than the previous record. Those operations are the most expensive way to relieve suffering, and it is clearly time to invest far more in *preventing* emergencies and conflicts, and in buttressing the new democracies, even as we put out the world's fires. As U.N. secretary-general Boutros Boutros-Ghali argues in his *Agenda for Peace,* prevention can prove far less costly—and produce far greater results—than relying on expensive and sometimes ineffective rescue operations.

As the international community shifts toward prevention—as it must—it makes the most sense to focus on eradicating poverty's worst manifestations early in the lives of children, breaking the cycle of poverty from generation to generation. At the World Summit for Children, the international community identified the basic package of high-impact, low-cost interventions that can make a difference in the short and medium term, while helping to build long-term development. Now it has only to make them work, albeit on a massive scale.

The overall price tag for reaching all the year 2000 goals for children and women, which would overcome most of the worst aspects of poverty, would be an extra $25 billion per year. The developing countries themselves are trying to come up with two-thirds of that amount by reordering their domestic priorities and budgets, while the remaining third—slightly more than $8 billion per year—should come from the industrialized world in the form of increased or reallocated official development assistance (ODA) and debt relief. That is a small price for meeting the basic needs of virtually every man, woman, and child in the developing world in nutrition, basic health, basic education, water and sanitation, and family planning within this decade.

In Russia and the other former Soviet republics, such aid could produce rapid grassroots results at an affordable cost, easing pain and helping to buy time until democratic and macroeconomic reforms show concrete progress. Plans for restoring democracy to Cambodia, Haiti, and Mozambique will need to alleviate suffering among the poor quickly; and targeting the essential needs of children and women can produce the biggest impact at the lowest cost. International relief programs for Somalia must rapidly give way to assistance that constitutes an investment in human development, and no such investment has been found to be more cost-effective than primary health care, nutrition, and basic education for children and women. The road to power for many of the world's extremist movements—whether based in religion or political ideology—is paved with the unmet needs of the poor.

Sadly, the U.S. has stagnated or regressed over the past decade with respect to children, even while much of the developing world has been making impressive progress. The United States has provided little leadership for that progress, except for that provided by the bipartisanship of Congress, which actively encouraged U.S. support to child survival and development programs abroad. But by increasing investment in American children and strengthening American families, and by reordering foreign assistance to reflect that new priority, the United States, the world's sole superpower, could once more set the global standard and give a major boost to human development and economic growth.

First, few actions would have more immediate impact than the signature and ratification this year of the historic Convention on the Rights of the Child. President Bill Clinton's signature of the convention and its submission to the U.S. Senate for early ratification (as has been urged by bipartisan leadership) would send an important message to the world, bringing the rights of children close to becoming humanity's first universal law.

Second, the United States needs to demonstrate a new culture of caring for its own children. The much-needed reordering of priorities for American children, women, and families is already under way, with initiatives on Head Start, universal immunization, parental leave, family planning, and health services for all. A "Culture of Caring," the American plan in response to the World Summit for Children that was issued at the end of the Bush administration—in January 1993 —provides a useful base for bipartisan action.

Third, the United States needs "20/20 vision." It should support the May 1991 proposal of the United Nations Development Programme, which had two components: It called on developing countries to devote at least 20 per cent of their budgets to directly meeting the basic human needs of their people, roughly double current average levels. It also argued that 20 per cent of all international development aid should go to meet those same basic needs: primary health care, nutrition, basic education, family planning, and safe water and sanitation. Today, on average, less than 10 per cent of already inadequate levels of ODA are devoted to that purpose. Different ways of defining and reporting social sector allocations within national and ODA budgets make precise quantification of those proportions somewhat difficult, and efforts are therefore underway to achieve a common form of reporting. But even if subsequent research changes the target percentages, the "20/20 vision" concept underscores the importance of restructuring both sets of budgets in line with the priorities established at the World Summit for Children, which may require—on average—a doubling of existing allocations.

On the ODA side, the United States today devotes less than $1 billion to basic human needs. Of the projected $25 billion extra annually that will be required globally by mid-decade to meet the World Summit year 2000 goals, the U.S. share would be $2 billion. The roughly $3 billion total would then still be less than 20 per cent of all U.S. foreign and military assistance. It is a small price to pay for jumpstarting solutions to so many of the overwhelming problems of population, democracy, and the worst aspects of poverty, to say nothing about saving tens of millions of young lives this decade. The additional funds can be obtained from reductions in the military and security component of the U.S. international affairs budget.

Fourth, the new spirit of democratic change and economic reform in Africa will not survive if its creditors do not give it some debt relief: Together, the sub-Saharan African countries pay $1 billion in debt service to foreign creditors every month, and its debt is now proportionally three or four times heavier than that of Latin America. At the November 1992 Organization of African Unity-sponsored International Conference on Assistance to African Children, donor countries and lending agencies alike pledged to promote more debt relief while expanding or restructuring ODA in order to help Africa protect and nurture its children. Here again the

United States could help lead the way, preventing Africa from deteriorating into a continent of Somalias. The G-7 Summit in Tokyo in July 1993 should make a definitive commitment to debt relief, with much of the local currency proceeds going to accelerate programs for children, women, and the environment through a variety of debt-swapping mechanisms. With the right mixture of domestic and international support, and with apartheid ending in South Africa, we could see dramatic progress in most of Africa by the year 2000. That could include a food revolution every bit as green as Asia's—but African countries will need help. The alternative could be a return to authoritarian rule, corruption, and conflict throughout large parts of the continent.

Fifth, the United States must actively support multilateral cooperation. With human development and poverty alleviation increasingly accepted as the focus for development cooperation in the 1990s, the United States has an opportunity to transform rhetoric into reality. Active U.S. support and leadership along those lines in the World Bank, the International Monetary Fund, the regional banks, and throughout the U.N. system will go a long way toward overcoming, in our time, the worst aspects of poverty in the South, where it is most acute. Land-mark U.N. conferences have been scheduled on human rights (1993), population (1994), and women (1995); U.S. leadership at those conferences and at the U.N. summit on social development in 1995 will strengthen their impact. The U.S. role will also be critical in reducing poverty in the North and in the transitional societies of Eastern Europe and the former Soviet Union.

Finally, the United States must strengthen its commitment to the United Nations. The new administration's initiative to seek restoration of U.S. funding for the United Nations Population Fund is a welcome step—a step that Congress should rapidly implement. That and a decision to rejoin the United Nations Educational, Scientific, and Cultural Organization (UNESCO) would not only give an important boost to family planning and global education, but—together with full payment of its U.N. arrears—it would signal long-term U.S. commitment to the United Nations as the global village's central vehicle for development cooperation and safeguarding the peace.

Focusing on children as a means of attacking the worst aspects of poverty will not solve all the world's problems, but it would make a historic contribution—at this all-too-brief juncture of opportunity —to the better world we all seek. It could change the course of history.

NO
Editors of *The Economist*

THE KINDNESS OF STRANGERS

> The old jibe about aid—"poor people in rich countries helping rich people in poor countries"—has plenty of truth in it. Donors need to learn from past mistakes if they want to help poor countries grow.

Anybody who tried to see the case for aid by looking merely at the way it is allotted would quickly give up in despair. The richest 40% of the developing world gets about twice as much per head as the poorest 40%. Big military spenders get about twice as much per head as do the less belligerent. El Salvador gets five times as much aid as Bangladesh, even though Bangladesh has 24 times as many people and is five times poorer than El Salvador.

Since 1960, about $1.4 trillion (in 1988 dollars) has been transferred in aid from rich countries to poor ones. Yet relatively little is known about what that process has achieved. Has it relieved poverty? Has it stimulated growth in the recipient countries? Has it helped the countries which give it? Such questions become more pressing as donor governments try harder to curb public spending. This year, two of the biggest players in the international aid business are looking afresh at their aims and priorities.

Brian Atwood, appointed by the Clinton administration to run America's Agency for International Development (AID), inherited an organisation encumbered over the years with 33 official goals by a Congress that loved using aid money to buy third-world adherence to its pet ideas. Now, faced with a sharp budget cut, Mr Atwood is trying to pare down to just four goals: building democracy, protecting the environment, fostering sustainable economic development and encouraging population control. Not, however, anything as basic as the relief of poverty.

A few blocks away from Mr Atwood's Washington office, the World Bank is going through a similar exercise. Set up in 1946, the Bank has become the most powerful of all the multilateral development organisations. But a critical internal report recently accused the Bank of caring more about pushing out loans than about monitoring how well the money was spent. Now the Bank hopes to improve the quality of its lending. It is also wondering about its future. Some of its past borrowers in East Asia are now rich enough to turn lenders themselves. More should follow. The Bank is trying to move into new areas, such as cleaning up the environment and setting up social-welfare systems. But some people wonder how long it will really be needed.

AID and the World Bank are unusual (although their critics rarely admit as much) in their openness and in the rigour with which they try to evaluate what they do. But other donors will also have to think about which kinds of aid to abandon as their budgets stop expanding. In the 1980s the official development assistance[1] (ODA) disbursed by members of the OECD's [Organization for Economic Cooperation and Development's] Development Assistance Committee (DAC)—21 rich countries plus the European Commission—increased by about a quarter in real terms; but between 1991 and 1992, the DAC's disbursements rose by just 0.5%. Development Initiatives, an independent British ginger group [a driving force within a larger group], believes "the end of an era" may have come; it reckons that aid budgets around the world are ceasing to grow at all. Almost the only exception is Japan, which provides a fifth of DAC aid and plans a substantial increase over the next five years.

Most multilateral donors, such as the UN agencies, also have budgets frozen. A rare exception is the European Development Fund [EDF], the aid arm of the European Union, which is taking a rapidly rising share of member-states' aid budgets. The EDF's secrecy and its mediocre reputation with recipient countries make some bilateral donors unhappy. "British officials are concerned about having to devote increasing quantities of their aid, which they regard as successful, to the European programme," reports Robert Cassen, a British aid expert.

Figure 1

More from the Market: Net Resource Flows to Developing Countries [in] $bn, Constant 1991 Prices and Exchange Rates

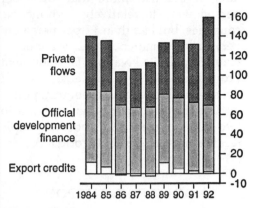

Source: OECD

NEEDED: A CASE FOR GIVING

Some developing countries—mainly the faster-growing ones perceived as "emerging markets"—have found the international capital markets to be increasingly willing suppliers of finance (see Figure 1). But demands for ODA are still appearing in new forms and from new sources. Astute third-world countries are giving old projects a green tinge to profit from fashionable enthusiasm for the environment. The countries of Eastern Europe and the former Soviet Union are competing with the third world for help. And the proportion of aid spent on relieving disasters has soared from 2% five years ago to around 7% today.

But with the clamour for more money goes increasing uncertainty about what aid is for and what it has achieved. The naive taxpayer might imagine that aid's main purpose was to relieve poverty. Yet only relatively small amounts of ODA go to the poorest of countries or to projects that benefit mainly the poorest of people. A study of America's aid programme conducted by the Overseas Development Council (ODC), a Washington, DC, think-tank, found that more than $250 per person went to relatively high-income countries, but less than $1 per person to very low-income countries. Mahbub ul Haq of the United Nations Development Programme (UNDP), a fierce critic of aid's failure to reach the poorest, points out that the ten countries that are home to two-thirds of the world's poorest people receive only one-third of world aid.

NOT HELPING THE POOR

Within poor countries, too, aid is rarely concentrated on the services that benefit the poorest. The World Bank reckons that, of all the aid going to low-income countries in 1988, a mere 2% went on primary health care and 1% on population programmes. Even the aid that is spent on health and education tends to go to services that benefit disproportionately the better-off. Aid for health care goes disproportionately to hospitals (in 1988–89, for instance, 33% of Japan's bilateral aid for health went on building hospitals); aid for education, to universities. In sub-Saharan Africa in the 1980s, only $1 of ODA went on each primary pupil; $11 on each secondary pupil; and $575 on each university student.

Such spending patterns often reflect the priorities of the recipient governments. Some donors have tried to persuade governments to distribute aid differently. They have had mixed success —not surprisingly, for their own motives in aid-giving often override the goal of poverty relief.

One such motive, powerful even since the end of the cold war, is the pursuit of national security. Most governments are coy about the role that national security plays in their aid budgets, but the biggest donor of all, the United States, is blatant: roughly a quarter of its $21 billion foreign-aid budget takes the form of military assistance, and roughly a quarter of the total budget goes to Israel and Egypt alone. "The United States has spent a lot less money on development than on advancing political and military goals," says John Sewell of the ODC. This year, America's aid budget protects the shares of Israel and Egypt. America also sees aid to Eastern Europe and to the countries of the former Soviet Union primarily in strategic terms.

"National security" is also now being used as an argument for giving more weight to all sorts of other goals in the drawing-up of aid budgets. Environmentalists claim that some types of environmental damage, such as global warming and the thinning of the ozone layer, may be worsened by poor-country growth, and they argue that rich-country aid donors should in their own interests take special care to minimise such risks. Others say aid should be used to parry the threats to rich countries posed by the trade in illegal drugs, by population growth and by third-world poverty.

If the goal of national security can conflict with that of poverty relief, then the commercial interests of aid donors can do so even more. Japan's approach has at least the merit of simplicity: its development assistance goes mainly to countries that are most likely to become its future customers. All DAC countries tie some aid—the average is about a quarter—to the purchase of their own goods and services. One problem with tying is that it forces countries to pay over the odds for imports: on average, some estimates suggest, recipients pay 15% more than prevailing prices. Another is that it often distorts development priorities. It is easier to tie aid to a large item of capital spending, such as a dam, road or hospital, than to a small rural project that may do more good. Not surprisingly, tying is especially common in transport, power generation and telecommunications projects.

Aid recorded as tied has been falling as a proportion of bilateral ODA, according to the OECD, which monitors the practice. That may be partly because of the rise in spending on disaster relief. It may also reflect an international agreement on guidelines for tied aid. But governments are clever at finding ways to use aid to promote exports. It has, for example, taken two official investigations to uncover some of the links between British aid to Malaysia and British arms sales to that country.

Some kinds of ODA are given in the sure knowledge that the money will be spent mainly in the donor country, but without explicit tying. One example is technical assistance. Of the $12 billion or so which goes each year to buy advice, training and project design, over 90% is spent on foreign consultants. Half of all technical assistance goes to Africa —which, observes UNDP's Mr Haq, "has perhaps received more bad advice per capita than any other continent". Most thoughtful people in the aid business regard technical assistance as one of the least effective ways to foster development.

Stung by the claims of their aid lobbies that too little help goes to the poor, some governments are trying to steer more money through voluntary bodies, such as charities and church groups. Such bodies, known in the trade as non-governmental organisations or NGOs, have proliferated at astonishing speed in both the rich and poor worlds. The OECD counted 2,542 NGOs in its 24 member countries in 1990, compared with 1,603 in 1980. The growth in the south may have been faster still. Roger Riddell, of the Overseas Development Institute in London, who has made a special study of NGOs and development, talks of a "veritable explosion" in their numbers; he mentions 25,000 grassroots organisations in the Indian state of Tamil Nadu alone. The public and private money dispensed by NGOs amounted to 13% of total net ODA flows in 1990, and the share has been creeping up.

NGOs may be better than central governments at handling small projects and more sensitive to what local people really need. But even NGOs, according to Mr Riddell, usually fail to help the very poorest. "If government and official aid programmes fail to reach the bottom 20% of income groups, most NGO interventions probably miss the bottom 5–10%," he guesses. And, as more aid is channelled through NGOs, some groups may find it harder to retain the element of local participation which is their most obvious strength. More searching questions might be asked about whether they are efficiently run, or achieve their purported goals: a study of projects supported by the Ford Foundation in Africa in the late 1980s found "very few successes to talk about, especially in terms of post-intervention sustainability".

AND WHAT ABOUT GROWTH?

When the modern panoply of official aid institutions grew up after the second world war, the intention was not to relieve poverty as such but to promote economic growth in poor countries. Aid was seen as a transitional device to help countries reach a point from which their economies would take off of their own accord. Its use was to remove shortages of capital and foreign exchange, boosting investment to a point at which growth could become self-sustaining.

In their baldest form, such views sit oddly beside the fact that, in many of the countries that have received the most aid and have the highest levels of capital investment, growth has been negligible. For at least 47 countries, aid represented more than 5% of GNP [gross national product] in 1988. Many of those countries were in sub-Saharan Africa, where GDP [gross domestic product] per head has been virtually flat for a quarter of a century. Yet, as David Lindauer and Michael Roemer of the Harvard Institute for International Development point out in a recent study, some of them were investing a share of GDP almost as large as that of much faster growing South-East Asian countries: Cameroon, Côte d'Ivoire, Kenya, Tanzania and Zambia all invested at least 20% of GDP, a figure comparable with that for Indonesia or Thailand.

Such rough comparisons may prove little, but they draw attention to an awkward point. Some third-world countries have enjoyed fast economic growth with relatively little aid per head. In particular, some Asian success stories, such as China and Vietnam, had little or no aid at a time when donors were pouring money into Africa (although China is now the World Bank's largest single customer). If some countries can achieve economic growth with little aid, while other countries which get a great deal of aid do not

grow at all, what if anything is aid good for?

One way to try to answer that question is to review the experience of individual countries and aid projects. In the late 1980s there were two valiant attempts to do just this: one conducted by a team led by Mr Cassen, the other on a more modest scale by Mr Riddell. Mr Cassen's team argued that "the majority of aid is successful in terms of its own objectives", but added that "a significant proportion does not succeed." Aid had worked badly in Africa; better in South Asia. Where aid did not work, the reason was sometimes that donors failed to learn from their mistakes or the mistakes of other donors; and sometimes that a recipient country failed to make the most of what was offered to it.

As for the impact of aid on economic growth, Mr Cassen concluded cautiously that one could not say that aid failed to help. In some countries, indeed, he found evidence that it did increase growth. Mr Riddell was similarly tentative. Aid, he concluded, "can assist in the alleviation of poverty, directly and indirectly" and "the available evidence... fails to convince that, as a general rule, alternative strategies which exclude aid lead in theory or have led in practice to more rapid improvements in the living standards of the poor than have been achieved with aid."

These are hardly ringing endorsements. But these evaluations of individual aid programmes and projects are more positive in their findings than attempts to establish broader links between aid and growth, which have usually failed entirely. Plenty of economists have picked holes in the original idea that aid would boost investment: why should it, some ask, when governments may simply use income from aid as an excuse to spend tax revenues in other, less productive ways?

Other economists, such as Howard White of the Institute of Social Studies at The Hague, who has reviewed many of the economic studies of the effects of aid on growth, point to the difficulties of generalising. Given the various transfers that count as "aid", the many conditions that donors attach, the differing importance of aid in national economies and the complexity of economic growth, there are simply too many variables to say much that is useful.

THIRD-WORLD DUTCH DISEASE

Since the start of the 1980s, many donors have come to believe that the quality of a country's economic management will do most to determine whether aid will do some good. Aid in the 1980s was frequently used, especially by the World Bank, as a prod to encourage countries to begin "structural adjustment" programmes. In some cases, the economic performance of these countries did improve—Ghana is one of the Bank's favourite examples. In other cases, it did not. A review by the IMF [International Monetary Fund] of 19 low-income countries which had undergone structural adjustment found that their current-account deficits averaged 12.3% of GDP before adjustment and 16.8% in the most recent year; and that their external debt had grown from 451% of exports to 482%.

Why was this? Were countries encouraged to adopt the wrong policies? Did they ignore the advice they were given? Or did the aid itself do some damage? Stefan de Vylder, a Swedish economist, argued for the last of these explanations at a conference in Stockholm in March.

Figure 2

Friends in Need: Aid* as % of GDP, 1992

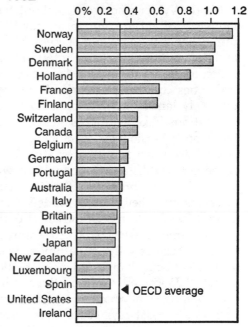

*Net official development assistance

Source: OECD

He argued that large volumes of aid (such as those associated with structural adjustment programmes) could damage an economy's international competitiveness; and countries where export performance was especially bad tended to be "rewarded" with low-interest loans and grants.

The damage to competitiveness, Mr de Vylder believes, is a version of "Dutch disease". This was the term coined in the 1970s to describe how Holland's exports of natural gas boosted its real exchange rate and thereby harmed its export competitiveness. Mr White thinks something similar happened in Sri Lanka between 1974 and 1988, when a sharp increase in aid contributed to a divergence between the nominal and real exchange rates; this hurt the growth of the country's manufactured exports.

Mr de Vylder also worries about the tendency of aid to compensate for failure rather than to reward success. Bilateral donors have increasingly found that much of the aid they give to some countries goes towards paying back money unwisely lent by international financial institutions. Take Zambia as an example. Between 1974 and 1987, Zambia had entered into seven stand-by or structural agreements with the IMF—one every two years. Each was broken by the Zambian government. When, in 1987, Mr de Vylder visited Zambia to assess the latest bout of economic disaster, he asked a minister how seriously the government was worried at being lambasted by every aid donor. "Concerned?" mused the minister, seeming somewhat surprised. Then: "Oh no. They always come back." The minister was right, says Mr de Vylder. Shortly afterwards, the international fi-nancial institutions were again knocking on the door, asking for a new agreement.

It is easy, with aid, to find examples of individual projects that do some good. Most of those who criticise aid argue that if the quality were better—if donors tried harder to learn from each other's mistakes, if they were less keen to reap commercial gain, if they concentrated harder on meeting basic human needs— then there would be far fewer failures. All that is true; but—other things being equal —there would also be much less aid. Will poor countries do worse, over the next 30 years, if rich countries decline to give or lend them another $1.4 trillion? At that price, the answer should be "Yes". Given the way that aid works at present, it is only "Maybe".

NOTES

1. Defined as aid administered with the promotion of economic development and welfare as the main objective; concessional in character; and with a grant element of at least 25%.

POSTSCRIPT

Should the Developed North Increase Aid to the Less Developed South?

There can be no argument that most of the people in most of the countries of the South live in circumstances that citizens in the developed countries of the North would find unacceptable. There is also no question that most of the LDCs were subjugated and held in colonial bondage by the developed countries. Apart from these points, there is little agreement on the causes and the solutions to the plight of the South.

Many LDC specialists blame colonialism for the LDCs' lack of development, past and present. This view is held in many of the LDCs and is also represented widely in Western scholarly opinion. Johan Galtung's "A Structural Theory of Imperialism," *Journal of Peace Research* (1971) is a classic statement from this perspective. This belief has led to the LDCs' demand for a New International Economic Order (NIEO), in which there would be a greater sharing of wealth and economic power between the North and the South. More on the common views and efforts of the LDCs can be found in Darryl C. Thomas, *The Theory and Practice of Third World Solidarity* (Greenwood, 1995). It is also possible to argue that continued poverty in the LDCs, especially amid the general prosperity of the economically developed countries, will increase anger among the people of the economically less developed countries, decrease global stability, and have a variety of other negative consequences. For a discussion of the growing military capabilities of the LDCs, consult Donald M. Snow, *Distant Thunder: Third World Conflict and the New International Order* (St. Martin's Press, 1993).

Other analysts argue that colonialism actually benefited many dependencies by introducing modern economic techniques and that those former colonies that have remained close to the industrialized countries have done the best. Still others have charged that some LDCs have followed policies that have short-circuited their own development. This point of view sees calls for an NIEO as little more than an attempt by the South to increase their power and to reorder the international system. Steven D. Krasner's *Structural Conflict: The Third World Against Global Liberalism* (University of California Press, 1985) is written from this point of view.

There are also disagreements about how much the North should aid the South, irrespective of who has caused their problems. Humanitarian concerns, as well as a sense that all the world's people will eventually be more prosperous if the 80 percent who live in poverty in the South can develop, argue for greater aid, a view represented in David Aronson, "Why Africa Stays Poor and Why It Doesn't Have To," *The Humanist* (March/April 1993).

ISSUE 10

Is There a Global Environmental Crisis?

YES: Hilary F. French, from "Forging a New Global Partnership to Save the Earth," *USA Today Magazine*, a publication of the Society for the Advancement of Education (May 1995)

NO: Julian L. Simon, from *More People, Greater Wealth, More Resources, Healthier Environment* (1994)

ISSUE SUMMARY

YES: Hilary F. French, a senior researcher at the Worldwatch Institute in Washington, D.C., warns that an international effort must be made to stabilize the planet before environmental deterioration reaches the point of no return.

NO: Julian L. Simon, a professor of economics and business administration, counters that the current gloom-and-doom about a "crisis" of our environment is not supported by scientific facts.

We live in an era of almost incomprehensible technological boom. In a very short time—less than a lifetime in many cases—technology has brought some amazing changes. If you talked to a 100-year-old person, he or she would remember a time before airplanes, before automobiles were common, before air conditioning, before electric refrigerators, and before medicines were available that could control polio and a host of other deadly diseases. A centenarian would also remember when the world's population was 25 percent of what it is today, when uranium was considered to be useless, and when mentioning ozone depletion, acid rain, or global warming would have engendered uncomprehending stares.

There are three points to bear in mind here. One is that technology and economic development have been a proverbial two-edged sword. Most people in the economically developed countries (EDCs) and even many people in the less developed countries (LDCs) have benefited mightily from modern technology. For these people, life is longer, easier, and filled with material riches that were the stuff of science fiction not long ago. Yet we are also endangered by the byproducts of progress: There is a burgeoning world population that now equals about 5.6 billion people; resources are being consumed at an exponential rate; cities have smog alerts and mountainous piles of trash in overused landfills; acid rain is damaging forests; and extinction claims an alarming array of species of flora and fauna yearly.

The second notable point is that most of this has occurred so rapidly. It is probable that between 80 and 90 percent of all technological advancement has occurred only within the last 100 years, which is a mere 2.9 percent of humankind's 3,500 years of recorded history. The speed of change is important because it says that if there is a critical problem, then it must be addressed quickly.

In many ways, the issue revolves around whether or not environmental safety requires us to alter drastically some of our consumption patterns; to pay more in taxes and higher prices for often expensive technologies that clean the environment; to use more expensive or less satisfactory substitutes for products that threaten the environment or resources that are scarce; and to alter (some might say lessen) our lifestyles by conserving energy.

Sustainability is one term that is important to this debate. Sustainable development means progress that occurs without further damaging the ecosystem. *Carrying capacity* is another key term. The question is whether or not there is some finite limit to the number of people that the Earth can accommodate. Carrying capacity is about more than just numbers. It also involves how carefully people manage the planet's resources and how that management will affect their lifestyles. If you live to be 100, you may well share the Earth with a world population of 10 billion, almost twice what it is today. Can the world carry 10 billion people while using resources as rapaciously as we do today? Can 10 billion environmentally careful people survive?

This leads to the third notable point, which is that individual countries and the global community collectively have begun to try to figure out how to protect the environment while maintaining—indeed, increasing and spreading—economic prosperity as well. In June 1992 most of the world countries and a huge array of private organizations gathered in Rio de Janeiro, Brazil, to attend the United Nations Conference on Environment and Development (UNCED), popularly called the Rio Conference. The conference represented a major international effort under the auspices of the UN to address sustainability. Among other things, UNCED reached two agreements: a convention to cut down emissions that create global warming and a convention to protect biodiversity. Many developed countries resisted strong language in the two treaties. President George Bush refused to sign the biodiversity treaty, although he did sign the global warming convention. When Bill Clinton became president, he reversed the U.S. position by signing the biodiversity treaty. After several years, there still has been little done by the wealthier nations to assist poorer countries in developing environmental safeguards.

For Hilary F. French and others, UNCED represented only a beginning. In the following selections, she claims that if a strong commitment to sustainable development is made, global disaster can be headed off. Julian L. Simon, in response, argues that worries about population, the environment, and resources are overwrought.

YES

Hilary F. French

FORGING A NEW GLOBAL PARTNERSHIP TO SAVE THE EARTH

In June, 1992, more than 100 heads of state and 20,000 non-governmental representatives gathered in Rio de Janeiro for the United Nations Conference on Environment and Development (UNCED). It resulted in the adoption of Agenda 21, an ambitious 500-page blueprint for sustainable development. In addition, Rio produced treaties on climate and biological diversity, both of which could lead to domestic policy changes in all nations. Significantly, the conference pointed to the need for a global partnership if sustainable development was to be achieved.

Since Rio, a steady stream of international meetings have been held on the many issues that were on its agenda. For instance, the September, 1994, International Conference on Population and Development in Cairo put the spotlight of world attention on the inexorable pace of population growth and the need to respond to it through broad-based efforts to expand access to family planning, improve women's health and literacy, and ensure child survival.

The pace of real change has not kept up with the increasingly loaded schedule of international gatherings, though. The initial burst of international momentum generated by UNCED is flagging, and the global partnership it called for is foundering due to a failure of political will. While a small, committed group of individuals in international organizations, national and local governments, and citizens' groups continues trying to keep the flame of Rio alive, business as usual largely is the order of the day in the factories, farms, villages, and cities that form the backbone of the world economy.

As a result, the relentless pace of global ecological decline shows no signs of letting up. Carbon dioxide concentrations are mounting in the atmosphere, species loss continues to accelerate, fisheries are collapsing, land degradation frustrates efforts to feed hungry people, and the Earth's forest cover keeps shrinking. Many of the development and economic issues that underpin environmental destruction are worsening. Income inequality is rising, Third World debt is mounting, human numbers continue growing at daunting rates, and the amount of poor people in the world is increasing.

The global partnership that is needed to reverse these trends will have several distinct features. It will involve a new form of relationship between the industrialized North and the developing South. Another feature will be a division of responsibility among different levels of governance worldwide. Problems are solved best at the most decentralized level of governance that is consistent with efficient performance of the task. As they transcend boundaries, decision-making can be passed upward as necessary—from the community to the state, national, regional, and, in some rare instances, global level. A third requirement is the active participation of citizens in village, municipal, and national political life, as well as at the United Nations [UN].

Above all, the new partnership calls for an unprecedented degree of international cooperation and coordination. The complex web of ecological, economic, communication, and other connections binding the world together can build a secure future for its citizens by acting alone.

PROTECTING THE GLOBAL ENVIRONMENT

One of the primary ways the world community has responded to the environmental challenge is through the negotiation of treaties and other types of international accords. Nations have agreed on more than 170 ecological treaties—more than two-thirds of them since the 1972 UN Conference on the Human Environment. In 1994, the climate and biological diversity conventions as well as the long-languishing Law of the Sea treaty received enough ratifications to enter into force. In addition, governments signed a

new accord on desertification and land degradation.

These agreements have led to some measurable gains. Air pollution in Europe has been reduced dramatically as a result of the 1979 treaty on transboundary air pollution. Global chlorofluorocarbon (CFC) emissions have dropped 60% from their peak in 1988 following the 1987 treaty on ozone depletion and its subsequent amendments. The killing of elephants has plummeted in Africa because of the 1990 ban on commercial trade in ivory under the Convention on International Trade in Endangered Species of Wild Flora and Fauna. Mining exploration and development have been forbidden in Antarctica for 50 years under a 1991 accord.

The hallmark of international environment governance to date is the Montreal Protocol on the Depletion of the Ozone Layer. First agreed to in September, 1987, and strengthened significantly twice since then, it stipulates that the production of CFCs in industrial countries must be phased out altogether by 1996. It also restricts the use of several other ozone-depleting chemicals, including halons, carbon terachlorides, methyl chloroform, and hydrochlorofluorocarbons. Developing countries have a 10-year grace period in which to meet the terms of the original protocol and its amendments.

While this is a momentous international achievement, the world will have paid a heavy price for earlier inaction. Dangerous levels of ultraviolet radiation will be reaching the Earth for decades to come, stunting agricultural productivity and damaging ecological and human health.

The lessons learned in the ozone treaty are being put to a severe test as the international community begins to confront a more daunting atmospheric challenge—the need to head off climate change. Less than two years after it was signed in Rio, the Framework Convention on Climate Change became international law in March, 1994, when the 50th country (Portugal) ratified it. The speed with which the treaty was ratified was in part a reflection of the fact that it contains few real commitments.

The pact's deliberately ambiguous language urges, but does not require, industrial nations to stabilize emissions of carbon—the primary contributor to global warming—at 1990 levels by the year 2000. Developing nations face no numerical goals whatsoever, though all signatories must conduct inventories of their emissions, submit detailed reports of actions taken to implement the convention, and take climate change into account in all their social, economic, and environmental policies. No specific policy measures are required, however.

As of late 1994, most industrial countries had established national greenhouse gas targets and climate plans, but they vary widely in effectiveness. Among the most ambitious and comprehensive are those of Denmark, the Netherlands, and Switzerland, none of which have powerful oil or coal industries to contend with. Through the use of efficiency standards, renewable energy programs, and limited carbon taxes, these plans are likely to limit emissions significantly in those nations.

According to independent evaluations by various nongovernmental organizations (NGOs), most of the climate plans issued so far will fall short of stabilizing national emissions and the other goals they have set for themselves. For example, Germany and the U.S., two of the largest emitters, have issued climate plans that fail to tackle politically difficult policies—the reduction of coal subsidies in Germany and the increase of gasoline taxes in the U.S. Neither country is likely to meet its stated goals. Reports from Japan suggest that it, too, is unlikely to achieve its stabilization target. In another failure of will, long-standing efforts by the European Union to impose a hybrid carbon/energy tax have failed so far, despite strong support from the European Community.

Even if the goal of holding emissions to 1990 levels in 2000 is met, this falls far short of stabilizing atmospheric concentrations of greenhouse gases, which will require bringing carbon emissions 60–80% below the current levels. As a result, several European countries and the U.S. have voiced cautious support for strengthening the treaty to promote stronger actions, though they have not said exactly how.

As with protecting the atmosphere, preserving biological diversity is something all nations have a stake in and no one country effectively can do alone. One of the most important achievements of the 1993 Convention on Biological Diversity was its recognition that biological resources are the sovereign property of nation-states. When countries can profit from something, they have an incentive to preserve it.

Genetic diversity is worth a lot. The protection that genetic variability affords crops from pests, diseases, and climatic and soil variations is worth $1,000,000,000 to U.S. agriculture. Over all, the economic benefits from wild species to pharmaceuticals, agriculture, forestry, fisheries, and the chemical industry adds up to more than $87,000,000,000 annually—over four percent of the U.S. gross domestic product. Though international pharmaceutical companies have been extracting genes from countries without paying for years, the convention says that gene-rich nations have a right to charge for access to this valuable resource and encourages them to pass legislation to set the terms....

Besides providing a forum for future negotiations, the convention calls for a number of actions by governments to preserve biological wealth. Possible steps in the future include discussions of a protocol on biotechnology, as well as deliberations on international standards for biodiversity prospecting agreements.

The oceans are another natural resource whose protection requires international collaboration. Not only did the Law of the Sea receive sufficient ratifications to enter into force in 1994, agreement also was reached on modifications to the original agreement that are expected to mean that the U.S. and other industrial countries will join in. The rebirth of this treaty comes just in time for the world's oceans and estuaries, which are suffering from overfishing, oil spills, land-based sources of pollution, and other ills....

Just as the Law of the Sea is coming into force, however, its rules are being overtaken by events in one important area—overfishing. In particular, the original treaty failed to resolve the issue of fish stocks that straddle the boundaries of EEZs [Exclusive Economic Zones] and species that migrate long distances. The UN has convened a series of meetings to discuss possible international action to deal with a situation that has seen seafood catch per person fall eight percent since 1989.

CURBING LAND DEGRADATION

The latest addition to the international repertoire of environmental treaties is a convention intended to curb land degradation, adopted in June, 1994. According to the UN Environment Program, the livelihoods of at least 900,000,000 people in about 100 countries are threatened by desertification, which affects about one-quarter of the Earth's land area: The degradation—caused by overgrazing, overcropping, poor irrigation practices, and deforestation, and often exacerbated by climatic variations—poses a serious threat to efforts to raise agricultural productivity worldwide.

The desertification treaty supplies a framework for local projects, encourages national action programs, promotes regional and international cooperation on the transfer of needed technologies, and provides for information exchange and research and training.

Protecting the environment and combating poverty are recognized to be interlinked priorities. The Cairo conference looked at the complex interconnections among population growth, deteriorating social conditions, sexual inequity, environmental degradation, and a range of other issues. A sustainable future can not be secured without an aggressive effort to fight poverty and meet basic social needs.

Trends during the last several decades suggests a mixed record on improving human welfare. Even though impressive progress has been made in boosting immunization rates, reducing infant mortality, and increasing life expectancy, one in three children remains malnourished, more than 1,000,000,000 people lack safe water to drink, and about 1,000,000,000 adults can not read or write. The share of the world's population living in poverty has declined steadily, but the actual numbers continue to rise to more than 1,000,000,000 individuals. Rather than shrinking, the gap between the rich and the poor is growing. In 1960, the richest 20% of the world earned 30 times as much income as the poorest 20%; by 1991, the difference had risen to 61 times as much....

As for poverty, unemployment and social integration, efforts to combat these problems have decreased in recent years, as recession-ridden nations have found it harder and harder to appropriate funds. Few countries have reached the international target of devoting .07% of their gross national product to development assistance, and the amounts that are spent often are not targeted well. Because donor nations have tended to skew their disbursements toward their own security interests, the 10 countries that are home to two-thirds of the world's poorest people get just 32% of total aid expenditures. The richest 40% of the developing world receives twice as much aid per person as the poorest 40%.

Under the proposed 20:20 Compact on Human Development, developing countries would agree to devote 20% of their domestic resources to human priorities and donors would target 20% of their aid funds for such purposes. If this initiative succeeds, it will be making a major contribution to a more sustainable world....

GRASSROOTS OPPOSITION TO SELLING RESOURCES

... Achieving sustainable development requires protecting the rights of local people to control their own resources —whether it be forests, fish, or minerals. Yet, nations and individuals also are

discovering that, if today's transnational challenges are to be mastered, a wider role for international institutions is inevitable.

To respond to this need, considerable reforms are necessary in the United Nations to prepare it for the world of the future. The UN Charter, for example, was written for a different era. Neither "environment" nor "population" even appear in the document. Moreover, though the need for more effective international institutions is clear, people the world over justifiably are worried by the prospect of control of resources being centralized in institutions that are remote from democratic accountability....

Even in the best of circumstances, the slow pace of international diplomacy and the rate at which environmental and social problems are growing worse are difficult to reconcile. The best hope for improving the process of global governance lies with people. Just as national policymaking can not be considered in isolation from public pressure, global policymaking increasingly must consider an organized and influential international citizenry.

... In Rio, the 20,000 concerned citizens and activists who attended from around the globe outnumbered official representatives by at least two to one. More than 4,000 NGOs participated in the Cairo conference, where they widely were credited with helping to shape the terms of the debate....

FORMIDABLE OBSTACLES

Despite their impressive contributions, citizens' groups working at the global level face formidable obstacles. International law traditionally has functioned as a compact among nations, with no provisions for public participation comparable to those that are taken for granted at the national level in democracies around the world. There is nothing yet resembling an elected parliament in the United Nations or any of its agencies. Though the UN has begun to experiment with occasional public hearings on topics of special concern, these continue to be rare events. No formal provisions are made for public review and comment on international treaties or is there a mechanism for bringing citizen suits at the World Court. International negotiations often are closed to public participation, and access to documents of critical interest to the public generally is restricted.

The UN Economic and Social Council is reviewing the rules for the participation of citizens' groups in the UN system at large. Some of those involved in the debate advocate making it easier for groups to be involved, taking the Rio experience as their guide. Others resist this view, worrying about the system being overwhelmed by sheer numbers or about whom the citizens groups are accountable to. The outcome of these deliberations remains to be seen, but it seems likely that the UNCED process has set a new standard for participation that the UN system will have difficulty backing away from.

When it comes to openness and accountability, GATT [General Agreement on Tariffs and Trade] has been subject to particularly strong criticism for its secretive procedures. When a national law is challenged as a trade barrier under GATT, the case is heard behind closed doors by a panel of professors and bureaucrats steeped in the intricacies of world trade law, but not in the needs of the planet. Legal briefs and other critical information generally are unavailable to the public, and there is no opportunity for citizens' groups to testify or make submissions. Governments are discussing rules on public participation for the Trade and Environment Committee of GATT's successor, the World Trade Organization. Preliminary reports suggest that the fight for public access will be a long and hard-fought battle.

Despite a checkered history regarding openness, the World Bank has instituted two new policies that others would do well to emulate. Under an information policy, more of its documents will be available publicly and an information center has been established to disseminate them. The second change—the creation of an independent inspection panel —will provide an impartial forum where board members or private citizens can raise complaints about projects that violate the financial organization's policies, rules, and procedures. Though both initiatives were watered down in the negotiating process, they nonetheless represent sizable chinks in the World Bank's armor. It will be up to the concerned public to test the limits of these new policies and to press for them to be strengthened— and replicated elsewhere.

Besides access to information, the public must become a fuller partner in the development process itself. All too often, "development" has served the purposes of a country's elite, but not its poorest members. A growing body of evidence suggests that, for a project to succeed, the planning process must include the people it is supposed to benefit. In other words, aid should be demand-driven, rather than imposed from above. Several bilateral aid agencies have developed new ways of fostering widespread participation in the development planning process, and the World Bank has come up with a new strategy along these lines. The challenge, as always, will be moving from words to action.

Despite public support for far-reaching changes, the international response to the interlinked threat of ecological collapse and social disintegration remains seriously inadequate. Fifty years ago, with large parts of Europe and Asia in shambles in the wake of World War II, the world community pulled together with an impressive period of institution-building that set the tone for the next half-century. The time has come for a similar burst on innovation to forge the new global partnership that will enable the world to confront the daunting challenges that await it in the next millennium.

If the changes called for in this article are made and the power of public commitment to sustainable development is unleashed, the planet can head off global ecological collapse and the social disintegration that would be sure to accompany it. However, if complacency reigns and international forums generate lots of talks and paper, but little action, the future does not look bright. The choice is ours to make.

NO

Julian L. Simon

MORE PEOPLE, GREATER WEALTH, MORE RESOURCES, HEALTHIER ENVIRONMENT

INTRODUCTION

This is the economic history of humanity in a nutshell: From 2 million or 200,000 or 20,000 or 2,000 years ago until the 18th Century there was slow growth in population, almost no increase in health or decrease in mortality, slow growth in the availability of natural resources (but not increased scarcity), increase in wealth for a few, and mixed effects on the environment. Since then, there has been rapid growth in population due to spectacular decreases in the death rate, rapid growth in resources, widespread increases in wealth, and an unprecedentedly clean and beautiful living environment in many parts of the world, along with a degraded environment in the poor and socialist parts of the world.

That is, more people and more wealth has correlated with more (rather than less) resources and a cleaner environment—just the opposite of what Malthusian theory leads one to believe. The task before us is to make sense of these mind-boggling happy trends.

The current gloom-and-doom about a "crisis" of our environment is all wrong on the scientific facts. Even the U. S. Environmental Protection Agency acknowledges that U.S. air and our water have been getting cleaner rather than dirtier in the past few decades. Every agricultural economist knows that the world's population has been eating ever-better since World War II. Every resource economist knows that all natural resources have been getting more available rather than more scarce, as shown by their falling prices over the decades and centuries. And every demographer knows that the death rate has been falling all over the world—life expectancy almost tripling in the rich countries in the past two centuries, and almost doubling in the poor countries in just the past four decades.

The picture also is now clear that population growth does not hinder economic development. In the 1980s there was a complete reversal in the consensus of thinking of population economists about the effects of more people. In 1986, the National Research Council and the National Academy of Sciences completely overturned its "official" view away from the earlier worried view expressed in 1971. It noted the absence of any statistical evidence of a negative connection between population increase and economic growth. And it said that "The scarcity of exhaustible resources is at most a minor restraint on economic growth."

This U-turn by the scientific consensus of experts on the subject has gone unacknowledged by the press, the antinatalist [anti-birth] environmental organizations, and the agencies that foster population control abroad.

Here is my central assertion: Almost every economic and social change or trend points in a positive direction, as long as we view the matter over a reasonably long period of time.

For proper understanding of the important aspects of an economy we should look at the long-run trends. But the short-run comparisons—between the sexes, age groups, races, political groups, which are usually purely relative—make more news. To repeat, just about every important long-run measure of human welfare shows improvement over the decades and centuries, in the United States as well as in the rest of the world. And there is no persuasive reason to believe that these trends will not continue indefinitely.

Would I bet on it? For sure. I'll bet a week's or month's pay—anything I win goes to pay for more research—that just about any trend pertaining to material human welfare will improve rather than get worse. You pick the comparison and the year.

THE FACTS

Let's quickly review a few data on how human life has been doing, beginning with the all-important issue, life itself.

The Conquest of Too-Early Death

The most important and amazing demographic fact—the greatest human achievement in history, in my view—is the decrease in the world's death rate.... It took thousands of years to increase life expectancy at birth from just over 20 years to the high 20's about 1750. Then, about 1750, life expectancy in the richest countries suddenly took off and tripled in about two centuries. In just the past two centuries the length of life you could expect for your baby or yourself in the advanced countries jumped from less than 30 years to perhaps 75 years. What greater event has humanity witnessed than this conquest of premature death in the rich countries? It is this decrease in the death rate that is the cause of there being a larger world population nowadays than in former times.

Then starting well after World War II, since the 1950s, the length of life you could expect in the poor countries has leaped upwards by perhaps fifteen or even twenty years, caused by advances in agriculture, sanitation, and medicine.

Let's put it differently. In the 19th century the planet Earth could sustain only one billion people. Ten thousand years ago, only 4 million could keep themselves alive. Now, 5 billion people are living longer and more healthily than ever before, on average. The increase in the world's population represents our victory over death.

Here arises a crucial issue of interpretation: One would expect lovers of humanity to jump with joy at this triumph

Figure 1
Copper Prices Indexed by Wages

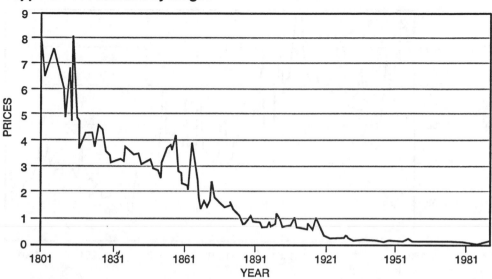

of human mind and organization over the raw killing forces of nature. Instead, many lament that there are so many people alive to enjoy the gift of life.... And it is this worry that leads them to approve the Indonesian, Chinese and other inhumane programs of coercion and denial of personal liberty in one of the most precious choices a family can make—the number of children that it wishes to bear and raise.

The Decreasing Scarcity of Natural Resources

Throughout history, the supply of natural resources always has worried people. Yet the data clearly show that natural resource scarcity—as measured by the economically-meaningful indicator of cost or price—has been decreasing rather than increasing in the long run for all raw materials, with only temporary exceptions from time to time. That is, availability has been increasing. Consider copper,

which is representative of all the metals. In Figure 1 we see the price relative to wages since 1801. The cost of a ton is only about a tenth now of what it was two hundred years ago.

This trend of falling prices of copper has been going on for a very long time. In the 18th century B.C.E. [before the Common Era] in Babylonia under Hammurabi—almost 4000 years ago—the price of copper was about a thousand times its price in the United States now relative to wages. At the time of the Roman Empire the price was about a hundred times the present price.

In Figure 2 we see the price of copper relative to the consumer price index. Everything that we buy—pens, shirts, tires—has been getting cheaper over the years because we know how to make them cheaper, especially during the past 200 years. Even so, the extraordinary fact is that natural resources have been get-

Figure 2
Copper Prices Divided by CPI

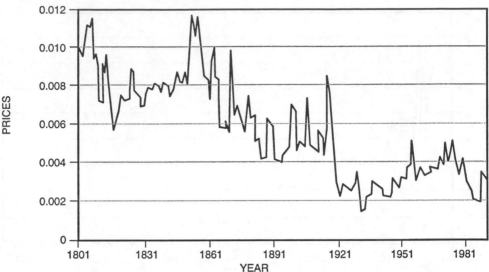

ting cheaper even faster than consumer goods.

So by any measure, natural resources have been getting more available rather than more scarce. ...

Regarding oil, the shocking price rises during the 1970s and 1980s were not caused by growing scarcity in the world supply. And indeed, the price of petroleum in inflation-adjusted dollars has returned to levels about where they were before the politically-induced increases, and the price of gasoline is about at the historic low and still falling. Concerning energy in general, there is no reason to believe that the supply of energy is finite, or that the price of energy will not continue its long-run decrease forever. ...

Food is an especially important resource. The evidence is particularly strong for food that we are on a benign trend despite rising population. The long-run price of food relative to wages is now only perhaps a tenth as much as it was in 1800 in the United States. Even relative to consumer products the price of grain is down, due to increased productivity, just as with all other primary products.

Famine deaths due to insufficient food supply have decreased even in absolute terms, let alone relative to population, in the past century, a matter which pertains particularly to the poor countries. Per-person food consumption is up over the last 30 years. And there are no data showing that the bottom of the income scale is faring worse, or even has failed to share in the general improvement, as the average has improved.

Africa's food production per person is down, but by 1994 almost no one any longer claims that Africa's suffering results from a shortage of land or water or sun. The cause of hunger in Africa is a combination of civil wars and collectivization of agriculture, which periodic droughts have made more murderous.

Here let us digress from the general discussion to a resource which has been of special historical interest... in the Netherlands—agricultural land. Let's consider it as an example of all natural resources. Though many people consider land to be a special kind of resource, it is subject to the same processes of human creation as other natural resources. The most important fact about agricultural land is that less and less of it is needed as the decades pass. This idea is utterly counter-intuitive. It seems entirely obvious that a growing world population would need larger amounts of farmland. But the title of a remarkable prescient article in 1951 by Theodore Schultz tells the story: "The Declining Economic Importance of Land."

The increase in actual and potential productivity per unit of land have grown much faster than population, and there is sound reason to expect this trend to continue. Therefore, there is less and less reason to worry about the supply of land. Though the stock of usable land seems fixed at any moment, it is constantly being increased—at a rapid rate in many cases—by the clearing of new land or reclamation of wasteland. Land also is constantly being enhanced by increasing the number of crops grown per year on each unit of land and by increasing the yield per crop with better farming methods and with chemical fertilizer. Last but not least, land is created anew where there was no land.

There is only one important resource which has shown a trend of increasing scarcity rather than increasing abundance. That resource is the most important of all—human beings. Yes, there are more people on earth now than ever before. But if we measure the scarcity of people the same way that we measure the scarcity of other economic goods—by how much we must pay to obtain their services—we see that wages and salaries have been going up all over the world, in poor countries as well as in rich countries. The amount that you must pay to obtain the services of a barber or a cook has risen in India, just as the price of a barber or cook—or economist—has risen in the United States over the decades. This increase in the price of peoples' services is a clear indication that people are becoming more scarce even though there are more of us.

About pollution now: Surveys show that the public believes that our air and water have been getting more polluted in recent years. The evidence with respect to air indicates that pollutants have been declining, especially the main pollutant, particulates. (See Figure 3.) With respect to water, the proportion of monitoring sites in the United States with water of good drinkability has increased since the data began in 1961. (See Figure 4.)

Every forecast of the doomsayers has turned out flat wrong. Metals, foods, and other natural resources have become more available rather than more scarce throughout the centuries. The famous Famine 1975 forecast by the Paddock brothers—that we would see millions of famine deaths in the United States on television in the 1970s—was followed instead by gluts in agricultural markets. Paul Ehrlich's primal scream about "What will we do when the [gasoline] pumps run dry?" was followed by gasoline cheaper than since the 1930s. The Great Lakes are not dead; instead they offer better sport fishing than ever. The main pollutants, especially the particulates which have killed people

Figure 3

National Ambient Concentrations of Pollutants

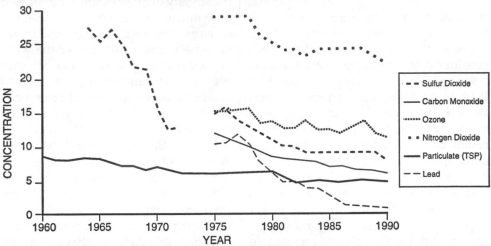

Source: Council on Environmental Quality, Environmental Quality, 22nd Annual Report, 1992, p. 276
Council on Environmental Quality, Environmental Quality 1981, 12th Annual Report, 1981, p. 243
Sulfur 1964 through 1972: EPA (1973): 32 stations

for years, have lessened in our cities. (Socialist countries are a different and tragic environmental story, however!)

... But nothing has reduced the doom-sayers' credibility with the press or their command over the funding resources of the federal government....

With respect to population growth: A dozen competent statistical studies, starting in 1967 with an analysis by Nobel prizewinner Simon Kuznets, agree that there is no negative statistical relationship between economic growth and population growth. There is strong reason to believe that more people have a positive effect in the long run.

Population growth does not lower the standard of living—all the evidence agrees. And the evidence supports the view that population growth raises it in the long run.

Incidentally, it was those statistical studies that converted me in about 1968

from working in favor of population control to the point of view that I hold today. I certainly did not come to my current view for any political or religious or ideological reason.

The basic method is to gather data on each country's rate of population growth and its rate of economic growth, and then to examine whether—looking at all the data in the sample together—the countries with high population growth rates have economic growth rates lower than average, and countries with low population growth rates have economic growth rates higher than average. All the studies agree in concluding that this is not so; there is no correlation between economic growth and population growth in the intermediate run.

Of course one can adduce cases of countries that seemingly are exceptions to the pattern. It is the genius of statistical inference, however, to enable us to

Figure 4

National Ambient Water Quality in Rivers and Streams, 1973–1990

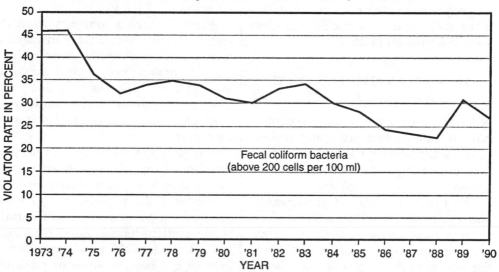

Source: Statistical Abstract of the United States, various issues

draw valid generalizations from samples that contain such wide variations in behavior. The exceptions can be useful in alerting us to possible avenues for further analysis, but as long as they are only exceptions, they do not prove that the generalization is not meaningful or useful.

The research-wise person may wonder whether population density is a more meaningful variable than population growth. And indeed, such studies have been done. And again, the statistical evidence directly contradicts the common-sense conventional wisdom. If you make a chart with population density on the horizontal axis and either the income level or the rate of change of income on the vertical axis, you will see that higher density is associated with better rather than poorer economic results....

The most important benefit of population size and growth is the increase it

brings to the stock of useful knowledge. Minds matter economically as much as, or more than, hands or mouths. Progress is limited largely by the availability of trained workers. The more people who enter our population by birth or immigration, the faster will be the rate of progress of our material and cultural civilization.

Here we need a qualification that tends to get overlooked: I do not say that all is well everywhere, and I do not predict that all will be rosy in the future. Children are hungry and sick; people live out lives of physical or intellectual poverty, and lack of opportunity; war or some new pollution may finish us off. What I am saying is that for most relevant economic matters I have checked, the aggregate trends are improving rather than deteriorating.

Also, I don't say that a better future happens automatically or without effort. It will happen because women and men will struggle with problems with muscle and mind, and will probably overcome, as people have overcome in the past— if the social and economic system gives them opportunity to do so.

THE EXPLANATION OF THESE AMAZING TRENDS

Now we need some theory to explain how it can be that economic welfare grows along with population, rather than humanity being reduced to misery and poverty as population grows.

The Malthusian theory of increasing scarcity, based on supposedly-fixed resources—the theory that the doomsayers rely upon—runs exactly contrary to the data over the long sweep of history. Therefore it makes sense to prefer another theory.

The theory that fits the facts very well is this: More people, and increased income, cause problems in the short run. Short-run scarcity raises prices. This presents opportunity, and prompts the search for solutions. In a free society, solutions are eventually found. And in the long run the new developments leave us better off than if the problems had not arisen.

To put it differently, in the short-run, more consumers mean less of the fixed available stock of goods to be divided among more people. And more workers laboring with the same fixed current stock of capital mean that there will be less output per worker. The latter effect, known as "the law of diminishing returns," is the essence of Malthus's theory as he first set it out.

But if the resources with which people work are not fixed over the period being analyzed, then the Malthusian logic of diminishing returns does not apply. And the plain fact is that, given some time to adjust to shortages, the resource base does not remain fixed. People create more resources of all kinds.

When we take a long-run view, the picture is different, and considerably more complex, than the simple short-run view of more people implying lower average income. In the very long run, more people almost surely imply more available resources and a higher income for everyone.

I suggest you test this idea against your own knowledge: Do you think that our standard of living would be as high as it is now if the population had never grown from about four million human beings perhaps ten thousand years ago? I don't think we'd now have electric light or gas heat or autos or penicillin or travel to the moon or our present life expectancy of over seventy years at birth in rich countries, in comparison to the life expectancy of 20 to 25 years at birth in earlier eras, if population had not grown to its present numbers....

THE ROLE OF ECONOMIC FREEDOM

Here we must address another crucial element in the economics of resources and population—the extent to which the political-social-economic system provides personal freedom from government coercion. Skilled persons require an appropriate social and economic framework that provides incentives for working hard and taking risks, enabling their talents to flower and come to fruition. The key elements of such a framework are economic liberty, respect for property, and fair and sensible rules of the market that are enforced equally for all.

The world's problem is not too many people, but lack of political and economic freedom. Powerful evidence comes from an extraordinary natural experiment that occurred starting in the 1940s with three pairs of countries that have the same culture and history, and had much the same standard of living when they split apart after World War II—East and West Germany, North and South Korea, Taiwan and China. In each case the centrally planned communist country began with less population "pressure," as measured by density per square kilometer, than did the market-directed economy. And the communist and non-communist countries also started with much the same birth rates.

The market-directed economies have performed much better economically than the centrally-planned economies. The economic-political system clearly was the dominant force in the results of the three comparisons. This powerful explanation of economic development cuts the ground from under population growth as a likely explanation of the speed of nations' economic development.

THE ASTOUNDING SHIFT IN SCHOLARLY CONSENSUS

So far we've been discussing the factual evidence. But in 1994 there is an important new element not present twenty years ago. The scientific community of scholars who study population economics now agrees with almost all of what is written above. The statements made above do not represent a single lone voice, but rather the current scientific consensus.

The conclusions offered earlier about agriculture and resources and demographic trends have always represented the consensus of economists in those fields. And ... the consensus of popula-tion economists also is now not far from what is written here.

In 1986, the U.S. National Research Council and the U.S. National Academy of Sciences published a book on population growth and economic development prepared by a prestigious scholarly group. This "official" report reversed almost completely the frightening conclusions of the previous 1971 NAS report. "Population growth [is] at most a minor factor.... The scarcity of exhaustible resources is at most a minor constraint on economic growth," it now says. It found benefits of additional people as well as costs.

A host of review articles by distinguished economic demographers in the past decade have confirmed that this "revisionist" view is indeed consistent with the scientific evidence, though not all the writers would go as far as I do in pointing out the positive long-run effects of population growth. The consensus is more toward a "neutral" judgment. But this is a huge change from the earlier judgment that population growth is economically detrimental.

By 1994, anyone who asserts that population growth damages the economy must either turn a blind eye to the scientific evidence, or be blatantly dishonest intellectually.

SUMMARY AND CONCLUSION

In the short run, all resources are limited. An example of such a finite resource is the amount of time allotted to me to speak. The longer run, however, is a different story. The standard of living has risen along with the size of the world's population since the beginning of recorded time. There is no convincing economic reason why these trends toward a better life should not continue indefinitely.

The key theoretical idea is this: The growth of population and of income create actual and expected shortages, and hence lead to price run-ups. A price increase represents an opportunity that attracts profit-minded entrepreneurs to seek new ways to satisfy the shortages. Some fail, at cost to themselves. A few succeed, and the final result is that we end up better off than if the original shortage problems had never arisen. That is, we need our problems though this does not imply that we should purposely create additional problems for ourselves.

I hope that you will now agree that the long-run outlook is for a more abundant material life rather than for increased scarcity, in the United States and in the world as a whole. Of course such progress does not come about automatically. And my message certainly is not one of complacency. In this I agree with the doomsayers—that our world needs the best efforts of all humanity to improve our lot. I part company with them in that they expect us to come to a bad end despite the efforts we make, whereas I expect a continuation of humanity's history of successful efforts. And I believe that their message is self-fulfilling, because if you expect your efforts to fail because of inexorable natural limits, then you are likely to feel resigned; and therefore to literally resign. But if you recognize the possibility—in fact the probability—of success, you can tap large reservoirs of energy and enthusiasm.

Adding more people causes problems, but people are also the means to solve these problems. The main fuel to speed the world's progress is our stock of knowledge, and the brakes are (a) our lack of imagination and (b) unsound social regulations of these activities. The ultimate resource is people—especially skilled, spirited, and hopeful young people endowed with liberty—who will exert their wills and imaginations for their own benefit, and so inevitably they will benefit not only themselves but the rest of us as well.

REFERENCES

Schultz, Theodore W., "The Declining Economic Importance of Land," *Economic Journal,* LXI, December, 1951, pp. 725–740.
National Research Council, Committee on Population, and Working Group on Population Growth and Economic Development, *Population Growth and Economic Development: Policy Questions* (Washington, D.C.: National Academy Press, 1986).

POSTSCRIPT

Is There a Global Environmental Crisis?

Some, such as French, say that we have exceeded the boundaries of responsibility. Others who take this view classify environmental issues as affecting national security. This perspective can be found in Gareth Porter, "Environmental Security as a National Security Issue," *Current History* (May 1995) and in Jessica Tuchman Matthews, "The Environment and International Security," in Michael T. Klare and Daniel C. Thomas, eds., *World Security: Challenges for a New Century* (St. Martin's Press, 1994). Simon and other technological optimists contend that we already have or can devise the technology to continue our development and enhance the existence of less developed countries while protecting—even improving—the environment. They may be correct, and it certainly is more comforting to believe Simon's optimistic view than to accept French's more dire outlook.

Even if Simon is correct, it is important not to ignore the costs of sustainable development. Simon does not deny that these exist. Because of population and economic development patterns, the less developed countries require particular care and assistance. It is easy to preach about not cutting down Brazilian rain forests or not poaching cheetah skins in Kenya. But what do you say to the poor Brazilian who is trying to scratch out a living by clearing cropland or grazing land? What do you tell the equally poor Kenyan who is trying to earn a few dollars in order to supply food for his family? Questions such as these have brought environmental issues much closer to the forefront of world political concerns. One exploration of efforts to balance costs and benefits can be found in Frances Cairncross, "Environmental Pragmatism," *Foreign Policy* (Summer 1994).

If the changes that need to occur are going to be put in place before further massive environmental degradation occurs, there will have to be a massive flow of expensive technology and financial assistance from the developed to the less developed countries. The EDCs resisted LDC demands for vastly increased aid at the Rio Conference. Based on their perceived economic self-interest, EDCs watered down the global warming and biodiversity treaties. Some refused to sign one or the other of them. You can learn more about the international response in Nazli Choucri, ed., *Global Accord: Environmental Challenges and International Responses* (MIT Press, 1995).

Would you be willing to pay an environmental protection tax of, say, 1 percent of your earnings to the United Nations for global programs? Would you be willing to forgo driving your car most of the time? Would you be willing to accept UN-mandated restrictions on the economic activity of your country? If not, what *is* the answer?

PART 3

THEY SHALL BEAT THEIR SWORDS INTO PLOWSHARES, AND THEIR SPEARS INTO PRUNING HOOKS. NATION SHALL NOT LIFT UP SWORD AGAINST NATION. NEITHER SHALL THEY LEARN WAR ANY MORE

International Security and World Politics

Whatever we may wish, war, terrorism, and other forms of physical coercion are still important elements of international politics. Countries calculate both how to use the instruments of force and how to implement national security. There can be little doubt, however, that significant changes are under way in this realm as part of the changing world system. Strong pressures exist to expand the mission and strengthen the security capabilities of international organizations and to reduce or eliminate nuclear weapons worldwide. This section examines how countries in the international system are addressing these issues.

- Was Dropping Atomic Bombs on Japan Justifiable?

- Does the World Need to Have Nuclear Weapons at All?

- Should a Permanent UN Military Force Be Established?

ISSUE 11

Was Dropping Atomic Bombs on Japan Justifiable?

YES: Donald Kagan, from "Why America Dropped the Bomb," *Commentary* (September 1995)

NO: John Rawls, from "Fifty Years After Hiroshima," *Dissent* (Summer 1995)

ISSUE SUMMARY

YES: Donald Kagan, a professor of history and classics, contends that using the atomic bombs on Japan was justified because a costly invasion was the only other strategy that would have compelled the Japanese to surrender.

NO: Political philosopher John Rawls examines the dropping of the atomic bombs on Japan from the perspective of just-war theory and finds that the attack did not satisfy the principles governing the just conduct of war.

At 8:16 A.M. on August 6, 1945, an American B-29 bomber that its pilot, Colonel Paul W. Tibbets, had named the *Enola Gay* after his mother dropped a single atomic bomb on the city of Hiroshima, Japan. The city was of such peripheral military importance that it had been spared the fierce bombing attacks that had devastated many other Japanese cities. Indeed, the coming of the lone B-29 and its three escorts seemed of such little consequence that, instead of seeking shelter, many in Hiroshima had gone about their business. As it turned out, it did not make much difference whether or not those in the center of the city had ignored the approaching enemy bomber. Forty-three seconds after the *Enola Gay*'s bombardier released the bomb, nicknamed "Little Boy," there was a tremendous flash. Both the people on the streets of Hiroshima and those in their shelters were incinerated. Somewhere between 80,000 and 120,000 Japanese died instantly; a more accurate toll is impossible because many victims simply were vaporized. Three days later another B-29 dropped a second bomb, dubbed "Fat Man." This time the target was Nagasaki. Another 50,000 people died of burns, blast, and radiation.

The question is: Was it necessary?

One factor that makes this question so compelling more than a half century later is that there are so many ways to frame the issue. One approach relates to whether the use of atomic weapons was, or today would be, so terrible as to be unique in its moral implications or whether a nuclear weapon is simply one more weapon of war that bears no special onus.

There are grounds to argue that nuclear weapons are a category unto themselves. The Hiroshima bomb erupted in a huge fireball of several million degrees in temperature that flattened or set on fire a 13-square-mile city. At 8:00 A.M. there were 76,000 buildings in Hiroshima. At 8:00 P.M. 48,000 of those structures were entirely obliterated; another 12,000 were severely damaged. Of the 340,000 residents, almost half were already dead or were doomed by radiation poisoning.

Yet, for all the massive instantaneous death and destruction, it is also possible to argue that it was just more of the same. The ferocity of World War II, combined with the technological capabilities of the combatants, had already wreaked unparalleled havoc. At least 40 million people were dead by August 6, 1945; the two atomic attacks increased the war's death toll by less than one half of one percent. Moreover, the massive bombing of largely civilian targets was common. The Japanese themselves had terror-bombed Shanghai; the Germans had sent bombers and rockets against London; Americans and British bombers had utterly destroyed numerous German cities. And fire-bomb raids on Tokyo had consumed perhaps 84,000 civilians. As such, some people have argued that the atomic bombing of Japan was not a seminal event at all; it was merely the continuation of strategic bombing, only with a much more effective weapon.

Another approach to evaluating the necessity of the atomic attacks in 1945 is to ask whether or not they were necessary to end the war. Historians continue to debate whether the Japanese would have soon surrendered anyway; whether some sort of nondeadly demonstration of the bomb could have frightened Tokyo into surrendering and preclude the necessity of destroying two cities and their populations; and whether an invasion of the Japanese main islands would have been necessary to subdue Japan and, if so, how high American and Japanese casualties would have been compared to the death toll in Hiroshima and Nagasaki.

A third approach to considering the use of atomic bombs, then or now, has to do with the just conduct of war. Dating back as far as Aristotle, and particularly focusing on the writings of two Christian theological philosophers, Saint Augustine and Saint Thomas Acquinas, there is a long line of thought based on Western cultural tradition that relates to what in Latin is called *jus in bello* (just conduct of war). There are two principal standards of *jus in bello*. First, war should be waged according to the standard of "proportionality"; that is, the amount of force used should be proportionate to the threat. Second, the use of war should engage the standard of "discrimination"; noncombatants should not be intentional targets, and attacks on military targets should be conducted in a way that will minimize civilian casualties.

The following selections contain elements of each of these three approaches. Donald Kagan argues that the atomic attacks on Japan were necessary, even advisable. John Rawls argues that the barbarity of war does not free a civilized society from the duty to make moral choices.

YES

Donald Kagan

WHY AMERICA DROPPED THE BOMB

The 50th anniversary of the use of atomic bombs on Hiroshima and Nagasaki has produced a wholly predictable debate over the necessity and morality of that decision. Or perhaps debate is the wrong word. All too typical of [the] commemorative activities was a proposed exhibit on Hiroshima at the Smithsonian Institution in Washington; the script for this exhibit presented a picture, in the words of an irate *Wall Street Journal* editorial, of a "besieged Japan yearning for peace" and lying "at the feet of an implacably violent enemy—the United States." Although the exhibit was subsequently canceled, it encapsulated a point of view that has now endured for a full half-century, and shows no sign of waning.

*   *   *

On August 6, 1945 the American war plane *Enola Gay* dropped an atomic bomb on Hiroshima, killing between 70,000 and 100,000 Japanese. Three days later another atomic device was exploded over Nagasaki. Within a few days Japan surrendered, and the terrible struggle that we call World War II was over.

At the time, the American people cheered the bombings without restraint, and for the simplest of reasons. As the literary historian Paul Fussell, then a combat soldier expecting to take part in the anticipated invasion of Japan, would later recall:

> We learned to our astonishment that we would not be obliged in a few months to rush up the beaches near Tokyo assault-firing while being machine-gunned, mortared, and shelled, and for all the practiced phlegm of our tough façades we broke down and cried with relief and joy. We were going to live.

At that moment, few if any Americans doubted that the purpose of this first use of atomic bombs was to bring the war to the swiftest possible end, and thereby to avert American casualties.

But the moment was short-lived. As early as 1946, challenges to the dominant opinion appeared and soon multiplied. To a large extent, the early revisionists ... were influenced by the emerging cold war, whose origins, for the most part, they attributed to American policy under President Truman. As one exemplar of the new revisionist movement put it:

The bomb was dropped primarily for its effect not on Japan but on the Soviet Union. One, to force a Japanese surrender before the USSR came into the Far Eastern war, and two, to show under war conditions the power of the bomb. Only in this way could a policy of intimidation [of the Soviet Union] be successful.

... In 1965, in *Atomic Diplomacy: Hiroshima and Potsdam*, Gar Alperovitz picked up the main themes of the earlier writers, arguing for them now on the basis of new documentation and in a cultural climate—the climate of the mid-60's—newly hospitable to revisionist interpretations of American motives and behavior. According to Alperovitz, the bombs were not needed "to end the war and save lives—and... this was understood by American leaders at the time." Their aim, he wrote, was political, not military; their target was not Japan but the Soviet Union.

The chief villain was Harry Truman, who, in Alperovitz's reading, was bent on reversing Franklin D. Roosevelt's policy of peaceful accommodation with the Soviets. Thus, when he learned of the prospect of the bomb, Truman decided to delay the Allied [U.S.-U.K.-U.S.S.R.] meeting at Potsdam until the weapon could be tested. If it worked, he could take a tougher line in Eastern Europe and, perhaps, end the war before the Soviets were able to make gains in East Asia. In his eagerness to achieve these political goals, Truman failed to give proper attention to Japanese peace feelers; refused to change the demand

for unconditional surrender, which was a barrier to Japanese acceptance of peace terms; and did not wait to see if Soviet entry into the Asian war might by itself cause Japan to surrender. In short, the confidence provided by the American monopoly on atomic weapons allowed Truman to launch, at Japan's expense, a "diplomatic offensive" against the Soviet Union, one which would play a role of great importance in engendering the subsequent cold war.

Because of his more detailed arguments, resting in part on newly available documents; because protest over the Vietnam war was raising questions about the origins of the cold war; and because a new generation of American diplomatic historians, trained or influenced by early revisionists... had come onto the academic scene, Alperovitz's book enjoyed great influence and established the direction which the debate over Hiroshima has taken up to this very day. Indeed, Alperovitz is in many ways the "dean" of atomic revisionism....

* * *

Alperovitz's eminence is all the more remarkable in that both his chief thesis and most of his arguments have, from their first appearance, been shredded by other scholars, his fellow revisionists among them.... [R]evisionist critics found, in the words of a 1974 summary of their views, that

the book strained the evidence, failed critically to assess sources, neglected the Roosevelt period, addressed the wrong questions, exaggerated the impact of the bomb, misunderstood Truman, and forced events into a dubious pattern.

This new generation of revisionists, notably Martin J. Sherwin and Barton J.

Bernstein, stressed the essential continuity between the policies of Truman and those of Roosevelt, who had also insisted on secrecy and on keeping information about the atomic bomb away from the Soviets. Where Sherwin found no evidence of an elaborately planned showdown or "strategy of delay" in dealing with the Russians, Bernstein was even more emphatic. In his view, the hope of using the atomic bomb to produce and "cement" a peace that was to America's liking was only "a tasty bonus," and was in no way "essential to propel American leaders in 1945 to use the bomb on Japan."

These, the findings of two of the most scholarly revisionist historians, amounted to a rejection of a basic tenet of the tradition as represented by Alperovitz. And yet, even as they demolished his arguments, the new revisionists remained wedded to a number of his major conclusions. By the time these newer scholars appeared on the scene, condemnation of the bomb had become a central element in the larger revisionist project of proving the general error and evil of American policy, and for many it could not be abandoned, whatever the cost in faithfulness to the evidence. And so, even as they conceded that the bomb had not been used to advance the incipient cold-war political interests of the U.S., they shifted the central ground of argument to another question. Granting that the bomb had been used to bring the war to a swift end in order to avoid an invasion of Japan and the consequent loss of American lives, they proceeded to question whether it was either a necessary or a morally acceptable means to that end. Their answer was: no.

* * *

That, in a nutshell, is the answer that is still being given today, and where the argument has to be engaged. For the school that I have called "revisionist" now represents something more like a scholarly consensus, not to say a conventional wisdom universally parroted by educators, pundits, and the popular media. . . .

Let us begin with the first line of revisionist attack, which is to question whether an invasion of Japan would have been so costly in American lives as to justify the use of atomic bombs in order to avoid it.

In his memoirs, President Truman wrote that an invasion of the Japanese home islands would have entailed the loss of 500,000 American lives. In their own respective memoirs, Secretary of War Henry Stimson and Secretary of State James Byrnes proposed the figure of one million lives, or one million casualties overall. The revisionists have pounced on both these estimates, producing lengthy arguments to show that they are impossible and leaving the impression that the numbers were cut from whole cloth to justify the bombings after the fact. All this is meant to undermine the probity of American leaders by showing them to be liars: if anticipated casualties at the time were fewer than the claims made after the war, the revisionists argue, then fear of such casualties could not have been the motive for dropping the bomb.

But some anticipations of casualties at the time were in fact quite high. A study done in August 1944 for the Joint Chiefs of Staff projected that an invasion of Japan would "cost a half-million American lives and many more that number in wounded." . . . There is every reason to believe that such round, frightening numbers lingered in the minds of Truman and Stimson long after they were first received, and that they haunted all future deliberations.

More precise estimates were made nearer in time to the use of the bombs. In preparation for a meeting with President Truman scheduled for June 18, 1945, the army's Chief of Staff, General George C. Marshall, asked General Douglas MacArthur for a figure of American casualties in the projected invasion of Kyushu.... Marshall was shocked by MacArthur's reply: 105,050 battle casualties (dead and wounded) in the first 90 days alone, and another 12,600 casualties among American noncombatants. Marshall called these figures unacceptably high.

* * *

In connection with that same meeting on June 18, the document that has received the most attention by revisionists is a study by the Joint War Plans Committee, prepared on June 15. It estimated that casualties in an invasion of southern Kyushu on November 1, followed some months later by an assault on the Tokyo plain, would be a relatively low 40,000 dead, 150,000 wounded, and 3,500 missing, for a total of 193,500 casualties in the entire two-pronged operation.

There are, however, several problems with these estimates. To begin with, they did not include naval casualties, although experience at Okinawa showed these were certain to be numerous. A separate estimate did exist for such losses —9,700 in the Kyushu invasion—but it excluded the unknowable number of casualties that would be suffered by American soldiers and sailors on transports struck by kamikaze attacks. Intercepted Japanese military messages revealed that

the Japanese had about 10,000 planes, half of them kamikazes, to defend the home islands. In addition, the Japanese counted on flying bombs, human torpedoes, suicide-attack boats, midget suicide submarines, motorboat bombs, and navy swimmers to be used as human mines. All of these "had been used at Okinawa and the Philippines with lethal results," and the intercepts showed that they were now being placed on Kyushu.

The report offering the figure of 40,000 dead, moreover, was peppered with disclaimers that casualties "are not subject to accurate estimate" and that the estimate was "admittedly only an educated guess." Indeed, when the report went from the original committee up to the Joint planners, it omitted the casualty figures altogether on the grounds that they were "not subject to accurate estimate." The document then went to Assistant Chief of Staff General John E. Hull. In his accompanying memorandum to General Marshall, Hull suggested that losses in the first 30 days in Kyushu would be on the order of those taken at Luzon, or about 1,000 casualties per day. Hull's memorandum, and not the committee report listing specific figures, was read out by Marshall at the June 18 conference with the President.

At the meeting itself, Fleet Admiral William D. Leahy, chairman of the Joint Chiefs, suggested that Luzon was not as sound an analogy as Okinawa. There, American casualties had run to 75,000, or some 35 percent of the attacking force. "Marshall," writes the historian Edward Drea, "allowed that 766,700 assault troops would be employed against Kyushu. Although unstated, a 35-percent casualty rate translated to more than a quarter-million American casualties." As for the President, he was very mindful of the bloodbath at Okinawa, and he demanded the "Joint Chiefs' assurance that an invasion of Kyushu would neither repeat that savagery nor degenerate into race war." There is no evidence that Truman ever saw or heard the omitted low figures for the entire operation that had been drawn up by the Joint War Plans Committee.

But whatever the value of any of these estimates, they soon became obsolete. Marshall's calculation rested on the assumption that Kyushu would be defended by eight Japanese divisions, or fewer than 300,000 men, and that American domination of the sea and air would make reinforcement impossible. Intercepts of Japanese military communications soon made a mockery of those expectations. By July 21, the estimate of Japanese troops on Kyushu had grown to 455,000; by the end of the month, to 525,000. Colonel Charles A. Willoughby, MacArthur's intelligence officer, took note of the new situation: "This threatening development, if not checked, may grow to a point where we attack on a ratio of one (1) to one (1), which is not the recipe for victory." Soon the number of Japanese troops on Kyushu rose to 680,000 and, on July 31, a medical estimate projected American battle and non-battle casualties needing treatment at 394,859. This figure, of course, excluded those killed at once, who would be beyond treatment.

Years later, in a letter, Truman described a meeting in the last week of July at which Marshall suggested the invasion would cost "at a minimum one-quarter-of-a-million casualties, and might cost as much as a million, on the American side alone, with an equal number of the enemy. The other military and naval men present agreed." If Truman's recollection was accurate, this may have been the last such estimate before the dropping of the bomb; but whether accurate or not, there can be no doubt that Marshall's own concern did not abate even after Hiroshima. On the very next day he sent a message to MacArthur expressing alarm at the Japanese strength on southern Kyushu, and asking for alternative invasion sites. On August 11, five days after Hiroshima, three days after the Soviets had entered the war, and two days after Nagasaki, when the Japanese had still not surrendered, Marshall thought it would be necessary "to continue a prolonged struggle" and even raised the possibility of using atomic bombs as tactical weapons against massed enemy troops during the invasion.

As the foregoing suggests, it was, and remains, impossible to make convincing estimates of the casualties to be expected in case of an American invasion of the Japanese home islands. From the beginning the debate has been tendentious, distracting attention from more important questions. The large numbers offered by Stimson and Truman in their memoirs may not have been accurate, but the attacks on those numbers by the revisionists are at least as suspect. No one can be sure that the true figure would have been closer to the lower than to the higher estimates.

In any case, what matters is not what American leaders claimed after the war, but what they believed before the atomic bombs were used. On that point, there can be no doubt. In discussions that were not shaped by attempts to justify using the bomb, since it had not yet even been tested, men like Truman, Stimson, and Marshall were deeply worried over the scale of American casualties—whatever their precise number—that were certain to be incurred by an invasion. The President could not face another Okinawa, much less something greater. That is all we need to know to understand why he and his associates were prepared to use the bomb.

Yet this conclusion, supported both by the evidence and by common sense, has been furiously resisted by revisionists and their large cohorts of fellow-travelers. Thus, a 1990 account of the current state of the question reports: "The consensus among scholars is that the bomb was not needed to avoid an invasion of Japan and to end the war within a relatively short time... an invasion was a remote possibility." This would have been welcome news indeed to General Marshall, who as we have seen was deeply concerned about the difficulty and human cost of such an invasion right up to the moment of surrender.

* * *

A second pillar of the argument that the dropping of the bomb was unnecessary goes as follows. The Japanese had already been defeated, and it was only a brief matter of time before continued conventional bombing and shortages caused by the naval blockade would have made them see reason. They were, in fact, already sending out peace feelers in the hope of ending the war. If the Americans had been more forthcoming, willing to abandon their demand for unconditional surrender and to promise that Japan could retain its emperor, peace could have come without either an invasion *or* the use of the bomb.

This particular case rests in large part on a quite rational evaluation of the condition of Japan and its dismal military prospects in the spring of 1945, and on the evidence that Japanese officials were

indeed discussing the possibility of a negotiated peace, using the Soviets as intermediaries. But neither of these lines of argument proves the point; nor do both of them taken together.

Even the most diehard military leaders of Japan knew perfectly well how grim their objective situation was. But this did not deter them from continuing the war, as the most reputable study of the Japanese side of the story makes clear. Although they did not expect a smashing and glorious triumph, they were confident of at least winning an operational victory "in the decisive battle for the homeland." Since *any* negotiated peace would be considered a surrender which would split the nation apart, Japan's militarists wanted to put it off as long as possible, and to enter negotiations only on the heels of a victory.

Some thought an American invasion could be repelled. Most hoped to inflict enough damage to make the invaders regroup. Others were even more determined; they "felt that it would be far better to die fighting in battle than to seek an ignominious survival by surrendering the nation and acknowledging defeat."

Premier Kantaro Suzuki supported the army's plan, and was content to prosecute the war with every means at his disposal—for that, after all, was "the way of the warrior and the path of the patriot." At a conference on June 8, 1945, in the presence of the emperor, the Japanese government formally affirmed its policy: "The nation would fight to the bitter end."

In spite of that, some Japanese officials did try to end the war by diplomatic negotiation before it was too late. Early efforts had been undertaken by minor military officials, who approached American OSS officers in Switzerland in April; but they were given no support from Tokyo. In July, some members of the Japanese government thought they could enlist the help of the Soviet Union in negotiating a peace that would not require a surrender or the occupation of the home islands. It is hard to understand why they thought the USSR would want to help a state it disliked and whose territory it coveted, especially when Japanese prospects were at their nadir; but such indeed was their hope.

The officials sent their proposals to Naotake Sato, the Japanese ambassador in Moscow. Their messages, and Sato's responses, were intercepted and must have influenced American plans considerably.

Sato warned his interlocutors in Tokyo that there was no chance of Soviet cooperation. An entry in the diary of Secretary of the Navy James V. Forrestal for July 15, 1945 reports "the gist of [Sato's] final message... Japan was thoroughly and completely defeated and... the only course open was quick and definite action recognizing such fact." Sato repeated this advice more than once, but the response from Tokyo was that the war must continue.

Revisionists and others have argued that the United States could have paved the way by dropping the demand for unconditional surrender, and especially that the U.S. should have indicated the emperor would be retained. But intercepts clearly revealed (according to Gerhard Weinberg in *A World at Arms*) that "the Japanese government would not accept the concept of unconditional surrender even if the institution of the imperial house were preserved." And then there were the intercepts of military messages, which led to the same conclusion—namely, as Edward J. Drea writes, that "the Japanese civil authorities

might be considering peace, but Japan's military leaders, who American decision-makers believed had total control of the nation, were preparing for war to the knife."

The demand for unconditional surrender had in any case been asserted by Roosevelt and had become a national rallying cry. Truman could not lightly abandon it, nor is there reason to think that he wanted to. Both he and Roosevelt had clear memories of World War I and how its unsatisfactory conclusion had helped bring on World War II. In the former conflict, the Germans had not surrendered unconditionally; their land had not been occupied; they had not been made to accept the fact of their defeat in battle. Demagogues like Hitler had made use of this opportunity to claim that Germany had not lost but had been "stabbed in the back" by internal traitors like the socialists and the Jews, a technique that made it easier to rouse the Germans for a second great effort. In 1944, Roosevelt said that "practically all Germans deny the fact that they surrendered during the last war, but this time they are going to know it. And so are the Japs."

In the event, Truman did allow the Japanese to keep their emperor. Why did he not announce that intention in advance, to make surrender easier? Some members of the administration thought he should do so, but most feared that any advance concession would be taken as a sign of weakness, and encourage the Japanese bitter-enders in their hope that they could win a more favorable peace by holding out. And there were also those who were opposed to any policy that would leave the emperor in place. These, as it happens, were among the more liberal members of the administration, men like Dean Acheson and Archibald MacLeish. Their opposition was grounded in the belief that, as MacLeish put it, "the throne [was] an anachronistic, feudal institution, perfectly suited to the manipulation and use of anachronistic, feudal-minded groups within the country." It is also worth pointing out, as did the State Department's Soviet expert, Charles Bohlen, that a concession with regard to the emperor, as well as negotiations in response to the so-called peace feelers on any basis other than unconditional surrender, might well have been seen by the Soviets as a violation of commitments made at Yalta and as an effort to end the war before the Soviet Union could enter it.

* * *

What if the U.S. had issued a public warning that it had the atomic bomb, and described its fearful qualities? Or warned the Japanese of the imminent entry of the Soviet Union into the fighting? Or, best of all, combined both warnings with a promise that Japan could keep its emperor? Again, there are no grounds for believing that any or all of these steps would have made a difference to the determined military clique that was making Japan's decisions.

Even after the atomic bomb had exploded at Hiroshima on August 6, the Japanese refused to yield. An American announcement clarified the nature of the weapon that had done the damage, and warned that Japan could expect more of the same if it did not surrender. Still, the military held to its policy of resistance and insisted on a delay until a response was received to the latest Japanese approach to the Soviet Union. The answer came on August 8, when the Soviets declared war and sent a large army against Japanese forces in Manchuria.

The foolishness of looking to the Soviets was now inescapably clear, but still Japan's leaders took no steps to end the fighting. The Minister of War, General Korechika Anami, went so far as to deny that Hiroshima had been struck by an atomic bomb. Others insisted that the U.S. had used its only bomb there, or that world opinion would prevent the Americans from using any others they might have. Then on August 9 the second atomic bomb fell on Nagasaki, again doing terrible damage.

The Nagasaki bomb convinced even Anami that "the Americans appear to have 100 atomic bombs... they could drop three per day. The next target might well be Tokyo." Even so, a meeting of the Imperial Council that night failed to achieve a consensus to accept defeat. Anami himself insisted that Japan continue to fight. If the Japanese people "went into the decisive battle in the homeland determined to display the full measure of patriotism... Japan would be able to avert the crisis facing her." The chief of the army general staff, Yoshijiro Umezu, expressed his confidence in the military's "ability to deal a smashing blow to the enemy," and added that in view of the sacrifices made by the many men who had gladly died for the emperor, "it would be inexcusable to surrender unconditionally." Admiral Soemu Toyoda, chief of the navy's general staff, argued that Japan could now use its full air power, heretofore held in reserve in the homeland. Like Anami, he did not guarantee victory, but asserted that "we do not believe that we will be possibly defeated."

These were the views of Japan's top military leaders *after* the explosion of two atomic bombs and the Soviet attack on Manchuria.

Premier Suzuki and the others who were by now favoring peace knew all this was madness. The Allies would never accept the military's conditions —restrictions on the extent of Japanese disarmament, on the occupation of Japan, and on trials of Japanese leaders for war crimes—and the continuation of warfare would be a disaster for the Japanese people. To break the deadlock he took the extraordinary step of asking the emperor to make the decision. (Normally no proposal was put to the emperor until it had achieved the unanimous approval of the Imperial Council.) At 2 A.M. on August 10, Emperor Hirohito responded to the premier's request by giving his sanction to the acceptance of the Allied terms. The Japanese reply included the proviso that the emperor be retained.

There was still disagreement within the American government on this subject. Public opinion was very hostile to the retention of the emperor, and in particular, as Gerhard Weinberg has written, "the articulate organizations of the American Left" resisted any concessions and "urged the dropping of additional atomic bombs instead." At last, the U.S. devised compromise language that accepted the imperial system by implication, while providing that the Japanese people could establish their own form of government.

Although the Japanese leaders found this acceptable, that was not the end of the matter. Opponents of peace tried to reverse the decision by a *coup d'etat*. They might have succeeded had General Anami supported them, but he was unwilling to defy the emperor's orders. He solved his dilemma by committing suicide, and the plot failed.

Had it succeeded, the war would have continued to a bloody end, with Japan under the brutal rule of a fanatical military clique. Some idea of the thinking of this faction is provided by an intercept of an August 15 message to Tokyo from the commander of Japan's army in China:

> Such a disgrace as the surrender of several million troops without fighting is not paralleled in the world's military history, and it is absolutely impossible to submit to the unconditional surrender of a million picked troops in perfectly healthy shape. . . .

It was the emperor, then, who was decisive in causing Japan to surrender. What caused him to act in so remarkable a way? He was moved by the bomb— and by the Soviet declaration of war. . . . But statements by the emperor and premier show clearly that they viewed the Soviet invasion as only another wartime setback. It was the bomb that changed the situation entirely.

On hearing of this terrible new weapon, Emperor Hirohito said, "We must put an end to the war as speedily as possible so that this tragedy will not be repeated." Suzuki said, plainly, that Japan's "war aim had been lost by the enemy's use of the new-type bomb." Finally, the central role of the bomb was made graphically clear in the Imperial Rescript of August 14, in which the emperor explained to his people the reasons for the surrender. At its heart was the following statement:

> The enemy has begun to employ a new and most cruel bomb, the power of which to do damage is indeed incalculable, taking the toll of many innocent lives. Should we continue to fight, it would not only result in an ultimate collapse and obliteration of the Japanese nation, but it

would also lead to the total extinction of human civilization. Such being the case, how are We to save the millions of Our subjects...? This is the reason why We have ordered the acceptance of the provisions of the Joint Declaration of the Powers.

There can be, in short, no doubt that the actual use of atomic weapons was critical in bringing a swift end to the war, and that mere warnings would not have sufficed.

* * *

Finally, whether or not they condemn American policy on instrumental grounds, some critics assail it on purely humanitarian ones. In particular they have asked whether it was necessary to drop the bomb on a *city*. Should it not have been used for the first time on a desert island, or some uninhabited place, as a demonstration?

This suggestion was put forward even before the bomb was dropped, but it failed to win support. A demonstration outside Japan, it was felt, would not be effective in persuading the Japanese themselves; and if it were announced for some location within Japan, the Japanese might place Allied prisoners on the site, and make extraordinary efforts to shoot down the carrying plane. Also, in August 1945 the Americans had but two bombs, and using one for a demonstration would leave only the other. There was the danger that one or both of the devices might fizzle, or that, even if the first one worked, those Japanese who wished to continue the war might deny, as in the event some did, that the blast came from a new weapon, or might argue, as others did, that the Americans had no more in their arsenal.

J. Robert Oppenheimer, who, as director of the research project at Los Alamos,
was on the committee that selected the target cities, averred that to his mind no mere display would be sufficiently impressive to shock the Japanese into surrender. Even the Franck Report, signed by scientists urging a demonstration, doubted that this would break the will or ability of Japan to resist, and reluctantly approved use against Japan if all else failed. Leo Szilard, the scientist most vigorous in his opposition to the early use of the bomb, also conceded that "the war has to be brought to a successful conclusion and attacks by atomic bombs may very well be an effective method of warfare." It is important to recognize that only in hindsight has moral revulsion been expressed against the use of atomic weapons on cities. As McGeorge Bundy points out in his book *Danger and Survival*, "*no one* put [the idea] forward before Hiroshima.... No one ever said simply, do not use it on a city *at all*."

* * *

Still, the moral question must be addressed. It has been argued that the nuclear bomb is a weapon like no other, so terrible that nothing can justify its use, and that its use in 1945 made its future use more likely. But events have not borne this out: in the 50 years since Hiroshima and Nagasaki, nuclear weapons have not been used in warfare, and it is not impossible that their first use helped deter a repetition.

Moreover, the sharp distinction between nuclear weapons and others on moral grounds seems questionable. In a single raid on Tokyo on March 9–10, 1945, incendiary bombs from American planes killed 80,000–100,000 Japanese (as many as at Hiroshima on August 6), wounded a similar number, and destroyed more than 250,000 buildings, leaving hundreds of thousands homeless. It is hard to see how the continuation of such bombing until there were no more targets would have been a moral improvement over Hiroshima. Distinguishing nuclear weapons from all others would seem, in fact, to give greater moral sanction to the use of weapons and tactics no less horrible.

If the moral complaint is to be fairly lodged, it must be lodged against any and all warfare that attacks innocents—which means, in effect, the overwhelming majority of wars to the present time. It is a historical axiom that the longer and more sharply contested a war, the greater the brutality with which it is fought. The British began World War II refusing to employ aerial bombardment; they dropped leaflets on Germany instead. Before the war was over, they had carried out the fire bombing of Dresden, killing tens of thousands of civilians. Similarly, American doctrine at the beginning of the war was that indiscriminate bombing of cities was both wrong and unwise. Before long, however, Hitler's bombing of Rotterdam and later of London, Japan's sneak attack on Pearl Harbor and its brutal treatment of prisoners of war, its bombing of Shanghai, the rape of Nanking, the forced prostitution of Korean women, and the Bataan death march made Americans change their minds. "Precision" bombings of targets in or near cities gave way to more indiscriminate destruction launched out of anger and with the purpose of destroying the enemy's morale, thereby (again) bringing the war to an earlier end.

In the history of warfare such developments are typical rather than unusual. It is right to do all we can to reduce the horrors of war. But to prevent them entirely, it will be necessary to prevent war.

* * *

Let us sum up. It is, I think, clear that any strategy other than the employment of atomic weapons would have failed to compel a Japanese surrender short of an invasion of the home islands. Even at a low estimate, the two planned invasions would have brought 193,500 American casualties and, as Robert J. Maddox puts it, "only an intellectual could assert that 193,500 anticipated casualties were too insignificant to have caused Truman to use atomic bombs." The Japanese, moreover, had plans to kill Allied prisoners of war as the fighting approached the camps where they were being held; so the swift surrender brought on by the bomb saved still more American lives.

And what about Japanese casualties? The experience of Luzon, Iwo Jima, and Okinawa showed that such casualties would have been many times greater than those suffered by Americans—invasion or no invasion. American planes would have dealt with many more Japanese cities as they had dealt with Tokyo, and would have repeated their attacks on the capital as well. The American navy would have continued its blockade, and starvation would have taken off countless civilians. In sum, the cost would have been greater than that exacted by the bombs. As a former president of the Japanese Medical Association has said, "When one considers the possibility that the Japanese military would have sacrificed the entire nation if it were not for the atomic bomb attack, then this bomb might be described as having saved Japan." It is a terrible thought, but the evidence suggests that he is right.

Gar Alperovitz, in the name of many other critics of U.S. policy, has as-

sailed "America's continued unwillingness to confront the fundamental questions about Hiroshima" because "we
Americans clearly do not like to see
our nation as vulnerable to the same
moral failings as others." Americans certainly share the same weaknesses as the
rest of the human race. They need not,
however, shrink from a confrontation of
the "fundamental questions" surrounding Hiroshima. An honest examination
of the evidence reveals that their leaders, in the tragic predicament common to
all who have engaged in wars that reach
the point where every choice is repugnant, chose the least bad course. Americans may look back on that decision with
sadness, but without shame.

NO
John Rawls

FIFTY YEARS AFTER HIROSHIMA

The fiftieth year since the bombing of Hiroshima is a time to reflect about what one should think of it. Is it really a great wrong, as many now think, and many also thought then, or is it perhaps justified after all? I believe that both the fire-bombing of Japanese cities beginning in the spring of 1945 and the later atomic bombing of Hiroshima on August 6 were very great wrongs, and rightly seen as such. In order to support this opinion, I set out what I think to be the principles governing the conduct of war—*jus in bello*—of democratic peoples. These peoples have different ends of war than nondemocratic, especially totalitarian, states, such as Germany and Japan, which sought the domination and exploitation of subjected peoples, and in Germany's case, their enslavement if not extermination.

Although I cannot properly justify them here, I begin by setting out six principles and assumptions in support of these judgments. I hope they seem not unreasonable; and certainly they are familiar, as they are closely related to much traditional thought on this subject.

1. The aim of a just war waged by a decent democratic society is a just and lasting peace between peoples, especially with its present enemy.

2. A decent democratic society is fighting against a state that is not democratic. This follows from the fact that democratic peoples do not wage war against each other; and since we are concerned with the rules of war as they apply to such peoples, we assume the society fought against is nondemocratic and that its expansionist aims threatened the security and free institutions of democratic regimes and caused the war.

3. In the conduct of war, a democratic society must carefully distinguish three groups: the state's leaders and officials, its soldiers, and its civilian population. The reason for these distinctions rests on the principle of responsibility: since the state fought against is not democratic, the civilian members of the society cannot be those who organized and brought on the war. This was done by its leaders and officials assisted by other elites who control and staff the state apparatus. They are responsible, they willed the war, and for doing that, they are criminals. But civilians, often kept in ignorance and swayed by state propaganda, are not. And this is so even if some civilians

knew better and were enthusiastic for the war. In a nation's conduct of war many such marginal cases may exist, but they are irrelevant. As for soldiers, they, just as civilians, and leaving aside the upper ranks of an officer class, are not responsible for the war, but are conscripted or in other ways forced into it, their patriotism often cruelly and cynically exploited. The grounds on which they may be attacked directly are not that they are responsible for the war but that a democratic people cannot defend itself in any other way, and defend itself it must do. About this there is no choice.

4. A decent democratic society must respect the human rights of the members of the other side, both civilians and soldiers, for two reasons. One is because they simply have these rights by the law of peoples. The other reason is to teach enemy soldiers and civilians the content of those rights by the example of how they hold in their own case. In this way their significance is best brought home to them. They are assigned a certain status, the status of the members of some human society who possess rights as human persons. In the case of human rights in war the aspect of status as applied to civilians is given a strict interpretation. This means, as I understand it here, that they can never be attacked directly except in times of extreme crisis, the nature of which I discuss below.

5. Continuing with the thought of teaching the content of human rights, the next principle is that just peoples by their actions and proclamations are to foreshadow during war the kind of peace they aim for and the kind of relations they seek between nations. By doing so, they show in an open and public way the nature of their aims and the

kind of people they are. These last duties fall largely on the leaders and officials of the governments of democratic peoples, since they are in the best position to speak for the whole people and to act as the principle applies. Although all the preceding principles also specify duties of statesmanship, this is especially true of 4 and 5. The way a war is fought and the actions ending it endure in the historical memory of peoples and may set the stage for future war. This duty of statesmanship must always be held in view.

6. Finally, we note the place of practical means-end reasoning in judging the appropriateness of an action or policy for achieving the aim of war or for not causing more harm than good. This mode of thought—whether carried on by (classical) utilitarian reasoning, or by cost-benefit analysis, or by weighing national interests, or in other ways—must always be framed within and strictly limited by the preceding principles. The norms of the conduct of war set up certain lines that bound just action. War plans and strategies, and the conduct of battles, must lie within their limits. (The only exception, I repeat, is in times of extreme crisis.)

* * *

In connection with the fourth and fifth principles of the conduct of war, I have said that they are binding especially on the leaders of nations. They are in the most effective position to represent their people's aims and obligations, and sometimes they become statesmen. But who is a statesman? There is no office of statesman, as there is of president, or chancellor, or prime minister. The statesman is an ideal, like the ideal of the truthful or virtuous individual. Statesmen are presidents or prime ministers who become statesmen through their exemplary performance and leadership in their office in difficult and trying times and manifest strength, wisdom, and courage. They guide their people through turbulent and dangerous periods for which they are esteemed always, as one of their great statesmen.

The ideal of the statesman is suggested by the saying: the politician looks to the next election, the statesman to the next generation. It is the task of the student of philosophy to look to the permanent conditions and the real interests of a just and good democratic society. It is the task of the statesman, however, to discern these conditions and interests in practice; the statesman sees deeper and further than most others and grasps what needs to be done. The statesman must get it right, or nearly so, and hold fast to it. Washington and Lincoln were statesmen. Bismarck was not. He did not see Germany's real interests far enough into the future and his judgment and motives were often distorted by his class interests and his wanting himself alone to be chancellor of Germany. Statesmen need not be selfless and may have their own interests when they hold office, yet they must be selfless in their judgments and assessments of society's interests and not be swayed, especially in war and crisis, by passions of revenge and retaliation against the enemy.

Above all, they are to hold fast to the aim of gaining a just peace, and avoid the things that make achieving such a peace more difficult. Here the proclamations of a nation should make clear (the statesman must see to this) that the enemy people are to be granted an autonomous regime of their own and a decent and full life once peace is securely reestablished. Whatever they may be told by their leaders, whatever reprisals they may reasonably fear, they are not to be held as slaves or serfs after surrender, or denied in due course their full liberties; and they may well achieve freedoms they did not enjoy before, as the Germans and the Japanese eventually did. The statesman knows, if others do not, that all descriptions of the enemy people (not their rulers) inconsistent with this are impulsive and false.

* * *

Turning now to Hiroshima and the firebombing of Tokyo, we find that neither falls under the exemption of extreme crisis. One aspect of this is that since (let's suppose) there are no absolute rights —rights that must be respected in all circumstances—there are occasions when civilians can be attacked directly by aerial bombing. Were there times during the war when Britain could properly have bombed Hamburg and Berlin? Yes, when Britain was alone and desperately facing Germany's superior might; moreover, this period would extend until Russia had clearly beat off the first German assault in the summer and fall of 1941, and would be able to fight Germany until the end. Here the cutoff point might be placed differently, say the summer of 1942, and certainly by Stalingrad. I shan't dwell on this, as the crucial matter is that under no conditions could Germany be allowed to win the war, and this for two basic reasons: first, the nature and history of constitutional democracy and its place in European culture; and second, the peculiar evil of Nazism and the enormous and uncalculable moral and political evil it represented for civilized society.

The peculiar evil of Nazism needs to be understood, since in some circumstances a democratic people might better accept defeat if the terms of peace offered by the adversary were reasonable and moderate, did not subject them to humiliation and looked forward to a workable and decent political relationship. Yet characteristic of Hitler was that he accepted no possibility at all of a political relationship with his enemies. They were always to be cowed by terror and brutality, and ruled by force. From the beginning the campaign against Russia, for example, was a war of destruction against Slavic peoples, with the original inhabitants remaining, if at all, only as serfs. When Goebbels and others protested that the war could not be won that way, Hitler refused to listen.

Yet it is clear that while the extreme crisis exemption held for Britain in the early stages of the war, it never held at any time for the United States in its war with Japan. The principles of the conduct of war were always applicable to it. Indeed, in the case of Hiroshima many involved in higher reaches of the government recognized the questionable character of the bombing and that limits were being crossed. Yet during the discussions among allied leaders in June and July 1945, the weight of the practical means-end reasoning carried the day. Under the continuing pressure of war, such moral doubts as there were failed to gain an express and articulated view. As the war progressed, the heavy fire-bombing of civilians in the capitals of Berlin and Tokyo and elsewhere was increasingly accepted on the allied side. Although after the outbreak of war Roosevelt had urged both sides not to commit the inhuman barbarism of bombing civilians, by 1945 allied leaders came to assume that Roosevelt would have used the bomb on Hiroshima. The bombing grew out of what had happened before.

* * *

The practical means-end reasons to justify using the atomic bomb on Hiroshima were the following:

The bomb was dropped to hasten the end of the war. It is clear that Truman and most other allied leaders thought it would do that. Another reason was that it would save lives where the lives counted are the lives of American soldiers. The lives of Japanese, military or civilian, presumably counted for less. Here the calculations of least time and most lives saved were mutually supporting. Moreover, dropping the bomb would give the Emperor and the Japanese leaders a way to save face, an important matter given Japanese samurai culture. Indeed, at the end a few top Japanese leaders wanted to make a last sacrificial stand but were overruled by others supported by the Emperor, who ordered surrender on August 12, having received word from Washington that the Emperor could stay provided it was understood that he had to comply with the orders of the American military commander. The last reason I mention is that the bomb was dropped to impress the Russians with American power and make them more agreeable with our demands. This reason is highly disputed but urged by some critics and scholars as important.

The failure of these reasons to reflect the limits on the conduct of war is evident, so I focus on a different matter: the failure of statesmanship on the part of allied leaders and why it might have occurred. Truman once described the Japanese as beasts and to be treated as such; yet how foolish it sounds now to call the Germans or the Japanese barbarians and beasts! Of the Nazis and Tojo militarists, yes, but they are not the German and the Japanese people. Churchill later granted that he carried the bombing too far, led by passion and the intensity of the conflict. A duty of statesmanship is not to allow such feelings, natural and inevitable as they may be, to alter the course a democratic people should best follow in striving for peace. The statesman understands that relations with the present enemy have special importance: for as I have said, war must be openly and publicly conducted in ways that make a lasting and amicable peace possible with a defeated enemy, and prepares its people for how they may be expected to be treated. Their present fears of being subjected to acts of revenge and retaliation must be put to rest; present enemies must be seen as associates in a shared and just future peace.

*   *   *

These remarks make it clear that, in my judgment, both Hiroshima and the fire-bombing of Japanese cities were great evils that the duties of statesmanship require political leaders to avoid in the absence of the crisis exemption. I also believe this could have been done at little cost in further casualties. An invasion was unnecessary at that date, as the war was effectively over. However, whether that is true or not makes no difference. Without the crisis exemption, those bombings are great evils. Yet it is clear that an articulate expression of the principles of just war introduced at that time would not have altered the outcome. It was simply too late. A president or prime minister must have carefully considered these questions, preferably long before, or at least when they had the time and leisure to think things out. Reflections on just war cannot be heard in

the daily round of the pressure of events near the end of the hostilities; too many are anxious and impatient, and simply worn out.

Similarly, the justification of constitutional democracy and the basis of the rights and duties it must respect should be part of the public political culture and discussed in the many associations of civic society as part of one's education. It is not clearly heard in day-to-day ordinary politics, but must be presupposed as the background, not the daily subject of politics, except in special circumstances. In the same way, there was not sufficient prior grasp of the fundamental importance of the principles of just war for the expression of them to have blocked the appeal of practical means-end reasoning in terms of a calculus of lives, or of the least time to end the war, or of some other balancing of costs and benefits. This practical reasoning justifies too much, too easily, and provides a way for a dominant power to quiet any moral worries that may arise. If the principles of war are put forward at that time, they easily become so many more considerations to be balanced in the scales.

Another failure of statesmanship was not to try to enter negotiations with the Japanese before any drastic steps such as the fire-bombing of cities or the bombing of Hiroshima were taken. A conscientious attempt to do so was morally necessary. As a democratic people, we owed that to the Japanese people—whether to their government is another matter. There had been discussions in Japan for some time about finding a way to end the war, and on June 26 the government had been instructed by the Emperor to do so. It must surely have realized that with the navy destroyed and the outer islands taken, the war was lost. True, the Japanese were deluded by the hope that the Russians might prove to be their allies, but negotiations are precisely to disabuse the other side of delusions of that kind. A statesman is not free to consider that such negotiations may lessen the desired shock value of subsequent attacks.

Truman was in many ways a good, at times a very good president. But the way he ended the war showed he failed as a statesman. For him it was an opportunity missed, and a loss to the country and its armed forces as well. It is sometimes said that questioning the bombing of Hiroshima is an insult to the American troops who fought the war. This is hard to understand. We should be able to look back and consider our faults after fifty years. We expect the Germans and the Japanese to do that—"*Vergangenheitsverarbeitung*" —as the Germans say. Why shouldn't we? It can't be that we think we waged the war without moral error!

None of this alters Germany's and Japan's responsibility for the war nor their behavior in conducting it. Emphatically to be repudiated are two nihilist doctrines. One is expressed by Sherman's remark, "War is hell," so anything goes to get it over with as soon as one can. The other says that we are all guilty so we stand on a level and no one can blame anyone else. These are both superficial and deny all reasonable distinctions; they are invoked falsely to try to excuse our misconduct or to plead that we cannot be condemned.

The moral emptiness of these nihilisms is manifest in the fact that just and decent civilized societies—their institutions and laws, their civil life and background culture and mores—all depend absolutely on making significant moral and political distinctions in all situations. Certainly war is a kind of hell, but why should that mean that all moral distinctions cease to hold? And granted also that sometimes all or nearly all may be to some degree guilty, that does not mean that all are equally so. There is never a time when we are free from all moral and political principles and restraints. These nihilisms are pretenses to be free of those principles and restraints that always apply to us fully.

POSTSCRIPT

Was Dropping Atomic Bombs on Japan Justifiable?

History is valuable only insofar as we learn from it. The challenge, of course, is to draw the right lessons from history. The debate over the atomic bombing of Japan offers an insight into our past that we can apply to our present and future. One thing to do is to learn even more about the events and thoughts that culminated in the bombing of Hiroshima and Nagasaki. Numerous articles have been written in conjunction with the 50th anniversary of the bombings. These include Barton J. Bernstein, "The Atomic Bombings Reconsidered," *Foreign Affairs* (January/February 1995); Thomas Powers, "Was It Right?" *The Atlantic Monthly* (July 1995); and Michael B. King, "Shock Treatment," *National Review* (April 3, 1995).

Jus in bello is one issue to consider. Rawls lays out a number of standards of just conduct of war and of just cause of war (*jus ad bellum*). It is valuable to ponder these, to read more about the morality of war, and to apply it to current history and the future. Two good books on the morality of war are Douglas P. Lackey, *The Ethics of War and Peace* (Prentice-Hall, 1989) and Michael Walzer, *Just and Unjust Wars* (Basic Books, 1992). The issue of just war does not apply only to nuclear weapons issues. One could ask, for example, whether or not some of the conventional war tactics used by the United States–led UN forces to defeat Iraq in 1991 violated the principles of *jus in bello*. Two readings that will help you to ponder this question are Jeffrey P. Whittman, "Utilitarianism and the Laws of Land Warfare," *Public Affairs Quarterly* (Fall 1993) and Nicholas G. Fotion, "The Gulf War: Cleanly Fought," *The Bulletin of Atomic Scientists* (October 1991).

Beyond the purely moral issue, there are some current policy implications of the debate over atomic (now nuclear) weapons. If, as some people argue, it is impossible to use nuclear weapons without violating the standards of discrimination and proportionality of *jus in bello,* then that is one argument for eliminating nuclear weapons altogether. Another issue involves the slow but perceptible movement of the global community toward holding leaders and sometimes soldiers responsible for the conduct of war outside the boundaries of *jus ad bellum* and *jus in bello.* That began with the Nuremberg and Tokyo war crime trials after World War II and has been revived by the current international tribunal investigating and prosecuting war crimes in the Balkans and in Rwanda. It could well be that any leader who orders the use of nuclear weapons or any soldier who drops or launches them could end up on trial for committing a war crime.

ISSUE 12

Does the World Need to Have Nuclear Weapons at All?

YES: Alex Roland, from "Keep the Bomb," *Technology Review* (August/September 1995)

NO: Joseph Rotblat, from "A Nuclear-Weapon-Free World," *Technology Review* (August/September 1995)

ISSUE SUMMARY

YES: Professor of history Alex Roland contends that we should keep the bomb to protect the world from conventional warfare.

NO: Joseph Rotblat, an emeritus professor of physics, contends that outlawing nuclear weapons altogether might well produce a world that is much more secure than the present world armed with nuclear weapons.

Efforts to control weapons of war go back to nearly the beginning of written history. Although progress was rarely made, it can be argued that the limited killing power of weapons made arms control agreements seem low priority. That changed rapidly as the destructive capability of weapons grew exponentially during the industrial and then the technological ages. The first, albeit ineffective, multilateral arms negotiations were the Hague Conferences (1899, 1907). The awful toll and fearsome weapons of World War I prompted renewed arms control efforts. Conferences in Washington and London set limits to battleship tonnage among the world's leading naval powers. There were other arms negotiations and agreements in the 1920s and 1930s, and in 1928 some 23 countries signed the Kellogg-Briand Treaty and forswore resorting to war. The outbreak of World War II in 1939 was evidence that these various efforts had failed to either keep the peace or reduce the devastation of war.

The arms control efforts were spurred yet again by the horror of World War II and then by the existence—and use on Hiroshima and Nagasaki, Japan, in 1945—of potentially civilization-ending atomic weapons. In January 1946 the UN established the International Atomic Energy Agency to try to limit the use of nuclear technology to peaceful purposes. Later that year, the UN also called for the "general regulation and reduction of armaments and armed forces" and established a Commission for Conventional Armaments.

Still, for almost 20 years nuclear weapons building and testing mushroomed unimpeded. Then, in 1963, the first major nuclear arms control agreement was signed, and by it most countries agreed to cease testing nuclear weapons in the atmosphere. Arms control efforts strengthened in the 1970s and continued to speed up. The cost of weaponry; the fact that each superpower had over 10,000 long-range nuclear weapons and myriad shorter-range systems; the ever-increasing speed, power, and accuracy of those weapons; and the moderation of the cold war all prompted this acceleration.

Several of the arms control agreements are worth noting: the two Strategic Arms Limitation Talks treaties (SALT I and II, 1972 and 1979); the Intermediate-range Nuclear Forces (INF) Treaty (1987); and the two Strategic Arms Reduction Talks treaties (START I and II, 1991 and 1993). The SALT treaties limited the number of weapons systems that each superpower could possess. The INF Treaty eliminated an entire type of missile—those missiles with an intermediate range (500–5,500 km). It was the first step toward actually reducing the number of nuclear weapons. The START treaties took up the abolition of the intercontinental-range (over 5,500 km) U.S. and Soviet missiles and, later, those of the successor states that had inherited Soviet nuclear arms (Belarus, Kazakhstan, Russia, and Ukraine). Like the INF treaty, the START treaties pledged the signatories to reduce their nuclear arsenals. Unlike the INF treaty, the reductions agreed to are substantial.

Under START II, which superseded START I, Russia will possess all the former Soviet intercontinental-range nuclear weapons delivery systems (missiles, bombers) and their associated weapons (warheads, bombs). Arsenals will be slashed to 3,500 weapons for the United States and 2,997 for Russia by the year 2003. The two sides agreed to eliminate all multiple-warhead land-based missiles.

The question before us here is, If the two nuclear behemoths can slim down their nuclear systems by approximately 75 percent, as they did comparing the SALT II and START II limits, then why not reduce the two sides' weapons (including both long-range weapons and the still-formidable short-range systems of bombs and artillery shells) to zero? Before we move to that debate, it is important to note that the closer one comes to zero, the more important others' nuclear arsenals become. Three countries (and their number of weapons) that have substantial arsenals are China (284), France (534), and Great Britain (200). Israel, India, Pakistan, and perhaps North Korea also have nuclear weapons, and Belarus, Kasakhstan, and Ukraine each continue to possess old Soviet weapons.

The following selections carry the debate over nuclear weapons into the future. Alex Roland outlines a number of reasons why it would not be wise to eliminate nuclear weapons in the foreseeable future. Joseph Rotblat contends that attaining a nuclear-free world is neither wishful thinking nor a perilous path but, rather, attainable and desirable.

YES

Alex Roland

KEEP THE BOMB

A Marine Corps major in the late 1970s decorated the door of his office at the Pentagon with a poster trumpeting "Ban the Bomb!" Barely visible at the bottom margin was the riposte: "Make the World Safe for Conventional War."

The poster was intended to be funny. Its premise, however, is not. With the world's major military powers paralyzed in a nuclear balance of terror, conventional war between them—the large-scale, mechanized, resource-intensive campaigning made familiar by the two world wars—has become unthinkable, lest it escalate into nuclear war. The result has been a far more peaceful world over the last 50 years than the one that surely would have existed without nuclear weapons. They have done more good than harm in the world.

Those of us who lived through the Cold War are not accustomed to thinking of nuclear weapons in these terms. Especially in the 1950s, when the insanity of the Cold War was at its peak, just the opposite seemed likely. Atmospheric testing of nuclear weapons poisoned the air. Krushchev threatened to bury us. In response, we prepared to bury ourselves in bomb shelters. The besetting question about nuclear war was not if, but when.

And the danger was real. At the climax of the Cold War, during the Cuban Missile Crisis of 1962, the superpowers came closer than ever before or since to unleashing their nuclear arsenals.

To those who formed their opinions about nuclear weapons during this early and dangerous era, nuclear weapons seemed likely to kill more people than any other technology in human history. Happily, such a cataclysm has never occurred. Instead, consider how many deaths have been *prevented* by nuclear weapons. An ever-growing body of evidence suggests that the number of people whose lives have been saved by nuclear weapons reaches into the hundreds of millions.

Through most of human history, death in war has been constant, horrible, and scant. Harvard sociologist Pitirim Sorokin estimated that war casualties in the Roman empire ranged from .07 percent to .36 percent of the empire's population. By comparison, the Soviet Union lost an estimated 14 percent of its population in World War II.

The reason that ancient warfare did not wipe out more people was not human kindness but limited technology. Killing was simply a labor-intensive enterprise. Virtually all deaths in combat came from sword stroke, spear thrust, or the discharge of some muscle-powered missile. Fights to the death were the exception rather than the rule. Armies losing ground in an engagement would more often flee than fight; victors seldom had the energy or the will to hunt them down. Even in naval warfare, where the sinking of a ship held out promise of mass casualties, most battles were decided by boarding, hand-to-hand combat, and the capture of prisoners. Humans were surely bloody in tooth and claw, but their reach was limited.

Two revolutions broke through this ceiling. The invention of gunpowder in the late Middle Ages allowed soldiers and sailors to kill their enemies at greater distance and in greater numbers. In her book *World Military and Social Expenditures*, Ruth Sivard, former chief of the economics division of the U.S. Arms Control and Disarmament Agency, has compared global war casualties over the past five centuries. Her research shows that with the aid of gunpowder, worldwide deaths in warfare quadrupled from an estimated 1.5 million during the sixteenth century to 6.2 million during the seventeenth.

Worse still, the Industrial Revolution mechanized warfare, further expanding its reach. Vast quantities of weapons could now be produced to supply armies of unprecedented size. Inventions such as the steamboat, railroad, and telegraph allowed those armies to be transported around the globe, resupplied for indefinite campaigns, and directed from afar in their grisly business. According to Sivard, global deaths caused by war increased from 6.4 million during the eighteenth century to 20 million in the nineteenth.

And the power to kill has continued to grow exponentially. The twentieth century has the grim distinction of being the most deadly in human history, with approximately 103 million war-related deaths so far. The first half of the century and the world wars that scarred it may be seen as the culmination of the gunpowder and industrial revolutions.

But after the midcentury mark, things changed. According to Sivard's calculations, 84 percent of the casualties from war in this century occurred before 1950. Moreover, the ratio of casualties to world population is now decreasing. By the latter measure, the rate of war-related deaths in the second half of the twentieth century is one-tenth that in the first half, lower than in the second half of the nineteenth century, and almost as low as in the first half of the nineteenth century.

The world has not been this safe since 1850. And the peace holds. The so-called proxy wars, in which the superpowers armed and aided the protagonists—Korea, Vietnam, Angola—have subsided. Certainly conventional armed conflict has persisted in the form of the Falklands War, the Iran-Iraq War, the Gulf War, and the war in Bosnia, but these remain localized conflicts with relatively limited casualties. It is hard to imagine an approaching cataclysm on the trajectory set up by the Napoleonic Wars, our Civil War, and the two world wars.

Had there been conventional war in the second half of the twentieth century on the scale seen in the first half, we could have expected more war deaths than occurred throughout recorded history up to the twentieth century—and more than piled up in the two world wars combined.

Extrapolating from Sivard's figures, we can reasonably project that another world war, say in the decade of the 1980s, could have killed 250 million people—5 percent of the world population—even if the combatants used only conventional weapons.

Since Sivard calculates that some 17 million people died in war between 1949 and 1990, we might conclude that more than 230 million people have been spared from the trajectory of death laid out by the Industrial Revolution and the world wars. Those people lived because of nuclear weapons.

With the advent of nuclear weapons, humans finally succeeded in devising an instrument of war so terrible that other means had to be found to settle political conflicts. Surely there has been no lack of conflict. Surely man's inhumanity to man is still a potent force in world affairs. Surely the United Nations and other institutions of collective security have proven ineffective. Yet the fear of conflict in many cases has become more powerful than the forces of conflict themselves.

Throughout the seventeenth, eighteenth and nineteenth centuries, visionaries... hoped that cannons, ships, and other artifacts of humanity's triumph over nature would make war too horrible to pursue. But only in the desert of New Mexico, in the summer of 1945, did the scientists and engineers of the Manhattan Project finally realize that goal. J. Robert Oppenheimer looked at the result of their labors and feared, "Now I have become death." For the victims of Hiroshima and Nagasaki, his fears proved true enough. But the legacy of that bomb has been life for hundreds of millions of people.

What reason is there to think that, in the absence of these terrible weapons, there would have been conventional war on such a massive scale? At no time in human history have two major powers, divided by ideology and ambition and united by proximity and conflicting interests, resisted the temptation to settle their differences on the battlefield. The rhetoric of the Cold War, and the huge conventional military forces amassed by both sides, give every reason to suspect that without nuclear weapons there would have been a World War III by now. Perhaps it would have come during one of the Berlin crises, or the Korean or Vietnam wars, or one of the countless other confrontations between East and West. But come it would have.

Still, it may be argued, the success of nuclear weapons in preventing World War III is hardly grounds for believing that these horrendous instruments have not posed—and do not still pose—a threat to humanity that entirely outweighs the fragile peace they have so far forced upon us. What about proliferation? What about the possibility of terrorists brandishing these weapons on the world stage? What about the argument of Admiral Noel Gaylor (a cold warrior turned peace activist) that these weapons, like all others in human history, will be used eventually—with the results that will obliterate the transient gains of the last 40 years?

Predictions of the imminent use of nuclear weapons have been made since 1946, and all have proven false. The darkest forecasts accompanied China's acquisition of nuclear weapons in the 1960s. But Mao and his successors have been true to their promise to use nuclear weapons only to ensure that China would not be attacked. Indeed, unlike the other major powers, China does not rattle the nuclear sabre.

Six to twelve nations now possess nuclear weapons, and the technology is within the reach of many more states and even some terrorist groups. Yet none have used them; most have foregone even developing them. The record grows stronger every year.

And what if nuclear weapons were to be used again? What if, for example, India and Pakistan—widely regarded as having nuclear weapons or the capacity to acquire them—drove each other, *in extremis*, to push the button? The casualties would surely be horrendous, but they would amount to only a fraction of the number that would have been killed by now without nuclear weapons.

The argument made here is not new. Historian Bruce Mazlish made a similar case in the 1960s; so have political scientists Kenneth Waltz and John Mearsheimer. But all of them wrote during the Cold War, too close to the event for their ideas to win broad acceptance.

Now the Cold War is over. What it has wrought may finally be viewed without the passions bred by fear. The great bloodletting engendered by the Industrial Revolution has peaked. We need to acknowledge this blessing and preserve the relative peace that it has brought—even if the price of peace is to live in apprehension, even dread, of our own capabilities for destruction.

Keep the bomb. Save the world from conventional war.

NO
Joseph Rotblat

A NUCLEAR-WEAPON-FREE WORLD

The iniquitous characteristics of nuclear weapons—enormous destructive power, indiscriminate killing of civilian populations, a legacy of death and disease in people yet unborn—make the atomic bomb repugnant to every sensible person. From the beginning there has been a nearly universal desire to get rid of it. The very first resolution of the United Nations [U.N.], adopted unanimously by the General Assembly in January 1946, called for eliminating nuclear weapons. Subsequent U.N. declarations have repeated this call. The five nuclear-weapon states became legally committed to nuclear abolition when they signed the Non-Proliferation Treaty (NPT), agreeing, in Article VI, to proceed in good faith to complete nuclear disarmament. This is still their stated objective.

Clearly, a nuclear-weapon-free world is not the weird idea of a fringe group but the desired objective of much of the global community. All the same, such an idea could not be considered seriously during the Cold War. The two superpowers were locked in a mortal, ideological struggle in which nuclear weapons played a major role. The world was polarized and the period was dominated by a relentless nuclear arms race.

Today's general state of strife and violence has made some people hanker after the "stability" of the Cold War. But there never was any stability. At no time was either side satisfied that its nuclear arsenal was sufficient to ensure its security. Each superpower felt compelled to keep improving its offensive potential and developing new defensive capabilities. As time went on the race became extremely costly, imposing unbearable economic burdens, particularly on the Soviet Union. I believe that the nuclear arms race, had it continued, would have ended in a nuclear holocaust and the destruction of our civilization. Fortunately, a sane leader emerged: Mikhail Gorbachev, who in a very bold move—one that later contributed to his downfall—stopped the nuclear arms race.

The collapse of communism and the disintegration of the Soviet Union created an entirely new political climate: erstwhile enemies have become friends and partners. Today there is no more excuse for the nuclear powers to avoid fulfilling their obligations under Article VI of the NPT. Yet they have not embarked on a program of complete nuclear disarmament. Despite views such as that of Gen. Charles Horner, chief of the U.S. Space Command, who has said "the nuclear weapon is obsolete. I want to get rid of them all," the U.S. Pentagon's recent nuclear posture review concluded that the "Post-Cold War environment requires the nuclear deterrent." This sentiment is echoed in the policies of Russia, France, and the United Kingdom.

The main argument advanced by the nuclear states as an excuse for retaining their weapons is the so-called "breakout" syndrome. According to this view, the genie is out of the bottle. Nuclear weapons cannot be disinvented; knowledge about them cannot be expunged. Therefore, this line of reasoning asserts, even if nations agreed to get rid of all nuclear weapons, a rogue state could still build a new nuclear arsenal at some time in the future. That state could then blackmail other countries, perhaps the whole world.

The fallacy of the disinvention argument is that it ignores ways by which a civilized society deals with undesirable products of technological advance: through the application of law—in this case by making the acquisition of nuclear weapons an illegal act punishable under international law. In putting forward their argument, the nuclear states have assumed, without supporting evidence, that a treaty to eliminate nuclear weapons would not be effective in preventing breakout.

The prevention of breakout is admittedly a serious problem that troubles even political and military leaders who want to get rid of nuclear weapons. For example, former Secretary of Defense Robert McNamara has said, "I strongly advocate a return, by all nuclear powers, insofar as practicable, to a non-nuclear world"—his

qualification referring to the necessity of maintaining protection against breakout. But a recent study of this problem by Pugwash, an international group of scientists who meet regularly to address security issues and other global concerns, concluded that preventing breakout, while not easy, is possible with the aid of two verification systems: one technological and the other social/political.

Some two to three decades will be needed to put into place the technological elements of the necessary safeguard system, including dismantling all warheads under international control, disposing of highly enriched uranium and plutonium, and establishing much more stringent supervision over the various processes involved in the peaceful use of nuclear energy.

Time will also be needed to introduce the necessary social and political changes, some of which contain an element of public education. One such innovation is the acceptance of the universal validity of a treaty to abolish nuclear weapons. Once a certain number of states —including the present nuclear states— have agreed to such a treaty, a resolution of the Security Council can make it binding on all states without exception. The treaty would make the possession of nuclear weapons a criminal offense, with any transgression punishable by the United Nations under international law.

An important feature of the treaty to eliminate nuclear weapons will be a clause that mandates all states to pass laws making it the right and duty of every citizen to notify an international authority of any suspected attempt to violate the treaty. This will make every citizen —each of us—the treaty's custodian. The scientific community will play a special role in monitoring the activities of scientists and the purchase of specialized equipment for making nuclear weapons. Whistleblowing will be encouraged and immunity will have to be assured.

With these two verification systems, technological and social/political, the probability of undetected nuclear proliferation will be vanishingly small. This system is not absolutely foolproof; there can be no 100 percent guarantee that breakout will not occur. But the likelihood of such an occurrence will be much less than it is at present, when we face an abundance of nuclear weapons.

Who is likely to violate the treaty? Not a state governed by rational leaders, because they will realize that any advantage gained from the acquisition of a few bombs would be transient, and very costly in view of the severe retribution by the family of nations. Of course, this argument does not apply to a fanatical leader or to a group of terrorists, but such a danger exists now. Should a terrorist group acquire an atomic bomb, place it somewhere in a city, and then demand a ransom, all the thousands of nuclear warheads in the world's arsenals will be useless to deal with the threat. However,

such an event is much more likely to occur now, when there are so many nuclear weapons and the materials to make them are available in a developing black market, than in a world in which there are no nuclear weapons.

Thus, while a nuclear-weapon-free world will not be absolutely safe against a nuclear threat, it will be safer than the present world, and much safer than the world we are likely to have in the next 20 to 30 years if the nuclear powers refuse to take definite steps to eliminate these weapons. This is so because the long-term alternative to a nuclear-weapon-free world is not the present world but a world where a large number of states have accepted the argument—now used by the nuclear states—that any nation that feels threatened in any way is entitled to its own nuclear deterrent.

The lesson from 50 years of the nuclear age is that nuclear weapons are not needed for world security; indeed, they are a menace to world peace. A nuclear-weapon-free world is both desirable and feasible; only political will is needed to make it a reality.

POSTSCRIPT

Does the World Need to Have Nuclear Weapons at All?

Do arms, nuclear or otherwise, provoke war or provide security? There is no doubt that arms make war possible and also sometimes help create the tensions that are fertile ground for war. But the relationship is complex. Arms may instead be amassed because of war-producing tension. Many analysts argue that weapons are necessary for survival in a predatory world. This logic suspects that disarmament would actually increase the likelihood of war or domination by tempting aggressors to cheat and spring their weapons on an unsuspecting and defenseless victim. One recent study of the relationship between arms control and political tension is Vally Koubi, "International Tensions and Arms Control Agreements," *American Journal of Political Science* (February 1993).

The power of nuclear weapons makes the relationship between weapons and war particularly important. The contention that nuclear arms are dangerous and that they decrease security is the prevailing view among political leaders, scholars, and others. But it is not a universally accepted view. British prime minister Winston Churchill once suggested that nuclear weapons may have rendered nuclear war and even large-scale conventional war between nuclear powers too dangerous to fight. Some would point to the absence of a U.S.–USSR war during decades of overt confrontation as proof that nuclear arms do provide security. A few commentators have even suggested that the way to end war is to have all countries armed with invulnerable nuclear retaliatory forces. This, the logic goes, would create a nuclear checkmate system, in which aggression would mean the aggressor's fiery destruction. The proverbial catch-22 in such arguments, of course, is that nuclear weapons are extremely powerful, and if deterrence does not work, then the apocalypse is possible.

It is also possible that the spread of nuclear weapons cannot be contained unless the current nuclear powers agree to disarm. The Nuclear Nonproliferation Treaty was renewed in 1995, but many nonnuclear countries expressed the view that it should not be construed as a way to freeze into place two unequal tiers of countries: those with and those without nuclear weapons. It may also be that without total nuclear disarmament, current "minor" nuclear powers could become major nuclear powers. On this issue from China's point of view, see Shen Dingli, "Towards a Nuclear-Weapon-Free World: A Chinese Perspective," *Bulletin of the Atomic Scientists* (March/April 1994). Nonproliferation is also considered in Mitchell Reiss, *Bridled Ambition: Why Countries Constrain Their Nuclear Capabilities* (Johns Hopkins University Press, 1995).

ISSUE 13

Should a Permanent UN Military Force Be Established?

YES: Lukas Haynes and Timothy W. Stanley, from "To Create a United Nations Fire Brigade," *Comparative Strategy* (vol. 14, 1995)

NO: John F. Hillen III, from "Policing the New World Order: The Operational Utility of a Permanent U.N. Army," *Strategic Review* (Spring 1994)

ISSUE SUMMARY

YES: Lukas Haynes, a former assistant to the president of the Carnegie Endowment for International Peace, and Timothy W. Stanley, vice president for policy of the United Nations Association–National Capital Area, propose a standing UN military force of international volunteers to better enable the United Nations to meet its peacekeeping mission.

NO: John F. Hillen III, a defense policy analyst at the Heritage Foundation, criticizes the idea of a permanent UN army on several grounds and concludes that such a force is unworkable.

More than any single purpose, the United Nations was established with the hope that it could help save "succeeding generations from the scourge of war which ... has brought untold sorrow to mankind." These opening words of the UN Charter (its constitution) reflect a realization born of World War I, World War II, and the advent of the atomic age, that whatever the toll of past warfare, the future cost could be far, far worse.

The UN seeks to maintain and restore peace through a variety of methods. These include creating norms against violence, providing a forum to debate conflicts as an alternative to war, efforts to prevent the proliferation of weapons, diplomatic intervention (such as mediation), and the placing of diplomatic and economic sanctions. Additionally, and at the heart of the issue here, the UN can dispatch troops under its banner or authorize member countries to use their forces to carry out UN mandates.

UN forces involving a substantial number of military or police personnel have been used more than two dozen times in the organization's nearly 50-year history and have involved troops and police from more than 75 countries. There is, therefore, a significant history of such UN forces. Nevertheless, recent events and attitude changes have engendered renewed debate over the military role of the UN.

The increased number of UN operations is one factor. Of all UN missions, about half are currently active. Furthermore, several of the recent missions, including the UN presence in Bosnia, Somalia, and Rwanda, have included large numbers of troops and, thus, have been very costly. Increased calls for UN peacekeeping operations and the sometimes sizable nature of those operations have inflated the UN's annual peacekeeping budget from $235 million in 1987 to approximately $3 billion in 1995.

A second factor that has sparked controversy about UN forces is the successes and failures of their missions. Often UN forces have played an important part in the peace process; other times they have been unsuccessful. The limited mandate (role, instructions) and strength (personnel, armaments) of UN forces has frequently left them as helpless bystanders. A third shift that has raised issues about UN forces is the change in the international system. The cold war has ended; some people hope for and are trying to promote a new world order. A part of that initiative is for countries to keep faith with the ideal within the UN charter and to use force only unilaterally, for immediate self-defense, unless they are authorized to use force by the UN or a regional organization (such as the Organization of American States). What this means is that collective action under UN auspices is becoming more normal; unilateral action by a country is becoming the exception.

Two potential changes in the operation of UN forces are related to the issue here. The first is to increase the mission of UN forces. To date, UN forces have operated according to two concepts: *collective security* and *peacekeeping*. Collective security is the idea that aggression against anyone is a threat to everyone. Therefore, the collective body should cooperate to prevent and, if necessary, defeat aggression. The second long-standing UN role of peacekeeping usually involves acting as a buffer between two sides to provide an atmosphere that will allow them to settle their differences, or at least not fight. Neither collective security nor peacekeeping, however, precisely applies to situations such as domestic civil wars where there is no international aggressor or clearly identifiable aggressor. Some people consider this a gap in what the UN does to prevent the scourge of war and, therefore, would augment the UN's role to include *peacemaking*. This would involve intervening in either international or civil wars, with or without the consent of any of the participants, to *make* the warring parties desist.

The second, and related, potential change for UN forces relates to proposals to create, at maximum, a standing UN army or, at least, a ready reserve of troops that would remain with the forces of their home countries but would train for UN operations and be instantly available to the UN.

In the following selections, Lukas Haynes and Timothy W. Stanley argue that a permanent UN military force would pave the way to lasting international peace and security for the next century. John F. Hillen III argues that such proposals are mostly ill-conceived and should not be supported.

YES

Lukas Haynes and
Timothy W. Stanley

TO CREATE A UNITED NATIONS
FIRE BRIGADE

As the United Nations [UN] fiftieth anniversary year, 1995 seems a most appropriate time to consider a standing United Nations fire brigade to function directly under the council on a truly international basis. A second Security Council meeting at heads of government level, if one is rescheduled in 1995, could help launch such an initiative. The first such summit occurred in January 1992 at a time of growing optimism that, with the end of the Cold War, the United Nations might at last begin to fulfill the aspirations of its founders to "save succeeding generations from the scourge of war." The UN Secretary-General was accordingly invited to design a strategy for peace maintenance and those recommendations became Boutros Boutros-Ghali's *Agenda for Peace*.

Subsequently, the world has learned the hard way the truth of the adage attributed to Carl von Clausewitz that "strategy may be simple, but it is not thereby easy" as applied to any strategy for peace. Whether called peacekeeping, peacemaking, peace-enforcement, or even humanitarian intervention, UN activities have encountered serious conceptual and practical difficulties. The few successes seem balanced by an equal number of partial failures or inconclusive results. Consequently, the broad topic of peacekeeping has become the subject of intense professional and academic analyses and discussions.

It is not our purpose in this article to review the literature or to outline possible solutions to the many dilemmas of international intervention in the proliferation of ethnic and civil conflicts around the world. Rather we offer a proposal for addressing low-intensity conflicts before they rage out of control. This article expands the now common concept of a UN standing force and lays out in detail the specifics of a relatively modest, if novel, international fire brigade. The brigade is designed mainly for facilitating a rapid UN response to selected humanitarian disasters, requiring some elements of military force, to enable civilian relief agencies to operate (as in Rwanda).

A standing UN fire brigade could be available for immediate airlift upon Security Council authorization without the delay of assembling national

From Lukas Haynes and Timothy W. Stanley, "To Create a United Nations Fire Brigade," *Comparative Strategy*, vol. 14 (1995). Copyright © 1995 by Taylor and Francis, Inc. Reprinted by permission. All rights reserved. Notes omitted.

contributions. Composed of individual volunteers, it would need no parliament to debate why its troops might die on foreign soil.

At first, the brigade would best be used in human disasters of the Somali or Rwandan type where a military presence is needed to secure civilian relief efforts amid chaos. When the warlords first intimidated the small Pakistani UN unit at Mogadishu in 1993, immediate deployment of a brigade might have reopened food supply lines without the need for large-scale U.S. intervention. Similarly in Rwanda, early deployment of the brigade might have reduced the slaughter and prevented much of the mass migration panic that cost the lives of tens of thousands of people. Such a standing UN unit, if well-trained and well-equipped, could have been deployed in days, rather than the months required under current UN procedures.

Such a force would be no panacea for world instability, nor would it substitute for improvised UN peacekeeping or coalition war-fighting. But it would be a new and flexible tool in the United Nations' meager kit, specially suited for rapid deployment to potential conflagrations where no major country is willing or able to act quickly. It would have to be initiated on an experimental basis, with a small augmented infantry brigade structure as the nucleus. A force numbering about 5,000 would seem adequate to test and develop the concept while remaining manageable and affordable. Because it would be truly international, the fire brigade would symbolize a commitment by the world community to check the advance of ethnic fires sweeping across the globe (or at least mitigate their human consequences).

Is the proposed fire brigade politically and economically feasible and could it be effective? Would the brigade's initially limited functions prove to be worth the investment? Could it evolve into more ambitious experiments in cooperative security?

To answer such questions one must consider the relevant precedents, today's international environment for collective security, the specifics of the proposed brigade, and the reasonable objections in principle and practice that can be raised against the concept.

PRECEDENTS FOR A UN FIRE BRIGADE

Proposing a standing force is neither novel nor radical. The first UN secretary general, Norway's Trygve Lie, proposed a "UN guard" of 5,000 to be under the control of the secretary general, and ultimately responsible to the Security Council. Its creation was blocked by the cold war. In 1992 Secretary General Boutros Boutros-Ghali urged that heavily armed and specially trained "peace-enforcement" units be made available on call, but his *Agenda for Peace* left the operational details vague. Between these initiatives by UN secretaries general 45 years apart, there have been numerous proposals by scholars and diplomats for "UN armies" ranging from 50,000 to 500,000 strong. None now seems politically viable, operationally feasible, or financially affordable.

Nonetheless, a blue ribbon commission of 28 former heads of state, including Gerald Ford, Helmut Schmidt, and

Mikhail Gorbachev, concluded in summer 1994 that:

> Given the reluctance of Governments to place their own soldiers in harm's way... the creation of a modest-size standing force of volunteers under UN auspices... backed up by regional or sub-regional peace-keeping forces [be considered for rapidly] pre-empting conflicts or intervening to head off humanitarian tragedies. [Their rationale:] Internal and ethnic conflicts threaten to produce a chain reaction... destabilizing entire regions. Stability may only be regained if the international community begins to intervene in cases of genocide or other blatant breakdowns of governmental authority and does not hide behind self-serving and disingenuous excuses.

INTERNATIONAL ENVIRONMENT FOR COLLECTIVE SECURITY

In the new international environment, the nature of conflict has indeed changed, particularly for the less developed world. Strategic pressures on the major powers to intervene for cold war reasons have disappeared. But these causes have been replaced by unprecedented demands to halt or contain highly publicized atrocities committed against civilian populations by poorly armed, often paramilitary, groups.

Western governments have been hard-pressed to respond effectively to this new generation of conflict. The United Nations has become the depository and scapegoat for security problems that command limited national interest but generate rhetoric and at least the appearance of action by timid governments.

The inadequacy of UN capabilities is most evident in recent developments. During 1994 an overburdened UN Security Council authorized Russia, France, and the United States to intervene in Georgia, Rwanda, and Haiti, respectively. Some call this "sphere-of-influence" intervention, when larger countries reassert influence in smaller countries they have traditionally dominated. These states presumably seek UN authorization of unilateral intervention for greater international legitimacy, but such UN practice may come to undermine the international community if it hopes to defend the primacy of international law and the ideal of sovereign equality of states.

There is also a real post–Persian Gulf War fear among less developed countries that cooperation among the major powers will afford them new opportunities for exploitation of smaller states. This perception could hasten the already growing political-economic chasm between North and South. Ironically, however, imperial or strategic designs have not yet been the problem. The major powers have demonstrated no real enthusiasm for foreign intervention, contributing to what *The Washington Post*'s Jim Hoagland calls the *five* horsemen of the Apocalypse: War, Disease, Famine, Death, and *Indifference*.

All the major powers have demonstrated a genuine aversion to sustaining casualties abroad. There are too many contributing factors for analysis here, but whatever the causes, unwillingness to shed blood of even an "all volunteer" U.S. military establishment seems to be a fact of life (for example, in congressional debate about Haiti); a fact in odd contradiction to U.S. claims of being the sole superpower.

Who then will deal with the world's numerous brushfires? The ability of the United Nations to monitor potential instability has improved and the Security

Council has become "seized" of a nearly endless list of trouble spots where the major powers do not want to intervene. To meet the growing demand for its services, the United Nations has done much to improve the management of UN peace operations both in the field and in New York. Central to the reform has been a restructuring of the United Nations Department of Peacekeeping Operations (DPKO) to integrate vertically different aspects of its activities including the political, military, and humanitarian dimensions. The DPKO also has worked to link forward-planning and more uniform peacekeeping training procedures to the later stages of managing UN peace operations. Logistic and air transport services for UN operations continue to be contracted out, but equipment is now being stockpiled at a UN complex and Italy and organization-wide communication is vastly improved....

Despite these reforms, traditional peacekeeping methods have proved inadequate or simply inappropriate to the more assertive tasks assigned in Bosnia, Rwanda, and Somalia. In each of these cases the United Nations was initially unprepared for immediate action and the United States, wary of an expanding peacekeeping budget, was opposed to additional funding. Inability to head off the crises early resulted in unthinkable human suffering and led to more costly interventions later. In Somalia alone, the United States eventually had to spend a billion dollars.

Having no preventive deployment or emergency relief capability, the UN Security Council authorized a traditional peacekeeping force of African troops in Rwanda, but it lacked the proper equipment and the United Nations had to turn to the United States for armored vehicles and airlift. As a Rwandan exodus to Tanzania and Zaire poured through the conflict zones, the United Nations entered into a petty negotiation with the Pentagon for badly needed armored vehicles and struggled to shape a peacekeeping force that would meet U.S.-imposed peacekeeping criteria....

The good news is that Somalia and Rwanda can now be added to a growing list of humanitarian emergencies, including efforts in northern Iraq and Sarajevo, where military forces have been used to provide relief to civilians. More importantly, while the post–cold war foreign policy of Russia is still evolving, neither it nor China has sought to block Security Council action to address such crises.

As the United States and an under-equipped United Nations have tried to shoulder the world's security burdens, some relevant conclusions can be drawn. Quicker response could save hundreds of thousands of lives and hundreds of millions, if not billions, of dollars, if the United Nations can get "fires" under control and avert catastrophes that are more costly to address later.

Military units can perform exceptionally well in battling humanitarian disasters when objectives are precise and the proper resources are provided. Even small forces, such as the French sent to Rwanda, can be successful in securing havens for refugees and restoring a semblance of order. But armed humanitarian intervention requires capabilities for using force that traditional peacekeeping missions do not have.

Lacking a viable international alternative, the United States will continue to come under strong internal and external pressures to respond as the depictions of human misery increase in the media. Haiti and Rwanda prove that the United

States is reluctant to endanger its credibility by intervening where its interests are not clearly at stake, and humanitarian concern always wanes when U.S. blood is spilled. That national sensitivity undermines political support for responses, erodes staying power, and weakens our ability to mount future ventures (the controversy over Haiti again being a case in point).

So if the United States cannot be the world's policeman and will only rarely fight "fires" that are flaming out of control, the need for a UN fire brigade becomes obvious.... Before exploring the specifics of the [UN] force we envision, it must be made clear that this proposal is for an emergency fire brigade or perhaps a temporary constabulary, not a standing "global police force," let alone a "UN army."

SPECIFICS OF A UN FIRE BRIGADE

Mission

The brigade's primary purpose would be for armed humanitarian intervention, including refugee relief in situations of a scale suitable for the force to operate successfully in a low-intensity, low-tech combat environment. Obviously it would take some time at least to develop and train the force, even as an experimental model. Its mission would evolve as its capability improved and world events unfolded. For training purposes, however, we believe its primary function should be to safeguard refugee and civilian relief personnel in Rwanda- or early Somalia-type scenarios; to fight as a cohesive, integrated unit in low-intensity combat; and to conduct an orderly fighting withdrawal if its deployment as a deterrent should fail.

A secondary and more evolutionary function would be to serve as the nucleus and command center to which other UN peacekeeping units could be attached as states would make them available. The brigade's combat capabilities could someday provide the cutting edge for peace enforcement or peacemaking assignments....

The brigade also could be used for preventive deployment as an adjunct to preventive diplomacy..., to protect or rescue UN civilian or military personnel in untenable situations..., to enforce economic sanctions on land..., to police or enforce formal peace agreements where low-level violence continues..., or to protect unarmed microstates from externally based coups.... Larger scale peacekeeping or enforcement actions would have to be left to other forces or coalitions with greater numbers and greater firepower; but after an experimental force of 5,000 had proved itself, we think its utility and efficiency could be much improved if it became 10,000 strong.

Legal Basis

The brigade could be created under Article 43 of the United Nations Charter undertaking "to make available to the Security Council, on its call, armed forces, assistance and facilities, including rights of passage."... [Or] Article 40, which grants the Security Council special provisional powers to prevent aggravations of security crises.... The brigade would operate as an extension of the Security Council's authority.... It would not be within the jurisdiction of the secretary general or the brigade command to deploy or to decide the legality of a deployment. The Secretariat could send the brigade only after the Security Council had mandated it to do so.

Command and Control

The force would be headed by a commander appointed by the Security Council from outstanding general officers with UN experience. The commander would require a normal command and staff that included liaison officers trained to work with civilian relief agencies. The brigade would be complemented by a director general at UN headquarters with a civilian-military staff to handle its myriad and novel tasks. The director general would be the key link between the force commander and the UN secretary general and should also be appointed by the council. The chain of command would run from the council to the secretary general to the force's director general to the brigade commander....

Personnel

We envisage worldwide recruitment through national authorities of active military personnel of all ranks and grades who volunteer. A national endorsement should provide a large pool of candidates. Informal soundings among officers with prior UN service suggest there would be far more highly qualified volunteers than needed. Priority should to go marine- or ranger-like elite units, which most countries maintain. Selection should be based on the needs of the force for skills and experience. Informally, some quota system would be needed to distribute the representation of Europeans, Asians, Africans, and Latin Americans. No more than about 5% of the total should be from one country and no more than 20–25% from a single region. Fluency in two foreign languages would be a must, with English as the operating language since it is the lingua franca of international aviation, commerce, shipping, and unofficially, UN peacekeeping.

Relationship With National Services

What relationship would the volunteers have with their national services? Personnel selected would be placed on extended leaves from their parent services for up to 5 years, thereby remaining eligible for Geneva Convention treatment as well as for the new conventions being drafted for the safety and protection of UN personnel. They would also be carried on national rolls for retirement and family benefit purposes.... National fiscal cost and potential drain on readiness of the international volunteers would be insignificant with at most a couple of hundred people from a single country, and these costs would be partly offset by the international skills returning veterans would bring back. Volunteers would not, however, be "assigned or attached" for UN duty. They would become international military servants analogous to civil servants who join the UN Secretariat for a tour.

Compensation

All personnel should be paid directly by the United Nations at whichever is highest: their national pay, or the UN reimbursement rate of about $12,000 per year, plus a bonus for hazardous duty. To minimize insult to the principle of equal pay for equal work and risks, pay envelopes for each rank should be equalized, with those earning more having the difference deposited into home savings accounts. Depending on the mix of national pay levels, the total for a force of 5,000 could be under $100 million per year. If the entire brigade were paid at the highest rates (U.S. salaries), those costs would double and could put the concept above the threshold of financial feasibility. We believe, however, that this elite UN brigade would still attract the best soldiers from their respective countries even if the standard rate of $12,000 (which is relatively high on world average) was lower than U.S. salaries.

Personnel should also have distinctive UN uniforms and be subject to discipline by the force itself, except that general court martial offenses would be referred to national military authorities. Personnel deemed unfit for the sophisticated, sensitive, and cooperative demands of the foreign brigade could be repatriated.

Basing

Since extensive training and joint exercises with national forces would be required, initial basing should be at a single location, which ideally would be donated by a host country from surplus military facilities worldwide. It would be politically preferable that the base not be in the territory of one of the Permanent Five of the Security Council.... Later on, if the experimental phase succeeds enough to warrant expansion, it would be desirable to have elements of the force dispersed close to likely operating areas in Africa, Asia, and the Middle East.... At such forward locations, stocks of heavier equipment could be maintained and supplies for air mobility would be emphasized.

Equipment

The embryo force would have to develop a table of organization and equipment (TO&E) for its three self-sustaining battalions, of roughly 1,200 men each, organized into four line companies each of about 200. Each battalion would need a headquarters facility and limited combat and service support. Trucks, jeeps, and armored personnel carriers would be the primary vehicles and armament, augmented by a few air transportable light tanks, artillery, and antiaircraft guns. Observation aircraft and helicopters with some gunship capacity would accompany each battalion. Based on U.S. Army costing models, the procurement costs for each such battalion would range from $100 million to $120 million and the annual operations and maintenance account would run to about $16 million....

Cost

Even with the most optimistic assumptions, the brigade would annually cost roughly $100 million for personnel plus another $100 million (half for equipment and half for operations and maintenance). Costs of both inter- and intra-theater airlift could also be considerable, whether provided commercially or reimbursably by the United States or another country's air force. So one is talking about $200 million per year for a 5,000-strong brigade, not an insignificant sum for the United Nations' perennially underfunded peacekeeping budget. Obviously, a stronger force of 10,000 would cost more.

On the other hand the cost pales in comparison to post-disaster relief and cleanup efforts, let alone the $50 billion plus in U.S. incremental costs for Desert Shield/Desert Storm which its allies had to reimburse. A UN fire brigade could have mitigated the former and perhaps prevented the need for the latter by deterring Iraq. To lend some perspective, the entire UN peacekeeping budget for 1992 would have paid for only 2 days of the Persian Gulf War.

One new way of raising money would be a special levy based not on the United Nations' antiquated and inequitable present peacekeeping formula, but prorated for each country's share of world gross domestic product (GDP) and a fraction of 1% of its actual military expenditures. Some less developed countries that now spend just a few thousand dollars on UN peacekeeping pour tens of millions of dollars into their own military establishments. Of the total obligation,... a portion could be met by acceptable donations of equipment, basing, support and facilities to the UN brigade.

OBJECTIONS RAISED AGAINST A UN FIRE BRIGADE

The UN standing force concept has attracted a number of objections. A fundamental objection goes to the competence, in both the legal and practical sense, of the United Nations to mount humanitarian and other interventions required by international or internal conflict that call for a significant military presence (as in Rwanda)....

Quite to the contrary, the founders of the United Nations, who were hardly wide-eyed one-worlders, envisioned that sovereign member states would enable the United Nations to do exactly that. Indeed, the UN charter requires members to earmark forces for the Security Council. Legally and conceptually, the United Nations was designed to keep the peace by peaceful means if possible, but it would employ concerted military force as a last resort to enforce the peace rather than repeat the failures of the League of Nations by relying on independent national actions.

Critics of assertive multilateralism further allege that the United Nations cannot effectively command a force of soldiers who can fight with the requisite discipline, training, and morale....

In truth, trained and equipped individuals actually fight in combat, not governments. For example, no one ever accused

the multinational French Foreign Legion of lacking morale and discipline under fire. The UN Blue Helmets have worked very well within their limits, although the standards of cooperation and communication for peacekeeping are not as demanding as the levels of discipline, teamwork, and mutual confidence required in combat....

The importance of integration at the level of individuals does require explanation. Several former UN force commanders have told us that efforts to join national units into emergency defense forces simply could not overcome national differences in doctrines and chains of command. Most argued that an integrated force of individual professionals who trained together and had uniform equipment and doctrines would be more effective and perceive less cause for animosity....

Many critics of a UN volunteer force conveniently overlook the North Atlantic Treaty Organization (NATO), which has operated integrated commands and staffs as well as operational elements such as the Allied Command Europe (ACE) Mobile Force, assorted naval standing forces, and the Airborne Warning and Control System (AWACS) with considerable success. NATO is now moving to even more ambitious combined joint task forces....

Major questions arise also from the wariness of small states about foreign intervention in internal affairs notwithstanding that Article II, paragraph 7 of the UN Charter (which reaffirms the sovereignty principle) specifically "shall not prejudice the application of enforcement measures under Chapter VII." The fear of the Un Security Council as a vehicle for power domination of the weak remains a political obstacle. It once appeared that the Security Council resolution authorizing Chapter VII force for the protection of Kurds was a rare and dangerous precedent. Nevertheless, in the cases of Somalia, Rwanda, and now Haiti, the Security Council has again invoked Chapter VII to authorize military responses aimed largely at human suffering. Events and the day-to-day diplomacy of the Security Council have gradually expanded the range of threats that are seen to undermine international security under Chapter VII. Threats naturally covered include cross-border aggression, but increasingly civil and tribal wars, genocide, and mass movements of victims are being added.

It is significant that Security Council activism on Somalia, Rwanda, and Haiti engendered relatively little opposition among smaller UN states, though the foreign interventions in those countries stretched the traditional application of Chapter VII. A case can be made that the greatest success of the United Nations since its creation has been to delegitimize the use of force to change internationally recognized borders. (Obviously, the case of the former Yugoslavia still threatens to be a troubling exception.) ...

Yet some critics in the United States and other developed countries see even the smallest UN "owned and operated" force as a potential threat to their nation's control of their own policies and forces, or even a step toward world government. People cry out not for world government but for at least incremental steps toward world governance to deal with global problems, and especially, mass slaughter or starvation. One can assume that large populations will probably continue to come under mortal threats from groups seeking to benefit from ethnic cleansing or promoting civil strife. In many such cases, no major power will

have an interest in intervening and whole communities will be exposed to catastrophes that the world should not be willing to tolerate at the end of the twentieth century. The Permanent Five are, of course, protected from UN intervention by their ability to veto any Security Council action. In terms of national readiness, we have stressed that the instrument of international force being proposed here involves not units of the U.S. armed forces, but selected individual volunteers from around the world including a few U.S. soldiers who are willing to serve under UN command.

The objection also arises that the existence of even the small ready forces we envisage could create the temptation to use them, and unwittingly drag the United Nations (and with it [member countries]) into some far-distant quagmire. Here, the issue must be joined. The purpose of the brigade would be to enhance UN capabilities, and indeed to be used, but only on Security Council deliberation when a clear international and regional consensus demands a response and no single country is willing to intervene. This proposal rests on the logical assumption that the secretary general would not recommend, and the council would not deploy, the force in situations that are already beyond its capacity or judged so by UN representatives in the field and at headquarters. This includes situations where a more organized belligerent faction could actually muster sufficient force to defeat the brigade. ...

Success in the field would depend on clearly defined mandates by the UN Security Council. Granted the councils' record has been mixed and in the past its decisions have been taken with poor information and often without understanding the limits of UN resources or the consequences of failure.... A UN brigade, with clearly limited capabilities and finite funding, would not suffer from the illusion and misperception surrounding ad hoc Security Council creations that additional troops will somehow materialize and necessary funding will be found at some later date. Hopefully..., an institutionalized UN brigade command... would inject necessary pragmatism into Security Council deliberations....

Generally the UN brigade would be most effective in the beginning phase of a crisis either to deter or prevent an escalation of conflict, or in the worst scenario, to establish safe havens for hundreds of thousands of refugees. Even the modest deployment of 2,500 French troops to Rwanda succeeded in initially establishing safe zones in part of the country, although of course they could not deal with the mass exodus into Zaire and were soon called home by domestic pressures. At least, they bought some time for other forces to arrive. The proposed UN brigade would have been even more effective and could have stayed longer, with its exact missions depending on evolving circumstances.

There are also the important issues of credibility or backup for the brigade if it gets into trouble, and logistic support while it is deployed. For the latter we envisage short, 60- to 90-day deployments until the brigade can be relieved by regularly assembled UN peacekeeping or enforcement units. With its light equipment, resupply (by air) of its basic combat stocks should not pose an obstacle....

The backup problem is more serious because no unit should be put in harm's way without provisions for reinforcement, air support, and, if necessary, evacuation. In that regard, another advan-tage of an international brigade would be its credibility. It would be defending no national military prestige, its missions would be altruistic, and retreat or evacuation would do it no dishonor. It would be better to withdraw than yield to "mission creep" that costs lives.

Reinforcement capability would certainly be needed but that cannot be built into the brigade without making initial costs unmanageable. Therefore, our recommendation is that in its experimental phase and prior to each deployment, one or more of the Permanent Five of the Security Council with force projection capabilities (the United Kingdom, France, Russia, or the United States), but probably not China, or if appropriate to the area one of the regional powers, would agree to perform the reinforcement role on a contingency basis....

Why would one of these powers agree to be a contingency backup, especially if their national interests did not seem to require their participation at the outset? First, they would be protecting the international interests in the performance and well-being of the first truly international brigade. Second, the brigade's long-term survival and success would save Security Council members the cost of future unilateral interventions, and perhaps even mitigate potential major power conflicts....

CONCLUSION

We have discussed the applicable experience and outlined the limited circumstances and careful deliberation that would govern the UN fire brigade's deployment. While there always would be professional doubters, and objections to the force's cost would be raised, we believe that once a UN brigade was in being, it would attract media and public interest and support around the world. Politicians tend to take pride in the symbols they help to create, and even the smallest countries would see the brigade as a symbol of a new United Nations committed to causes that hardly could be construed as major power interests.

In sum, the case for a UN fire brigade must rest on the world security advantages of having such a dual purpose force available for rapid dispatch to a "fire" before it gets out of control. Any major power could do a better job with its own forces and with smaller incremental costs. The trouble is that they often will not do so, while at present the United Nations cannot....

In the end it is the people's will that should matter most. In opinion polls Americans have repeatedly indicated that they support intervention abroad for humanitarian purposes, and under a United Nations flag. Despite congressional concerns, Americans realize the angers of ethnic and civil violence (the cause of 89 of the world's 92 conflicts) and want to help civilians who comprise 90% of those conflicts' victims.... [T]he United Nations must be redesigned for more effective response. The small, pioneering step of a truly international UN volunteer brigade could pave the way toward further mobilizations of the world's will and resources. To get the ball rolling would be an innovative birthday experiment on the occasion of the United Nations' fiftieth anniversary in 1995. We believe few initiatives would do more to help the cause of lasting international peace and security for the next century.

NO

John F. Hillen III

POLICING THE NEW WORLD ORDER: THE OPERATIONAL UTILITY OF A PERMANENT U.N. ARMY

Proposals to create a U.N. Army are not new. They are designed to provide a mechanism and structure that will allow the U.N. to exercise its mandate while circumventing the problem that usually hobbles U.N. operations: the lack of a common political will. Political obstacles aside, there are operational reasons for rejecting a standing U.N. Army. The most important reason for this rejection is that such a force is redundant if employed at the lower end of the U.N. military operations spectrum (observation missions and first generation peacekeeping) but incapable of having any real impact at the upper end (second generation peacekeeping and enforcement).

In the three years immediately following the end of the Cold War, there was a heady optimism about the renewed capacity of the United Nations to enforce resolutions concerning international peace and security. Now, due to the apparent impotency of United Nations forces in Bosnia and Somalia, the mood has swung back toward the pessimism characteristic of the Cold War era. This has not stopped debate about mechanisms that the U.N. can use to enforce its resolutions, including an idea that never quite seems to go away for long: a permanent U.N. Army. Proponents say that such a force could rise above the ebb and flow of national interests and provide a genuinely useful security tool for the United Nations. However, what many of these observers fail to realize is that the limited operational capabilities of a permanent U.N. Army would rarely allow it to influence situations like Bosnia and Somalia. In some respects, it is a worthwhile idea, but it is self-defeating in that the force could make little impact on the very problems it was created to alleviate....

A RECURRING THEME

The idea of a permanent force for the U.N. is not envisaged by the U.N. Charter: it is in fact a concept that seeks to rectify a weakness in the Charter.

Article 43 of the U.N. Charter was intended to create for the U.N. continued access to the massive forces of the victorious World War II alliance. Even the most modest of proposals for U.N. forces constituted under Article 43 visualized 12 Army divisions, 900 combat aircraft, and almost 50 capital warships. The charter structure for using these forces visualized a fairly consistent process. The Security Council could determine a threat to international peace and security (Article 39), order action to redress such a threat by land, sea, and air forces under U.N. authority (Article 42), and call said forces to its service through the agreements reached according to Article 43. However, this security structure was doomed from the start because the critical agreements of Article 43 never materialized.

Thus, all proposals for a permanent U.N. Army have a common goal: to provide the U.N. with the mechanism and structure necessary to exercise its mandate: to maintain international peace and security....

[C]urrent proposals for a permanent U.N. Army are fueled by the desire for a tool that the U.N. can employ without being buffeted by the tides of a fickle international community. This most recent revival of the call for a permanent U.N. force does not seek to harness international consensus for the United Nations... but to institutionalize a security mechanism for the U.N. that does not rely on that consensus. The contemporary rationale for a permanent U.N. force is that it can circumvent the lack of political resolve in such situations as Bosnia.

THE SPECTRUM OF U.N. MILITARY OPERATIONS

Operations involving military personnel conducted under the auspices of the United Nations or its mandates span a broad operational spectrum. This spectrum ranges from unarmed peace observation missions to the conduct of war against an intransigent state. The operational nature of a U.N. military mission can be determined by many different factors, most of which can be subsumed under two categories: 1) the environment in which the force operates; and 2) the level of military effort or force used.

The environment in which the operation takes place could range from completely benign to very hostile. This important factor in the planning of U.N. military missions largely determines the size, nature, and composition of the U.N. force and its tasks. The level of military effort and the force employed reflects the environment and/or opposing forces as well as the nature of the tasks to be performed. By measuring these factors in all U.N. military operations, one can actually plot the spectrum of operations. While it is a continuous spectrum, there are discernible mission subsets: 1) Observation Missions; 2) First Generation Peacekeeping; 3) Second Generation Peacekeeping; and 4) Enforcement Actions.

The first two sets of U.N. military operations share many of the same operational characteristics. These are largely derived from the "principles of peacekeeping" which were recently articulated by the Under Secretary-General for peacekeeping operations.

1. They are United Nations operations. The forces are formed by the U.N. at the outset, commanded in the field

by a U.N.-appointed general, under the ultimate authority of the U.N. Secretary-General, and financed by member states collectively.

2. Peacekeeping forces are deployed with the consent of all the parties involved and only after a political settlement had been reached between warring factions.

3. The forces are committed to strict impartiality. Military observers and peacekeepers can in no way take sides with or against a party to the conflict.

4. Troops are provided by member states on a voluntary basis. During the Cold War era, the superpowers or even "big five" [the permanent members of the Security Council—China, France, Great Britain, the Soviet Union (now Russia), and the United States] rarely participated in these missions, and the majority of troops were supplied by the so-called "middle nations" to reinforce the concept of neutrality.

5. These units operate under rules of engagement that stress the absolute minimum use of force in accomplishing their objectives. This is usually limited to the use of force in self-defense only, but some missions have used force in "situations in which peacekeepers were being prevented by armed persons from fulfilling their mandate."

These five principles are especially applied in earnest in *observation missions.* There have been fifteen of these missions to date, and they represent the low end of the operational spectrum....

FIRST GENERATION PEACEKEEPING

Another class of U.N. military operations guided by the "principles of peacekeep-

ing" are first generation peacekeeping missions. These operations were all initiated during the Cold War era, as an improvised response to "the failure of collective security and the success of early U.N. peace observation missions." There were seven operations of this kind.... Three are still operational: Cyprus, the Golan Heights, and Lebanon, in their 29th, 19th and 15th years respectively. These operations share the salient feature of observation missions. Because peacekeeping forces are deployed after a political settlement and because they must remain strictly neutral, they rely on the goodwill and cooperation of the belligerents to accomplish their mission.

These forces differ from observation missions in that they are made up of entire military units from U.N. member states. These units are organically equipped, organized, trained, and armed (albeit lightly) for combat. They therefore possess some modicum of offensive capability and a credible defensive capacity. First generation peacekeeping forces have usually been deployed in a "buffer" role, physically occupying and controlling neutral territory between belligerents. These missions have focused primarily on ensuring the continued separation of the previously warring factions.

First generation peacekeeping missions do not generally have ambitious tasks: missions are derived from political objectives. The main objective is to contain the armed conflict in order to provide a stable atmosphere in which the conflict can be politically resolved. First generation peacekeeping missions (with the exception of parts of the U.N. intervention in the Congo) have no mandate or capacity to impose a political solution on the belligerents. After all, if deployed in accordance with the "principles of peacekeeping" there should be no need for forceful action in an atmosphere of cooperation. However, the operational environment has generally been more bellicose than that experienced by observation missions and there have been over 750 U.N. peacekeepers killed in these seven missions. That environment, and the more complicated military tasks involved for these combat units place these operations higher on the operational spectrum.

SECOND GENERATION PEACEKEEPING

Second generation peacekeeping missions share some operational characteristics with their Cold War predecessors but transcend the "principles of peacekeeping." The U.N. has initiated five of these operations since the relaxation of the superpower confrontation in 1987–1989: in Namibia, Cambodia, the former Yugoslavia, Somalia and Mozambique. In the main these operations are far more ambitious in their objectives, which include disarming the warring factions, maintaining law and order, restoring civil government and its associated functions, setting up and supervising elections, and delivering humanitarian aid. What makes these second generation tasks so challenging is that they very often take place in an atmosphere of continued fighting between factions, civil turmoil, and general chaos. The rate of U.N. fatalities in these missions is climbing.

There are considerable differences between these missions and those of the first two classes. While second generation peacekeeping forces are formed and deployed with unprecedented Security Council consensus, the warring parties often do not want them. Unlike first generation peacekeeping, a cease-fire is not a *sine qua non* [essential] for U.N. deployment. The U.N. forces involved in these operations face the prospect of having little or no cooperation from the factions on the ground, since second generation peacekeeping missions often consist of heavily armed combat units possessing considerable offensive capability, frequently contributed by the major powers.

The large and combat-heavy force structure of second generation peacekeeping forces means that they are able not only to protect themselves and other U.N. personnel, but also to attempt to impose an agreement on unwilling belligerents. The risks inherent in this have been most graphically portrayed in Bosnia and Somalia. In each case, military force has been employed against particular parties in the conflict. In Bosnia, it has mainly consisted of an enforced flight ban against the Serbs and the low level use of force to protect the delivery of humanitarian aid and keep supply lines open. In Somalia, the U.N. authorized the capture by force of Mohammed Aideed, again clearly taking sides in the attempt to impose a political solution. The offensive use of military force in these missions has not produced great dividends for the "peacekeepers" as yet.

The operational characteristics of most second generation peacekeeping missions bear little resemblance to the five "principles of peacekeeping." 1) While they are U.N. operations, they sometimes must rely nonetheless on other organizations or member states for complex operational capabilities that the U.N. does not possess. The use of NATO to enforce the Bosnian flight ban and a U.S. military task force to initially intervene in Somalia are two examples of this. 2) There has been no concrete political settlement in some cases and there is hardly an environment of consent for a U.N. presence. 3) As mentioned above, the doctrine of strict neutrality has not been followed. 4) The forces of the permanent members of the Security Council are often heavily involved. 5) The rules of engagement have been enlarged substantially to allow second generation peacekeepers the capacity to impose a solution on the local parties through the use of force.

In most respects, these missions are only one step short of full-scale enforcement operations. The U.N. has recognized that, considering the innocuous forces and methods employed, traditional peacekeeping can only succeed under favorable political conditions. But second generation peacekeeping military forces are caught on the horns of a prickly dilemma. While lesser operations are governed by the principles of peacekeeping and higher operations are governed by the principles of war, second generation peacekeeping operations are quite simply ungoverned by doctrine of any kind.

ENFORCEMENT

Enforcement actions represent the high end of the operational spectrum, taking place in a bellicose and adversarial environment that necessitates the use of large-scale military force. The operational characteristics of these campaigns are those of war. The role of military forces in this enterprise is obviously more clear cut than the somewhat ambiguous parameters of action in peacekeeping missions. There is no cooperation from the enemy and therefore no need for impartiality. The forces can use purely military doctrine to calculate the force

needed to impose the dictates of the U.N. resolution on the aggressor. From a military point of view, this is the only type of U.N. operation where the force can actually create the environment it needs to guarantee success. The only two examples of U.N. collective security operations of this type are Korea in 1950–1953 and Kuwait in 1990–1991.

Each of these situations presented a unique set of circumstances for the exercise of collective security under the auspices of the U.N. In each case the command and control of the operation and the majority of forces were provided by the United States, leading many to dismiss these operations as American wars. However, both were multinational operations authorized by the legislative bodies of the U.N. The fact that the U.N. was essentially following the U.S. lead in both cases illustrates an important characteristic of large-scale enforcement actions. They must have the wholesale participation of a great power in order to bring about the huge resources, sacrifices, and political will required to wage modern war against an intransigent state. Only a few states or groups of states can provide the complex infrastructure and large forces necessary to undertake complicated military enterprises like Operation Desert Storm.

THE PERMANENT U.N. ARMY

Having described the types of military operations in which a U.N. force operates, we must now briefly address the different types of permanent U.N. force proposed. This paper will not consider Article 43-type proposals which would create, on paper, a huge force available to the U.N. for any operation up to major enforcement actions. The main reason for this is that there appears to be no chance that an Article 43 agreement will be signed in the foreseeable future. This is the main reason that [U.N. Secretary-General Boutros] Boutros-Ghali's *An Agenda for Peace* calls for the mobilization of a large force separate from Article 43 agreements. It is an effort to bypass the perpetual deadlock surrounding that luckless article.

Boutros-Ghali proposes "units that would be available on call and would consist of troops that have volunteered for such service." This plan would identify units from member states that could be called upon to build a U.N. force "package" when the Security Council authorizes a mission. Communications units, logistics units, transportation units, medical units, and other expensive sophisticated support elements would be earmarked by member states for U.N. service as well as the traditional light infantry units. These units would have to concentrate the majority of their training on U.N. duties and it has been recommended that their deployments be financed through national defense budgets. Needless to say, the response to these proposals from member states has been tepid at best. "Such modeling assumes that there will be major cuts in national armies as a result of diminishing East-West tensions and that this reduction could be matched by a growth in U.N. military capabilities." That assumption has proved to be naive in the extreme.

The proposal addressed here calls for a supra-national force of U.N. volunteers. Much like the civilian bureaucrats and officials employed by the U.N., these soldiers would be international civil (military) servants. They would be volunteers for international service and would not be under military obligation to any member state: only to the United Nations. They would be recruited, trained, equipped, and paid by the United Nations. The force proposed is usually infantry brigade-size, five to six thousand troops, with organic support and transportation capabilities. There are countless practical difficulties associated with forming such a force, but let us for the moment assume that it can be formed, trained, and deployed by the U.N.

THE UTILITY OF A U.N. ARMY

Naturally, even the most enthusiastic proponents of this small U.N. force recognize that its utility is limited by its size and capabilities. The most important advantage of this force is its rapid reaction capability. Since it is not drawn from member states, with all the attendant difficulties of that process, it can be deployed at the discretion of the Secretary-General on very short notice. The key element contributing to its success would be timeliness. "Clearly, a timely intervention by a relatively small but highly trained force, willing and authorized to take combat risks and representing the will of the international community, could make a decisive difference in the early stages of a crisis." This force would be akin to a small kitchen fire extinguisher, whose greatest utility is in the very earliest stages of a possible fire.

But operationally, we must ask where such a force could really enhance the credibility of the U.N. It is not needed for observation missions, as they are composed of experienced individual military observers. In addition, these missions are formed to observe a previously concluded political settlement. An unarmed observation mission would never be undertaken in a situation where dangerous tensions are at the boiling point and the rapid deployment of combat troops is needed.

Would timely and rapid intervention by such a small force make any difference in first generation peacekeeping missions? As these are also only initiated in response to a completed political agreement, would a rapid deployment force greatly increase the efficiency of the peacekeepers on the ground? "Even a full contingent of peacekeeping troops cannot prevent renewal of hostilities by a determined party. Maintenance of the cease-fire ultimately depends on the willingness of the parties to refrain from fighting." On the other hand, rapid deployment can have a favorable impact. In the case of Cyprus, "Canadian troops arrived... within twenty-four hours of UNFICYP's [U.N. force in Cyprus's] approval. A symbolic presence is perhaps all that is needed in the first days of a cease-fire anyway."

Surprisingly, it is in the conduct of second generation peacekeeping missions that U.N. Army enthusiasts foresee the greatest utility for such a permanent force, despite the bellicose environment frequently associated with these missions. To use this force in such a mission would mean that the U.N. would continue its selective abandonment of its "principles of peacekeeping" which it articulated to define success. In fact, the force is targeted for these difficult missions because "few, if any, governments are willing to commit their own troops to a forceful ground role in a situation which does not threaten their own security and which may well prove to be both violent and open ended."

Thus the paradox of using a permanent U.N. force in these operations is exposed. On the one hand it is proposed as a mechanism to circumvent the unwillingness of member states to get involved in difficult missions such as those of the second generation of peacekeeping. It will replace the ground troops which were never committed by reluctant member states. On the other hand, it is acknowledged that this small and symbolic force would be deployed to impose a solution on an armed party which has not accepted a solution through diplomatic channels. It is genuinely hard to imagine how the timely intervention of such a force could have forced a different outcome in Bosnia or Somalia.

In Bosnia, without the conclusion of a political settlement, any U.N. force in limited numbers operating under peacekeeping rather than enforcement rules of engagement is bound to be hostage to its environment. Because the lack of consensus among member states keeps the mandate and size of the force small and innocuous, any U.N. force is powerless to influence the environment in which it operates. Therefore, dozens of U.N. resolutions on the conflict go unenforced. Rapid reaction by a U.N. military force would not have changed this. Neither unarmed observers nor light infantry with soft-skinned armored vehicles can impose or enforce action in a bellicose combat environment. In both cases, the force is merely a tripwire and its operating imperative is almost solely based on its moral strength as a symbol.

In Somalia, the dilemma stems from the fact that "the basic distinction between peacekeeping and enforcement action... has been blurred. The forceful measures taken by U.S. troops to disarm warring factions, while fully within the mandate of UNOSOM II [U.N. force in Somalia], have highlighted the particular risks of attempting to combine the coercive use of force with peacekeeping objectives." Once again, the basic question is how to use the force to effect the political objectives. Any permanent U.N. force would be faced with exactly the same question no matter when it arrived. Only it might get to face that dilemma a bit sooner.

Naturally, a small, permanent U.N. force would have no great utility in enforcement action either. The fact that large-scale enforcement actions are taking place means that diplomacy or previous intervention has failed. The only scenario in which a permanent U.N. force could be involved at this end of the spectrum was if it was deployed, came under heavy attack, or suffered a similar failure to pacify a volatile environment, and withdrew prior to large scale intervention authorized by an Article 42 resolution.

The only outstanding use of such a force would be in preventative deployments, of which Macedonia is the only current example. In this case, the force does not seek to exercise any sort of operational capability other than limited observation and patrolling. It is a human tripwire, a symbol of the will of the international community. Any violent actions directed against this force (or the peace it seeks to keep) will have to be met with a U.N. response that transcends the organic capacity of this very small and lightly armed force. The soldiers involved are in an unenviable position, as they are powerless to influence their own environment. Their fate rests on the goodwill of the belligerents and the credibility of the United Nations in the eyes of the opposing factions. That bluff has been called in the past and the casualty lists are fast approaching 1000.

OPERATIONAL QUESTIONS

In short, preventative deployment by a permanent U.N. force begs a whole series of operational questions:

1. Under what circumstances will the force be deployed? Guidelines for intervention must be clearly defined. After all, "demand for U.N. peacekeeping since early 1992 has begun to outstrip the supply, whether that supply is measured in money or in national political will." Resources ultimately come from the member states, and are limited no matter what form they take. It is easy to imagine the small force being called upon for almost every potential conflict.
2. Will the U.N. force be governed by the "principles of peacekeeping" or will it be expected to enforce or impose solutions on belligerent factions? If the time-consuming negotiations necessary to obtain the consent of all parties are still underway, the rapid deployment capabilities of this force will have little utility.
3. What explicit mechanisms would be needed to determine the composition and missions of follow-on forces to relieve the rapid reaction force? There must be an organized process by which the crisis is evaluated, and intervention is either continued, upgraded, or abandoned. The involvement of a permanent U.N. force in an open-ended commitment would completely negate its utility.

While such guidelines are necessary, in some cases they will be inadequate to address the *sui generis* [unique] conflicts of the post–Cold War era. On the one hand, doctrine governing the use of a U.N. force must be stringent enough to provide real direction. On the other hand, that same doctrine will rule out intervention in many pressing crises. The doctrine guiding the use of U.N. force must cover a bewildering myriad of crises. It must also have a mechanism which forces decisionmakers to evaluate its immediate utility in a timely manner.

The deployment of a permanent U.N. rapid reaction force would catapult issues onto the U.N. agenda which member states are not ready to address. It could quite easily upset a natural control measure in an organization made up of nation-states. "States may well prefer a situation in which the provision of military force for U.N. activities is managed in an *ad hoc* manner, thereby giving them a greater degree of control over events."

There have been situations where the U.N. Security Council has called for troops to staff operations and the member states have simply failed to comply (Somalia 1992, Georgia 1993). It is reasonable to assume that these same member states would not support the deployment of a force controlled by the Secretary-General, which would require them to provide quick reinforcements. The reaction of member states to calls for collective operations are an important barometer of their willingness to act in common with others. A mechanism which forces or circumvents that common ground could backfire.

CONCLUSION

Even when one completely ignores these attendant political difficulties discussed briefly, it is still obvious that the operational utility of a permanent U.N. force is extremely limited. The value of such a force lies in its preventative role. Other than that role, it does not fit naturally into the spectrum of U.N. military operations conducted since 1948. Even in a preventative role, its small size, limited operational capabilities, and constrained mandate would limit its effectiveness to operations at the low end of the spectrum.

And at this end of the spectrum, there is not only little need for rapid deployments, but little need for forces other than those constituted by traditional means. When acting as a tripwire and in a symbolic role, an *ad hoc* blue-helmet force or an expensive permanent U.N. Army are scarcely different in terms of operational effectiveness or political viability. The past approach to staffing U.N. operations at the low end of the spectrum has always been adequate, has never been seen as responsible for mission failures, and is an important mechanism for involving states in the maintenance of international peace and security. The strategic utility of such a force is marginal when compared with the current system for staffing U.N. operations at the low end of the spectrum.

Many supporters want the U.N. force to solve problems in operations at the upper end of the operational spectrum. This force could never have the complex operational infrastructure and capabilities to make a difference in missions which entail even modest enforcement operations. The whole issue of staffing and directing U.N. operations at the high end of the spectrum needs much greater attention. Second generation peacekeeping and enforcement missions are quite obviously much more reliant on the vigorous political backing of powerful member states. Beyond the politics involved, these missions require the leadership of a major power for two reasons: 1) large-scale enforcement against an intransigent party is an immensely complicated and expensive enterprise; and 2) only a very few member states have the actual military capability to command and control such a campaign. A small force only under the control of the Secretary-General cannot affect these types of situations.

This dilemma stems from the nature of the post–Cold War world and the attendant difficulties of military intervention. It cannot be solved by the implementation of a single mechanism whose operational utility is very limited.

POSTSCRIPT

Should a Permanent UN Military Force Be Established?

The debate over the creation of a permanent international police force, even an army, is being debated seriously in many forums. A good place to begin more reading is with the report issued by Boutros Boutros-Ghali, *An Agenda for Peace: Preventive Diplomacy, Peacemaking and Peacekeeping* (United Nations, 1992). For more on the debate from a broader perspective, read David DeWitt, David Haglund, and John Kirton, eds., *Building a New Global Order: Emerging Trends in International Security* (Oxford University Press, 1994) and Thomas R. Cusak and Richard Stoll, "Collective Security and State Survival in the Interstate System," *International Studies Quarterly* (Winter 1994).

The nature of the UN mission is the broadest issue that relates to whether or not to create a standing UN military force. Many observers argue that a standing force would not only be more effective at peacekeeping, it would also be better at peacemaking. Other analysts are more skeptical of the possibility or wisdom of a standing UN force and its possible uses. One study from this perspective is Laura Neack, "UN Peace-Keeping: In the Interest of Community or Self?" *Journal of Peace Research* (1995). There is also concern about the ethics of humanitarian intervention by the UN or by other outside forces. This is expressed in David Fisher, "The Ethics of Intervention," *Survival* (Winter 1994).

In addition to the broader issues regarding the expansion of UN international security operations, there are a number of more parochial concerns. One is the cost of these operations. The budget for UN peacekeeping operations has soared. Many countries have not kept up with their funding obligations to support these missions. Member countries are behind in their assessments for UN peacekeeping operations by about $2.5 billion. The United States owes the largest debt, $1.26 billion as of October 1995. Many countries have criticized the United States for being in arrears. This criticism of the United States is especially intense because it occupies a permanent, veto-wielding seat on the Security Council, which has primary responsibility for peacekeeping. There is a clause in the UN Charter that states that member countries that have not met their financial obligations to the UN can lose their voting privilege. That fact and the U.S. debt led the British ambassador to charge what many British have been waiting more than 200 years to say: that the United States is seeking representation without taxation. The U.S. Congress sees things quite differently, however, and it has refused to pay the full amount assessed by the United Nations.

PART 4

Values and International Relations

In this era of increasing global interdependence, the state of relations among countries will become an ever more vital concern to all the world's people. This section examines issues of global concern and issues related to the values that affect relations and policy making among nations.

■ Should Foreign Policymakers Minimize
  Human Rights Concerns?

■ Are Efforts to Promote Democracy
  Culturally Biased and Self-Serving?

ISSUE 14

Should Foreign Policymakers Minimize Human Rights Concerns?

YES: Alan Tonelson, from "Jettison the Policy," *Foreign Policy* (Winter 1994/ 1995)

NO: Michael Posner, from "Rally Round Human Rights," *Foreign Policy* (Winter 1994/1995)

ISSUE SUMMARY

YES: Alan Tonelson, a fellow of the Economic Strategy Institute in Washington, D.C., contends that the United States' human rights policy has collapsed and ought to be jettisoned.

NO: Michael Posner, executive director of the Lawyers Committee for Human Rights, maintains that Tonelson's argument is flawed and that the United States should continue to incorporate human rights concerns into its foreign policy decisions.

This debate on the role of human rights and other moral issues in determining foreign policy is one over which realists and idealists disagree strongly.

Realists are averse to applying moral standards to foreign policy. When Adolf Hitler's Nazi Germany invaded Joseph Stalin's communist Soviet Union, Sir Winston Churchill, the prime minister of democratic Great Britain, offered aid to Stalin. When a critic in Parliament challenged the decision of the prime minister, he replied: "If Hitler had invaded Hell, ... [I would] make favorable reference to the devil." It is not that realists are amoral. Instead, they agree with the view of Secretary of State George Shultz (1982–1989) that "we ... have ... to accept that our passionate commitment to moral principles [cannot] be a substitute for sound foreign policy in a world of hard realities and complex choices." This is true, he argues, because "moral impulse, noble as it might be, [can] lead either to futile and perhaps dangerous global crusades, on the one hand, or to escapism and isolationism, equally dangerous, on the other." Similarly, Hans Morgenthau, one of the founders of the academic realists' school, argued that it is unconscionable as well as risky for a state to abandon realpolitik in favor of moralism. He contended that "while the individual has a moral right to sacrifice himself" in defense of a moral principle, "the state has no right to let its moral disapprobation ... get in the way of successful political action, itself inspired by the moral principle of national survival."

Idealists, in contrast, believe that it is both right and wise to consider human rights when making foreign policy decisions. Richard Falk, a leading idealist scholar, criticizes realists for their "tendency to discount... the normative aspirations of society." Some policymakers agree with this view. President Jimmy Carter declared during a speech marking the 30th anniversary of the Universal Declaration of Human Rights of 1948 that Americans should be "proud that our nation stands for more than military might or political might," that "our pursuit of human rights is part of a broad effort to use our great power and our tremendous influence in the service of creating a better world in which human beings can live," and that "human rights is the soul of our foreign policy." Idealists also reject the realists' contention that a country will be at a disadvantage if it applies moral standards to foreign policy making in a dangerous world. Secretary of State Cyrus Vance (1977–1980) once commented that it is a "dangerous illusion" to believe that "pursuing values such as human rights... is incompatible with pursuing U.S. national interests" because we can "never be secure in a world where freedom was threatened everywhere else."

The end of the cold war has, in many ways, made the issue of human rights more acute. During the cold war the human rights abuses of friendly regimes were often ignored in the interests of solidarity as the West faced the threat from the Soviet-led communists. That threat has ended, of course, and with it has died the easy standard that an anticommunist dictator is better than no anticommunist government at all. Idealists now argue that we act on our principles without the fear that we are empowering an enemy. Realists rejoin that the end of the cold war did not mean the end of power politics.

The debate over whether or not to incorporate human rights standards into foreign policy making is not simply a matter of intellectual speculation. The controversy also involves important policy choices. If democracy truly does promote peace, then perhaps the United States, Canada, and other democracies should pressure, even force if possible, other nondemocratic regimes to change. The United States, backed by the United Nations, did that in Haiti. Should the same standard apply to friendly nondemocratic regimes such as Saudi Arabia, which is ruled by a feudal monarchy? Also, what should a country do when the dictates of realpolitik point in one direction and human rights concerns point in another?

YES
Alan Tonelson

JETTISON THE POLICY

President Bill Clinton's team-up with the Haitian military and his [recent] acknowledgment that trade sanctions would not hasten democracy's development in China are only the latest signs that America's human rights policy has collapsed. The signs of America's failure to achieve the policy's objectives appear everywhere: from the halls of power in defiant Beijing to the streets of Port-au-Prince, from the mountains of Bosnia to the tenant farms of rebellious Chiapas in southern Mexico. At least as important, the policy has antagonized or simply turned off numerous democratic countries, as well as endangered a broad range of U.S. strategic and economic interests in key regions around the world.

No one can fairly blame U.S. policy for the world's continuing—and in many respects worsening—human rights situation. But Washington has been so ineffective in combating human rights violations in so many places for so long, and so many of its efforts at promoting democracy—especially their unilateral elements—have entailed such high costs, that the usual explanations seem inadequate.

Rather than blame Secretary of State Warren Christopher's alleged incompetence and Clinton's allegedly naive campaign promises, or struggle to better "balance" human rights concerns with other major U.S. interests, Americans might instead begin asking a fundamental question: Does any government-centered human rights policy make sense in the post–Cold War era? All the evidence indicates that such policies, however morally compelling, are obsolete—swamped, ironically, by the very forces that only yesterday inspired such bipartisan optimism in a new age of human rights progress. The immense tides of information, technology, goods, and capital that now flow so effortlessly across borders have turned Washington's efforts into Cold War relics, as antiquated as fallout shelters—and, in their own way, as falsely comforting.

Since the Cold War spawned U.S. human rights policy, its post–Cold War collapse should come as no surprise. American leaders have spoken out against oppression abroad through-out U.S. history, and the American people fought two global hot wars as well as a cold war against imperialist adversaries. But a systematic, dedicated policy to promote greater respect worldwide for human rights dates back only to the 1970s. Unfortunately, the policy was never rooted in a rigorous critique of prevailing American approaches to world affairs, or in a careful search for alternatives, but in a politically inspired temper tantrum by foreign policy professionals of the Left and Right.

Of course, as left-of-center human rights advocates argued, Washington's Cold War alliances with anticommunist dictators sometimes backfired. Of course, as right-of-center human rights advocates argued, American leaders episodically kept quiet about communist oppression whenever they pursued détente-like policies. And, of course, there was much heartfelt concern at the grassroots level about the moral tone and impact of American foreign policy. But the high-profile politicians and activists across the political spectrum who created and debated official human rights policies were, at bottom, simply venting frustrations over the compromises with evil that no foreign policy in an imperfect, anarchic world can avoid, and using human rights debates to push broader, more questionable agendas.

Liberals and other left-wing opponents of the Vietnam War used the human rights issue to push the broader view that millennial change was sweeping over world affairs, and that the United States could abandon the use of force and power-politicking altogether. They asserted that America's essential foreign policy objectives could be secured with more morally and aesthetically pleasing tools like foreign aid, diplomacy, and acceding to the (usually legitimate) interests of even hostile powers. The political Right used the human rights issue to attack détente with the Soviet Union and the larger belief that peaceful coexistence with other nuclear superpowers not only was necessary, but also could improve national security by reducing tensions and even produce mutually beneficial agreements.

Not surprisingly, given such political and polemical origins, human rights policy rarely advanced U.S. national interests in the 1970s. Relations with both allies and adversaries worsened (including West European countries that criticized the policy's heavy-handed treatment of the former Soviet Union), dictatorial friends were often weakened without generating better replacements (as in Iran and Nicaragua), and equally dictatorial foes remained securely in power (throughout the communist bloc and much of the developing world).

More surprisingly, prominent human rights advocates rarely sounded troubled when their policies failed to significantly improve human rights practices worldwide. Did U.S. policy simply help replace a friendly autocrat with an equally ruthless and hostile successor, as in Iran and Nicaragua? Did American initiatives lead a target regime to crack down on dissenters or aspiring emigrants, as in the Soviet Union? Was America aiming at countries where it had no influence at all, as in Vietnam or Ethiopia?

When advocates did try to answer such questions, their responses spoke volumes about their real priorities. Symbolism was critical. Consistency was essential—never mind that the objects of human rights policy were countries that differed completely in their level of social and economic development, their significance to the United States, and their political relations with America. The United States had to go on record. Americans had to do "what they could"—implying, of course, that salving American consciences was the main point.

For those reasons, moderate critics of the policies were missing the point entirely when they labored mightily to reconcile human rights positions with American strategic and economic interests. U.S. efforts did score limited successes—securing the release of numerous political prisoners during the 1970s (especially in Latin America) and joining in rare global economic sanctions that did advance the cause of reform in South Africa—although how those successes made the United States appreciably more secure or more prosperous was never explained. But human rights activism was never primarily about enhancing national security and welfare, or even alleviating suffering abroad. It was an exercise in therapy. The bottom line, as Jimmy Carter made clear, was to give Americans a foreign policy they could feel good about.

By the early 1980s, human rights policy became bogged down in sterile debates over the relative merits of left- and right-wing dictators, or the relative importance of the more traditional political rights such as free expression and the vote versus social and economic rights (to a job or education). Advancing the national interest or achieving concrete results receded further into the background. Pushing one's left- or right-wing sympathies and elegantly rationalizing them became higher priorities.

HUMAN RIGHTS IN THE AGE OF CLINTON

The end of the Cold War generated broad optimism that human rights would take center stage, not only in U.S. foreign policy, but in world politics as a whole. Economic and trade issues aside, human rights dominated Clinton's intermittent foreign policy rhetoric during the 1992 campaign, as he and other Democrats repeatedly blasted George Bush's alleged indifference to human rights horrors in Tiananmen Square [China], Iraq, and the former Yugoslavia.

And so far—again, leaving economics aside—human rights issues have dominated Clinton's intermittent foreign policy making as president. His inaugural address promised to use American power if necessary whenever "the will and conscience of the international community is defied." His national security adviser Anthony Lake has made the "enlargement" of the world's roster of democratic countries one of America's top foreign policy priorities. And human rights considerations permeate the U.S. foreign policy agenda from Russia to China to Somalia to Bosnia to Haiti.

Clinton's priorities clearly reflected a rapidly emerging bipartisan conventional wisdom. The reasons for optimism were obvious to conservatives and liberals alike—although they disagreed sharply on what some of them were. Both were thrilled by the prospect of an America no longer forced to back dictators for anti-Soviet reasons. Both expected the collapse of Soviet power and Soviet stooges around the world to bring the blessings of national self-determination to numerous captive peoples. And both assumed that the global revolutions in communications and commerce would inevitably carry democratic political ideas and liberal economic practices into even the most repressive and backward societies.

But conservatives were more taken with the role that America, as the last superpower, could play unilaterally in fostering democracy and capitalism. Some even urged the United States to launch a global crusade to help the process along and create a worldwide Pax Democratica shaped by American political principles and by Reaganomics.

Liberals focused on multilateral approaches, churning out blueprints for creating a U.N. that could oust repressive regimes through sanctions or force of arms. As demonstrated most dramatically in 1991 by the establishment of safe havens for Iraq's Kurds, the international community, they argued, was acquiring the right to intervene in sovereign states' internal affairs when rights violations threatened international security or passed some unspecified threshold of savagery.

Yet none of the countries that the president or the world community has focused on have become significantly freer or more democratic places since Clinton's inauguration or since the Soviet Union's demise. In other areas of American concern, notably Russia and its "Near Abroad," the situation has arguably worsened in recent months. Bleaker still is the human rights outlook in those regions that have so far eluded either the administration's or the media's focus—from sub-Saharan Africa to suddenly shaky Mexico to the Arab world.

Even in Western Europe, democracy is deeply troubled as high unemployment and burgeoning immigrant populations have strengthened xenophobic politicians in many countries. And writers such as Jean-François Revel argue convincingly that the rampant corruption of social democratic systems in Italy and France has undermined the public trust in government that is crucial to the survival of democracy.

However, success stories are by no means unknown. So far, they include Taiwan, South Korea, and Chile, and even economically troubled countries such as Argentina, the Czech Republic, and the Baltic states. Nor can prospects for near-term improvement be written off completely in Russia and Mexico.

Still, one of the most comprehensive annual studies of the global human rights picture—the traditionally optimistic Freedom House's *Comparative Survey of Freedom*—concluded at the end of last year that "freedom around the world is in retreat while violence, repression and state control are on the increase." Of course, recent U.S. policy is not exclusively, largely, or even significantly responsible for that. But it is not apparent that official efforts have achieved many durable gains, either.

Even more disturbing has been the global reaction to U.S. human rights policies, especially their unilateral elements. Not a single major power, for example, emulated Washington's linkage of trade relations with human rights progress in China. Some of America's staunchest regional allies, such as Japan and Australia, openly criticized that strategy from the start. Other allies, principally the West Europeans, quietly worked overtime to cut deals with a booming economy that is already the world's third largest.

Furthermore, many East Asian governments—and many Asian voices outside government—have openly challenged U.S. human rights initiatives as arrogant efforts to impose Western values on proud, ancient societies that are doing quite well economically and socially, thank you. Similar resentments are widely expressed in the Arab world and other Islamic countries.

But the best evidence of failure is the administration's zig-zag record on numerous human rights fronts. Human rights issues are a large part of the president's most embarrassing retreats from campaign promises. Clinton has decided to follow the Bush administration's approach to China, finally agreeing that continued economic engagement is the best way to advance America's human rights and broader agendas with the world's most populous country. Even before his inauguration, the president had to endorse his predecessor's policy of returning Haiti's boat people, and in September 1994 he acquiesced in an agreement negotiated mainly by former president Jimmy Carter for joint U.S. administration of Haiti's democratic transition with the very military leaders he had condemned as murderers and rapists the week before. Moreover, bitter experiences in Somalia and Haiti in 1993 have so far led to a lowering of America's peacekeeping goals.

DECLINE IN PUBLIC SUPPORT

In part, U.S. human rights policies are failing because their consistently shaky strategic foundations have crumbled. During the Cold War, a plausible case could be made for denying an ideologically hostile rival superpower targets of opportunity by fostering democratic practices abroad. But in the absence of such a rival, the state of human rights around the world does not have, and has never had, any demonstrable effect on U.S. national security. America's rise to global prominence occurred primarily in periods when democracies were few and far between, and a combination of geography, power, wealth, and social cohesion will continue to be the country's best guarantees of security in a turbulent world.

In the wake of the Cold War, both liberal and conservative human rights advocates (including the president) have argued that democracies rarely fight each other—hence the more there are, the merrier and safer America will be. Yet the jury is still out: Significant numbers of democracies have existed together only in the last 50 years. Furthermore, U.S. leaders obviously have never bought the argument themselves—otherwise, they would not continue to be terrified by the prospect of democratic Germany and Japan carrying out independent foreign policies or going nuclear.

Moreover, strong domestic support for an active human rights policy has been difficult to detect. Although Americans often endorse vigorous human rights policies when talking with pollsters, they have not recently acted or voted as if they cared much about them. Carter made human rights a top foreign policy priority and was rewarded with early retirement —because he let the economy deteriorate and seemed ineffective in dealing with the Soviets. His 1980 opponent, Ronald Reagan, promised to uphold American values against an evil Soviet empire, but his most politically popular foreign policy position was his stand against the military threat he saw emanating from Moscow. And what happened when the greatest White House communicator since Franklin Roosevelt tried to mobilize public support for his Reagan Doctrine policies of arming "freedom fighters" combating pro-Soviet Third World regimes? He failed everywhere except in Afghanistan, where the Soviet occupation arguably threatened the oil-rich Persian Gulf.

What politicians and pundits do not understand—and may not want to understand—is that unlike their leaders, the American people evidently have learned from past mistakes. Vietnam has happened. The Iran hostage crisis has happened. As the 1992 election and its aftermath showed, when voters care deeply about issues—from the economy to [U.S. attorney general nominee] Zoe Baird's nanny problem—they are not shy about making their feelings known. And just as they never filled the streets or flooded Washington's phone banks protesting oppression around the world during the 1970s and 1980s, they have not been demanding the denial of tariff breaks to China or intervention in basket-case countries in the 1990s. If the American people retain any significant missionary impulse, or much optimism that the world craves American guidance on human rights issues, they are hiding their feelings well.

To a depressing degree, however, U.S. human rights policy grinds on along the same well-worn tracks. Despite the China trade decision, another China-like struggle over linking trade relations with human rights practices may be unfolding with Indonesia, and yet another looms with Vietnam. Both controversies have scary implications for America's economic position in rapidly growing Asia (where establishing long-term relationships and, consequently, a reputation for reliability are keys to business success) and other emerging markets.

And as during the 1970s and 1980s, today's human rights skeptics unwittingly play along, accepting the basic assumptions driving human rights policy but pleading for moderation, perspective, and "balancing" human rights considerations with America's strategic and economic objectives.

In the process, critics have periodically aired stronger objections, calling human rights policy arrogant, naive, inconsistent —a juvenile protest against life's built-in imperfections. They are largely correct. Yet two even greater obstacles to a successful government-led U.S. human rights policy are embedded in the very nature of the post–Cold War world.

The first concerns the phenomenon of failed states that has been exposed by the retreat of Soviet power in Eastern Europe and by the end of Cold War confrontation in much of the Third World—in Bosnia, Georgia, Haiti, Somalia, Rwanda, and elsewhere. The often horrendous general conditions and specific outrages that have resulted from the breakdown of governments in those regions are usually described as "human rights violations," but the phrase trivializes the problem. At worst, they are endemic features of deep-rooted ethnic conflicts. At best, they are symptoms of a monumental struggle over issues not of liberalization or democratization, but of minimal coherence or further fragmentation. Welcome to the dark side of national self-determination, as Colonel E. M. House warned Woodrow Wilson nearly 75 years ago.

Outside Western Europe, North America, and East Asia, most "countries" around the world simply do not deserve that label. They may have the trappings of statehood—postage stamps, U.N. membership—but their populations lack a sense of mutual loyalty and obligation, and their politics lack strong institutions, a commitment to the rule of law, and even a tradition of public service as anything more than an opportunity for theft and vengeance. They are straining to reach minimal viability not even as nation-states but as societies. The conceit behind the idea that even the best designed policies, or a few billion dollars' worth of foreign aid, or "how to" democracy courses can make a real difference is, to put it kindly, immense.

As for U.S. human rights policies toward more advanced repressive countries, they are swamped by a similar problem—by the very global economic and cultural interaction responsible for much of the optimism of human rights advocates. Precisely because ideas and capital and technology—and, to a somewhat lesser extent, people—can cross borders so easily, official rhetoric and even sanctions get lost in the shuffle. Government words and deeds form merely one small breeze in the gales of commerce and culture blowing around the world today. Western and American values will not be the only seeds dropped by those winds. But if we consider their spread and growth to be essential, then we are better advised to lead from strength— to energetically add to America's already vast commercial, cultural, and ideological influence around the world, rather than seek to replace it with legislation or executive orders or official oratory.

Leave aside for the moment the op-ed level arguments that dominated the China most-favored-nation debate—for example, over which country has the most leverage, over whether economic relations with America strengthen the Chinese government's economic base and help pacify the population, over whether other countries will rush in to replace American suppliers and investors. Say Americans were to start from scratch on an imaginary campaign to reform China. What would the most promising tools be? "Sense of the Congress" resolutions? Cutbacks in the numbers of American

companies that the Chinese can work for or do business with, and that pay Chinese employees higher wages and provide safer working conditions than do China's state-owned enterprises? Or would America send as many businesspeople to China as quickly as it could? The answer should be obvious even to those who do not believe in business-created utopias.

The China issue, however, along with [the recent] controversy over the North American Free Trade Agreement, does bring up one bona fide human rights issue where more effective U.S. government action is needed: the question of how most of America's workforce can benefit from trade with countries that repress labor rights. American workers are already exposed to strong competition from hundreds of millions of workers in developing countries who are highly educated, highly productive, and organized by the world's leading multinational corporations, but who are paid a fraction of what their U.S. counterparts earn and who are systematically denied the right to form independent unions and bargain collectively for wages that bear some relationship to productivity increases, for decent workplaces, and for nonwage benefits—rights and conditions until recently taken for granted in North America and Western Europe. Many more such workers will soon be coming into the world economy from China's interior (as opposed to its already booming coastal regions), from South and Southeast Asia, and, farther down the road, from Russia and Eastern Europe.

Even if all of them work for politically and socially progressive American companies, which they will not, the capacity of those workers to export will exceed by orders of magnitude their capacity to consume. Lack of labor rights is hardly the only reason, but it can create major competitive advantages. As Labor Secretary Robert Reich noted in an April 1994 speech, the problem is part and parcel of the inherent difficulties of commerce between countries at greatly differing levels of economic and social development in an age of highly mobile capital and technology.

Unlike other human rights issues, moreover, labor rights controversies and their resolutions are already having concrete effects on the lives of millions of Americans. But they are best seen not as human rights issues at all, but as challenges in managing interdependence —in ensuring that the great integrative forces shaping the world economy work for the long-term benefit of the great majority of the American people, not against it.

Nor can labor rights controversies be successfully resolved by acting out the stylized morality plays that make up human rights policy today—by issuing the same threats and voluminous reports, by trotting out the same dissidents in front of the press, by fasting, or by any other attempts to dictate the social and economic priorities of other countries. Instead, labor rights problems require

a raft of new trade, technology, foreign investment, and other policies designed to increase America's economic power.

A vibrant industrial base that creates millions of new high-wage jobs can give America the economic leverage needed to negotiate beneficial economic agreements with the rest of the world. A prosperous America can generate enough markets, capital, and technology to give other countries powerful incentives to conform to U.S. labor, environmental, and other standards voluntarily—not as acknowledgements of American moral superiority or as acts of surrender, but simply as the price of access.

As Americans will discover in many foreign policy fields, crusades to bring about utopian change around the world will rarely achieve their goals. The best bets lie in measures that enable the country to survive, flourish, and bargain successfully in the deeply flawed world that we will remain stuck with for many decades. Americans wishing their government to act in moral ways might consider focusing on their own country —which suffers its share of problems and moral outrages, but is also blessed with the institutions and social cohesion to make serious reform more than a pipe dream.

NO

Michael Posner

RALLY ROUND HUMAN RIGHTS

Alan Tonelson has written a provocative but premature obituary to international human rights. He asserts that the tragedies in Bosnia, Somalia, and Haiti prove that it is no longer useful or productive for the U.S. government to challenge state-sponsored murder and torture in other countries and to emphasize human rights as an element of its foreign policy.

Tonelson's postmortem is flawed in at least four basic assumptions: In a relatively short space, he manages to misrepresent the origins of human rights, its scope and objectives, reasonable measures to judge the effectiveness of U.S. human rights policy, and the view of key U.S. allies with respect to this policy.

According to Tonelson, the emphasis on human rights was a product of the Cold War, designed principally to challenge the Soviet Union. From his perspective, the starting point for the discussion was the 1970s. He is wrong, both about the purpose and the timing. Contrary to Tonelson's narrow world view, attention to international human rights has evolved steadily over the last five decades.

The international community in fact began to focus on human rights immediately after World War II. Shaken by the Holocaust and determined to make amends for their slow and inadequate response to the murder of millions of innocent victims, the United States and its allies sought to take steps to prevent similar future occurrences. The United Nations Charter, adopted in 1945, made human rights a central purpose of that new organization. Governments pledged to take joint and separate actions to encourage a more just, humane world.

A year later, the U.N. created its own Commission on Human Rights, with former first lady Eleanor Roosevelt serving as its first chair. Under her stewardship, the commission moved quickly to draft a body of human rights principles—the Universal Declaration of Human Rights, adopted by the U.N. General Assembly in 1948. Working closely with the U.S. Department of State, Roosevelt helped develop two other key treaties, the International Covenant on Civil and Political Rights and the International Covenant on Economic, Social and Cultural Rights. Many other countries participated in those early

From Michael Posner, "Rally Round Human Rights," *Foreign Policy* (Winter 1994/1995).

developments and many more, including virtually all key American allies, now view the treaties as the basis for international consideration of those rights.

Official U.S. attention to those issues increased significantly in the 1970s with congressional efforts like the Jackson-Vanik Amendment, which linked trade with the Soviet Union to its willingness to allow emigration by Soviet Jews. As president, Jimmy Carter greatly expanded U.S. initiatives in the area and gave human rights a much higher profile.

Nongovernmental organizations also came of age at that time. Amnesty International was awarded the 1977 Nobel Peace Prize in recognition of its unique role in human rights advocacy. Several key U.S.-based human rights organizations, including Helsinki Watch (now part of Human Rights Watch) and the Lawyers Committee for Human Rights, were also founded during that period. Thus, over the past 50 years, significant progress has been made in developing human rights law and in setting practical objectives for its implementation.

SCOPE AND OBJECTIVES

Tonelson offers a confusing and sometimes contradictory view of the scope and objectives of U.S. human rights policy. On one hand, he criticizes politicians and activists for using human rights "to push broader, more questionable agendas." On the other hand, he urges that we pursue labor rights, not because it is the right thing to do, but to protect the economic well-being of "millions of Americans."

Tonelson also builds straw men, only to tear them down. He refers repeatedly to "human rights advocates," a term he never defines. Using that broad rubric, he notes that conservatives are using

human rights to foster "democracy and capitalism." He then accuses liberals of using human rights to advocate using U.N. sanctions or military force "to oust repressive regimes." While some have indeed used the language of human rights to pursue these broad political objectives, in doing so they are going beyond the core meaning of human rights, which is to challenge governments when they mistreat their own people.

Human rights advocates such as Amnesty International and hundreds of national rights advocacy groups around the world rely on international human rights standards that set minimum requirements for governments. States that ratify international treaties make a pledge to abide by those core legal principles, which include commitments not to torture their own people, subject them to slavery, or engage in political murder. Tonelson blithely dismisses efforts by human rights groups and others to challenge such violations as "an exercise in therapy." On the contrary, human rights advocacy has evolved into a worldwide movement aimed at exposing and combating official misconduct and alleviating suffering. There is now ample evidence that by exposing violations and challenging the violators, lives are being saved.

The international treaties provide a foundation for such efforts, but set forth only broad basic principles. The civil and political covenant, for example, requires governments to allow for a free press, for the right to hold public meetings, and for the right to speak freely. It also requires popular participation in choosing a government. But it neither spells out how that should be accomplished, nor suggests a specific political structure or system. Those who seek to wrap broader economic and political agendas in the flag of human rights, including some in the Clinton administration, are overloading the system.

The treaties are also silent on the sanctions that may be imposed on governments that systematically violate basic human rights. Although there is nothing to prevent the U.N. Security Council from invoking the language of human rights to help justify military action, there is nothing in the treaties that compels it, or even suggests that it should do so.

Some governments, including that of the United States, have linked their provision of bilateral aid and trade privileges to human rights. In the last 20 years, the United States has occasionally withheld or delayed the provision of bilateral aid—particularly military aid—in situations where a sustained pattern of violations was occurring. The connection to military aid is the most direct, given the possibility that the weapons being provided will be used to commit further violations.

It is much more difficult to impose trade sanctions, in part because there is much less agreement on the usefulness of trade restrictions as an instrument of leverage. The Jackson-Vanik Amendment, which restricted trade to the former Soviet Union, was an exception for two reasons: U.S. economic opportunities in the USSR were limited, and such sanctions had bipartisan support in the broader effort to challenge Soviet influence worldwide.

The recent controversy over the linkage between trade and human rights in China was not surprising, given the economic opportunities at stake. Yet the Clinton administration's decision to de–link the two issues by renewing China's most-favored-nation trading status does not mean that future human rights initiatives should be avoided, or that long-term international pressure on the human rights front will be ineffective.

MEASURES OF EFFECTIVENESS

Tonelson's sole criterion for measuring human rights progress appears to be whether U.S. strategic interests are being advanced. That is the wrong place to start. While governments that respect human rights are likely to be more stable and reliable strategic allies, the protection and promotion of basic rights worldwide is important in itself. Consistent with our values and traditions, the U.S. government should promote international initiatives designed to alleviate suffering and to challenge governments that deny basic freedoms to their own people.

Tonelson argues that since human rights are being violated all around the world, the human rights policy must be failing, and therefore should be abandoned. That is akin to arguing that since thousands of businesses go bankrupt each year, we must abandon the free market system. While progress on human rights cannot be evaluated with the precision of a profit and loss statement, there are several useful measures of effectiveness.

The first measure is public attention to and awareness of human rights issues. Twenty years ago it was rare to see any reference to international human rights in the news media. By contrast, in any newspaper today one is likely to see several articles, often including one or more front-page stories, where human rights issues are featured prominently. While growing awareness does not automatically lead to greater respect for human rights, it is an important step toward that goal. Most governments are surprisingly thin-skinned on these issues and will go out of their way to avoid being stigmatized by a broad public spotlight

A second measure of progress is the extent to which indigenous human rights activists are raising the issue in their own countries. Apparently Tonelson does not see such activists from his perch in Washington, since he makes no reference to the proliferation of national advocates and organizations. In the 1970s there were perhaps a few dozen human rights organizations around the world. Today, there are hundreds of such organizations operating in countries throughout the world. Every day the groups are busy documenting abuses, filing lawsuits, and challenging their own governments when they violate basic human rights. Most of the groups are underfunded and work in very difficult circumstances. Those who participate in such activism frequently do so at personal risk. But they carry on, often relying on international diplomatic pressure from the U.S. government and influential parties to protect them and help reinforce the legitimacy of their efforts.

Many of the Asian governments, like those of China and Singapore, that are most critical of U.S. human rights policy and seek to characterize it as Western-based and culturally biased are among the declining number of regimes that absolutely prevent any independent human rights groups from operating. Their claims of cultural relativism can only be sustained if they can continue to prevent their own people from raising human rights issues. But they are fighting a losing battle. Recent experience in countries as diverse as Chile, Kuwait, Nigeria, South Africa, and Sri Lanka leave no doubt that where people are allowed to organize and advocate their own human rights, they will do so. The common denominators in this area are much stronger than the cultural divisions.

Finally, look around the world and note that progress continues to be made on human rights issues. Contrast the Latin America today with the one of 15 years ago. Tonelson's own criteria also lead him to assert that none of the countries on which Washington has focused its attention since 1991 have become any freer or more democratic. On that he is simply wrong. A great majority of South Africans, among others, would undoubtedly disagree with him.

Even in the many places where governments do continue to commit serious violations, Tonelson offers no viable alternative to challenging the violators. His suggestion that the United States abandon ship rather than risk the embarrassment of future failure adds little more than a rhetorical flourish to his argument.

The fourth broad mistake in Tonelson's analysis is his assertion that U.S. human rights policy is a failure because it has "antagonized or simply turned off numerous democratic countries." To support his proposition, he notes that not a single "major power" followed the Clinton administration's lead in linking human rights and trade in China. He also notes that some of America's strongest allies in the region, such as Australia and Japan, were openly critical of the policy.

While Tonelson is correct in identifying discomfort and in some cases opposition to the U.S. approach, his analysis is incomplete and therefore misleading. A number of key U.S. allies—Canada, Great Britain, the Netherlands, Sweden, Australia—include human rights as a component in their own foreign policies. But they often prefer to pursue those concerns on a multilateral rather than a bilateral basis. Historically, the U.S. government has disdained multilateral institutions, viewing U.N. debates as an exercise in damage control. In the 1980s, U.S. representatives to the U.N. repeatedly opposed resolutions that called for the appointment of special experts to investigate and report on the situations in Guatemala, Haiti, and El Salvador, among others—preferring to address those situations in a less-confrontational manner.

Tonelson also misses another important point, which is the declining U.S. ability to act unilaterally. During the Cold War, the United States invested billions of dollars in bilateral military and economic aid. Most of the money went to the support of strategic allies in the geopolitical confrontation with the Soviet bloc. A number of governments, such as those in El Salvador, Haiti, Indonesia, Liberia, the Philippines, and Zaire, were committing serious human rights violations. In those situations, the United States had enormous influence and could threaten to cut off aid as a means of ultimate leverage. Following the collapse of the Soviet Union, however, Congress drastically reduced foreign aid—particularly military aid—and, concomitantly, U.S. influence and ability to act unilaterally.

To date, both the Clinton administration and the human rights community have been slow to accept the new reality. The real failure of Clinton's China policy was not that he tried to link trade and human rights, but that he tried to do it alone. American companies quickly mobilized when they realized that not only would they be shut out of a huge market, but that their overseas competitors would jump in to fill the void. So while it remains an open question whether linking trade to human rights is a politically viable option for advancing the cause of human rights, in China or elsewhere, it is clear that whatever America's tactical approach is, it can no longer act alone if it is going to be effective.

Concern for human rights is far from obsolete—either as a set of U.N. principles or as an element of U.S. foreign policy. In looking to the future, these issues are likely to loom more prominently than ever before, particularly in those societies that are in transition, such as China, India, Mexico, Nigeria, and Russia. To be effective, U.S. policymakers and activists need to rethink strategies while working more in concert with others who regard human rights as a vital international concern.

POSTSCRIPT

Should Foreign Policymakers Minimize Human Rights Concerns?

There are times when promoting human rights standards and the realpolitik pursuit of the national interest can both be furthered by the same policy choice. Defeating dangerously militaristic and unconscionably evil Nazi Germany is one such clear example. At other times, the degree to which human rights and realpolitik point in the same direction is less clear. When President Bill Clinton broadcast his address to the nation in November 1995, he asked Americans to support the deployment of U.S. troops to Bosnia on the grounds that "it's in our interest to do so and because it's the right thing to do." Clinton argued that it was in U.S. national interest to intervene "because problems that start beyond our borders can quickly become problems within them." Among other potential evils, he cited terrorism, the spread of weapons of mass destruction, and the possibility that continued violence in Bosnia "could spread like a poison throughout the region, eat away at Europe's stability, and erode our partnership with our European allies." The humanitarian concern, Clinton said, was the "quarter of a million men, women, and children who have been shelled, shot, and tortured to death." There are other times when pressing other countries on human rights and following realpolitik policy are probably very different. China is one such case. Some people call for trade and other sanctions on China in retaliation for its human rights violations. Yet, China is at least a potential great power and an important economic actor. Even after criticizing President George Bush for not putting trade sanctions on China, Clinton, once in the White House, followed the same policy and has chosen realpolitik over human rights.

To study the divergent realist and idealist approaches to morality in foreign policy, begin with Hans Morgenthau's classic *Politics Among Nations* (Alfred A. Knopf, 1985) and the review of this book by leading idealist scholar Stanley Hoffmann in *The Atlantic Monthly* (November 1985). More recent expositions would include Lea Brilmayer, *American Hegemony: Political Morality in a One Superpower World* (Yale University Press, 1994); George F. Kennan, "On American Principles," *Foreign Affairs* (March/April 1995); Walter Russell Mead, "Lucid Stars: The American Foreign Policy Tradition," *World Policy Journal* (Winter 1995); and Richard Falk, *On Humane Governance* (Penn State Press, 1995). From a practitioner's point of view, there are numerous memoirs by former presidents and secretaries of state. The most recent of these is James A. Baker III, *The Politics of Diplomacy* (G. P. Putnam's Sons, 1995). An idealist orientation can be found in Cyrus Vance, *Hard Choices* (Simon & Schuster, 1982).

ISSUE 15

Are Efforts to Promote Democracy Culturally Biased and Self-Serving?

YES: Kishore Mahbubani, from "The Dangers of Decadence: What the Rest Can Teach the West," *Foreign Affairs* (September/October 1993)

NO: Aung San Suu Kyi, from "Transcending the Clash of Cultures: Freedom, Development, and Human Worth," *Journal of Democracy* (April 1995)

ISSUE SUMMARY

YES: Kishore Mahbubani, deputy secretary of foreign affairs, contends that Westerners need to be sensitized to the perceptions of the rest of the world about the West's culturally biased standards of democracy.

NO: Aung San Suu Kyi, the leader of Burma's National League for Democracy, disputes the claim that democracy is a Western concept that is alien to indigenous values.

Take a survey of your friends. Ask how many of them are in favor of democracy and its concomitant civil liberties, such as freedom of speech, assembly, and the press. It would be surprising if any of the people you asked came out solidly against democracy. Nevertheless, democracy is far from universally practiced. Some governments egregiously violate the standards of democracy as they are practiced in the United States, Canada, Western Europe, and elsewhere. Many governments violate them at least sometimes, according to some critics.

Why is there a gap between the rhetorical support of democracy and its practice? There are two reasons. One, of course, is that some governments really do not mean what they say. The second reason is a lot more complex and is the focus of this issue. It may be that "violations" of democracy and the other noble standards of civil liberties and rights are, to a degree, matters of perception and culture. It may be that practices that we sometimes condemn in others are not abuses as such. Rather, they may be actions that we disapprove of because of our cultural biases.

One thing to ask yourself is where rights, concepts of civil liberties, and civil rights come from in the first place. Some people believe that one or more deities bestow rights on mortals. Other people would argue that there is such a thing as "natural rights." These are based on the essence of being human and were theoretically possessed by people when they lived in a "state of nature," that is, before they joined into governments. The "right to free speech" is one possible inherent right. Philosophers such as Jean-Jacques Rousseau (1712–1778) and John Locke (1632–1704) believed that people joined in societies and created governments to improve themselves. It was, therefore, illogical to reason that people would surrender any of their rights.

This view of human rights based on natural rights is not accepted by everyone. There have been other philosophers, such as Thomas Hobbes (1588–1679), who have argued that people submitted to government for protection from a state of nature that was brutal, not idyllic. As such, individuals traded away some of their rights in order to gain protection from the state.

Yet other people contend that rights are not inherent, at least for the most part. Instead, those who hold this view argue that rights, or at least many of them, are culturally based. Proponents of this view would assert that differing standards prove cultural origins rather than condemn one or another standard to illegitimacy. Western (especially American) culture, for example, places a high value on individual rights. The right of the individual comes before the good of the society or a class of citizens. Many other cultures put a much higher value on communitarian values. This means that when the rights of the individual and the good of the society clash, the presumption is that societal good is the more important standard. When students protesting in Tiananmen Square and elsewhere in China were attacked and killed by government troops in 1989, the West condemned China for violating the right to democracy, the right to free speech, and other rights. The Chinese government contended that the students' rights did not extend to trying to undermine the socialist movement that had done much to benefit Chinese society.

The contention that democracy and other standards of civil liberties and rights are culture-based, and therefore not universal, leads to the charge by some analysts that trying to insist that others abide by your standards leads to cultural imperialism. Many people in China, for example, see American-style democracy as divisive, even dangerous. Chinese officials argue that the country faces so many huge problems that it cannot afford the luxury of what they see as the interminable debate and political gridlock of Western democracies. Instead, as communists, they believe in what they call "democratic centralism." What this means is that since the government is supported by the mass, then it is democratic and has the authority to make decisions centrally, which all are then obligated to follow.

Others would argue that although that standards of democracy differ, there is a basic standard: that the people should be sufficiently empowered to be able to participate significantly in the governance of their country.

The issues of democracy are complex. In the following selections, Kishore Mahbubani argues that Western values are neither universally good nor always appropriate for other cultures. Aung San Suu Kyi rejects this view and contends that there is a basic standard of democracy by which all governments can be judged.

YES
Kishore Mahbubani

THE DANGERS OF DECADENCE: WHAT THE REST CAN TEACH THE WEST

In key Western capitals there is a deep sense of unease about the future. The confidence that the West would remain a dominant force in the 21st century, as it has for the past four or five centuries, is giving way to a sense of foreboding that forces like the emergence of fundamentalist Islam, the rise of East Asia and the collapse of Russia and Eastern Europe could pose real threats to the West. A siege mentality is developing.... It will therefore come as a great surprise to many Westerners to learn that the rest of the world fears the West even more than the West fears it, especially the threat posed by a wounded West.

[P]ower is shifting among civilizations. But when the tectonic plates of world history move in a dramatic fashion, as they do now, perceptions of these changes depend on where one stands. The key purpose of this essay is to sensitize Western audiences to the perceptions of the rest of the world.

The retreat of the West is not universally welcomed. There is still no substitute for Western leadership, especially American leadership. Sudden withdrawals of American support from Middle Eastern or Pacific allies, albeit unlikely, could trigger massive changes that no one would relish. Western retreat could be as damaging as Western domination.

By any historical standard, the recent epoch of Western domination, especially under American leadership, has been remarkably benign. One dreads to think what the world would have looked like if either Nazi Germany or Stalinist Russia had triumphed in what have been called the "Western civil wars" of the twentieth century. Paradoxically, the benign nature of Western domination may be the source of many problems. Today most Western policymakers, who are children of this era, cannot conceive of the possibility that their own words and deeds could lead to evil, not good. The Western media aggravate this genuine blindness. Most Western journalists travel overseas with Western assumptions. They cannot understand how the West could be seen as anything but benevolent. CNN is not the solution. The same visual images transmitted simultaneously into living rooms across the globe can trigger opposing perceptions. Western living rooms applaud when cruise missiles strike Baghdad. Most living outside see that the West will deliver swift retribution to nonwhite Iraqis or Somalis but not to white Serbians, a dangerous signal by any standard.

THE ASIAN HORDES

[Some Western analysts warn of] the challenge posed by Islamic and Confucian civilizations. Since the bombing of the World Trade Center [in February 1993], Americans have begun to absorb European paranoia about Islam, perceived as a force of darkness hovering over a virtuous Christian civilization. It is ironic that the West should increasingly fear Islam when daily the Muslims are reminded of their own weakness. "Islam has bloody borders," Huntington says. But in all conflicts between Muslims and pro-Western forces, the Muslims are losing, and losing badly, whether they be Azeris, Palestinians, Iraqis, Iranians or Bosnian Muslims. With so much disunity, the Islamic world is not about to coalesce into a single force.

Oddly, for all this paranoia, the West seems to be almost deliberately pursuing a course designed to aggravate the Islamic world. The West protests the reversal of democracy in Myanmar, Peru or Nigeria, but not in Algeria. These double standards hurt. Bosnia has wreaked incalculable damage. The dramatic passivity of powerful European nations as genocide is committed on their doorstep has torn away the thin veil of moral authority that the West had spun around itself as a legacy of its recent benign era. Few can believe that the West would have remained equally passive if Muslim artillery shells had been raining down on Christian populations in Sarajevo or Srebrenica.

Western behavior toward China has been equally puzzling. In the 1970s, the West developed a love affair with a China ruled by a regime that had committed gross atrocities during the Great Leap Forward and the Cultural Revolution. But when Mao Zedong's disastrous rule was followed by a far more benign Deng Xiaoping era, the West punished China for what by its historical standards was a minor crackdown: the Tiananmen incident.

Unfortunately, Tiananmen has become a contemporary Western legend created by live telecasts of the crackdown. Beijing erred badly in its excessive use of firearms but it did not err in its decision to crack down. Failure to quash the student rebellion could have led to political disintegration and chaos, a perennial Chinese nightmare. Western policymakers concede this in private. They are also aware of the dishonesty of some Western journalists: dining with student dissidents and even egging them on before reporting on their purported "hunger strike." No major Western journal has exposed such dishonesty or developed the political courage to say that China had virtually no choice in Tiananmen. Instead sanctions were imposed, threatening China's modernization. Asians see that Western public opinion—deified in Western democracy—can produce irrational consequences. They watch with trepidation as Western policies on China lurch to and fro, threatening the otherwise smooth progress of East Asia.

Few in the West are aware that the West is responsible for aggravating turbulence among the more than two billion people living in Islamic and Chinese civilizations. Instead, conjuring up images of the two Asian hordes that Western minds fear most—two forces that invaded Europe, the Muslims and the Mongols— [alarmists] posit a Confucian-Islamic connection against the West. American arms sales to Saudi Arabia do not suggest a natural Christian-Islamic connection. Neither should Chinese arms sales to Iran. Both are opportunistic moves, based not on natural empathy or civilizational alliances. The real tragedy of suggesting a Confucian-Islamic connection is that it obscures the fundamentally different nature of the challenge posed by these forces. The Islamic world will have great difficulty modernizing. Until then its turbulence will spill over into the West. East Asia, including China, is poised to achieve parity with the West. The simple truth is that East and Southeast Asia feel more comfortable with the West.

This failure to develop a viable strategy to deal with Islam or China reveals a fatal flaw in the West: an inability to come to terms with the shifts in the relative weights of civilizations.... [One essay illustrates] the nature of the problem: first, "In the politics of civilizations, the peoples and governments of non-Western civilization no longer remain the objects of history as targets of Western colonization but join the West as movers and shapers of history," and second, "The West in effect is using international institutions, military power and economic resources to run the world in ways that will maintain Western predominance, protect Western interests and promote Western political and economic values." This combination is a prescription for disaster.

Simple arithmetic demonstrates Western folly. The West has 800 million people; the rest make up almost 4.7 billion. In the national arena, no Western society would accept a situation where 15 percent of its population legislated for the remaining 85 percent. But this is what the West is trying to do globally.

Tragically, the West is turning its back on the Third World just when it can finally help the West out of its economic doldrums. The developing world's dollar output increased in 1992 more than that of North America, the European Community and Japan put together. Two-thirds of the increase in U.S. exports has gone to the developing world. Instead of encouraging this global momentum by completing the Uruguay Round [trade agreement], the West is doing the opposite. It is trying to create barriers, not remove them. French Prime Minister Edouard Balladur tried to justify this move by saying bluntly in Washington that the "question now is how to organize to protect ourselves from countries whose different values enable them to undercut us."

THE WEST'S OWN UNDOING

... If other civilizations have been around for centuries, why are they posing a challenge only now? A sincere attempt to answer this question reveals a fatal flaw that has recently developed in the Western mind: an inability to conceive that the West may have developed structural weaknesses in its core value systems and institutions. This flaw explains, in part, the recent rush to embrace the assumption that history has ended with the triumph of the Western ideal: individual freedom and democracy would always guarantee that Western civilization would stay ahead of the pack.

Only hubris can explain why so many Western societies are trying to deft the economic laws of gravity. Budgetary discipline is disappearing. Expensive social programs and pork-barrel projects multiply with little heed to costs. The West's low savings and investment rates lead to declining competitiveness vis-à-vis East Asia. The work ethic is eroding, while politicians delude workers into believing that they can retain high wages despite becoming internationally uncompetitive. Leadership is lacking. Any politician who states hard truths is immediately voted out. Americans freely admit that many of their economic problems arise from the inherent gridlock of American democracy. While the rest of the world is puzzled by these fiscal follies, American politicians and journalists travel around the world preaching the virtues of democracy. It makes for a curious sight.

The same hero-worship is given to the idea of individual freedom. Much good has come from this idea. Slavery ended. Universal franchise followed. But freedom does not only solve problems; it can also cause them. The United States has undertaken a massive social experiment, tearing down social institution after social institution that restrained the individual. The results have been disastrous. Since 1960 the U.S. population has increased 41 percent while violent crime has risen by 560 percent, single-mother births by 419 percent, divorce rates by 300 percent and the percentage of children living in single-parent homes by 300 percent. This is massive social decay. Many a society shudders at the prospects of this happening on its shores. But instead of traveling overseas with humility, Americans confidently preach the virtues of unfettered individual freedom, blithely ignoring the visible social consequences.

The West is still the repository of the greatest assets and achievements of human civilization. Many Western values explain the spectacular advance of mankind: the belief in scientific inquiry, the search for rational solutions and the willingness to challenge assumptions. But a belief that a society is practicing these values can lead to a unique blindness: the inability to realize that some of the values that come with this package may be harmful. Western values do not form a seamless web. Some are good. Some are bad. But one has to stand outside the West to see this clearly, and to see how the West is bringing about its relative decline by its own hand.

NO

Aung San Suu Kyi

TRANSCENDING THE CLASH OF CULTURES: FREEDOM, DEVELOPMENT, AND HUMAN WORTH

At its third meeting, held at San José, Costa Rica, 22–26 February 1994, the World Commission on Culture and Development set itself three goals, the third of which was "to promote a new cultural dynamic: the culture of peace and culture of development." The Commission undertook to "endeavour to recommend the concrete measures that could promote, on a national and international scale, a culture of peace" and went on to state that "a culture of peace, culture of democracy and culture of human rights are indivisible. Their effective implementation must result in a democratic management and ... the prevention of intercultural conflicts."

Peace as a goal is an ideal which will not be contested by any government or nation, not even the most belligerent. And the close interdependence of the culture of peace and the culture of development also finds ready acceptance. But it remains a matter of uncertainty how far governments are prepared to concede that democracy and human rights are indivisible from the culture of peace and therefore essential to sustained development. There is ample evidence that culture and development can actually be made to serve as pretexts for resisting calls for democracy and human rights. It is widely known that some governments argue that democracy is a Western concept alien to indigenous values; it has also been asserted that economic development often conflicts with political (i.e., democratic) rights and that the second should necessarily give way to the first. In the light of such arguments culture and development need to be carefully examined and defined that they may not be used, or rather, misused, to block the aspirations of peoples for democratic institutions and human rights....

BEYOND ECONOMICS

While the concept of human development is beginning to assume a dominant position in the thinking of international economists and administrators,

From Aung San Suu Kyi, "Transcending the Clash of Cultures: Freedom, Development, and Human Worth," *Journal of Democracy* (April 1995). Originally presented before a meeting of the World Commission on Culture and Development in Manila, November 21, 1994. Copyright © 1994 by Aung San Suu Kyi. Reprinted by permission. Notes omitted.

the Market Economy, not merely adorned with capital letters but seen in an almost mystic haze, is increasingly regarded by many governments as the quick and certain way to material prosperity. It is assumed that economic measures can resolve all the problems facing their countries. Economics is described as the *"deus ex machina,* the most important key to every lock of every door to the new Asia we wish to see"; and "healthy economic development" is seen as "essential to successfully meeting the challenge of peace and security, the challenge of human rights and responsibilities, the challenge of democracy and the rule of law, the challenge of social justice and reform and the challenge of cultural renaissance and pluralism."

The view that economic development is essential to peace, human rights, democracy, and cultural pluralism, and the view that a culture of peace, democracy, and human rights is essential to sustained human development, may seem on the surface to differ only in the matter of approach. But a closer investigation reveals that the difference in approach itself implies differences of a more fundamental order. When economics is regarded as the most important key to every lock of every door it is only natural that the worth of man should come to be decided largely, even wholly, by his effectiveness as an economic tool. This is at variance with the vision of a world where economic, political, and social institutions work to serve man instead of the other way round; where culture and development coalesce to create an environment in which human potential can be realized to the full. The differing views ultimately reflect differences in how the valuation of the various components of the social and

national entity are made; how such basic concepts as poverty, progress, culture, freedom, democracy, and human rights are defined; and, of crucial importance, who has the power to determine such values and definitions.

The value systems of those with access to power and of those far removed from such access cannot be the same. The viewpoint of the privileged is unlike that of the underprivileged. In the matter of power and privilege the difference between the haves and the have-nots is not merely quantitative, for it has far-reaching psychological and ideological implications.... It is not enough merely to provide the poor with material assistance. They have to be sufficiently empowered to change their perception of themselves as helpless and ineffectual in an uncaring world.

The question of empowerment is central to both culture and development. It decides who has the means of imposing on a nation or society their view of what constitutes culture and development and who determines what practical measures can be taken in the name of culture and development. The more totalitarian a system, the more power will be concentrated in the hands of the ruling elite, and the more culture and development will be used to serve narrow purposes.... [W]hen [culture] is bent to serve narrow interests it becomes static and rigid, its exclusive aspects come to the fore, and it assumes coercive overtones. The "national culture" can become a bizarre graft of carefully selected historical incidents and distorted social values intended to justify the policies and actions of those in power. At the same time, development is likely to be seen in the now-outmoded sense of economic growth. Statistics, often unverifiable, are reeled off to prove the success of official measures.

Many authoritarian governments wish to appear in the forefront of modern progress, but are reluctant to institute genuine change. Such governments tend to claim that they are taking a uniquely national or indigenous path toward a political system in keeping with the times. In the decades immediately after the Second World War, socialism was the popular option. But increasingly since the 1980s, democracy has gained ground. . . .

It is often in the name of cultural integrity as well as social stability and national security that democratic reforms based on human rights are resisted by authoritarian governments. It is insinuated that some of the worst ills of Western society are the result of democracy, which is seen as the progenitor of unbridled freedom and selfish individualism. It is claimed, usually without adequate evidence, that democratic values and human rights run counter to the national culture, and therefore to be beneficial they need to be modified—perhaps to the extent that they are barely recognizable. The people are said to be as yet unfit for democracy; therefore, an indefinite length of time has to pass before democratic reforms can be instituted.

The first form of attack is often based on the premise, so universally accepted that it is seldom challenged or even noticed, that the United States of America is the supreme example of democratic culture. What tends to be overlooked is that although the United States is certainly the most important representative of democratic culture, it also represents many other cultures, often indelicately enmeshed. Among these are the "I-want-it-all" consumer culture. . . .

Many of the worst ills of American society, increasingly to be found in varying degrees in other developed countries, can be traced not to the democratic legacy but to the demands of modern materialism. Gross individualism and cutthroat morality arise when political and intellectual freedoms are curbed on the one hand while on the other hand fierce economic competitiveness is encouraged by making material success the measure of prestige and progress. The result is a society where cultural and human values are set aside and money value reigns supreme. . . .

It is precisely because of the cultural diversity of the world that it is necessary for different nations and peoples to agree on those basic human values which will act as a unifying factor. When democracy and human rights are said to run counter to non-Western culture, such culture is usually defined narrowly and presented as monolithic. In fact the values that democracy and human rights seek to promote can be found in many cultures. Human beings the world over need freedom and security that they may be able to realize their full potential. The longing for a form of governance that provides security without destroying freedom goes back a long way. Support for the desirability of strong government and dictatorship can also be found in all cultures, both Eastern and Western: the desire to dominate and the tendency to adulate the powerful are also common human traits arising out of a desire for security. A nation may choose a system that leaves the protection of the freedom and security of the many dependent on the inclinations of the empowered few, or it may choose institutions and practices that will sufficiently empower individuals and organizations to protect their own freedom and security. The choice will decide how far a nation will progress along the road to peace and human development.

Many of the countries in the Third World now striving for meaningful development are multiracial societies where there is one dominant racial group and a number—sometimes a large number —of smaller groups: foreign, religious, or ethnic minorities. As poverty can no longer be defined satisfactorily in terms of basic economic needs, "minority" can no longer be defined merely in terms of numbers....

Once again, as in the case of poverty, it is ultimately a question of empowerment. The provision of basic material needs is not sufficient to make minority groups and indigenous peoples feel they are truly part of the greater national entity. For that they have to be confident that they too have an active role to play in shaping the destiny of the state that demands their allegiance. Poverty degrades a whole society and threatens its stability, while ethnic conflict and minority discontent are two of the greatest threats to both internal and regional peace. And when the dispossessed "minority" is in fact an overwhelming majority, as happens in countries where power is concentrated in the hands of the few, the threat to peace and stability is ever-present even if unperceived.

The Commission for a New Asia notes that:

the most rapid economic transformation is most likely to succeed within the context of international peace and internal political stability, in the presence of social tranquility, public order and an enlightened and strong government, and in the absence of societal turbulence and disorder.

This comment highlights the link between economic, political, and social concerns. But there is a danger that it could be interpreted to imply that peace, stability, and public order are desirable only as conditions for facilitating economic transformation rather than as ends in themselves. Such an interpretation would distort the very meaning of peace and security. It could also be used to justify strong, even if unenlightened, government and any authoritarian measures that such a government may take in the name of public order.

EMPOWERING THE PEOPLE

If material betterment, which is but a means to human happiness, is sought in ways that wound the human spirit, it can in the long run only lead to greater human suffering. The vast possibilities that a market economy can open up to developing countries can be realized only if economic reforms are undertaken within a framework that recognizes human needs....

Again we come back to empowerment. It decides how widespread will be the benefit of actions taken in the name of culture and development. And this in turn will decide the extent of the contribution such actions can make to genuine peace and stability. Democracy as a political system which aims at empowering the people is essential if sustained human development, which is "development of the people for the people by the people," is to be achieved....

The argument that it took long years for the first democratic governments to develop in the West is not a valid excuse for African and Asian countries to drag their feet over democratic reform. The history of the world shows that peoples and societies do not have to pass through a fixed series of stages in the course of development. Moreover, latecomers should be able to capitalize on the experiences of the pioneers and avoid the mistakes and obstacles that impeded early progress. The idea of "making haste slowly" is sometimes used to give backwardness the appearance of measured progress. But in a fast-developing world, too much emphasis on "slowly" can be a recipe for disaster.

There will be as many kinds of democracies as there are nations which accept it as a form of government. No single type of "Western democracy" exists; nor is democracy limited to a mere handful of forms such as the American, British, French, or Swiss. Each democratic country will have its own individual characteristics. With the spread of democracy to Eastern Europe, the variety in the democratic style of government will increase. Similarly, there cannot be one form of Asian democracy; in each country the democratic system will develop a character that accords with its social, cultural, and economic needs. But the basic requirement of a genuine democracy is that the people should be sufficiently empowered to be able to participate significantly in the governance of their country.

The 30 articles of the Universal Declaration of Human Rights are aimed at such empowerment. Without these rights, democratic institutions will be but empty shells incapable of reflecting the aspirations of the people and unable to withstand the encroachment of authoritarianism.

The democratic process provides for political and social change without violence. The democratic tradition of free discussion and debate allows for the settlement of differences without resort to armed conflict. The culture of democracy and human rights promotes diversity and dynamism without disintegration; it is indivisible from the culture of development and the culture of peace. It is only by giving firm support to movements that seek to empower the people through democratic means that the United Nations and its agencies will truly be able to promote the culture of peace and the culture of development.

TOWARD A GLOBAL COMMUNITY

Let me in conclusion summarize my argument. The true development of human beings involves much more than mere economic growth. At its heart there must be a sense of empowerment and inner fulfillment. This alone will ensure that human and cultural values remain paramount in a world where political leadership is often synonymous with tyranny and the rule of a narrow elite. People's participation in social and political transformation is the central issue of our time. This can only be achieved through the establishment of societies which place human worth above power, and liberation above control. In this paradigm, development requires democracy, the genuine empowerment of the people. When this is achieved, culture and development will naturally coalesce to create an environment in which all are valued, and every kind of human potential can be realized. The alleviation of poverty involves processes which change the way in which the poor perceive themselves and their world. Mere material assistance is not enough; the poor must have the sense that they themselves can shape their own future. Most totalitarian regimes fear change, but the longer they put off genuine democratic reform; the more likely it is that even their positive contributions will be vitiated: the success of national policies depends on the willing participation of the people. Democratic values and human rights, it is sometimes claimed, run counter to "national" culture, and all too often the people at large are seen as "unfit" for government. Nothing can be further from the truth. The challenge we now face is for the different nations and peoples of the world to agree on a basic set of human values, which will serve as a force in the development of a genuine global community. True economic transformation can then take place in the context of international peace and internal political stability. A rapid democratic transition and strengthening of the institutions of civil society are the *sine qua non* for this development. Only then will we be able to look to a future where human beings are valued for what they are rather than for what they produce. If the UN and its agencies wish to assist this development, they must support those movements which seek to empower the people, movements which are founded on democracy, and which will one day ensure a culture of peace and of development.

POSTSCRIPT

Are Efforts to Promote Democracy Culturally Biased and Self-Serving?

The points discussed by Kishore Mahbubani and Aung San Suu Kyi are not just matters of abstract concern; they are importantly related to the conduct of international relations. Many have argued that countries should make foreign policy decisions based at least partly on questions of how democratic another government is.

Some people care about democracy in other countries because they believe that nondemocratic governments are reprehensible and should be shunned on normative grounds. Other people believe that democratic governments are simply more peaceful and that working toward a world in which all governments are democratic will lead to a world that is much less violent. The German philosopher Immanuel Kant argued in *Perpetual Peace* (1795) that the spread of democracy would change the world by eliminating war. This would result, Kant reasoned, because "if the consent of the citizens is required in order to decide that war should be declared . . . nothing is more natural than that they would be very cautious in commencing such a poor game, decreeing for themselves all the calamities of war." Modern scholarship has taken up the question of whether or not democratic regimes are more peaceful and has found that they generally are. For some recent studies on this subject, consult James Lee Ray, *Democracy and International Conflict* (University of South Carolina Press, 1995) and Arie M. Kacowicz, "Explaining Zones of Peace: Democracies as Satisfied Powers," *Journal of Peace Research* (Summer 1995).

The belief that there is a connection between democracy and foreign policy is also shared by many policymakers. "We ought to be promoting the democratic impulses around the world," President Bill Clinton has commented. "Democracies are our partners. They don't go to war with each other. They're reliable friends in the future." This view played a part in Clinton's decision to use force to overthrow Haiti's military junta. "History has taught us that preserving democracy in our own hemisphere strengthens American security and prosperity," the president told Americans during a nationally televised address. For more on the standard of democracy as a factor in U.S. foreign policy, read Tony Smith, *America's Mission: The United States and the Worldwide Struggle for Democracy in the Twentieth Century* (Princeton University Press, 1994).

Still, advocating democracy does not fully solve the issue of what constitutes a democracy and what fails to meet that standard. A particularly non-Western argument is that democracy should be measured by the equality within a society, not by the procedural steps (such as contested elections) by which some societies judge democracy. On this topic, read Frederick C. Turner and Marita Cabrallo de Cilley, "Equality and Democracy," *International Social Science Journal* (Spring 1993). For more on the standards in some non-Western countries, see Zhera F. Arat, *Democracy and Human Rights in Developing Countries* (Lynne Rienner, 1991) and Axel Hadenius, *Democracy and Development* (Cambridge University Press, 1992). One also has to be aware of the argument that some societies are not as suited as others for Western-style democracy and that, at the very least, economically developed countries like the United States have to be patient with the development of less fortunate countries. This discussion is examined in Jacques Barzun, "Is Democratic Theory for Export," *Society* (March/April 1989).

PART 5

Political Identification

Many political analysts believe that the sovereignty of the state (country) is declining, that the political identification of people with the state is begining to weaken, and that people are beginning to refocus their loyalties on their nationalities. This section takes up issues that relate to the movement of people from state to state and to the value and strength of nationalism.

■ Should Serbia Be Treated Leniently?

■ Should Immigration Be Restricted?

■ Will the World Fragment into Antagonistic Cultures?

■ Is Self-Determination a Right of All Nationalities?

ISSUE 16

Should Serbia Be Treated Leniently?

YES: Marten van Heuven, from "Rehabilitating Serbia," *Foreign Policy* (Fall 1994)

NO: Hodding Carter, from "Punishing Serbia," *Foreign Policy* (Fall 1994)

ISSUE SUMMARY

YES: Marten van Heuven, a retired U.S. foreign service officer and an analyst at the RAND Corporation, contends that long-term stability in the Balkans can be reached only with the cooperation of Serbia and, therefore, future relations should be aimed at working with, rather than punishing, Serbia.

NO: Hodding Carter, a former U.S. State Department spokesman, argues that Serbia has been responsible for a great deal of suffering in the Balkans and must therefore be dealt with severely.

Yugoslavia was established in the aftermath of World War I. There was no historical precedent for any place called Yugoslavia. Rather, its creation forced within the same country a polyglot range of people, including Serbs from Serbia and closely related Montenegrins from Montenegro (both countries had been independent since 1878), Croats, Slovenians, Muslim Bosnians, Herzegovinians, Macedonians, Albanians, and others. The Croats, Slovenians, and some of the others had been part of the Austro-Hungarian empire, which collapsed in 1918.

It is helpful to know a bit about the earlier history to make some sense about what has occurred in the 1990s. The Balkans were for several centuries dominated by the Ottoman Turks, who were Muslims. Gradually, the fortunes of the Ottoman Empire declined. Several peoples, including the Serbs and Montenegrins, gained their independence in the late 1800s. Serbia had been independent before being conquered by the Ottoman Turks in 1389, and Serbs look back at a history of what they see as brutal oppression under Muslim domination.

The Balkan region has, over the last century or so, been the scene of almost continual turmoil. With both the Ottoman and the Austro-Hungarian empires tottering toward their collapse, there was considerable effort by various groups to revolt and gain independence and equally vigorous efforts by other countries around the region to gain or hold territory.

This instability continued into the twentieth century. General war was narrowly averted when the Austrians annexed Bosnia and Herzegovina, and their Muslims, in 1908. Peace did not last long, however. Various ambitions led to the First Balkan War in 1912, with Bulgaria, Greece, and Serbia at war with Turkey; then the Second Balkan War in 1913, with Bulgaria, Romania, and Turkey at war with Greece and Serbia. The following year, the spark that ignited World War I was struck in the Bosnian provincial capital of Sarajevo when Serbian nationalists assassinated the heir to the Austro-Hungarian throne, the Archduke Franz Ferdinand.

After World War I, Yugoslavia was created in part to reward the Serbs (who would dominate) and also to incorporate the disparate other groups whom, for one reason or another, the victorious powers did not want independent or did not want joined with their ethnic brethren in neighboring countries. There were, for example, Macedonians in the Yugoslav province of Macedonia and in the Greek province of Macedonia; and there were Albanians in Kosovo province and in Albania. Yugoslavia first had a king, then it was overrun by the Germans in World War II, and finally the guerrilla leader and communist Marshal Tito came to power after World War II. The force of Tito's control generally kept the country at ethnic peace until he died in 1980. The next 10 years saw the country begin to unravel. Croatia, Bosnia and Herzegovina, Macedonia, and Slovenia all declared their independence in June 1991. The mixture of Croats, Muslims, and Serbs living in Bosnia and of Serbs living in Croatia led to immediate fighting as Croats and Serbs sought to escape countries now dominated by another ethnic group. Most significant to this debate, Bosnian Serbs proclaimed the establishment of their own country.

The fighting in Bosnia was brutal as various factions sought to control territory and to expel other ethnic groups in a process called ethnic cleansing. Investigators charge that the brutality was directed by Bosnian Serb leaders to terrorize the Croats and Muslims. And the United Nations instituted economic sanctions against what remained of Yugoslavia in retaliation for its support of the Bosnian Serbs.

As the following articles by Marten van Heuven and Hodding Carter were being written, the fighting continued. UN peacekeeping forces had been unable to end the warfare. Since then, a peace accord was signed. The fact that the war ended, in many ways, does not change the issue that van Heuven and Carter are debating. Many have accused Serbian president Slobodan Milosevic and other Yugoslav leaders in Belgrade of being war criminals who should be tried. Moreover, it remains to be seen whether or not the Serbs will honor the peace accord's various pledges, such as agreeing to turn over accused war criminals and not trying to incorporate the autonomous Bosnian Serb areas into a Greater Serbia. Van Heuven argues that whatever has happened, we must deal with the present as we find it. There must be carrots for Serbia, he says, because sticks have not worked. Carter disagrees and contends that if crimes committed by the Serbs (and by others) go unpunished, it will be tantamount to rewarding barbarism and encouraging it in the future.

YES
Marten van Heuven

REHABILITATING SERBIA

Eventually, as fighting in Bosnia-Herzegovina subsides, U.S. efforts to shape a confederal structure that holds together Croats and Muslims will raise a key question: how to integrate the fragments of the former Yugoslavia into the European enterprise. In time, the European Union [EU] must lead the effort to return stability, security, and prosperity to the Balkans; further, that effort should focus on Serbia.

In the wake of territorial conquests and ethnic violence committed by Serb-controlled forces, it may appear counterintuitive to suggest that the West should lead an effort to lift the opprobrium of international sanctions and return Serbia to a respectable place and role in the Balkans. Western interests, however, require just that.

Early concerted Western action might have prevented Serb acquisition of most of Bosnia and part of Croatia. At present, however, it is not politically or militarily feasible for the West to roll back Serb territorial conquest.

Under the best imaginable circumstances, Serbia would be moving toward a post-Milošević, more-or-less-democratic country covering its original territory plus Montenegro and a large part of Bosnia-Herzegovina, guaranteeing minority rights for its Muslim population, living in general harmony with its neighbors, and building a market economy with the help of the West. For the West, such a scenario would be a preferable, if not an essential, departure from the injustices of territorial conquest and "ethnic cleansing." But that may not be realistic. An approach focused on Serbia is required under the more likely, even though less auspicious, scenario of a hegemonic and autocratic Serbia. It may encompass Montenegro, much of Bosnia-Herzegovina, and parts of Croatia (from which Croats have been forced to leave); have influence in Macedonia; pay little attention to minority rights; maintain an uneasy relationship with its neighbors; and be crippled by an economy scarred by United Nations [U.N.] sanctions.

Whatever the scenario for Serbia over the next two to five years, it will be the key power in the Balkans by virtue of its central location, newly acquired size, Serb ethnic cohesion, cultural ethos, military capacity, and strong-willed leadership. Serbia will inevitably exercise hegemonic influence. Budapest's talk of "normalization" in relations with Belgrade and its announcement in February 1994 that it wanted AWACS aircraft to vacate Hungarian airspace in the event that NATO were to order air-strikes against the Serbs provide evidence of growing ambiguity among Balkan states in continuing the political and economic isolation of Serbia. Growing porousness of the U.N. sanctions against Serbia demonstrates diminishing support for continued economic sanctions on the part of Bulgaria, Greece, and others. Moreover, Serbia still has friends in Moscow. It can, provided the right circumstances, also draw on historical associations with Great Britain and France. Given Serbia's strengths and the relative weakness of its neighbors, Serbian influence in and around what used to be Yugoslavia will be considerable.

One option for the United States, its Western European allies, and other regional powers is to attempt a policy of containment. Such a policy would put into action the judgment of the international community, as expressed in a series of U.N. Security Council resolutions, that Serbia bears major responsibility for aggression and violations of human rights. The point of such a policy would be to punish Serbia and deter other would-be hegemons. It would signal that such behavior will trigger a severe and enduring international response. The objectives would also be to keep strong pressure on the Serbs and to limit the influence of a contentious Serbia in the Balkans.

Such a policy, however, would encounter serious—and probably insurmountable—hurdles. In the Balkans, there are no obvious candidates to lead an effective policy of isolating Serbia. Even now, the economic cost of United Nations sanctions on Serbia's neighbors is forcing them to reevaluate their approach. In the Security Council, consensus to continue such a policy cannot be assumed. It is more likely that Moscow will increasingly disassociate itself from sanctions, thus driving a huge wedge into what is already a feeble international constraint. Further, none of the major European countries—Britain, France, or Germany—will be willing or able to lead a European attempt to isolate Serbia over the medium term and beyond. Nor would such a role, without a wholesale reversal of U.S. policy, be sought or carried out by the United States. Moreover, even a policy of isolation will ultimately have to be traded for improvements in Serbian conduct. The option of containing and isolating Serbia is, therefore, not sustainable in the short or the medium term.

The alternative option is to take today's situation as a point of departure for a carrot-and-stick approach. Through a sustained combination of incentives and disincentives, the West should allow Serbia to escape the position of international pariah by patiently but persistently negotiating changes in its conduct.

Important elements of the approach would be Serbian provisional—and later permanent—agreement with Croatia and Bosnia on borders; respect for the territorial integrity and independence of those two states, Macedonia, and other neighbors; adequate guarantees for the protection of minorities; basic human rights for the Albanian population in Kosovo; and a good faith effort by Belgrade to help deal with the consequences of displaced refugees. In return, U.N. sanctions would be lifted gradually. Serbia would, in due course, participate in the organizations from which it is now suspended; it would be eligible to receive West European regional economic assistance; and it could once again turn to the World Bank and the International Monetary Fund. A mixture of those elements would establish major incentives for Serbia to assume a responsible role in Balkan security and reconstruction.

Even though the West through inaction permitted Serb territorial conquest, and must now live with some of the results, it is important that the approach clearly indicate the unacceptability of aggression and human rights violations and penalize violations of internationally accepted norms. At some point it must hold individuals responsible for war crimes. It is important to recognize that the success of such an effort is likely to take years.

Serbia may be ready to proceed down such a path. It has achieved substantial territorial gains and seems assured of gaining permanent possession of considerable territory, even if it returns portions of Bosnia, and perhaps of Krajina, as part of a territorial settlement. It has achieved significant extension of its writ to encompass areas of significant Serbian population. However, sanctions have had a severe impact on the Serbian economy, and the Serbian population strongly desires to see them lifted. Not least, the prospect of escaping international opprobrium is attractive to Serbs, who have with doctrinaire rigidity defended the righteousness of their efforts to control all territory with Serb populations, despite broad condemnation.

Paradoxically, West European countries are now intent on stopping the war and preventing it from spreading. At the same time many within the Clinton administration, on Capitol Hill, and among the pundits feel that the United States should not have any part of an "unjust"

outcome that penalizes Bosnian victims of Serb aggression even if Bosnia agreed to it, since such an agreement would be regarded as having been given under duress. Nonetheless, such feelings are beginning to be overtaken by reality: Bosnia, however unfortunately, has lost the war with the Serbs. Even a partial lifting of the arms embargo is not likely to produce a significant change in the military situation. U.S. interests require an end to the fighting. The war is draining the effort at reform in the Balkans and Eastern Europe, and continued fighting will make for greater instability on the Continent. If not contained, the war could spill over, drawing in America's allies and requiring greater U.S. involvement with uncertain outcomes.

THE ASSISTANCE OF OUTSIDERS

Successful pursuit of the alternative option of offering carrots and sticks to Serbia would continue to require the involvement of outsiders. It was clear, even early in the breakup of Yugoslavia, that the extent of this Balkan conflict outstretched the capacity of the Yugoslavs themselves to cope successfully with their deepening divisions. Their tendency to see current events—and the future-exclusively with reference to the past makes them incapable of facing the future by themselves. Only outside elements—a "foreign factor"—can effectively shape the future. In 1990 and 1991, the fiction of Yugoslav unity stood in the way of effective outside involvement when it could have made a difference. Recognition of the independence of Slovenia and Croatia by the European Community (EC in early 1992, and of Bosnia by the EC and the United States in April 1992, came too late to avert Serbian expansion by diplomatic efforts such as the introduction of foreign observers or peacekeepers. Moreover, recognition of Bosnia in April 1992 was accorded with little consideration of the ramifications of leaving that country without any effective outside support. What has been achieved through truce and diplomatic agreement, however, has been largely due to the efforts of outsiders and the presence of foreign forces.

Earlier this year [1995], U.S. diplomatic initiatives succeeded—where others had failed—when the United States brought Bosnia's Croats and Muslims together and established a loose relationship between the new Bosnian federation and Croatia. Simultaneously, Russian diplomacy started to affect the Serbian stance —though not to the point of bringing Serbia to accept linkage with the new federation.

It would be too much, however, to expect the United States to lead for the long period that it will take to stabilize the situation in the former Yugoslavia. The U.S. diplomatic effort to put the fragments of Yugoslavia back together is bound to fall short, since it is unlikely that Washington will be prepared to stay for the many years that it will take to bring the Balkan situation back to some sort of normalcy. There will not be in any foreseeable future a final peaceful settlement in the Balkans. We will instead be facing the problem of long-term crisis management, preferably at a level short of violence. Moreover, the American people will not support a lengthy involvement.

The political mood in the United States has returned to caution about any U.S. role abroad that depends on the threat and possible application of military force. The U.S. military leadership is now resolutely opposed to all but the most lim-ited kinds of foreign intervention. The likelihood of U.S. approval for new U.N. peacekeeping operations has been circumscribed severely by Presidential Decision Directive 25 of May 1994, which severely restricts possible use of American military force in a U.N. peacekeeping force. The disinclination of the American public to see the United States send forces to the former Yugoslavia has reinforced the tendency of the Clinton administration to eschew the commitment of American military power. Washington is also seeking to reduce its financial share of the peacekeeping and peace-enforcing operations that the U.N. Security Council, with American agreement, has decided or may decide to authorize.

As for the U.N. peacekeeping operation in Bosnia, even though Lt. Gen. Sir Michael Rose, the U.N.'s Bosnia commander, has repeatedly requested more U.N. peacekeepers, and in spite of the clear U.S. interest in strengthening the U.N. military contingent, the United States initially told other Security Council members that it had difficulties agreeing to extend the U.N. Protection Force in Bosnia (UNPROFOR) mandate by six months and increase the force by 5,000 troops because it was unsure about congressional funding. The administration, moreover, has been consistent in its position that the United States will deploy its forces only after a peace agreement has been reached. That thinking, in terms of neat categories, suggests that Washington has not yet drawn the lesson from the turmoil of the past few years: that Balkan events tend to defy the rule books of U.S. strategists.

U.S.-Russian diplomacy to build on the truce around Sarajevo is also likely to lose momentum. Without sustained high-level backing and public explanation, U.S. diplomatic efforts will reach their limits, if they have not already done so. Lacking an effective U.S. partner, Russia will very likely be confined to insisting on a seat at the table. In Western Europe there is bound to be growing unease, if not dissatisfaction, with any prospect of those two powers again drawing the lines of a political settlement in the Balkans while marginalizing European participation. Moreover, the reintroduction of a substantial Russian role in Yugoslavia for the first time since Marshall Tito broke with Soviet communism is not likely to be regarded with equanimity by most countries in the region.

That situation creates an opportunity, but also a necessity, for the European Union (EU) to provide the "foreign factor" that will be required to keep the settlement process on course after the current hostilities end. The next two to five years will be a second chance for the EU. Its first attempt, during much of 1991, proved ineffective. The EU (then the EC) lacked an analytic consensus on the nature of the problem, the political resolve to carry through a policy, and the consistency that would have been essential to contain the crisis. Ultimately, the EC handed the issue over to the Security Council in the fall of 1991.

For more than two years the EC and the U.N. attempted, with success always just beyond reach, to achieve a political settlement along the lines of proposals made by former British foreign secretary David Owen and former U.S. secretary of state Cyrus Vance. Despite the failure of its first try, the EU is bound to make another attempt to respond to the need for the active engagement of the states most concerned over the long-term future of the Balkans. That course flows from the historical drive toward greater European integration, the desire to see the European Union succeed, the lessons learned from past failures, and French willingness—at present at least—to play an active role. More than five years will be required to steer through the treacherous political, economic, and military shoals present in the Balkans today. Even then the Yugoslav imbroglio may not be settled, but at least it will have been contained and the crisis will have been managed.

It needs to be clearly understood that the effort now required in the area goes well beyond the geographic extent and nature of the new Bosnian federation. The issues that the international community now faces in the Balkans include Croatia's place in the Balkans; a settlement in Krajina; the independence and security of Macedonia; minority rights within Serbia—particularly Kosovo—and neighboring countries; refugees; Greek policy with respect to Albania and Macedonia; and, ultimately, acceptable and accepted international monitoring and mediation. A way will also have to be found to commit the tribunal in the Hague to addressing the issue of crimes against humanity in the former Yugoslavia. The task is to gradually establish patterns—which will evolve over time—that will bring the various parts of the Balkans together in a way that reestablishes stability and security. Communication will provide opportunities for reconstruction and for addressing key issues, such as refugees.

Members of the EU—Britain, France, Germany, Greece, and Italy in particular—are the states most directly affected by the outcome. They are also the best placed to help shape it. Other countries that are also affected can be drawn into the diplomatic effort—Hungary, as a neighboring country and potential member of the EU; Austria, as a prospective new member of the EU; and Turkey, as a member of NATO [North Atlantic Treaty Organization]. Using the EU mechanism would afford the countries most directly affected a primary role. Some, such as France and perhaps Britain, could play a special role with Serbia. Germany could do the same in Croatia. Turkish involvement would provide some sense of security for the Muslim populations. EU diplomatic monitors and observers could become a crucial part of the diplomatic effort.

EU diplomacy, moreover, could be supported militarily. EU forces could be the backbone of a continuing UN force that would support the diplomatic effort to return the Balkans to a process of peaceful adjustment. Alternatively, the Western European Union (WEU) could provide the basic framework for a broad array of military tasks now carried out mostly by the UN. The WEU could use NATO's European assets. For certain contingencies, the EU and the WEU could even call for NATO backup.

Such an EU-oriented approach should leave room for both American and Russian participation. Optimally, one of the tasks of the EU would be to marshal and bring to bear American and Russian resources to support its effort. That approach would create limited roles for a United States that is hesitant about European commitments and for a Russia that perhaps wants, but should not have, a major role in the Balkans. Ultimately, Russia will probably be content with a lesser role, as long as Moscow is seen to be part of the process.

Though limited, the U.S. role would be significant. Perhaps it would be the indispensable element for achieving and maintaining consensus among the lead-

ing European countries in their effort to define objectives, choose strategies, and apply tactics. Americans could, moreover, give concerted support to European diplomatic efforts and contribute, including with military resources, to an effective EU-led mediation, pacification, and peacekeeping effort.

Other international organizations are less suited to provide the "foreign factor" that the Balkan situation requires. UNPROFOR, though it has been well served by various national military units, is likely to continue to be bedeviled by scarce resources, logistical difficulties, and command and control confusion. Further, the United Nations may find it difficult to sustain an engagement in Bosnia—even assuming the Security Council consensus to that effect continues —when other crises in the world make growing claims on its capabilities. France, whose military forces have, along with those of other countries, played a significant and praiseworthy role in the former Yugoslavia, has already indicated that it intends to reduce the number of its troops in UNPROFOR. Other countries may do likewise.

NATO, despite its apparent success in obtaining a truce around Sarajevo and other U.N. safe havens, has been a military instrument that its members have been reluctant to use. That condition is not likely to change. With the Russian interest and role in the Balkans, and with Russia now part of the Partnership for Peace, NATO members will be particularly loath to use their forces as the prime instrument for shaping a Balkan settlement.

Thus, the EU emerges as the most likely if not the only available instrument for the West to help shape the future of the Balkans. Having failed once, the

EU countries could fail again. It will be very difficult for the EU to settle on a common policy and the manner of its execution over the considerable period of time it will take to reestablish peaceful and orderly relations in the former Yugoslavia. But despite those difficulties, Balkan problems will not go away. Even if the EU, as such, fails to meet the challenge, key European countries will still face and must still accept the responsibility of seeking a coordinated approach.

Several factors, taken together, could make for EU success. First, there is no longer a question of whether the interests of EU countries are affected: The countries of Western Europe have learned that what happens in the Balkans affects what they perceive as their key interests. The Balkans are now viewed as a clear test of the viability of a common EU foreign and security policy. The Treaty of Maastricht requires, if not success, then at least a serious common effort. With elections and referenda giving new political shape to Western Europe, an emerging constellation of leaders will want a leading role in European security. In that capacity, they will be buttressed by leaders and citizens of countries on the periphery of the Balkans, who are all seeking to shield themselves from the serious economic dislocations, political turbulence, and flow of refugees caused by the Balkan conflict. Meanwhile, both the United States and Russia will have places, but not the dominant roles each used to play during the Cold War. The EU does have the resources to apply to issues so patently in its interest. Finally, the major European powers now see their concerns in the Balkans as best served by settlement, not war, thus creating an opening for diplomacy. As George Kennan has pointed out, the task will be difficult and painful, but the alternatives are worse.

In the process of establishing a new framework of relations and patterns of conduct that open the way toward greater democracy, more human rights, and economic reconstruction in the Balkans, a leading role by the EU countries is a major American interest. It calls for America to be supportive in various ways—with diplomacy, economic development aid, educational assistance, and conflict resolution. But it puts the main burden where it belongs, and where Washington has always wanted it: on European shoulders. It allows Washington more room to reassess previous commitments, such as its pledges to provide ground forces to implement a peace agreement in Bosnia and its unilateral commitment to retaliate against Serb violence in Kosovo. It would also be a significant step toward the broadening of the EU that President Bill Clinton articulated as America's policy goal for Europe in his speech to the French National Assembly.

In part because of Western inaction, the situation in the former Yugoslavia has reached a point where it is no longer possible to return to the political and territorial arrangements of the past. Although the West may want to maintain international sanctions on Serbia for its policies of territorial acquisition and ethnic cleansing, as suggested recently by David Gompert in *Foreign Affairs*, such an approach has been overtaken by events on the ground. We must now deal with the present as we find it. The Serbs have changed the map of the Balkans. Short of a massive Western military intervention, nothing can be done to roll them back.

The road toward a peaceful and prosperous Balkans will have to go through Belgrade. There must be carrots for Serbia, because a policy of sticks alone will not work. Outsiders—the European Union in particular—will and must play a major role, as they once again draw boundary lines in Southern Europe. The goal of a stable Balkans can be achieved only by cooperation with all the political elements of the former Yugoslavia, including its most significant and influential member—Serbia.

NO

Hodding Carter

PUNISHING SERBIA

A just solution in Bosnia and stability in the Balkans will be difficult to achieve under any circumstances. They will be impossible unless the United States takes and keeps the lead in both aims. Anything less on Washington's part will all but guarantee an aggressively unrepentant Serbia and a dismembered Bosnia, which in turn would seriously weaken NATO [North Atlantic Treaty Organization], further cripple the United Nations, and accelerate the trend toward global chaos.

Looking to the European Union (EU) for leadership... is an exercise in wishful thinking. The Clinton administration may or may not accept responsibility, but Europe is incapable of assuming it.

What are the long-range objectives that anyone who cares about the Balkans and a workable world order would want to achieve in Serbia? Van Heuven lists them as most outside observers would, a quibble here and an addition there notwithstanding: "Serbian... agreement with Croatia and Bosnia on borders; respect for the territorial integrity and independence of those two states, Macedonia, and other neighbors; adequate guarantees for the protection of minorities; basic human rights for the Albanian population in Kosovo; and a good-faith effort by Belgrade to help deal with the consequences of displaced refugees."

And what are we to do about war crimes and genocide, open aggression across internationally recognized borders, and studied contempt for U.N. Security Council resolutions, NATO intervention, and world opinion? As he puts it, "It is important that the approach clearly indicate the unacceptability of aggression and human rights violations and penalize violations of internationally accepted norms. At some point it must hold individuals responsible for war crimes."

Thus we have the bell that needs hanging—a rather large one—and the Serbian cat on which it should be hung. But the questions that arose as Yugoslavia disintegrated politically and militarily between 1990 and 1992 remain the critical ones. Who will bell the cat? And how?

Van Heuven does not dodge any of those questions. He offers an elaborate construct that has a number of worthwhile features. Ultimately, however,

From Hodding Carter, "Punishing Serbia," *Foreign Policy* (Fall 1994). Copyright © 1994 by The Carnegie Endowment for International Peace. Reprinted by permission.

what is both sad and mystifying about his good-faith effort to chart a course away from further disaster is that his heading leads inevitably toward it. At the end of his road, the cat's grin will be as large as its now-sated appetite was enormous. Meanwhile, another round of savage violence will lie just around the corner.

Along the way, van Heuven discounts the possibility that sanctions can be maintained, that the U.N. can pull itself together and operate effectively, that NATO will be energetically deployed, or that the United States will exert itself in a coherent, meaningful way. All of those are quite respectable propositions if the past is the only guide to the future. He then offers salvation in the form of the European Union, which, unfortunately for everyone, has been and remains an utterly implausible hope.

There is no question that Western Europe has an immense and direct stake in Balkan stability, but Europe's policy missteps have helped create and sustain the tragedy we now confront. From its rush to recognize Croatia and Slovenia without conditions in January 1992 to its campaign to force capitulation upon Bosnia in 1994, which looked suspiciously like an eagerness to reward Serbian aggression, Europe has managed to get it wrong at least as often as the Bush and Clinton administrations.

Usually, little good has resulted even when Europe has tried to do the right thing. Its best-intentioned and best-executed diplomatic effort, the combined European Community–U.N. diplomatic initiative, foundered on the obduracy of the Serbs and degenerated into bullying the Bosnians. The forthright decision by Paris, London, Ottawa, and other capitals to commit peacekeeping troops has been a longstanding rebuke to American timidity, but those commitments are increasingly problematic. Without any substantial movement toward settlement, "Bring the boys home" will soon have an irresistible appeal.

There are other, more sinister impediments to a European Union solution. Greece's support of Serbia—its "diminishing support for continued economic sanctions" as van Heuven delicately puts it—is as notorious as is its deliberate destabilization of Macedonia. Less noticed is the new Italian government's dramatic shift in policy. Virtually the first EU initiative of the incoming Italian foreign minister was a proposal to lift the sanctions on Serbia, or so it has been widely reported. Equally provocative reassertions of old Italian interests in the Balkans have already been advanced by members of Rome's unruly patchwork coalition. More can be expected.

It is extremely difficult to speak of a "European" policy toward the states that arose from what was once Yugoslavia, any more than it is possible to speak of a "unified Europe." To the extent that European foreign policy unity has been achieved in the past for the most part it has been forged on the American anvil. Without the support of the United States, the lowest common denominator prevails. That cannot be a welcome thought in Sarajevo or a discomfitting one in Belgrade.

Van Heuven concedes all that. The U.S. role "perhaps...would be the indispensable element for achieving and maintaining consensus among the leading European countries in their effort to define objectives, choose strategies, and apply tactics," he writes toward the end of his article. "The United States could, moreover, give concerted support to European diplomatic efforts and contribute, *including with military resources*, to an effective EU-led mediation, *pacification*, and peace-keeping effort" [emphasis added].

Yet that program implies a sustained American interest and involvement in the Balkans that has already been summarily dismissed with the phrase "it is unlikely that Washington will be prepared to stay for the many years that it will take to bring the Balkan situation back to some sort of normalcy." Politicians, the military, and the American public are all opposed to any policy that carries the risk of military involvement, van Heuven notes. The kind of American underpinning of an EU initiative that he envisions is precisely the kind of activity he believes is all but impossible.

There is another flaw in his logic, or at least a major contradiction. "The option of containing and isolating Serbia is, therefore, not sustainable in the short or the medium term," he says. If that is true, then the game is up and it is time for everyone to declare defeat and go home. If true, it is even more untenable to maintain that the EU can lead an effort that will take "more than five years" and must depend primarily on carrots that Serbia has reason to believe will appear on its table in due course without concessions. What possible "disincentives" are left, particularly since van Heuven believes that ending the arms embargo would not change the situation on the ground?

That, of course, remains a point of basic contention. For van Heuven it is a given that

> Bosnia, however unfortunately, has lost the war with the Serbs. Even a partial lifting of the arms embargo is not likely to produce a significant change in the military situation. U.S. interests require an end to the fighting.... If

not contained, the war could spill over, drawing in America's allies and requiring greater U.S. involvement with uncertain outcomes.

Those are assertions, not facts. Bosnia, the victim state, does not accept most of them and there is good reason to question others. Bosnia has not lost the war with the Serbs, though it has certainly lost lives and territory to aggression made possible and unstintingly supported by Serbia. As outside aid has begun to reach Bosnia, however inadequately, the Serbian tide has been checked.

It can be argued, and I would, that fully arming Bosnia so that it can deal directly with the internal threat while interdicting Serbia's cross-border replenishments of the Bosnian Serbs is a "sustainable" way to contain the situation. For that matter, a well-armed Bosnia might be able to roll back Serbian gains. The myth of Serbian invincibility is just that—a myth, ungrounded in discernible fact.

Self-defense is a right incorporated in the United Nations Charter, the answer that international law offers to aggression. So is member-nation action against an aggressor state. To minimize both indispensable props of a workable international system in the name of realpolitik is to encourage that system's disintegration. To place the quest for a phony peace above the requirements of justice is to guarantee the failure of both.

But let us assume that the war is indeed lost and that the Western- and Russian-backed partition proposal giving the Muslim-Croat federation 51 per cent of Bosnian territory is accepted at some point by all the players. The ensuing lull would be an interlude between slaughters, not a solution. None of the objectives summarized by van Heuven would be achieved. The Balkans would have neither stability nor justice, merely a pause between Munich and *blitzkrieg*, between Versailles and revanchism. Even a fully functioning Europe could not rescue the Balkans from its fate.

That is the final flaw in van Heuven's project. There is no possibility of a world order founded on law if a "hegemonic Serbia" based on the dismemberment of a member state of the U.N. is allowed to stand. Western Europe, now risen far above its bloody roots, will itself be at risk if the precedents being established in Bosnia are not checked, reversed, and penalized. Only yesterday it was possible to think of the "family feuds" of France and Germany as givens. The condescension that allows many observers to speak of the Balkans' "ethnic divisions" as immutable is Serbia's secret weapon. It is also an irresistible invitation to hungry politicians in other parts of Europe to rattle yesterday's skeletons for today's gain.

There is no doubt that Serbia must be brought back into the family of nations and that it has a key role to play in the Balkans of tomorrow. But the world must await a different Serbia from the one that now confronts the region. The Germany of 1994 is the linchpin of European security. The Germany of 1944 was a rogue state at war with the world. First comes compliance with basic norms; then comes cooperation.

ACCEPTING GENOCIDE

One other aspect of the Balkan violence deserves further note. The world has made "never again" a sick joke. Genocide, the word Washington dares not utter, has been perpetrated in Cambodia, Croatia, Bosnia, and Rwanda. There has

been limited outcry, but no purposeful response. "Again and again" is the certain result If the Serbian "crimes against humanity" documented by the U.N.'s war crimes tribunal go unpunished, or, even worse, are rewarded by accession to the fruits of those crimes, then humanity will again give up hard-won ground to barbarism.

The burden of leading the world community in the opposite direction falls on Washington. It is to this administration that pressure should be applied and petitions directed. President Bill Clinton, unlike his predecessor (the fecklessness of whose policy toward the Balkans is now admitted by some of its leading architects), "talks the talk," at least on alternate days. It is past time for him to do so more consistently and to "walk the walk" as well.

It is useful to remember that the more direct American involvement of recent months has already produced positive results. The agreement between Bosnian Croats and Muslims is one example. The limited deployment of NATO assets and pressure, which at least temporarily lifted the siege of Sarajevo, is another.

But those achievements are the products of a policy of fits and starts. Too often, friends and foes have been united in mutual bafflement about Washington's real intentions. Virtually everyone has reason to doubt this administration's staying power when it comes to matters involving possible military deployment.

The consequences of Serbian success will be felt most immediately and keenly by its neighbors. But a narrow issue of U.S. self-interest is involved here as well. Serbian success will be unavoidably and correctly viewed as an American failure of staggering proportions. No longer "bound to lead," we will be bound instead to witness the inexorable diminution of our influence. Many countries will tend to reach accommodations without American participation that are harmful to basic American interests, based on the accurate assessment that there are no penalties for doing so.

Former senator William Fulbright, Clinton's fellow Arkansan and occasional mentor, once spoke wisely of the "arrogance of power" as applied most notably to U.S. policy in Vietnam. But there are two possible kinds of arrogance. One is to have power and influence and abuse them. The other is to have both and, in a situation that cries out for their application, fail to use them.

It is true that the American public is confused about the state of the world and wary of overseas adventures. It is true that the military sees the Balkans as a morass. It is a given that mustering the West or the U.N. to live up to its resolutions is a task of gargantuan proportions. But it is also true that the president has the capacity, by speaking directly and consistently, to lay out the case for an activist policy and to marshal a majority behind it.

He can do so in the name of international law, of humanity, of the direct national interest in assuring that aggression carries penalties. He can do so by invoking the dire consequences of past American failures to measure up to its responsibilities and the hard-won but real success of the times when it did. He can lay out the evidence that American investigators, among others, have gathered, and utter the word Washington has elided so far—genocide.

There is something profoundly contemptuous of the American people in the argument that they are obsessed with their economic situation to the exclusion of all other considerations. There is no question that they are worried about the state of the economy and confused about America's role in a post–Cold War world. But in both respects, public opinion is like an unanchored ship. The circumstances increase rather than diminish the role of the helmsman.

As any cynic will duly note, all that is rhetoric. But it is the kind of rhetoric that American presidents invoke to create a majority for a focused purpose, a tool not available to that amorphous being called "Europe." There is no president, no commander in chief for Europe. There is one for the United States, as some in the military establishment need to be forcefully reminded. The United States remains first among equals in what remains of the Atlantic Alliance and is the most significant presence in the United Nations.

To be as clear as possible about what the United States can and should do, what its objectives should be, refer back to the two sets of purposes outlined by van Heuven and repeated earlier in this essay. *How* to achieve them is the essence of tactics. The objectives themselves are the essence of strategy. Both depend upon the full commitment of the United States, and first and foremost on that of its president.

Perhaps that asks too much of Clinton at this point in a beleaguered presidency. If so, no one should doubt what will follow. No one else, no conglomeration of countries, no other institution has the ability or will to take the lead in building a just and workable foundation for peace in the Balkans. If America cannot or will not lead, it will not be done, most certainly not by "Europe." The consequences of that failure will haunt the world for years to come.

POSTSCRIPT

Should Serbia Be Treated Leniently?

The most recent chapter in Balkan violence came to an uncertain close in late 1995. After a series of distressing events during the summer of 1995—including mortar attacks on children and Bosnian Serbs taking 377 UN peacekeepers hostage—the countries of the world, especially the United States, found the resolve to intervene forcefully. The Americans led a high-pressure diplomatic effort that soon convinced the presidents of Bosnia, Croatia, and Serbia (representing the Bosnian Serbs) to meet for face-to-face peace talks. After three weeks the Croats, Muslims, and Serbs all begrudgingly accepted a peace plan that technically maintains Bosnia and Herzegovina as a unified country with a single government but, in reality, divides the country's territory into two semiautonomous sections, one for Muslims and Croats and the other for Bosnian Serbs. The agreement will be enforced for a year or so by the NATO-led international force (IFOR) of 60,000 soldiers, including 20,000 American troops, that will patrol the 4-kilometer-wide demilitarized zone that divides the two sections of Bosnia. For more background on the Balkan fighting, read Susan L. Woodward, *Balkan Tragedy* (Brookings Institution, 1995) and Robert J. Donia and John V. A. Fine, Jr., *Bosnia and Hercegovina* (Columbia University Press, 1995).

The coming of peace has not, however, erased the reality of the ghastly crimes that were committed during the war. Even as the peace talks were under way in Ohio, the United Nations issued a report in November 1995 that condemned the Bosnian Serbs for engaging in "a consistent pattern of summary executions, rape, mass expulsion, arbitrary detentions, forced labor, and large-scale disappearances." Many observers are fearful that those responsible for these acts of barbarism will go unpunished. Richard J. Goldstone, a South African jurist and the chief prosecutor for the UN war crimes tribunal, worried publicly that it would be "unthinkable" if the peace accord did not include a provision that specified that all parties must "surrender those indicted" for trial. A good analysis of the peace negotiations is Roger Cohen, "Taming the Bullies of Bosnia," *The New York Times Magazine* (December 17, 1995). A more general study of the difficulty of ending such conflicts is I. William Zartman, ed., *Elusive Peace: Negotiating an End to Civil Wars* (Brookings Institution, 1995).

For a view that too much appeasement has already occurred in the Balkans, consult Nader Mousavizadeh, ed., *The Black Book of Bosnia* (Basic Books, 1995). The final issue is whether to forget, if not forgive, and allow Serbia to resume its seat at the United Nations or to take tough action until all war criminals have been tried and adjudged innocent or guilty.

ISSUE 17

Should Immigration Be Restricted?

YES: George J. Borjas, from "Know the Flow," *National Review* (April 17, 1995)

NO: Stephen Moore, from "Give Us Your Best, Your Brightest," *Insight* (November 22, 1993)

ISSUE SUMMARY

YES: George J. Borjas, an economist at the University of California, San Diego, refutes a number of what he considers myths about the impact of immigration.

NO: Stephen Moore, an economist with the Cato Institute in Washington, D.C., maintains that the net gains that the United States reaps from the contributions of immigrants far outweigh any social costs.

The world is awash in refugees and immigrants. For the most part, immigrants are people seeking a better standard of living, people seeking to escape restrictions on their human rights, or people seeking to flee violence in their native lands and find safety in a new country. Whatever their motivations, a vast number of people have left their countries in search of new ones.

There are some 125 million people living outside their native homelands. Most of these people chose to migrate, but more than 16 million are refugees, according to the UN High Commission on Refugees. Many countries are host to numerous refugees displaced by fighting, famine, and other calamities. There are more than 1 million Hutus huddled in Zaire because they fear that if they return to Rwanda they will face reprisals from the Tutsis. The fighting within Bosnia and Herzegovina and the other parts of the former Yugoslavia has displaced a million or more people, some 400,000 of whom are now in Germany. The United States is home to almost 200,000 refugees from Cuba, Haiti, and elsewhere.

Immigration is a traditional path to seeking a new life in a new place. The difficulty is that many countries are reacting to the increase in immigration pressure by closing, not opening, their doors. This is especially true of the countries of Western Europe. The United Nations estimates that since 1980, more than 15 million people have migrated to Western Europe. Three million of these asked for political asylum. Seven percent of France's population and 5 percent of Germany's are foreigners.

The reaction of many countries in Europe has been to tighten entry policies. Germany had one of the most liberal immigration policies, based on Article

16 of its constitution; it promised asylum to "people persecuted on political grounds." On July 1, 1993, Germany's immigration policy became among the most restrictive in Europe.

As in Europe, legal and illegal immigration has become the subject of heated debate in the United States. The case of the Haitians has been particularly important during the Clinton administration. As a presidential candidate he advocated allowing many more Haitians to enter the United States; as president, Clinton soon beat a retreat and followed essentially the same policy that George Bush had. There are numerous reasons why Americans tend to resist immigration. Many Americans believe that immigrants compete for jobs, a worrisome thought in an era of economic uncertainty. There is also a common notion that immigrants too often use expensive social services (such as education, housing, and health care) while paying little in taxes. Changes in American views on political asylum have also added to opposition to immigration. In the past large refugee groups from communist countries were allowed into the United States. Czechoslovakian, Hungarian, Polish, Romanian, and Soviet citizens made up the bulk of European immigrants during the 1960s, 1970s, and 1980s. Cambodians, Laotians, and Vietnamese accounted for the vast majority of Asian immigrants, and Cubans were the second largest single group from Latin America, after Mexicans. Arthur Helton, head of the Lawyers Committee for Human Rights, commented that the changed attitude "raises the question—was asylum just a cold war luxury all along? It seems so."

Racism may also play a part in the current debate over immigration policy. A national poll on immigration conducted in 1993 revealed that, of those Americans surveyed, half thought that it should be easier for people from Eastern Europe to emigrate to the United States. By contrast, 73 percent of the poll's respondents thought that it should be more difficult for Haitians to come to the United States, 59 percent favored making immigration more difficult for Africans, and 65 percent wanted to make it harder for Asians to seek residency and citizenship.

Should more immigrants be allowed into the United States? Or is fewer—even none—a better proposal? This is the issue taken up in the following selections by George J. Borjas and Stephen Moore. Borjas argues that unless we drastically change immigration policy, we will create a permanent underclass and a volatile social situation. Moore asserts that by pursuing liberal immigration policies, the United States can ensure that the twenty-first century, like the twentieth century, will be the American century.

YES

George J. Borjas

KNOW THE FLOW

The flow of legal immigrants has increased steadily since the 1930s, when only 500,000 immigrants were admitted during the entire decade. In the 1950s, 250,000 legal immigrants entered the United States *each year*. By the 1990s, nearly 900,000 legal immigrants were being admitted every year. A large number of people also enter the country illegally, despite the enactment of the Immigration Reform and Control Act of 1986. Last year [1994] the Border Patrol apprehended 1.1 million illegal aliens, more than two per minute. We have also witnessed a radical change in the national-origin mix of immigrants. Over two-thirds of immigrants during the 1950s originated in Europe or Canada. By the 1980s, only about 12 per cent originated in Europe or Canada, as against 37 per cent who originated in Asia and almost 50 per cent who originated in Latin America.

In view of these historic changes, it is not surprising that immigration has resurfaced as a pivotal issue. The debate has blurred the traditional lines between the Left and the Right, leading to odd political alliances: Bill Bennett siding with Fidel Castro and the California Teachers Association in proclaiming the evils of Proposition 187, Pat Buchanan siding with environmentalist groups to argue that the flow of legal immigrants must be reduced.

For the most part, the immigration debate focuses on economic issues. The stakes are high, and so it is not surprising that the participants use facts, factoids, and outright distortions to champion their point of view. For instance, depending on whose numbers we believe, immigrants either pay $27 billion more in taxes than they take out of the welfare system or take out $42 billion more than they pay. A number of myths permeate the field. Before we can engage in a serious debate, it is worth contemplating a simple question: What do we know about the economic impact of immigrants on the United States?

Myth: By historical standards, immigration today is not all that high.

In 1910, 14 per cent of the American population was foreign-born; by 1990, only 8 per cent was. This trend causes some observers to argue that immigration fears are blown out of proportion because, by historical standards, immigrants now make up a small proportion of the population. Yet by several measures immigration today is at or near record levels. Between 1901 and 1910, at the height of the Great Migration, 8.8 million legal immigrants entered the United States. If present trends continue, as many as 10 million legal immigrants, and perhaps another 3 million illegals, will have entered the country in the 1990s. The United States, therefore, will probably have admitted more immigrants in this decade than in any other decade in its history.

Moreover, because of the decline in the number of children borne by American women, immigration now accounts for nearly 40 per cent of the growth in population, compared to about 50 per cent at the beginning of the century. At least one of every three new workers who enters the U.S. labor market during the 1990s will be an immigrant. By this yardstick, immigrants play a crucial role in determining demographic and economic trends in the United States.

Myth: Immigrants do well in the labor market.

If the typical new immigrant were a highly skilled worker, we would be engaged in a very different discussion over immigration policy. Imagine the nature of the debate about Proposition 187 if the flow of illegal aliens was composed mainly of teachers, academics, and journalists. The country's intellectual elite would probably be manning the barricades to prevent the illegal entry of competing workers.

Most of the immigrants now entering the United States, however, are less skilled workers who have little hope of reaching economic parity with native workers during their lifetimes. Recent immigrants are not as skilled, in comparison to the native-born population, as earlier waves.

The typical immigrant who had just arrived in the U.S. in 1970 had 11.1 years of schooling, compared to 11.5 years for the typical native worker at that time. By 1990, the typical new arrival had 11.9 years of schooling, compared to 13.2 years for natives. In view of the widening gap in educational attainment, it is not surprising that the wage differential between immigrants and natives rose dramatically. The most recent arrivals enumerated in the 1970 census earned 16.6 per cent less than natives. By 1990, the wage disadvantage was 31.7 per cent.

The poor economic performance of recent immigrants at the time of entry would not be a cause for concern if the economic disadvantage diminished over time, as immigrants assimilated. The available evidence, however, suggests that the gap will not narrow substantially during the immigrants' working lives. The process of economic assimilation takes place mainly in the first two decades after arrival and narrows the wage gap by about 10 percentage points. This rate of assimilation allowed earlier immigrants, for whom the initial gap was less than 20 per cent, to almost catch up with natives, but it is not sufficient to permit recent immigrants, for whom the gap starts at more than 30 per cent, to reach economic parity.

Myth: Immigrants use welfare less than natives do.

Less skilled workers, whether immigrants or natives, are more likely to qualify for and participate in welfare programs. There is little doubt that immigrant use of welfare programs is on the rise. In 1970, immigrants were slightly less likely to receive cash benefits (such as Aid to Families with Dependent Children and Supplemental Security Income) than natives. In 1970, 5.5 per cent of newly arrived immigrant households received welfare, compared to 6 per cent of native households. By 1990, 8.3 per cent of newly arrived immigrant households received public assistance, compared to 7.4 per cent of native households.

Moreover, the welfare-participation rate of a given immigrant wave increases over time. The wave that arrived between 1965 and 1969 had a welfare participation rate of 5.5 per cent in 1970. By 1990, the participation rate of this cohort had risen to 9.8 per cent. It seems that assimilation involves not only learning about labor–market opportunities but also learning about the income opportunities provided by the welfare state.

The dollar benefits received by immigrant households that are on welfare have also increased rapidly. The typical native household on welfare received roughly $4,000 in cash benefits each year (in 1989 dollars) throughout the 1970–1990 period. In contrast, the typical immigrant household on welfare received about $3,800 in 1970 and about $5,400 in 1990.

As a result of the increasing participation of immigrants in welfare programs and the larger benefits they are collecting, immigrants now receive a disproportionate share of case benefits. In 1970, 6.8 per cent of U.S. households were headed by an immigrant, and these immigrant households received 6.7 per cent of all cash benefits, so that immigrants were slightly under-represented in the distribution of these welfare benefits. By 1990, the situation had changed drastically: 8.4 per cent of households were headed by an immigrant, and these households received 13.1 per cent of all cash benefits. Put differently, the cash benefits received by immigrant households in 1990 were 56 per cent higher than they would have been if immigrants had used the welfare system to the same extent as natives.

By contrast, immigrants do not receive a disproportionately high share of non-welfare income. In 1970, they received approximately 6.3 per cent of all non-welfare income, about the same as their proportion of the population. Because immigrants do not get a disproportionately high share of income, they also do not pay a disproportionately high share of taxes.

Myth: Immigrants pay their way in the welfare state.

A widely publicized 1994 study by the Urban Institute concluded that immigrants pay over $27 billion more in taxes than it costs to provide them with schooling and welfare services. On the other hand, Donald Huddle (in a study conducted for the Carrying Capacity Network, an anti–population-growth group) concluded that the net costs of immigration exceeded $40 billion. These accounting exercises inevitably incorporate many hidden and questionable assumptions.

To illustrate, let's conduct a simple, back-of-the-envelope calculation of the costs and benefits of immigration. As noted above, the 1990 census indicated that immigrants received about 13.1 per cent of all cash benefits distributed in the United States. At that time, roughly $181.3 billion was spent on all means-tested entitlement programs (including Food Stamps, Medicaid, etc.). If we assume that immigrants received 13.1 per cent of these expenditures, they accounted for $23.8 billion.

How much do immigrants pay in taxes? According to the census, the total non-welfare income of immigrant households was $284.7 billion. If the total tax rate (including federal, state, and local taxes) was 30 per cent, immigrant households paid about $85.4 billion in taxes. The calculation thus indicates that immigrants pay more in taxes ($85.4 billion) than they take out of the welfare system ($23.8 billion).

CHANGING THE ASSUMPTIONS

But this comparison assumes that immigrant taxes are used only to fund their use of entitlement programs. One can justify this assumption by arguing that all other government programs provide pure "public goods," so that spending on these programs is the same regardless of immigration. Immigrants, however, increase the congestion of amenities provided by government (e.g., parks, freeways, schools, jails). The cost of providing these public goods to the immigrant population is not zero.

Obviously, different assumptions about the cost of providing these goods will lead to different conclusions about whether immigrants pay their way in the welfare state. If the cost is zero, immigrants make a substantial contribution to the treasury. If, on the other hand, the average cost of providing services to immigrants equals the average cost of providing services to natives, immigrants should be charged for the various government programs as if they were natives. In 1990, 91.1 per cent of taxes were used to pay for programs other than means-tested entitlement programs. If we charge immigrants 91.1 per cent of their tax payments for using these other programs, then only 8.9 per cent of immigrants'

taxes are left to fund their use of means-tested entitlement programs. Immigrants would then contribute only $7.6 billion (or 8.9 per cent of the $85.4 billion they pay) to the funding of these programs. The tax burden resulting from immigration would be on the order of $16 billion.

The Urban Institute's claim that immigrants create a $27-billion "net surplus" for the United States assumes that immigrants do not increase the cost of any programs other than the ones included in the Institute's calculations (mainly welfare and education). Because we do not know by how much immigrants raise the cost of freeways, national parks, and even defense, accounting exercises that claim to estimate the fiscal impact of immigration should be viewed suspiciously.

Furthermore, the typical accounting exercise does not consider the long-run impact of immigration on government expenditures. For instance, some argue that immigrants make a net contribution to the Social Security system because they are paying into the system now and are not collecting benefits. But immigrants are on average about 30 years old when they enter the United States. As a result, many immigrants pay into the Social Security system for a much shorter time than natives, yet collect roughly the same benefits. In other words, a sizable bill will come due some day, and our children (as well as the immigrants' children) will have to pay it.

The accounting exercises also take a myopic view of expenditures on education. In California alone, it is estimated that roughly $1.7 billion was spent on educating the children of illegal aliens in 1993. These costs, however, must be weighed against the benefits of having a more educated work force later on. Moreover, immigrants who enter the

United States after they have completed their education import "free" human capital, from which substantial benefits might accrue.

Myth: Refugees and illegal aliens are the source of the immigration problem.

There are huge differences in educational attainment, earnings, and welfare propensities among groups of different national origins. In 1990, immigrants from France and Germany earned about 25 per cent more than natives, those from China and Peru earned 21 per cent less than natives, and those from El Salvador and Mexico earned 40 per cent less than natives. Similarly, only about 2 to 4 per cent of the households originating in South Africa, Taiwan, or the United Kingdom received public assistance, as opposed to 11 to 12 per cent of the households originating in Ecuador or Mexico and nearly 50 per cent of the households originating in Laos or Cambodia. In view of these differences, it is tempting to blame a relatively small number of groups for the disturbing trends in the economic impact of immigration.

The Urban Institute's study offers a typical example of this blame game. The data presented by the Institute's researchers indicate that 41 per cent of recent immigrants were high-school dropouts, compared to only 23 per cent of natives. Nevertheless, they conclude that the "low educational attainment or poor 'quality' of recent immigrants... is directly attributable to illegal immigrants and refugees, not to legal immigrants."

The researchers reach this conclusion by manipulating the data. In defining "legal immigrants," the study omits refugees, presumably because they are admitted under a different set of rules. The researchers also want to omit illegal aliens. The census, however, does not provide *any* information on who is legal and who is not, so they simply omit immigrants from Mexico (and several Central American countries). The rationale is that a large number of illegal aliens are Mexicans. It is also true, however, that a very large number of *legal* immigrants are Mexicans. In fact, Mexicans are the largest group in the legal immigrant flow, accounting for almost a quarter of the immigrants admitted legally in the 1980s. By excluding Mexicans from the calculation, the Urban Institute can conclude that "legal" (read: non-Mexican, non-refugee) immigrants don't look quite so bad. In other words, there is no immigration problem once we get rid of the "problem" immigrants.

The blame game also shows up in the Manhattan Institute's recent "Index of Leading Immigration Indicators," which dismisses the high propensity of immigrants to receive public assistance by noting that "immigrants are more likely than natives to receive welfare, but that is due mainly to very high rates of welfare use among refugees and the elderly." How we define both the native and the immigrant populations influences what we conclude about the economic and social benefits from immigration.... Over all, immigrants are more likely to be on welfare than natives (7.4 per cent of households headed by native-born Americans versus 9.1 per cent of households headed by immigrants are on welfare). If one looks only at the non-refugee population, however, the welfare gap between immigrants and natives essentially disappears. If we also omit the elderly, we find that non-refugee, non-Mexican immigrants are less likely to be on welfare than natives (6.7 versus 5.0 per cent, respectively).

But before we conclude that we have found the source of the immigration problem (that is, the refugees, the presumed illegals, and the elderly), there are two points that are worth remembering. Just as we can minimize the immigration problem by getting rid of the problem immigrants, we can play a similar game with the native population.... [E]ven highly "select" groups of immigrants (such as non-refugee, non-Mexican immigrants) are more likely to be on welfare than non-Hispanic white natives. More important, even if we were to find that these select groups of legal immigrants have the same propensity to be on welfare as a similarly select group of natives, we would still have a problem. After all, shouldn't our immigration policy strive to admit workers who do more than just replicate the social and economic problems of our native population? Yet, instead of considering the economic potential of applicants when handing out entry visas, our current policy awards entry visas mainly to applicants who have relatives already residing here.

Myth: Immigrants do not hurt the earnings of native workers.

Another reason to be concerned about the impact of unskilled immigrants is that they probably reduce the economic opportunities of unskilled natives. Economists have typically estimated the impact of immigration on native earnings by comparing the earnings of natives who reside in "immigrant" cities (such as Los Angeles and San Diego) with the earnings of natives who reside in cities where few immigrants live (such as Atlanta and Pittsburgh). These cross-city comparisons suggest that the average native wage is lower, but only slightly, in labor markets where immigrants tend to cluster. If one city has 10 per cent more immigrants than another, the native wage in the city with more immigrants is only about 0.2 per cent lower.

But this correlation does not necessarily indicate that immigrants have a negligible impact on native workers. Suppose immigration into Los Angeles lowers the earnings of natives in L.A. substantially. Native workers are not likely to stand idly by and watch their economic opportunities evaporate. Many will move out of the Los Angeles basin into other cities, and people who were considering moving to L.A. will now move elsewhere instead. As natives respond to immigration by voting with their feet (creating "the new white flight"), the adverse impact of immigration on the L.A. labor market is transmitted to the entire economy. In the end, all competing native workers are worse off from immigration, not simply those residing in cities where immigrants cluster.

There is some evidence that this "macro" effect of immigration on native earning opportunities is significant. The 1980s witnessed a substantial increase in the wage gap between workers who did not have a high-school diploma and workers with more education. The decade also witnessed the entry of large numbers of less skilled immigrants. Recent evidence suggests that perhaps a third of the 10-percentage-point decline in the relative wage of high-school dropouts between 1980 and 1988 can be attributed to the flow of less skilled immigrants.

Myth: Americans gain a lot from immigration.

A number of observers claim that immigration is very beneficial for natives. It is typically argued that immigrants spur economic growth, lower prices for American consumers, and increase the demand for goods and services produced by native-owned firms. It is telling that these claims are seldom, if ever, backed up by numbers. It is simply taken as a tenet of faith that Americans gain from immigration and that these benefits are substantial.

The belief that immigration spurs economic growth arises from the fact that there is a positive correlation between the number of immigrants in a particular city and the rate of economic growth in that city. This correlation is interpreted to mean that when immigrants enter a locality, economic growth follows. This interpretation, however, assumes that immigrants are not very smart. Why would anyone migrate to a city with a stagnant economy? Immigrants (like natives) look at economic conditions before deciding where to settle. The positive correlation between economic growth and immigration, therefore, might simply indicate that immigrants are smart in choosing where to live.

REDISTRIBUTION OF WEALTH

In any case, the numbers do suggest that natives, as a group, gain from immigration. Immigration, however, does more than just raise the national income that accrues to natives; it also induces a substantial redistribution of wealth. In particular, wealth is redistributed from native workers who compete with immigrant workers to those who employ immigrants and use immigrants' services. I have recently estimated that native workers, on the whole, lose about $133 billion a year, or 1.9 per cent of GDP in a $7-trillion economy, mainly because immigrants drive down the wages of compet-

ing workers. At the same time, employers and other users of immigrants' services, such as owners of large farms..., gain substantially. These gains are on the order of $140 billion, or 2 per cent of GDP. The net gain, therefore, is only on the order of 0.1 per cent of GDP, or about $7 billion. But although the net gain is small, *some* Americans gain very much. This simple fact explains why a small, well-financed, and powerful segment of the population finds it difficult to understand why most other Americans are so concerned about immigration.

Myth: Immigrants are more likely to be entrepreneurs, and these entrepreneurs are very successful.

It is often claimed that immigrants create more jobs than they take because a large number of them become successful entrepreneurs. Asserting that "immigrant companies have generated hundreds of thousands of good jobs in California," Ron Unz uses Silicon Valley and the computer industry to illustrate how immigrant entrepreneurship benefits our country.

Sentimentality aside, it simply is not true that the entrepreneurial spirit burns more brightly among immigrants than among natives. The Census Bureau's statistics indicate that only 6.8 per cent of immigrant workers in 1990 were self-employed, compared to 7 per cent of native workers. Although entrepreneurship is an important economic activity among some immigrant groups (15 per cent of Greek and 18 per cent of Korean immigrants were self-employed), it does not characterize the bulk of the immigrant population. Only 6 per cent of Vietnamese immigrants, 5 per cent of Mexican immigrants, and 3 per cent of Filipino immigrants were self-employed.

We should not use these statistics to denigrate the significant entrepreneurial contribution made by some immigrants. For instance, it might be that even though most immigrants do not become entrepreneurs, those who do are wildly successful and contribute significantly to the American economy. The proponents of this argument typically do not back up their assertion with data (since none exist)....

Myth: The melting pot works fast.

In 1990, 10 per cent of the people living in America were "second generation" (that is, were born here but had at least one parent born elsewhere). By 2050, if current trends continue, the share of second-generation Americans will increase to about 14 per cent, and an additional 9 per cent of the population will be the grandchildren of current immigrants. The impact of immigration depends not only on how immigrants perform in the U.S. economy but also on the economic performance of their offspring. Despite this, the current debate almost completely ignores the implications of immigration policy for the economic and social well-being of this country in the twenty-first century.

We ignore these implications at our peril. The experience of the children of earlier immigrant waves suggests that, although second-generation workers earn more than their immigrant parents, on average the intergenerational improvement is not that large. At best, the children of immigrants earn about 10 per cent more than their parents. Because recent immigrant waves are relatively unskilled and earn about 20 per cent less than natives throughout much of their lives, this pattern would imply that second-generation workers in the next century

may also have a substantial economic disadvantage.

There is also evidence that the huge wage differentials among different national-origin groups in a given generation are transmitted to their children. For example, in 1940 immigrants from the Philippines earned about 41 per cent less than immigrants from Italy. In 1970, second-generation Filipino-Americans earned 17 per cent less than second-generation Italian-Americans. Today's skill differentials among foreign-born groups become tomorrow's skill differentials among American-born ethnic groups. It might take up to four generations for the ethnic differences in economic status introduced by current immigration to disappear.

THE NEED FOR ACTION

We do not yet know how the welfare state and the multicultural agenda favored by many segments of the intellectual elite will alter the speed at which the melting pot does its job. A prudent observer can only conclude that these misguided policies will retard the forging of Americans. This factor, combined with the relatively low skills of recent immigrant waves and their high rates of welfare recipiency, might mean we are already witnessing the creation of a large new underclass. As other countries have learned at a very high cost, ethnicity matters, and it matters for a long time.

The debate over immigration policy is much too important to be guided by ignorance or by a distortion of the facts. The available evidence suggests reasons for conservatives, and even for open-border libertarians, to be worried about immigration. Perhaps if we can agree on the essence of the problem, we can proceed to a more rational discussion of the policy solutions.

Time is running out, however. The failure of the political system to address the problems caused by illegal aliens led to the enactment of Proposition 187, a proposition that many of us (even if we believe that illegal aliens create problems) view as ill-advised and ill-crafted. The longer the politicians bury their heads in the sand, the more likely that the Proposition 187 movement will spawn a "Proposition 188" to control legal immigration.

This resolution to the debate would be unfortunate, because it would probably lead to far more draconian measures than are justified. If we wish to pursue a more rational policy that nourishes some forms of legal immigration, that upholds the traditions that made America an "immigrant nation," and that takes advantage of the many economic, social, and cultural contributions that a well-chosen immigrant flow can confer upon the U.S., we will have to act soon and decisively.

NO

Stephen Moore

GIVE US YOUR BEST, YOUR BRIGHTEST

For many Americans, the word "immigration" immediately conjures up an image of poor Mexicans scrambling across the border near San Diego to find minimum-wage work and perhaps collect government benefits. Recent public opinion polls confirm that the attitude of the American public toward immigration is highly unfavorable. Central Americans are perceived as welfare abusers who stubbornly refuse to learn English, Haitians are seen as AIDS carriers, Russian Jews are considered to be mafiosi, and Asians are seen as international terrorists. The media reinforce these stereotypes by battering the public with negative depictions of immigrants.

The conception of immigrants as tired, poor, huddled masses seems permanently sketched into the mind of the public, just as the words are sketched irrevocably at the feet of the Statue of Liberty. But the Emma Lazarus poem simply does not describe the hundreds of thousands of people who are building new lives here in the 1990s. It would be more appropriate if the words at the base of the statue read: "Give us your best, your brightest, your most energetic and talented." Why? Because in large part those are the people who come to the United States each year.

Before we start slamming shut the golden door, it might be worthwhile to find out who the newcomers are and how they truly affect our lives.

Anyone who believes that immigrants are a drain on the U.S. economy has never visited the Silicon Valley in California. Here and in other corridors of high-tech entrepreneurship, immigrants are literally the lifeblood of many of the nation's most prosperous industries. In virtually every field in which the United States asserted global leadership in the 1980s—industries such as computer design and softwear, pharmaceuticals, bioengineering, electronics, superconductivity, robotics and aerospace engineering—one finds immigrants. In many ways these high-growth industries are the modern version of the American melting pot in action.

Consider Intel Corp. With profits of $1.1 billion in 1992, it is one of the most prolific and fast-expanding companies in the United States, employing tens of thousands of American workers. It is constantly developing exciting, cutting-edge technologies that will define the computer industry in the 21st century.

And it is doing all of this largely with the talents of America's newest immigrants. Three members of Intel's top management, including Chief Executive Officer Andrew S. Grove, from Hungary, are immigrants. Some of its most successful and revolutionary computer technologies were pioneered by immigrants, such as the 8080 microprocessor (an expanded-power computer chip), invented by a Japanese, and polysilicon FET gates (the basic unit of memory storage on modern computer chips), invented by an Italian. Dick Ward, manager of employee information systems at Intel, says: "Our whole business is predicated on inventing the next generation of computer technologies. The engine that drives that quest is brainpower. And here at Intel, much of that brainpower comes from immigrants."

Or consider Du Pont-Merck Pharmaceutical Co., an $800 million-a-year health care products company based in Wilmington, Del., which reports that immigrants are responsible for many of its most promising new product innovations. For example, losartan, an antihypertensive drug, was developed by a team of scientists that included two Chinese and a Lithuanian. Joseph Mollica, Chief Executive Officer of Du Pont-Merck, says that bringing together such diverse talent "lets you look at problems and opportunities from a slightly different point of view."

Intel and Du Pont-Merck are not alone in relying on immigrants. Robert Kelley Jr., president of SO/CAL/TEN, an association of nearly 200 high-tech California companies, insists: "Without the influx of Asians in the 1980s, we would not have had the entrepreneurial explosion we've seen in California." David N. K. Wang, vice president for worldwide business operations at Applied Materials Inc., a computer-technology company in California, adds that because of immigration, "Silicon Valley is one of the most international business centers in the world."

Take away the immigrants, and you take away the talent base that makes such centers operate. Indeed, it is frightening to think what would happen to America's global competitiveness if the immigrants stopped coming. Even scarier is the more realistic prospect that U.S. policymakers will enact laws to prevent them from coming.

New research has begun to quantify the contributions of immigrants to American industry. The highly respected National Research Council reported in 1988 that "a large fraction of the technological output of the United States [is] dependent upon foreign talent and that such dependency is growing." Noting that well over half of all scientists graduating with doctorate degrees from American universities and one in three engineers working in the United States are immigrants, the report states emphatically: "It is clear ... that these foreign-born engineers enrich our culture and make substantial contributions to the U.S. economic well-being and competitiveness."

The United States' competitive edge over the Japanese, Germans, Koreans and much of Europe is linked closely to its continued ability to attract and retain highly talented workers from other countries. A 1990 study by the national Science Foundation says, "Very significant, positive aspects arise from the presence of foreign-born engineers in our society."

For example, superconductivity, a technology that is expected to spawn hundreds of vital new commercial applications in the next century, was discovered by a physicist at the University of Houston, Paul C. W. Chu. He was born in China and came to the U.S. in 1972. His brilliance and inventiveness have made him a top contender for a Nobel Prize.

Of course, if Chu does win a Nobel, he will join a long list of winners who were immigrants in America. In the 20th century, between 20 percent and 50 percent of the Nobel Prize winners, depending on the discipline involved, have been immigrants to the United States. Today there are more Russian Nobel Prize winners living in the U.S. than there are living in Russia.

Public opinion polls consistently reveal that a major worry is that immigrants take jobs from American workers. The fear is understandable but misplaced. Immigrants don't just take jobs, they create jobs. One way is by starting new businesses. Today, America's immigrants, even those who come with relatively low skill levels, are highly entrepreneurial.

Take Koreans, for example. According to sociologists Alendro Portes and Ruben Rumbaut, "In Los Angeles, the propensity for self-employment is three times greater for Koreans than among the population as a whole. Grocery stores, restaurants, gas stations, liquor stores and real estate offices are typical Korean businesses." Cubans also are prodigious creators of new businesses. The number of Cuban-owned businesses in Miami has expanded from 919 in 1967 to 8,000 in 1976 to 28,000 in 1990. On Jefferson Boulevard in Dallas, more than 800 businesses operate, three-quarters of them owned by first- and second-generation Hispanic immigrants. Just 10 years ago, before the influx of Mexicans and other Central Americans, the neighborhood was in decay, with many vacant storefronts displaying "for sale" signs in the windows. Today it is a thriving ethnic neighborhood.

To be sure, few immigrant-owned businesses mature into an Intel. In fact, many fail completely. Like most new businesses in America, most immigrant establishments are small and only marginally profitable. The average immigrant business employs two to four workers and records roughly $200,000 in annual sales. However, such small businesses, as President Clinton often correctly emphasizes, are a significant source of jobs.

It should not be too surprising that immigrants are far more likely than average U.S. citizens to take business risks. After all, uprooting oneself, traveling to a foreign culture and making it requires more than the usual amount of courage, ambition, resourcefulness and even bravado. Indeed, this is part of the self-selection process that makes immigrants so particularly desirable. Immigrants are not just people—they are a very special group of people. By coming, they impart productive energies on the rest of us.

This is not just romanticism. It is well-grounded in fact. Countless studies have documented that immigrants to the United States tend to be more skilled, more highly educated and wealthier than the average citizen of their native countries.

Thomas Sowell, an economist and senior fellow at the Hoover Institution in Stanford, Calif., reports in his seminal study on immigration, "Ethnic America," that black immigrants from the West Indies have far higher skill levels than their countrymen at home. He also finds that the income levels of West Indies immigrants are higher than those of

West Indies natives, American blacks and native-born white Americans.

Surprisingly, even illegal immigrants are not the poverty-stricken and least skilled from their native countries. Surveys of undocumented immigrants from Mexico to the United States show that only about 5 percent were unemployed in Mexico, whereas the average unemployment rate there was about three times that level, and that a relatively high percentage of them worked in white-collar jobs in Mexico. In addition, surveys have found that illiteracy among undocumented Mexicans in the U.S. is about 10 percent, whereas illiteracy in Mexico is about 22 percent.

Perhaps the greatest asset of immigrants is their children, who tend to be remarkably successful in the U.S. Recently, the city of Boston reported that an incredible 13 of the 17 valedictorians in its public high schools were foreign-born—from China, Vietnam, Portugal, El Salvador, France, Italy, Jamaica and the former Czechoslovakia. Many could not speak a word of English when they arrived. Public high schools in Washington, Chicago and Los Angeles also report remarkably disproportionate numbers of immigrant children at the top of the class. Similarly, Westinghouse reports that over the past 12 years, about one-third of its prestigious National Science Talent Search winners have been Asians. Out of this group might emerge America's next Albert Einstein, who himself was an immigrant.

So one hidden cost of restricting immigration is the loss of immigrants' talented and motivated children.

In the past century, America has admitted roughly 50 million immigrants. This has been one of the largest migrations in the history of the world. Despite this infusion of people—no, because of it

—the United States became by the middle of the 20th century the wealthiest nation in the world. Real wages in America have grown more than eightfold over this period. The U.S. economy employed less than 40 million people in 1900; today it employs nearly 120 million people. The U.S. job machine had not the slightest problem expanding and absorbing the 8 million legal immigrants who came to this country in the 1980s. Eighteen million jobs were created.

But what about those frightening headlines? "Immigration Bankrupting Nation." "Immigrants Displacing U.S. Workers." "Foreigners Lured to U.S. by Welfare."

Here are the facts. The 1990s census reveals that roughly 6 percent of native-born Americans are on public assistance, versus 7 percent of the foreign-born, with less than 5 percent of illegal immigrants collecting welfare. Not much reason for alarm. Because immigrants tend to come to the United States when they are young and working, over their lifetimes they each pay about $20,000 more in taxes than they use in services, according to economist Julian Simon of the University of Maryland. With 1 million immigrants per year, the nation gains about $20 billion more than cost. Rather than fiscal burdens, immigrants are huge bargains.

Nor do immigrants harm the U.S. labor market. A comprehensive 1989 study by the U.S. Department of Labor concluded: "Neither U.S. workers nor most minority workers appear to be adversely affected by immigration—especially during periods of economic expansion." In the 1980s, the top 10 immigrant-receiving states —including California, Florida, Massachusetts and Texas—recorded rates of unemployment 2 percentage points below the U.S. average, according to the

Alexis de Tocqueville Institution in Arlington, Va. So where's the job displacement?

We are now witnessing in America what might be described as the return of the nativists. They are selling fear and bigotry. But if any of their allegations against immigrants are accurate, then America could not have emerged as the economic superpower it is today.

In fact, most Americans do accept that immigration in the past has contributed greatly to the nation's economic growth. But they are not so sanguine in their assessment of present and future immigrants. It is strangely inconsistent that Americans believe that so long-standing and crucial a benefit is now a source of cultural and economic demise.

Shortly before his death, Winston Churchill wrote, "The empires of the future are the empires of the mind." America is confronted with one of the most awesome opportunities in world history to build those empires by attracting highly skilled, highly educated and entrepreneurial people from all over the globe. The Andrew Groves and the Paul Chus of the world do not want to go to Japan, Israel, Germany, France or Canada. Almost universally they want to come to the United States. We can be selective. By expanding immigration but orienting our admission policies toward gaining the best and the brightest, America would enjoy a significant comparative advantage over its geopolitical rivals.

By pursuing a liberal and strategic policy on immigration, America can ensure that the 21st century, like the 20th, will be the American century.

POSTSCRIPT

Should Immigration Be Restricted?

In New York Bay on Liberty Island stands a 152-foot-high, world-renowned statue of a woman facing seaward. The Statue of Liberty greets those entering the harbor from the Atlantic, and its torch is meant to symbolically light the way of immigrants to nearby Ellis Island, which long served (1892–1943) as the chief point of entry for immigrants to the United States. Both the statue and Ellis Island are now part of the Statue of Liberty National Monument, which honors the important role that immigrants, both the famous and the forgotten, have played in American history.

To raise money in 1883 to build a pedestal for Frédéric Bartholdi's Statue of Liberty, a citizens' committee invited authors to write appropriate words of commemoration and to donate their manuscripts to the committee for a fund-raising auction. One author, Emma Lazarus, penned a sonnet, "The New Colossus," whose most famous lines read:

> Give me your tired, your poor,
> Your huddled masses, yearning to breathe free,
> The wretched refuse of your teeming shore.
> Send these, the homeless, tempest-tost to me,
> I lift my lamp beside the golden door.

These words can be found on a plaque on the pedestal of the Statue of Liberty. On the question of whether or not the words of the poet Lazarus should still govern U.S. policy, several points are important. The open door to immigration ended long ago. The decade 1911–1920 was the last, with an average annual rate of over 5 immigrants per 1,000 Americans. Since then the rate has risen and fallen; the 1931–1940 rate, at 0.4, was the lowest in history. Moore may be right that immigration should be encouraged, but those who argue that case need to account for changing conditions.

By the same token, those who oppose immigration also need to argue with care. Totaling up numbers of immigrants and quoting unemployment statistics are easy exercises in data collection. To say that A (immigration) causes B (unemployment) is another matter. They may not be related at all. Indeed, in a low-birthrate and graying America, it may be that immigrants provide new sources of labor for both high-skill jobs and those that many Americans disdain. Similar observations could be made about the logical validity of other pro and con arguments. The point is to be wary of inferences and illogical connections. For more discussions of the economic contributions of immigrants to the United States, read the companion articles by James C. Clad, "Lowering the Wave," and Michael Fix, "Myths About Immigrants," in *Foreign Policy* (Summer 1994). For a more extensive look at the data, consult Julian L. Simon, *Immigration: The Demographic and Economic Facts* (Cato Institute, 1995). Simon's study is also available at the Cato site on the Internet at: http://www.cato.org/pr-immig.html. Also worth examining is George J. Borjas, "The Economics of Integration," *Journal of Economic Literature* (December 1994), in which Borjas presents a highly detailed analysis of the evidence that he used for the selection that is presented in this debate. Reflecting an anti-immigration view is John O'Sullivan, "America's Identity Crisis," *National Review* (November 21, 1994). Nathan Glazer, in "Immigration and the American Future," *The Public Interest* (Winter 1995), and Lawrence E. Harrison, in "America and Its Immigrants," *National Interest* (Summer 1992), argue in favor of selective immigration that would allow only those with desirable skills into the United States. For a broader look at the global issues of immigration, see Wayne A. Cornelius, Phillip L. Martin, and James F. Hollifield, eds., *Controlling Immigration: A Global Perspective* (Stanford University Press, 1995).

ISSUE 18

Will the World Fragment into Antagonistic Cultures?

YES: Samuel P. Huntington, from "The Clash of Civilizations?" *Foreign Affairs* (May/June 1993)

NO: James Kurth, from "The *Real* Clash," *The National Interest* (Fall 1994)

ISSUE SUMMARY

YES: Professor of government Samuel P. Huntington hypothesizes that world politics is entering a new phase during which culture will be the fundamental source of division and conflict.

NO: Professor of political science James Kurth takes issue with Huntington's hypothesis and contends that the greatest clash will be within the West itself.

Many social scientists believe that the age of patriotism may be coming to an end. Two political entities govern our political world today, the nation and the state. The state has become the dominant political actor in the international system.

The traditional symbol of the origins of the state-based system is the Peace of Westphalia (1648). This peace treaty ended the Thirty Years' War and recognized the independence of the Protestant states (and by inference some of the Catholic states) of Europe from the secular control of the Papacy and, in some cases, the Holy Roman Empire. In other words, states became sovereign. At first, states were ruled by monarchs under the theory of divine right. Kings and emperors "owned" their realms and the people in them; national loyalty (patriotism) by the commoners grew only slowly. That changed with the coming of democracy, represented by the American Revolution (1776) and the French Revolution (1789). Democracy includes the idea of popular sovereignty, the notion that the people own the state. Rulers are mere leaders entrusted by the people with the governance of the state. Popular sovereignty also immeasurably strengthened the idea that there was a bond between the people (nation) and the state (political structure) and that the people ought to be loyal to (allegiance), even have affection for (patriotism), the state. The state and its government, in turn, would dedicate themselves to protecting the nation and making life better for its citizenry.

Arguably, states have held up their end of this implicit bargain over the years. By establishing sovereignty, they have helped their people to escape multiethnic empires. States have also consolidated feudal, tribal, and other smaller political units into larger structures that are better able to provide for the common defense and to promote the general welfare by creating more defensible and more efficient economic units.

Many observers believe that even if the state was once an efficacious entity, it has become outmoded because it can no longer adequately provide for the common defense or adequately promote the general welfare. The alleged inadequacy of the state stems from a combination of new technology, population growth, and increased demands for services. The technology-based advent of nuclear weapons and intercontinental ballistic missiles, other weapons of mass destruction and rapid means of delivery, and the possibility of nuclear terrorism mean that the ability of the state to protect its citizens is vastly diminished. Technology combined with rapidly expanding population also makes states much more complex. When the United States was founded, it contained but 2.5 million people; now there are 250 million. Cable television, superhighways, massive air pollution, and myriad other factors that the government now deals with did not exist in 1776. Demands for government services have also increased. The U.S. government now spends more per day than it spent per year in 1932; over one-third of all economic activity in the United States is attributable to government spending. Added to all of this is the fact that in an interdependent world, many of the most important issues are global problems that are beyond the ability of any one state to solve. Some analysts suggest that this mix of size, complexity, increasing demand, and interdependence has left states and their governments no longer able to promote the general welfare.

The upshot of these trends, some analysts contend, is that loyalty to the state is breaking down as people consciously or subconsciously realize that it no longer serves their needs. There are many signs of this, including the marked increase in the number of civil wars in recent years.

One significant question, which this debate addresses, is: What will the future be like in terms of political organization and loyalty? One scenario is that larger political structures will be established. Other analysts believe that the trend will be toward smaller political structures.

Another possibility is that cultures will coalesce and form groups of allied states or perhaps even single units. There is considerable evidence that people, feeling alienated from states, are identifying more strongly with cultural or other demographic groups. So-called religious fundamentalism has combined with an urge for cultural separatism and the return to an earlier (mostly mythical) time of cultural purity. In the following selections, Samuel P. Huntington contends that the future will be marked by such clashes between cultural groups. James Kurth foresees instead clashes within cultures, especially the West, between traditionalists and postmodern deconstructionists.

YES

Samuel P. Huntington

THE CLASH OF CIVILIZATIONS?

THE NEXT PATTERN OF CONFLICT

World politics is entering a new phase, and intellectuals have not hesitated to proliferate visions of what it will be—the end of history; the return of traditional rivalries between nation states, and the decline of the nation state from the conflicting pulls of tribalism and globalism, among others. Each of these visions catches aspects of the emerging reality. Yet they all miss a crucial, indeed a central, aspect of what global politics is likely to be in the coming years.

It is my hypothesis that the fundamental source of conflict in this new world will not be primarily ideological or primarily economic. The great divisions among humankind and the dominating source of conflict will be cultural. Nation states will remain the most powerful actors in world affairs, but the principal conflicts of global politics will occur between nations and groups of different civilizations. The clash of civilizations will dominate global politics. The fault lines between civilizations will be the battle lines of the future.

Conflict between civilizations will be the latest phase in the evolution of conflict in the modern world. For a century and a half after the emergence of the modern international system with the Peace of Westphalia [1648], the conflicts of the Western world were largely among princes—emperors, absolute monarchs and constitutional monarchs attempting to expand their bureaucracies, their armies, their mercantilist economic strength and, most important, the territory they ruled. In the process they created nation states, and beginning with the French Revolution the principal lines of conflict were between nations rather than princes.... This nineteenth-century pattern lasted until the end of World War I. Then, as a result of the Russian Revolution and the reaction against it, the conflict of nations yielded to the conflict of ideologies, first among communism, fascism-Nazism and liberal democracy, and then between communism and liberal democracy. During the Cold War, this latter conflict became embodied in the struggle between the two superpowers,... each of which defined its identity in terms of its ideology.

These conflicts between princes, nation states and ideologies were primarily conflicts within Western civilization, "Western civil wars," as [one scholar] has labeled them. With the end of the Cold War, international politics moves out of its Western phase, and its centerpiece becomes the interaction between the West and non-Western civilizations and among non-Western civilizations. In the politics of civilizations, the peoples and governments of non-Western civilizations no longer remain the objects of history as targets of Western colonialism but join the West as movers and shapers of history.

THE NATURE OF CIVILIZATIONS

... What do we mean when we talk of a civilization? A civilization is a cultural entity. Villages, regions, ethnic groups, nationalities, religious groups, all have distinct cultures at different levels of cultural heterogeneity. The culture of a village in southern Italy may be different from that of a village in northern Italy, but both will share in a common Italian culture that distinguishes them from German villages. European communities, in turn, will share cultural features that distinguish them from Arab or Chinese communities. Arabs, Chinese and Westerners, however, are not part of any broader cultural entity. They constitute civilizations. A civilization is thus the highest cultural grouping of people and the broadest level of cultural identity people have short of that which distinguishes humans from other species. It is defined both by common objective elements, such as language, history, religion, customs, institutions, and by the subjective self-identification of people. People have levels of identity:

a resident of Rome may define himself with varying degrees of intensity as a Roman, an Italian, a Catholic, a Christian, a European, a Westerner. The civilization to which he belongs is the broadest level of identification with which he intensely identifies. People can and do redefine their identities and, as a result, the composition and boundaries of civilizations change.

Civilizations may involve a large number of people, as with China, ... or a very small number of people, such as the Anglophone Caribbean. A civilization may include several nation states... or only one, as is the case with Japanese civilization. Civilizations obviously blend and overlap, and may include subcivilizations.... Civilizations are nonetheless meaningful entities, and while the lines between them are seldom sharp, they are real. Civilizations are dynamic; they rise and fall; they divide and merge. And, as any student of history knows, civilizations disappear and are buried in the sands of time.

Westerners tend to think of nation states as the principal actors in global affairs. They have been that, however, for only a few centuries. The broader reaches of human history have been the history of civilizations....

WHY CIVILIZATIONS WILL CLASH

Civilization identity will be increasingly important in the future, and the world will be shaped in large measure by the interactions among seven or eight major civilizations. These include Western, Confucian, Japanese, Islamic, Hindu, Slavic-Orthodox, Latin American and possibly African civilization. The most important conflicts of the future will occur along the cultural fault lines separating these civilizations from one another.

Why will this be the case?

First, differences among civilizations are not only real; they are basic. Civilizations are differentiated from each other by history, language, culture, tradition and, most important, religion. The people of different civilizations have different views on the relations between God and man, the individual and the group, the citizen and the state, parents and children, husband and wife, as well as differing views of the relative importance of rights and responsibilities, liberty and authority, equality and hierarchy. These differences are the product of centuries. They will not soon disappear. They are far more fundamental than differences among political ideologies and political regimes. Differences do not necessarily mean conflict, and conflict does not necessarily mean violence. Over the centuries, however, differences among civilizations have generated the most prolonged and the most violent conflicts.

Second, the world is becoming a smaller place. The interactions between peoples of different civilizations are increasing; these increasing interactions intensify civilization consciousness and awareness of differences between civilizations and commonalities within civilizations.... [As one commentator] has pointed out, "An Ibo may be... an Owerri Ibo or an Onitsha Ibo in what was the Eastern region of Nigeria. In Lagos, he is simply an Ibo. In London, he is a Nigerian. In New York, he is an African." The interactions among peoples of different civilizations enhance the civilization-consciousness of people that, in turn, invigorates differences and animosities stretching or thought to stretch back deep into history.

Third, the processes of economic modernization and social change throughout the world are separating people from longstanding local identities. They also weaken the nation state as a source of identity. In much of the world religion has moved in to fill this gap, often in the form of movements that are labeled "fundamentalist." Such movements are found in Western Christianity, Judaism, Buddhism and Hinduism, as well as in Islam. In most countries and most religions the people active in fundamentalist movements are young, college-educated, middle-class technicians, professionals and business persons. The "unsecularization of the world,"... has [been called] "... one of the dominant social facts of life in the late twentieth century." The revival of religion... provides a basis for identity and commitment that transcends national boundaries and unites civilizations.

Fourth, the growth of civilization-consciousness is enhanced by the dual role of the West. On the one hand, the West is at a peak of power. At the same time, however, and perhaps as a result, a return to the roots phenomenon is occurring among non-Western civilizations. Increasingly one hears references to trends toward a turning inward and "Asianization" in Japan,... the "Hinduization" of India, the... re-Islamization" of the Middle East, and now a... Russianization in Boris Yeltsin's country. A West at the peak of its power confronts non-Wests that increasingly have the desire, the will and the resources to shape the world in non-Western ways.

In the past, the elites of non-Western societies were usually the people who were most involved with the West, had been educated [in the West], and had absorbed Western attitudes and values.

At the same time, the populace in non-Western countries often remained deeply imbued with the indigenous culture. Now, however, these relationships are being reversed. A de-Westernization and indigenization of elites is occurring in many non-Western countries at the same time that Western, usually American, cultures, styles and habits become more popular among the mass of the people.

Fifth, cultural characteristics and differences are less mutable and hence less easily compromised and resolved than political and economic ones. In the former Soviet Union, communists can become democrats, the rich can become poor and the poor rich, but Russians cannot become Estonians and Azeris cannot become Armenians. In class and ideological conflicts, the key question was "Which side are you on?" and people could and did choose sides and change sides. In conflicts between civilizations, the question is "What are you?" That is a given that cannot be changed....

Finally, economic regionalism is increasing. The proportions of total trade that were intraregional rose between 1980 and 1989 from 51 percent to 59 percent in Europe, 33 percent to 37 percent in East Asia, and 32 percent to 36 percent in North America. The importance of regional economic blocs is likely to continue to increase in the future. On the one hand, successful economic regionalism will reinforce civilization-consciousness. On the other hand, economic regionalism may succeed only when it is rooted in a common civilization. The European Community rests on the shared foundation of European culture and Western Christianity. The success of the North American Free Trade Area depends on the convergence now underway of Mexican, Canadian and American cultures.

Japan, in contrast, faces difficulties in creating a comparable economic entity in East Asia because Japan is a society and civilization unique to itself. However strong the trade and investment links Japan may develop with other East Asian countries, its cultural differences with those countries inhibit and perhaps preclude its promoting regional economic integration like that in Europe and North America.

Common culture, in contrast, is clearly facilitating the rapid expansion of the economic relations between the People's Republic of China and Hong Kong, Taiwan, Singapore and the overseas Chinese communities in other Asian countries.... If cultural commonality is a prerequisite for economic integration, the principal East Asian economic bloc of the future is likely to be centered on China....

Culture and religion also form the basis of the Economic Cooperation Organization, which brings together ten non-Arab Muslim countries: Iran, Pakistan, Turkey, Azerbaijan, Kazakhstan, Kyrgyzstan, Turkmenistan, Tadjikistan, Uzbekistan and Afghanistan. One impetus to the revival and expansion of this organization, founded originally in the 1960s by Turkey, Pakistan and Iran, is the realization by the leaders of several of these countries that they had no chance of admission to the European Community....

As people define their identity in ethnic and religious terms, they are likely to see an "us" versus "them" relation existing between themselves and people of different ethnicity or religion.... Differences in culture and religion create differences over policy issues, ranging from human rights to immigration to trade and commerce to the environment. Geographical propinquity gives rise to conflicting territorial claims from Bosnia to Mindanao. Most important, the efforts of the West to promote its values of democracy and liberalism as universal values, to maintain its military predominance and to advance its economic interests engender countering responses from other civilizations. Decreasingly able to mobilize support and form coalitions on the basis of ideology, governments and groups will increasingly attempt to mobilize support by appealing to common religion and civilization identity.

The clash of civilizations thus occurs at two levels. At the micro-level, adjacent groups along the fault lines between civilizations struggle, often violently, over the control of territory and each other. At the macro-level, states from different civilizations compete for relative military and economic power, struggle over the control of international institutions and third parties, and competitively promote their particular political and religious values.

THE FAULT LINES BETWEEN CIVILIZATIONS

The fault lines between civilizations are replacing the political and ideological boundaries of the Cold War as the flash points for crisis and bloodshed.... As the ideological division of Europe has disappeared, the cultural division of Europe between Western Christianity, on the one hand, and Orthodox Christianity and Islam, on the other, has reemerged. The most significant dividing line in Europe ... may well be the eastern boundary of Western Christianity in the year 1500. This line runs along what are now the boundaries between Finland and Russia and between the Baltic states and Rus-

sia, cuts through Belarus and Ukraine separating the more Catholic western Ukraine from Orthodox eastern Ukraine, swings westward separating Transylvania from the rest of Romania, and then goes through Yugoslavia almost exactly along the line now separating Croatia and Slovenia from the rest of Yugoslavia. In the Balkans this line, of course, coincides with the historic boundary between the Hapsburg and Ottoman empires. The peoples to the north and west of this line are Protestant or Catholic; they shared the common experiences of European history—feudalism, the Renaissance, the Reformation, the Enlightenment, the French Revolution, the Industrial Revolution; they are generally economically better off than the peoples to the east; and they may now look forward to increasing involvement in a common European economy and to the consolidation of democratic political systems. The peoples to the east and south of this line are Orthodox or Muslim; they historically belonged to the Ottoman or Tsarist empires and were only lightly touched by the shaping events in the rest of Europe; they are generally less advanced economically; they seem much less likely to develop stable democratic political systems. The Velvet Curtain of culture has replaced the Iron Curtain of ideology as the most significant dividing line in Europe. As the events in Yugoslavia show, it is not only a line of difference; it is also at times a line of bloody conflict.

Conflict along the fault line between Western and Islamic civilizations has been going on for 1,300 years. After the founding of Islam, the Arab and Moorish surge west and north only ended at Tours in 732. From the eleventh to the thirteenth century the Crusaders attempted with temporary success to bring Christianity and Christian rule to the Holy Land. From the fourteenth to the seventeenth century, the Ottoman Turks reversed the balance, extended their sway over the Middle East and the Balkans, captured Constantinople, and twice laid siege to Vienna. In the nineteenth and early twentieth centuries as Ottoman power declined Britain, France, and Italy established Western control over most of North Africa and the Middle East.

After World War II, the West, in turn, began to retreat; the colonial empires disappeared; first Arab nationalism and then Islamic fundamentalism manifested themselves; the West became heavily dependent on the Persian Gulf countries for its energy; the oil-rich Muslim countries became money-rich and, when they wished to, weapons-rich. Several wars occurred between Arabs and Israel (created by the West). France fought a bloody and ruthless war in Algeria for most of the 1950s; British and French forces invaded Egypt in 1956; American forces went into Lebanon in 1958; subsequently American forces returned to Lebanon, attacked Libya, and engaged in various military encounters with Iran; Arab and Islamic terrorists, supported by at least three Middle Eastern governments, employed the weapon of the weak and bombed Western planes and installations and seized Western hostages. This warfare between Arabs and the West culminated in 1990, when the United States sent a massive army to the Persian Gulf to defend some Arab countries against aggression by another. In its aftermath NATO planning is increasingly directed to potential threats and instability along its "southern tier."

This centuries-old military interaction between the West and Islam is unlikely to decline. It could become more virulent. The Gulf War left some Arabs feeling proud that Saddam Hussein had attacked Israel and stood up to the West. It also left many feeling humiliated and resentful of the West's military presence in the Persian Gulf, the West's overwhelming military dominance, and their apparent inability to shape their own destiny. Many Arab countries, in addition to the oil exporters, are reaching levels of economic and social development where autocratic forms of government become inappropriate and efforts to introduce democracy become stronger. Some openings in Arab political systems have already occurred. The principal beneficiaries of these openings have been Islamist movements. In the Arab world, in short, Western democracy strengthens anti-Western political forces. This may be a passing phenomenon, but it surely complicates relations between Islamic countries and the West.

Those relations are also complicated by demography. The spectacular population growth in Arab countries, particularly in North Africa, has led to increased migration to Western Europe. The movement within Western Europe toward minimizing internal boundaries has sharpened political sensitivities with respect to this development. In Italy, France and Germany, racism is increasingly open, and political reactions and violence against Arab and Turkish migrants have become more intense and more widespread since 1990.

On both sides the interaction between Islam and the West is seen as a clash of civilizations. The West's "next confrontation," observes M. J. Akbar, an Indian Muslim author, "is definitely going to come from the Muslim world. It is in the sweep of the Islamic nations from the

Maghreb to Pakistan that the struggle for a new world order will begin." ...

Historically, the other great antagonistic interaction of Arab Islamic civilization has been with the pagan, animist, and now increasingly Christian black peoples to the south. In the past, this antagonism was epitomized in the image of Arab slave dealers and black slaves. It has been reflected in the on-going civil war in the Sudan between Arabs and blacks, the fighting in Chad between Libyan-supported insurgents and the government, the tensions between Orthodox Christians and Muslims in the Horn of Africa, and the political conflicts, recurring riots and communal violence between Muslims and Christians in Nigeria. The modernization of Africa and the spread of Christianity are likely to enhance the probability of violence along this fault line. ...

On the northern border of Islam, conflict has increasingly erupted between Orthodox and Muslim peoples, including the carnage of Bosnia and Sarajevo, the simmering violence between Serb and [mostly Muslim] Albanian, the tenuous relations between Bulgarians and their Turkish minority, the violence between [Orthodox] Ossetians and [Muslim] Ingush, the unremitting slaughter of each other by [Orthodox] Armenians and [Muslim] Azeris, the tense relations between Russians and Muslims in Central Asia, and the deployment of Russian troops to protect Russian interests in the Caucasus and Central Asia. Religion reinforces the revival of ethnic identities and restimulates Russian fears about the security of their southern borders. ...

The conflict of civilizations is deeply rooted elsewhere in Asia. The historic clash between Muslim and Hindu in the subcontinent manifests itself now not only in the rivalry between Pakistan and India but also in intensifying religious strife within India between increasingly militant Hindu groups and India's substantial Muslim minority. ... In East Asia, China has outstanding territorial disputes with most of its neighbors. It has pursued a ruthless policy toward the Buddhist people of Tibet, and it is pursuing an increasingly ruthless policy toward its Turkic-Muslim minority. With the Cold War over, the underlying differences between China and the United States have reasserted themselves in areas such as human rights, trade and weapons proliferation. These differences are unlikely to moderate. A "new cold war," Deng Xiaoping reportedly asserted in 1991, is under way between China and America.

The same phrase has been applied to the increasingly difficult relations between Japan and the United States. Here cultural difference exacerbates economic conflict. People on each side allege racism on the other, but at least on the American side the antipathies are not racial but cultural. The basic values, attitudes, behavioral patterns of the two societies could hardly be more different. The economic issues between the United States and Europe are no less serious than those between the United States and Japan, but they do not have the same political salience and emotional intensity because the differences between American culture and European culture are so much less than those between American civilization and Japanese civilization.

The interactions between civilizations vary greatly in the extent to which they are likely to be characterized by violence. Economic competition clearly predominates between the American and European subcivilizations of the West and between both of them and Japan. On the Eurasian continent, however, the proliferation of ethnic conflict, epitomized at the extreme in "ethnic cleansing," has not been totally random. It has been most frequent and most violent between groups belonging to different civilizations. In Eurasia the great historic fault lines between civilizations are once more aflame. This is particularly true along the boundaries of the crescent-shaped Islamic bloc of nations from the bulge of Africa to central Asia. Violence also occurs between Muslims, on the one hand, and Orthodox Serbs in the Balkans, Jews in Israel, Hindus in India, Buddhists in Burma and Catholics in the Philippines. Islam has bloody borders.

CIVILIZATION RALLYING: THE KIN-COUNTRY SYNDROME

Groups or states belonging to one civilization that become involved in war with people from a different civilization naturally try to rally support from other members of their own civilization. As the post–Cold War world evolves, civilization commonality,... the "kin-country" syndrome, is replacing political ideology and traditional balance of power considerations as the principal basis for cooperation and coalitions. It can be seen gradually emerging in the post–Cold War conflicts in the Persian Gulf, the Caucasus and Bosnia. None of these was a full-scale war between civilizations, but each involved some elements of civilizational rallying, which seemed to become more important as the conflict continued and which may provide a foretaste of the future.

First, in the Gulf War one Arab state invaded another and then fought a coalition of Arab, Western and other

states. While only a few Muslim governments overtly supported Saddam Hussein, many Arab elites privately cheered him on, and he was highly popular among large sections of the Arab publics. Islamic fundamentalist movements universally supported Iraq rather than the Western-backed governments of Kuwait and Saudi Arabia. Forswearing Arab nationalism, Saddam Hussein explicitly invoked an Islamic appeal. He and his supporters attempted to define the war as a war between civilizations. "It is not the world against Iraq," as Safar Al-Hawali, dean of Islamic Studies at the Umm Al-Qura University in Mecca, put it in a widely circulated tape. "It is the West against Islam." Ignoring the rivalry between Iran and Iraq, the chief Iranian religious leader, Ayatollah Ali Khamenei, called for a holy war against the West: "The struggle against American aggression, greed, plans and policies will be counted as a jihad, and anybody who is killed on that path is a martyr." "This is a war," King Hussein of Jordan argued, "against all Arabs and all Muslims and not against Iraq alone."

The rallying of substantial sections of Arab elites and publics behind Saddam Hussein caused those Arab governments in the anti-Iraq coalition to moderate their activities and temper their public statements. Arab governments opposed or distanced themselves from subsequent Western efforts to apply pressure on Iraq, including enforcement of a no-fly zone in the summer of 1992 and the bombing of Iraq in January 1993. The Western-Soviet-Turkish-Arab anti-Iraq coalition of 1990 had by 1993 become a coalition of almost only the West and Kuwait against Iraq.

Muslims contrasted Western actions against Iraq with the West's failure to protect Bosnians against Serbs and to impose sanctions on Israel for violating U.N. resolutions. The West, they alleged, was using a double standard. A world of clashing civilizations, however, is inevitably a world of double standards: people apply one standard to their kin-countries and a different standard to others.

Second, the kin-country syndrome also appeared in conflicts in the former Soviet Union. Armenian military successes in 1992 and 1993 stimulated Turkey to become increasingly supportive of its religious, ethnic and linguistic brethren in Azerbaijan. "We have a Turkish nation feeling the same sentiments as the Azerbaijanis," said one Turkish official in 1992.... Maybe we should show Armenia that there's a big Turkey in the region." President Turgut Özal agreed, remarking that Turkey should at least "scare the Armenians a little bit."... Turkish Air Force jets flew reconnaissance flights along the Armenian border; Turkey suspended food shipments and air flights to Armenia; and Turkey and Iran announced they would not accept dismemberment of Azerbaijan.... Russian troops [by contrast] fought on the side of the Armenians, and Azerbaijan accused the "Russian government of turning 180 degrees" toward support for Christian Armenia....

Conflicts and violence will also occur between states and groups within the same civilization. Such conflicts, however, are likely to be less intense and less likely to expand than conflicts between civilizations. Common membership in a civilization reduces the probability of violence in situations where it might otherwise occur. In 1991 and 1992 many people were alarmed by the possibility of violent conflict between Russia and Ukraine over territory, particularly Crimea, the Black Sea fleet, nuclear weapons and economic issues. If civilization is what counts, however, the likelihood of violence between Ukrainians and Russians should be low. They are two Slavic, primarily Orthodox peoples who have had close relationships with each other for centuries. As of early 1993, despite all the reasons for conflict, the leaders of the two countries were effectively negotiating and defusing the issues between the two countries....

Civilization rallying to date has been limited, but it has been growing, and it clearly has the potential to spread much further.... Populist politicians, religious leaders and the media have found it a potent means of arousing mass support and of pressuring hesitant governments. In the coming years, the local conflicts most likely to escalate into major wars will be those, as in Bosnia and the Caucasus, along the fault lines between civilizations. The next world war, if there is one, will be a war between civilizations.

THE WEST VERSUS THE REST

The West is now at an extraordinary peak of power in relation to other civilizations. Its superpower opponent has disappeared from the map. Military conflict among Western states is unthinkable, and Western military power is unrivaled. Apart from Japan, the West faces no economic challenge. It dominates international political and security institutions and with Japan international economic institutions. Global political and security issues are effectively settled by a directorate of the United States, Britain and France, world economic issues by a directorate of the United States, Germany and Japan, all of which maintain extraordinarily close relations with each other to the exclusion of lesser and largely non-Western countries. Decisions made at the U.N. Security Council or in the International Monetary Fund [IMF] that reflect the interests of the West are presented to the world as reflecting the desires of the world community. The very phrase "the world community" has become the euphemistic collective noun (replacing "the Free World") to give global legitimacy to actions reflecting the interests of the United States and other Western powers. Through the IMF and other international economic institutions, the West promotes its economic interests and imposes on other nations the economic policies it thinks appropriate. In any poll of non-Western peoples, the IMF undoubtedly would win the support of finance ministers and a few others, but get an overwhelmingly unfavorable rating from just about everyone else, Who would agree with Georgy Arbatov's characterization of IMF officials as "neo-Bolsheviks who love expropriating other people's money, imposing undemocratic and alien rules of economic and political conduct and stifling economic freedom."

Western domination of the U.N. Security Council and its decisions, tempered only by occasional abstention by China, produced U.N. legitimation of the West's use of force to drive Iraq out of Kuwait and its elimination of Iraq's sophisticated weapons and capacity to produce such weapons. It also produced the quite unprecedented action by the United States, Britain and France in getting the Security Council to demand that Libya hand over the Pan Am 103 bombing suspects and then to impose sanctions when Libya refused. After defeating the largest Arab army, the West did not hesitate to throw its weight around in the Arab world. The West in effect is using international insti-tutions, military power and economic resources to run the world in ways that will maintain Western predominance, protect Western interests and promote Western political and economic values.

That at least is the way in which non-Westerners see the new world, and there is a significant element of truth in their view. Differences in power and struggles for military, economic and institutional power are thus one source of conflict between the West and other civilizations. Differences in culture, that is basic values and beliefs, are a second source of conflict. [One commentator] has argued that Western civilization is the "universal civilization" that "fits all men." At a superficial level much of Western culture has indeed permeated the rest of the world. At a more basic level, however, Western concepts differ fundamentally from those prevalent in other civilizations. Western ideas of individualism, liberalism, constitutionalism, human rights, equality, liberty, the rule of law, democracy, free markets, the separation of church and state, often have little resonance in Islamic, Confucian, Japanese, Hindu, Buddhist or Orthodox cultures. Western efforts to propagate such ideas produce instead a reaction against "human rights imperialism" and a reaffirmation of indigenous values, as can be seen in the support for religious fundamentalism by the younger generation in non-Western cultures. The very notion that there could be a "universal civilization" is a Western idea, directly at odds with the particularism of most Asian societies and their emphasis on what distinguishes one people from another. Indeed, the author of a review of 100 comparative studies of values in different societies concluded that "the values that are most important in the West are least important worldwide."

In the political realm, of course, these differences are most manifest in the efforts of the United States and other Western powers to induce other peoples to adopt Western ideas concerning democracy and human rights. Modern democratic government originated in the West. When it has developed in non-Western societies it has usually been the product of Western colonialism or imposition.

The central axis of world politics in the future is likely to be, in Kishore Mahbubani's phrase, the conflict between "the West and the Rest" and the responses of non-Western civilizations to Western power and values. Those responses generally take one or a combination of three forms. At one extreme, non-Western states can, like Burma and North Korea, attempt to pursue a course of isolation, to insulate their societies from penetration or "corruption" by the West, and, in effect, to opt out of participation in the Western-dominated global community. The costs of this course, however, are high, and few states have pursued it exclusively. A second alternative, the equivalent of "band-wagoning" in international relations theory, is to attempt to join the West and accept its values and institutions. The third alternative is to attempt to "balance" the West by developing economic and military power and cooperating with other non-Western societies against the West, while preserving indigenous values and institutions; in short, to modernize but not to Westernize. . . .

THE CONFUCIAN-ISLAMIC CONNECTION

The obstacles to non-Western countries joining the West vary considerably. They are least for Latin American and East European countries. They are greater for the Orthodox countries of the former Soviet Union. They are still greater for Muslim, Confucian, Hindu and Buddhist societies. Japan has established a unique position for itself as an associate member of the West: it is in the West in some respects but clearly not of the West in important dimensions. Those countries that for reason of culture and power do not wish to, or cannot, join the West compete with the West by developing their own economic, military and political power. They do this by promoting their internal development and by cooperating with other non-Western countries. The most prominent form of this cooperation is the Confucian-Islamic connection that has emerged to challenge Western interests, values and power.

Almost without exception, Western countries are reducing their military power; under Yeltsin's leadership so also is Russia. China, North Korea and several Middle Eastern states, however, are significantly expanding their military capabilities. . . .

Centrally important to the development of counter-West military capabilities is the sustained expansion of China's military power and its means to create military power. Buoyed by spectacular economic development, China is rapidly increasing its military spending and vigorously moving forward with the modernization of its armed forces. It is purchasing weapons from the former Soviet states; it is developing long-range missiles; in 1992 it tested a one-megaton nuclear device. It is developing power-projection capabilities, acquiring aerial refueling technology, and trying to purchase an aircraft carrier. Its military buildup and assertion of sovereignty over the South China Sea are provoking a multilateral regional arms race in East Asia. China is also a major exporter of arms and weapons technology. It has exported materials to Libya and Iraq that could be used to manufacture nuclear weapons and nerve gas. It has helped Algeria build a reactor suitable for nuclear weapons research and production. China has sold to Iran nuclear technology that American officials believe could only be used to create weapons and apparently has shipped components of 300-mile-range missiles to Pakistan. North Korea has had a nuclear weapons program under way for some while and has sold advanced missiles and missile technology to Syria and Iran. The flow of weapons and weapons technology is generally from East Asia to the Middle East. There is, however, some movement in the reverse direction; China has received Stinger missiles from Pakistan.

A Confucian-Islamic military connection has thus come into being, designed to promote acquisition by its members of the weapons and weapons technologies needed to counter the military power of the West. It may or may not last. At present, however, it is, as [one analyst] has said, "a renegades' mutual support pact, run by the proliferators and their backers." A new form of arms competition is thus occurring between Islamic-Confucian states and the West. In an old-fashioned arms race, each side developed its own arms to balance or to achieve superiority against the other side. In this new form of arms competition, one side is developing its arms and the other side is attempting not to balance but to limit and prevent that arms build-up while at the same time reducing its own military capabilities.

IMPLICATIONS FOR THE WEST

This article does not argue that civilization identities will replace all other identities, that nation states will disappear, that each civilization will become a single coherent political entity, that groups within a civilization will not conflict with and even fight each other. This paper does set forth the hypotheses that differences between civilizations are real and important; civilization-consciousness is increasing; conflict between civilizations will supplant ideological and other forms of conflict as the dominant global form of conflict; international relations, historically a game played out within Western civilization, will increasingly be de-Westernized and become a game in which non-Western civilizations are actors and not simply objects; successful political, security and economic international institutions are more likely to develop within civilizations than across civilizations; conflicts between groups in different civilizations will be more frequent, more sustained and more violent than conflicts between groups in the same civilization; violent conflicts between groups in different civilizations are the most likely and most dangerous source of escalation that could lead to global wars; the paramount axis of world politics will be the relations between "the West and the Rest"; the elites in some torn non-Western countries will try to make their countries part of the West, but in most cases face major obstacles to accomplishing this; a central focus of conflict for the immediate future will be between the West and several Islamic-Confucian states.

This is not to advocate the desirability of conflicts between civilizations. It is to set forth descriptive hypotheses as to what the future may be like. If these are plausible hypotheses, however, it is necessary to consider their implications for Western policy. These implications should be divided between short-term advantage and long-term accommodation. In the short term it is clearly in the interest of the West to promote greater cooperation and unity within its own civilization, particularly between its European and North American components; to incorporate into the West societies in Eastern Europe and Latin America whose cultures are close to those of the West; to promote and maintain cooperative relations with Russia and Japan; to prevent escalation of local inter-civilization conflicts into major inter-civilization wars; to limit the expansion of the military strength of Confucian and Islamic states; to moderate the reduction of Western military capabilities and maintain military superiority in East and Southwest Asia; to exploit differences and conflicts among Confucian and Islamic states; to support in other civilizations groups sympathetic to Western values and interests; to strengthen international institutions that reflect and legitimate Western interests and values and to promote the involvement of non-Western states in those institutions.

In the longer term other measures would be called for. Western civilization is both Western and modern. Non-Western civilizations have attempted to become modern without becoming Western. To date only Japan has fully succeeded in this quest. Non-Western civilizations will continue to attempt to acquire the wealth, technology, skills, machines and weapons that are part of being modern. They will also attempt to reconcile this modernity with their traditional culture and values. Their economic and military strength relative to the West will increase. Hence the West will increasingly have to accommodate these non-Western modern civilizations whose power approaches that of the West but whose values and interests differ significantly from those of the West. This will require the West to maintain the economic and military power necessary to protect its interests in relation to these civilizations. It will also, however, require the West to develop a more profound understanding of the basic religious and philosophical assumptions underlying other civilizations and the ways in which people in those civilizations see their interests. It will require an effort to identify elements of commonality between Western and other civilizations. For the relevant future, there will be no universal civilization, but instead a world of different civilizations, each of which will have to learn to coexist with the others.

NO

James Kurth

THE *REAL* CLASH

What will be the central conflicts of world politics in our future? That is the question that dominates the current debates about international affairs. The most comprehensive, and most controversial, answer has been given by Samuel Huntington, whose concept of "the clash of civilizations" has provoked its own major clash of authors.

I intend to engage in this clashing. I will first review the current clash of definitions over the nature of the new era in international affairs. I will then review Huntington's central argument bearing on potential conflicts between Western civilization and other ones, particularly between the West and a grand alliance of the Islamic and the Confucian civilizations. I will conclude, however, by arguing that the *real* clash of civilizations, the one most pregnant with significance, will not be between the West and the rest, but one that is already underway within the West itself, particularly within its central power, the United States. This is a clash between Western civilization and a different grand alliance, one composed of the multicultural and the feminist movements. It is, in short, a clash between Western and post-Western civilizations.

THE CLASH OF DEFINITIONS

In the first few years after the Second World War, it was common for people to refer to the time that they were living through as the post-war period. But a post-war or post-anything period cannot last long, and eventually an era will assume a characteristic name of its own. . . .

Until recently, it was common to speak of the post-Cold-War era, but to continue to refer to the current period in this way—fully five years after the end of the Cold War—does seem to be stretching things a bit. . . . And yet there is just as clearly no commonly accepted designation for this indisputably new era that we are now in. . . .

The problem is not that there are no reasonable contending definitions of the new era but rather that there are too many of them. Indeed, by 1993, there had developed at least four major candidates for the definition of the post-

Cold War central axis of international conflict. Analogous to the war-centered definitions of past eras, these were: (1) trade wars, particularly between the United States, Japan, and Western Europe; (2) religious wars, particularly involving Islam; (3) ethnic wars, particularly within the former Soviet Union, the former Yugoslavia, and the "failed states" of Africa; and (4) renewed cold wars, particularly involving Russia or China. And then along came Samuel Huntington, who published a now-famous article, which in large measure subsumed the four different kinds of wars into "the clash of civilizations." ...

HUNTINGTON VERSUS HUNTINGTON

Huntington has had a long and exceptionally distinguished career as a political scientist. His distinctive contributions to political science have focused on political institutions, in particular the state, military organizations, and political parties. His books on these topics are seminal works that have made him one of the most read and respected political scientists in the world. Yet political institutions are virtually absent from his essay on the clash of civilizations. In fact, however, the origins, spread, and persistence of civilizations have been intrinsically linked with political institutions, such as traditional dynastic empires and modern nation states, and with the power that they have wielded. But different civilizations have produced different kinds of political institutions, and this will make for different kinds of clashes and conflicts. A Huntingtonian attention to political institutions will cause us to amend the Huntingtonian analysis of civilizational clashes.

Islamic civilization: A legacy of weak states: Islamic civilization was created and spread by military prowess and political power. There were times when there was a leading Islamic power, most prominently the Ottoman empire (sometimes known as "the Ottoman Ruling Institution"). The Ottoman empire was a true civilization-bearing state. However, there was never a time when there was only one strong Islamic power. Even the Ottoman empire had to deal with other Islamic empires in Persia and in India. Since the Ottomans' collapse at the end of the First World War, the Islamic civilization has been fragmented into many conflicting states.

The closest approximation today to a core state for the Islamic civilization is Iran, but it is largely isolated from the rest of the Islamic world by either its Shi'ite theology or its Persian ethnicity (and, temporarily at least, also its dismal economy). It is virtually impossible for Iran to become the core state for the Islamic civilization; it is, however, also virtually impossible for any other state to become so. The other large states who might seem to be potential leaders (Egypt, Turkey, Pakistan, and Indonesia) are so different from, and so contemptuous of, each other that no concerted policy toward the West or toward the rest (e.g., Orthodox, Hindu, or Confucian civilizations) is possible. Islam will remain a civilization without an empire or even a core state to carry out a civilizational foreign policy. This means that the clash between the West and Islam is not likely to take place at the level of conventional or even nuclear wars between Western states and Islamic states. (The [Persian] Gulf War is the exception that proves—and strengthens—the rule.) Rather, it will more likely take place between Western societies and Islamic groups, as a long series of terrorist actions, border skirmishes, and ethnic wars.

Confucian civilization—A legacy of a strong state: The story of Confucian civilization is precisely the opposite of that of Islam. Confucian civilization has been centered upon a core state for 2200 years, ever since the time of the Han dynasty. Whereas the history of Islamic civilization has been marked by long periods of fragmentation, punctuated by brief periods of unity, the history of Confucian civilization has been marked by long periods of unity (or at least deference to an imperial center), punctuated by brief periods of fragmentation.

Today, as in the past, Confucian civilization has only one contender for the role of core state, i.e., China.... All of the other Confucian countries (and they are few and mostly small—Korea, Taiwan, Hong Kong, and Singapore) can be expected to revolve around, or at least defer to, China. The clash between Confucian civilization and the West (or the rest—i.e., Orthodox or Hindu civilizations) will really take the form of a clash between China and some other state (or states). This means that what happens to the Chinese state will be crucial to the direction, and the timing, of a clash of civilizations.

Two generations ago, almost no one thought that the Confucian form of statecraft had any value in the modern world. For all the differences between Western liberals and Chinese communists, they both agreed about this. For the past decade or more, however, there has been a broad consensus that the Confucian societies have created states that are outstanding at industrial development.

These are South Korea, Taiwan, Singapore and (insofar as Confucianism rather than Shintoism or Buddhism should get the credit) Japan. They are the most successful trading states in the world.

The Chinese state must make the great transition from being a communist state to being a Confucian one. This is not going to be a smooth and easy process. The ideal Confucian state in the modern era has been the Singapore of Lee Kuan Yew. Its achievements have been extraordinarily great, but its size is extraordinarily small. (It is really a city-state, with a population of only 2.8 million.) The other successful Confucian states have also governed rather small countries, with the exception of only partly-Confucian Japan. So there is a crucial question: Will the modern Confucian state be able to govern 1.2 billion people?

There may indeed come a clash between Western and Confucian civilizations, but sometime soon there will intervene a clash between the communist past and the Confucian future in China itself. The nature of that internal clash will largely shape the nature and timing of the external one. A clash of civilizations that occurred after a long Chinese "time of troubles" would have different consequences than one that occurred in the near future.

In any event, the clash between the Western and Confucian civilizations, like the clash between Western and Islamic civilizations, is not likely to take place at the level of conventional or nuclear wars. Rather, it will more likely take place between Western-style or liberal capitalism and Confucian-style or state-guided capitalism, as a long series of economic conflicts, human-rights disputes with an economic dimension, and trade wars.

FROM CHRISTENDOM
TO "THE WEST"

A closer look at Huntington's list of major civilizations will raise a fundamental question about the nature of civilizations and the differences between them. He identifies "Western, Confucian, Japanese, Islamic, Hindu, Slavic-Orthodox, Latin American, and possibly African civilization." This is, on the face of it, a motley collection of terms. Four clearly identify a civilization with a religion (in Toynbee's term, a universal church). However, the two civilizations with the most advanced economies—the Western and the Japanese—are identified in secular terms. We have already noted that Japanese civilization is a result of a synthesis of *three* religions—Confucianism, Shintoism, and Buddhism—so in its case the use of a national term rather than a religious one seems logical.

The real anomaly in Huntington's list is the most powerful and most pervasive civilization of them all—Western civilization, which is identified with a term that is only a geographical direction. Instead of connoting the profound essence of the civilization, the term Western connotes something bland and even insipid, with no content at all. And instead of connoting the global sway of the civilization, the term Western connotes a locus that is limited and confined, with no breadth at all.

The problematic quality of Western civilization goes deeper than an anomalous term, however. It reaches to the most fundamental character of the civilization, to its definition and its direction.

The fact of the matter is that Western civilization is the *only* civilization that is explicitly *non-religious* or post-religious. This is the radical difference of the West from the other civilizations. It helps to explain why there are new conflicts between the West and the rest. It predicts that these conflicts will become more intense in the future. And it also points to a possible fatal flaw within Western civilization itself.

Three hundred years ago, no one knew that there was a Western civilization, not even those that were living within it. The term then, and the one that would be parallel to Huntington's terms for the other civilizations, was Christendom. The story of how Christendom became Western civilization and how most other civilizations have retained a religious identity is crucial for understanding the clash of civilizations in the future.

Western civilization is, as Huntington notes, the product of a series of great cultural and historical movements. The featured tableaux in this grand parade are the Renaissance, the Reformation, the Counter-Reformation, the Enlightenment, the French Revolution, and the Industrial Revolution. Huntington's own list does not include the Counter-Reformation. This may be natural enough for Americans; Europeans, however, have good reasons to include it.

The Enlightenment brought about the secularization of much of the intellectual class, the idea-bearing class, of what hitherto had been called Christendom. The civilization was now no longer called that, even though much of its ordinary population remained Christian. The French Revolution and the Industrial Revolution spread Enlightenment ideas and secularization to important parts of this population, but the Christian churches continued to be a vital force within the civilization. But ever since the Enlightenment, it has not been possible to refer to the civilization as Christendom.

For a time in the late eighteenth and early nineteenth century, "Europe" became the preferred term for the civilization. But this was also the very time that saw the rise of European settlements in the New World to the status of independent nations. This soon made impossible the term "European civilization."

For a brief and exuberant time in the nineteenth century, when this civilization seemed to be the only dynamic and growing one and with all the others in manifest decline and decay, the preferred term was just "Civilization" itself, since this civilization seemed to be the only one around. But this term, too, could not be sustained.

It was only at the beginning of the twentieth century that the term "Western civilization" was invented. The term registered the awareness that this civilization, unlike others, did not place religion at its core. It also registered the awareness that this civilization was only one among many. It was a civilization past the enthusiasms of faith and also past the exuberance of being a civilization so blessed that it was in a class by itself. In short, the term Western civilization was the product of a high degree of intellectualism, perhaps even a sickly self-consciousness. The term was itself a sign of the first appearance of decline. It is no accident that, almost as soon as it was invented, it began to be used in this pessimistic context, as in Oswald Spengler's *The Decline of the West* (1918). Had the term been left in the hands, or rather the minds, of Europeans alone, it probably would have had only a short and unhappy life.

It was the New World that was called in to redress the pessimism of the Old. The Americans breathed a new meaning into the term Western civilization, first as they dealt with the European immigrants in America and then as they dealt with the European nations in Europe itself. For Americans then, and for Huntington now, Western civilization was the ideas of "individualism, liberalism, constitutionalism, human rights, equality, liberty, the rule of law, democracy, free markets, the separation of church and state."

The new content of Western civilization became the American creed. Conversely, the new context for the American creed became Western civilization. The combination of American energy and European imagery gave the idea of Western civilization both power and legitimacy. The power helped the United States win both the Second World War against Nazi Germany and the Cold War against the Soviet Union. The legitimacy helped it to order the long peace within Western Europe that was so much intertwined with that Cold War. The term Western civilization has experienced, therefore, its own heroic age.

That age, however, is now over. It is over partly because the term no longer provides the United States legitimacy among the Europeans.... The main reason why the heroic age of the term is over is because it no longer provides any energy within the United States itself, and this is because it no longer has any legitimacy among Americans.

The decline of Western civilization is a tale that scholars have been telling ever since the *fin-de-siècle* [end] of the nineteenth century.... Now, at the *fin-de-siècle* of the twentieth century, the decline of that term is a sign of a much more advanced decline. The tale of the decline of "Western civilization" as a term is part of the longer tale of the decline of Western civilization itself. This is connected with certain transformations within the West that have matured in the 1990s.

THE GREAT TRANSFORMATIONS

One big event of the 1990s, of course, has been the end of the Cold War.... But the 1990s have also seen the maturing of other major developments that will have major consequences for international security and the national interest, and that will shape the clash of civilizations: first, there has been the transformation of the most advanced countries from industrial to post-industrial economies, and their associated transformation from modern to post-modern societies; second, there has been the transformation of the international economy into a truly global one.

The transformation from industrial to post-industrial economy: At the most obvious level, this means the replacement of industrial production with service processes. These changes have been noted and discussed for more than a generation.... It will prove useful for our purposes, however, to emphasize one dimension of this transformation—that of gender.

The agricultural economy was one that employed both men and women. They were, it is true, employed at different tasks, but they worked at the same place, the farm, which was also the home. The industrial economy largely employed men. They worked both at different tasks from those of women and at a different place, the factory, which was away from the home. The service economy is like the agricultural economy in that it employs both men and women. But it employs them at much the same tasks and at the same place, the office. Like the industrial economy, that place is away from the home. These simple differences in tasks and place have had and will continue to have enormous consequences for society.

The greatest movement of the second half of the nineteenth century was the movement of men from the farm to the factory. Out of that movement arose many of the political movements that shaped the history of the time—socialism and anti-socialism, revolutions, and civil wars. The full consequences of this movement from the farm to the factory culminated in the first half of the twentieth century with the Communist revolution in Russia, the National Socialist reaction in Germany, and the Second World War that included the great struggle between the two.

The greatest movement of the second half of the twentieth century has been the movement of women from the home to the office. Out of that movement there have already arisen political movements that are beginning to shape the history of our own time. One is feminism, with its political demands ranging from equal opportunity to academic deconstruction to abortion rights. Feminism has in turn produced a new form of conservatism. These new conservatives speak of "family values;" their adversaries call them "the religious right."

The full consequences of this movement from the home to the office will only culminate in the first half of the twenty-first century. They may not take the form of revolutions, civil wars, and world wars, as did the earlier movement of men from the farm to the factory. Feminists have constructed elaborate theories about how women are far less violent than men. But there are other factors at work.

The movement from farm to factory in large measure brought about the replacement of the extended family with the nuclear family. The movement from home to office is carrying this process one step further. It separates the parents from the children, as well as enabling the wife to separate herself from the husband... [S]plitting the nuclear family,... like the splitting of the atom's nucleus, will release an enormous amount of energy (which feminists see as liberating and conservatives see as simply destructive).

Some indication of that energy, and its direction, may be gleaned from the behavior of the children of split families or single-parent families, especially where they have reached a critical mass forming more than half the population, as in the large cities of America. In such locales, there is not much evidence of "Western civilization" or even of civility. For thousands of years, the city was the source of civilization. In contemporary America, however, it has become the source of barbarism.

The transformation of the international economy into a global one: At the most obvious level, this means the replacement of national production that is engaged in international trade with global production that is engaged in a world-wide market in trade, investment, and technology. These changes too have been noted and discussed for a generation.... We will only note one of these aspects. The globalization of production means the relocation of industrial production from high-wage and high-skill advanced-industrial countries to low-wage but high-skill newly-industrial countries (NICs). This is the de-industrialization of the advanced countries, the dark half of the post-industrial transformation that we dis-cussed above. The two transformations —from industrial to post-industrial and from international to global—are intimately connected.

The conjunction of two processes— the de-industrialization of the advanced countries and the industrialization of the less-advanced countries—means that the most advanced countries are becoming less modern (i.e. post-modern), while the less-advanced countries are becoming more modern. Or, viewing it from a civilizational perspective, the West is becoming less modern and the rest, especially Confucian civilization, are becoming more modern.

AMERICANIZATION VS. MULTICULTURALISM

The most significant development for Western Civilization, however, has occurred within its leading power, which was once its "defender of the faith." Increasingly, the political and intellectual elites of the United States no longer think of America as the leader, or even a member, of Western civilization. Western civilization means nothing to many of them. And in the academic world, Western civilization is seen as an oppressive hegemony that should be overturned.

The American political and intellectual class instead thinks of America as a multicultural society. The preferred cultures are those of African Americans, Latino Americans, and Asian Americans. These cultures are derived from the African, Latin American, Confucian, and Islamic civilizations rather than from the Western one. Together, they form a sort of series of beachheads or even colonies of these civilizations on the North American continent, and are now contesting the hegemony there of Western civilization.

The United States, however, has always had a large African American population, and it has long had a large Latino American one. Conversely, although the U.S. Asian American population has more than doubled since the changes brought by the immigration law of 1965, Asian Americans still represent only three percent of the U.S. population. The gross demographics of the United States are still much the same as they have been for decades. Something else had to be added to convert a long-existing multiracial demography into a multicultural ideology, establishing a multicultural society.

It is not merely the addition of large numbers of immigrants from different cultures in recent years. This is not the first time that the United States has experienced large numbers of immigrants from different cultures, with prospects for their acceptance of the dominant culture seemingly problematic. A similar condition existed a century ago, particularly from the 1880s to the 1920s, when the culture formed within the U.S. by Western Europeans (principally by those of British descent) had to confront large numbers of immigrants from Eastern and Southern Europe (principally Poles, Jews, and Italians). These immigrants were all from Western civilization, but this was no consolation to the Americans who were already here. Most of these "old-stock" Americans did not even know that they were part of Western civilization (the concept had hardly been invented yet), but rather thought of themselves in terms of religious, national, or (spurious) racial identities.

The reaction of the political and intellectual elites of that time to their multicultural reality was precisely the opposite of that of the political and intel-

lectual elites of today. They did not rejoice in multicultural society and dedicate themselves to making it even more multicultural. Rather, they undertook a massive and systematic program of Americanization, imposing on the new immigrants and on their children the English language, Anglo-American history, and American civics (what... Huntington has elsewhere termed the "American Creed")....

This grand project of Americanization was relentless and even ruthless. Many individuals were oppressed and victimized by it, and many rich and meaningful cultural islands were swept away. But the achievements of that project were awesome, as well as awful. In particular, when the United States entered into its greatest struggles of the twentieth century, first the Second World War and then the Cold War, it did so as a national state, rather than as a multicultural society.... It was because of the Americanization project that the United States could become the leader and the defender of Western civilization.

Indeed, one of the consequences of this grand project of Americanization was the spread within the American academic elite of the concept of the Western civilization. The political elite remained comfortable with Americanization of the mass population. The academic elite,... however, was in the business of teaching the elite of the future. For this purpose, simple Americanization was too rough and primitive. Rather than imposing Americanization unilaterally on people who were in some sense both European and American, it would be better to find a new common denominator for both Europeans and Americans. This became "Western civilization." As we have seen, very little in this Western civilization happened to contradict the American creed. All of the elements that Huntington identifies as being the elements of Western civilization were in the American creed also.

DECONSTRUCTING THE WEST

The presence of African Americans, Latino Americans, and Asian Americans might have been sufficient to create a multicultural ideology in the 1980s and 1990s. But these three groups alone probably would not have been sufficient to have that ideology adopted by much of the American political and intellectual elites, or to have it translated into policies aimed at establishing a multicultural society. Even a grand coalition between them would not have been grand enough to take power and make policy. A truly grand coalition had to include, indeed had to have as its core, a group that was much closer in social and educational background to the existing elite and much more central to the emerging post-industrial economy. That group, which was not really a group but a majority, was women. We have already noted the importance of women in the post-industrial economy and the consequent importance of feminism in post-modern politics.

The feminist movement is central to the multicultural coalition and its project. It provides the numbers, having reached a central mass first in academia and now in the media and the law. It promotes the theories, such as deconstructionism and post-modernism. And it provides much of the energy, the leadership, and the political clout.

The multicultural coalition and its feminist core despise the European versions of Western civilization, which they see as the work of "dead white European males." They also despise the American version or the American creed, particularly liberalism, constitutionalism, the rule of law, and free markets.... The multicultural project has already succeeded in marginalizing Western civilization in its very intellectual core, the universities and the media of America.

THE REAL CLASH

The ideas of the Enlightenment were invented in Britain in the aftermath of the religious wars of the seventeenth century. They were then adopted by the intellectual elite of the greatest power of the eighteenth century, France, which then proceeded to spread them throughout Europe. The ideas of the post-Enlightenment were invented in France in the aftermath of the mid-twentieth century. They were then adopted by the intellectual elite of the greatest power of the late twentieth-century, the United States, which is beginning to spread them throughout Western civilization.

The overthrow of the Enlightenment by the post-Enlightenment is also the overthrow of the modern by the post-modern and therefore of the Western by the post-Western. At the very moment of its greatest triumph, its defeat of the last great power opposing it, Western civilization is becoming non-Western. One reason is that it has become global and therefore extra-Western. But the real, and the fatal, reason is that it has become post-modern and therefore post-Western.

The real clash of civilizations will not be between the West and one or more of the Rest. It will be between the West and the post-West, within the West itself. This clash has already taken place within the brain of Western civilization, the American intellectual class. It is now spreading from that brain to the American body politic.

The 1990s have seen another great transformation, this time in the liberal and the conservative movements that have long defined American politics and that, whatever their differences, had both believed in the modern ideas represented by the American creed. Among liberals, the political energy is now found among multicultural activists. Liberalism is ceasing to be modern and is becoming post-modern. Among conservatives, the political energy is now found among religious believers. Conservatism is ceasing to be modern and is becoming pre-modern. Neither these liberals nor these conservatives are believers in Western civilization. The liberals identify with multicultural society or a post-Western civilization (such as it is). The conservatives identify with Christianity or a pre-Western civilization. A question thus arises about who, in the United States of the future, will still believe in Western civilization. Most practically, who will believe in it enough to fight, kill, and die for it in a clash of civilizations?

*   *   *

It is historically fitting that Samuel Huntington has issued a call to Western civilization and to Americans within it. In the seventeenth century, the first Hunt-ingtons arrived in America, as Puritans and as founders of the Massachusetts Bay Colony. In the eighteenth century, Samuel Huntington of Connecticut was a signer of the Declaration of Independence and a lender to General George Washington of the funds necessary to sustain his army at Valley Forge. In the nineteenth century, Collis P. Huntington was a builder of the transcontinental railroad. In the twentieth century, Samuel P. Huntington has been, for more than forty years, the most consistently brilliant and creative political scientist in the United States. Huntingtons have been present at the creation for most of the great events of American history, which in turn have been linked up with great movements of Western civilization—the Reformation, the Enlightenment, the French Revolution, and the Industrial Revolution. It is fitting indeed that, in our century, Samuel Huntington has been not just an analyst of Western civilization but an exemplar of its creative intelligence.

The American intellectual class of our time is present at the deconstruction of Western civilization. When that civilization is in ruins, however, it will be its glories, and not multiculturalism's barbarities, that will be remembered. And when that intellectual class has also passed away, it will be the brilliant achievements of Samuel Huntington, and not the boring clichés of the deconstructionists, that will be remembered also.

POSTSCRIPT

Will the World Fragment into Antagonistic Cultures?

One of the most readable recent essays on the future course of human governance is Benjamin R. Barber's "Jihad vs. McWorld," *The Atlantic Monthly* (March 1992). Barber ponders two possible paths. One is toward international integration, which he calls "McWorld." The other is toward international fragmentation, which Barber calls "Jihad," an Arabic term that means "struggle in defense of Islam." Barber thinks that both currents are strong, but he predicts that in the end McWorld will triumph. Huntington's view is essentially that Jihad will carry the day. Both Barber and Huntington implicitly agree, however, that the role of the state will decline as a primary focus of political loyalty and activity in the international system. Kurth rejects Jihad, but he also does not accept McWorld. Rather, he seems to assume the continuance of the state as the foremost focus of political organization. Another article that takes issue with Huntington is Richard E. Rubenstein and Jarle Crocker, "Challenging Huntington," *Foreign Policy* (Fall 1994).

Europe has witnessed the breakup of many countries, including Yugoslavia, the Soviet Union, and Czechoslovakia. Even the new, smaller countries sometimes have their own separatist movements. The Chechens, for example, are one among several national groups that wish to secede from Russia. Other countries are experiencing acute separatist pressures too. A referendum to endorse negotiating an end to the union of the province of Quebec with the rest of Canada was defeated by less than 1 percent in October 1995. See the debate between Jacques Parizeau, "The Case for a Sovereign Quebec," and Daniel Johnson, "The Case for a United Canada," in *Foreign Policy* (Summer 1995).

The list of current Jihad movements could go on, but that is not necessary to make the point that there is considerable evidence that people are searching for new loyalties to replace or supplement state-oriented patriotism. Whether the new attachments will develop into antagonistic cultures, whether the system will evolve toward greater global integration and governance, or whether the state will persist as the locus of loyalty and political power are uncertain. What is almost sure is that there are turbulent times ahead. There is considerable reading to supplement your knowledge in these areas. Two such readings are Michael Bruner, Allen Ketcham, Michael Preda, and Jim Norwine, "Postmodern Nationalism Among University Students in Texas," *Canadian Review of Studies in Nationalism* (Winter 1993) and Ted Robert Gurr, "Peoples Against States: Ethnopolitical Conflict and the Changing World System," *International Studies Quarterly* (September 1994).

ISSUE 19

Is Self-Determination a Right of All Nationalities?

YES: Michael Lind, from "In Defense of Liberal Nationalism," *Foreign Affairs* (May/June 1994)

NO: Amitai Etzioni, from "The Evils of Self-Determination," *Foreign Policy* (Winter 1992/1993)

ISSUE SUMMARY

YES: Michael Lind, executive editor of *The National Interest*, writes that nationalism, "the idea that every nation should have its own state," is the most powerful idea in the contemporary world. Prejudice against nationalism is a mistake, he argues; for practical, strategic reasons, and for reasons of principle, the United States should support legitimate efforts at self-determination.

NO: Amitai Etzioni, a professor of sociology at George Washington University, contends that self-determination movements have exhausted their legitimacy. It is time to see them for what they are—destructive.

President Woodrow Wilson stood before a joint session of Congress on January 8, 1918, to outline the goals of the United States in World War I. Trying to set America's war aims apart from what he saw, and rejected, as the power plays and land grabs that had long sullied and bloodied Europe, Wilson outlined a program that became known as the Fourteen Points. Wilson called for the self-determination of nationalities within the Austro-Hungarian, German, and Ottoman empires with which the United States was at war.

Not long before, Nikolai Lenin had similarly called for self-determination. Writing in his epic work *Imperialism*, the Bolshevik leader condemned colonialism as the domination of proletariat people by bourgeois, imperialist countries, and he advocated revolution and freedom for oppressed nations.

The idea of self-determination dates back to the mid-1700s and the idea of popular sovereignty. This concept rejected the theory that kings had the divine right to hold power, to control and even to own people within their realms. The theory of popular sovereignty holds that a people should be free from outside control and should control their own governments. The theory of self-determination was one of the ideological underpinnings of the late-eighteenth-century democratic revolutions in the United States and France.

Western-based ideas about independence spread around the world and gave intellectual justification to the ancient, some would argue instinctive, urge of groups of people not to be dominated by others. In the time of Wilson and Lenin there were about 40 independent countries; now there are nearly 200. The Spanish and Portuguese empires in the Americas collapsed in the early 1800s; the German, Austro-Hungarian, and Ottoman empires collapsed during World War I; the African and Asian colonial empires of the British, French, and other European imperialists collapsed in the 30 years following the end of World War II. Finally, in 1991, the Soviet Union collapsed. Some countries that were formed with a mix of various religious and ethnic groups have recently fallen apart or descended into internal warfare. The Czechs and Slovaks managed a national divorce peacefully, to their credit. The Bosnians, Croats, and Serbs were neither that lucky nor that civilized in Yugoslavia.

The debate at issue here is whether or not the idea of self-determination is a standard that should be supported. It is important to clarify a few terms before proceeding. The word *state*, as used by political scientists, means country. A state is a physical and political entity that possesses sovereignty. *Sovereignty* means autonomy, or freedom from outside control. *Nations* and *ethnic groups* (tribes) are groups of people who share a mutual identity based on some combination of history, culture, language, religion, and other characteristics. What differentiates nations and ethnic groups is that a nation can be said to have some sense of wanting independence or at least political autonomy, which is not necessarily the case for ethnic groups.

To return to the idea of national self-determination, it has evolved in this century mostly as an affirmation that nations have the right to break free from empires. That is what Wilson and Lenin were advocating; that is what has been affirmed by the United Nations in its 1960 declaration on the independence of colonial peoples and in various UN-sponsored human rights conventions. While old-style empires have disappeared, multiethnic and multinational states are still commonplace. Africa, for example, is a maze of cross-cutting ethnic and political boundaries created by the Europeans who carved the continent up with little or no regard to its population distribution. The periodic fighting since the late 1950s between the Hutus and Tutsis in what are now Burundi and Rwanda is part of that legacy. India, which has 24 different languages spoken by a million or more people, is considered an ethnic powder keg by many. The point is that the drive for self-determination did not end with the demise of traditional empires.

Michael Lind and Amitai Etzioni take up the debate about what our attitude should be as we approach the twenty-first century. Lind does not favor indiscriminate support for separatism. But he argues that U.S. interests may be better served by those who seek to break up multinational states than by those who seek to preserve them. Etzioni disagrees strongly, contending that we should oppose those forces that seek fragmentation and tribalism and support those that promote multicultural tolerance.

YES

Michael Lind

IN DEFENSE OF LIBERAL NATIONALISM

THE WORLD'S MOST POWERFUL FORCE

The simple idea that every nation should have its own state—accompanied by the corollary that one ethnic or cultural groups should not collectively rule over another—has been the most powerful political force of the past two hundred years. While particular nationalisms vary, this basic nationalist conception of an ideal world order has been remarkably unchanged for well over a century. "The world should be split into as many states as humanity is divided into nations," the Swiss international lawyer Johann Caspar Bluntschli wrote in 1870. "Each nation a state, each state a national being." When he wrote, nationalism as a considered doctrine, with its roots in the thought of Rousseau, Herder, Fichte and Mazzini, was already generations old. National sentiments, of course, long predated the doctrine, despite recent attempts to claim that national feelings are purely modern fabrications.

The nationalist ideal has survived one universalist assault after another: the Concert of Europe, which Metternich saw as a way of repressing anti-dynastic nationalism and republicanism; Hitler's supranational racist imperialism; the doomed Soviet effort to replace national loyalties with commitment to socialist universalism. Even the failure of the European Community to become a genuine federal state was foreseeable long before the troubles afflicting the Maastricht treaty and the crisis of the European Monetary System. It seems unlikely that liberal universalism will succeed where illiberal universalisms failed, in attempting to transfer loyalties from nations to supranational entities.

Despite all the evidence of the enduring power of nationalist sentiment, many statesmen, scholars and opinion leaders continue to treat nationalism as an anachronistic or dangerous relic of a previous age. Translated into policy, this prejudice against national self-determination usually means supporting the efforts of regimes to suppress secessionist movements by national minorities. The widespread conviction that nationalist secession is in itself dangerous and regressive helps explain the vehemence with which many observers blamed Germany for its allegedly premature recognition of

Slovenia, Croatia and Bosnia, and the criticism directed at the United States for allegedly engineering the independence of Eritrea.

This prejudice against nationalism—even liberal, democratic, constitutional nationalism—is a mistake. Reflexive support for multinational political entities, especially despotic ones, is as misguided as the automatic rejection of movements that seek the sovereignty of national homelands. For practical strategic reasons, as well as reasons of principle, the United States should identify itself with the most powerful idea in the contemporary world.

THE GREAT ILLUSION

Having survived so many setbacks since the wars of the French Revolution, will nationalism now end up in the dustbin of history along with its defeated universalist rivals? Scholars and writers... have been predicting the imminent obsolescence of the nation state for most of the twentieth century. In most cases, they have rested their argument on the economies of scale made possible by advances in technology—the transoceanic cable of yesterday, the computerized stock exchange and satellite television of today.

But this "interdependence" school, like Marxism, is based on a contradiction. It is simultaneously deterministic and prescriptive. If the world is inevitably growing more interdependent, then there is no reason to oppose particular nationalisms that are doomed in the long run anyway. Why oppose what is bound to wither away? On the other hand, if effort is needed to promote transnational integration, then clearly such integration is not preordained.

The mistake of prophets of a postnationalism world has been to leave out moral and political economies of scale. As a purely technical matter, it has probably been possible since Genghis Khan—certainly since Napoleon—for the earth to be governed from a single capital. That all attempts at world conquest have failed has nothing to do with technology and everything to do with the determination of diverse peoples not to be ruled by the conquering nation of the day. This is true of the latest attempt at world hegemony as well. Superior technology made it possible for the Western alliance to outinnovate and outproduce the Soviet bloc, but it was American, German and Japanese desires to protect national autonomy that kept those countries in a four-decade alliance. Why nations that will fight to the death to prevent surrendering their sovereignty to a conqueror would voluntarily surrender it to a supranational bureaucracy or a global elite of financiers and industrialists is a mystery that interdependence theorists have yet to explain.

THE 'STABILITARIANS'

A somewhat more plausible case against nationalism is made by "stabilitarians," or defenders of the present-day territorial status quo. The harmful effects of alteration of existing borders—even peaceful alteration—would, it is thought, outweigh the benefits. Every viewpoint has an address, of course. A national leader will view stability differently, depending on whether he thinks of his state as a status quo or a revisionist power. The belief of the Bush administration that the United States was a status quo power explains its efforts to keep both the Soviet empire and the Yugoslav federation intact.

While the breakup of a multinational state may create a regional power vacuum or a new balance-of-power pattern among its successor states, these results may be strategically desirable for some countries. Britain, for example, sought the independence of the Low Countries, the Hapsburgs the fragmentation of Italy, and successive Chinese empires the disunity of the nomads [to the northwest] in the Tarim Basin. A state may easily conclude that a power vacuum in a particular region is preferable to a rival power center. Given the threat the Soviet Union posed to the United States (and the threat its predecessor, the Romanov empire, posed to Great Britain) it is by no means clear that a consolidated entity on the territory of the Soviet Union is preferable to a balance-of-power system of rival successor states.

Assertions that successful secession by one or a few nations will produce runaway disintegration, thanks to the demonstration effect, deserve to be greeted with the same skepticism that should be directed at other straight-line extrapolations. The domino theory of nationalist disintegration is no more persuasive than similar domino theories. Secessionist activity tends to come in limited bursts: decolonization, the disintegration of the Soviet bloc and empire.

The potential for global disorder inherent in a world community with more states than exist at present is easy to exaggerate. To begin with, the number of possible new nation states is in the dozens, not the hundreds or thousands. While there are thousands of ethnic nations in the world, there are at most only dozens of national groups numerous, unified and compact enough conceivably to serve as the nuclei of sovereign nation states. The impossibility of basing nation states on tiny minorities like Sorbs or Wends in Germany or the Amish in the United States in no way discredits the potential for statehood of the Kurds [mostly in Turkey, Iraq, and Iran] or the Ibo [in Nigeria] or the Tibetans.

Even if the number of nation states were to increase by a dozen or two in the next few decades, through the peaceful or violent partition of several multinational countries, the very inequality of power among states would prevent too great a degree of disorder. A world of 200 or 250 effectively equal states would indeed be unmanageable, but not a world of the same number of nominally independent states, in which real power inheres in a handful of great powers, blocs and alliances. The breakup of nineteenth- and twentieth-century empires has produced, to date, almost two hundred states —well short of the 300 independent political units that existed in early-modern Germany, or the 500 that Charles Tilly has identified in the Europe of 1500. If the world survived the rapid expansion of the number of U.N. member states from 52 in 1946 to 183 today, surely it can survive a more incremental expansion by a dozen or two more.

Would the replacement of some of today's multinational states by new nation states lead to an increase in interstate war? History since the great wave of postwar decolonization in Africa and Asia gives some cause for reassurance in this regard. While many postcolonial states have been riven by ethnic conflict (reflecting the fact that they themselves are often ethnically heterogeneous), major interstate wars have been relatively infrequent.

Although prophets must be careful, it is possible that there would be less interstate conflict in a world of relatively homogeneous nation states than there is intrastate conflict between ethnic groups in multinational states. There are powerful incentives against engaging in cross-border war, whereas the penalties against a dominant ethnic group crushing others in the state it controls are very weak indeed.

Opponents of secessionist nationalism frequently argue that larger minorities, once they gain independence, may in turn oppress smaller minorities in the new national territory. The Quebecers, if independent, might be more inclined to oppress American Indians in Quebec. (The Balkan war is not terribly relevant, inasmuch as Slovenes, Croats and Yugoslav Muslims seceded in the first place to escape oppression in a multinational federation dominated by Serbs.)

Without condoning any injustice, the fact that a secessionist nation engages in oppressive behavior does not mean its complaints about its own oppression at the hands of a central government or dominant imperial ethnic group are not legitimate. Even criminals may be victims of crime. Inevitably, the replacement of a multinational empire or federation by a group of nation states will leave minorities that are too small or too dispersed without states of their own. This, in itself, is no argument for holding the multinational structure together, unless the multinational elite is significantly more virtuous than the successor national elites, which is rarely the case.

The relatively bloodless dissolution of the Soviet Union into its constituent republics, the separation of the Czech and Slovak republics, the accession of East Germany and, earlier, the Saarland to the German Federal Republic, as well as a number of cases of postcolonial independence, prove that national self-determination need not be accompanied by violence. Those concerned that national self-determination will lead to violence should support the strengthening of peaceful constitutional and diplomatic procedures for increasing the congruence of borders and nations, rather than support the status quo at all costs.

SMALL IS VIABLE

Is there a lower limit to the size of a viable nation state, imposed by the needs of defense or economics or minimum international order? If the viability of a state is defined as its military invulnerability in the absence of allies and economic autarky, then the only viable states would be isolationist, continental superpowers (rather like the Eastasia, Eurasia and Oceania of Orwell's *1984*).

As long as states are willing to cooperate in security alliances and engage in mutually beneficial trade, there is no reason why a small state like Portugal or Croatia should not be as viable as a great power like the United States. In an integrated North American market, an independent Quebec might prosper, even while preserving its distinctive French-American identity (though the transition might be painful). Indeed, smaller states may have advantages over the populous when it comes to economic progress (contrast Singapore and Hong Kong with China). Instead of specializing in one or a few crops, like states in a federation or provinces in an empire, an independent nation can take steps to diversify its economy as a buffer against market shocks. A sovereign state can also have a certain amount of leverage in both economic and military diplomacy—an advantage denied to a region subordinated to a single capital.

It might be thought that the costs of defense for a small nation state would be prohibitive. In fact, experience shows that small nation states do not spend more on defense as a share of GDP [gross domestic product] than do large countries. Indeed, during the Cold War the United States spent proportionately more on defense than its medium-sized allies like Germany and Japan, or small allies like Denmark and Portugal. A small state can act as a free rider, taking advantage of a powerful neighbor's interest in defending not only itself but its region. Of course such a neighbor may be a threat as well as an ally—but this is a risk that might be worth taking. After all, Kurds would be safer from Baghdad even in a weak Kurdish nation state than they can ever be as part of Iraq.

At any rate, an argument for the benefits of scale is an argument against small states of any kind—against small multinational states, like Switzerland, as much as small nation states like Slovenia. It is not in itself an argument against making nationality the basis of statehood wherever substantial geographical concentrations of linguistically and culturally similar people exist.

LIBERAL VS. ILLIBERAL NATIONALISM

Support in some circumstances for national self-determination need not mean support for nationalism in its tyrannical or imperial manifestations. It is important to draw a distinction between liberal and illiberal nationalism. Liberal nationalists tend to favor a linguistic-cultural definition of nationality and a liberal-constitutional (though not neces-

sarily democratic) organization of the state. Illiberal nationalists (who might more accurately be described as nativists, to employ a term that originated in American politics) favor a religious or genetic definition of nationality, as in Iran or Serbia, and usually (though not always) an authoritarian-populist constitution. It is as great a mistake to confuse liberal nationalism with illiberal nativism as it is to identify social democracy with Leninist communism. Illiberal nationalism is often responsible for terrible atrocities, as the carnage in Bosnia has shown. The problem, however, is with illiberalism and militarism, not with nationalism as such.

Liberal nationalism holds that, far from being a threat to democracy, nationalism —the correspondence of cultural nation and state—is a necessary, though not sufficient, condition for democracy in most places today. Modern democracy presupposes a degree of extrapolitical community. The linguistic-cultural nation is today generally accepted as the basis for the political community because it is the largest particular community that can still command sentimental loyalty and the smallest comprehensive community that still has features of universality, combining all ages and classes. The nation is a small humanity and a large association. "Few will burn with ardent love for the entire human species," Tocqueville observed. "The interests of the human race are better served by giving every man a particular fatherland than by trying to inflame his passions for the whole of humanity."

Some claim that national loyalty is irrational and atavistic, compared to "rational" patriotism or allegiance to a state that is not identified with any predominant linguistic or cultural group. There is nothing at all "irrational," however, about making the suprafamilial community with which one identifies the cultural nation, rather than the territorial state in the abstract. Quite apart from the psychological reasons, there are practical reasons. One is usually born into a cultural nation for life, but the state to which one owes allegiance may alter its borders, change its constitution, change its name, even cease to exist through conquest or merger. National communities, while by no means immortal themselves, tend to be more stable and long-lived. This being the case, to identify primarily, not with a historic linguistic-cultural nation, but with a possibly transient government or a paper constitution, would be the height of irrationality.

MULTINATIONAL DEMOCRACY IS NEITHER

The evidence that democracy almost never works in societies that are highly divided along linguistic and cultural lines is overwhelming. Examples of multinational countries that have failed are numerous: Cyprus, Lebanon, Sri Lanka, Sudan, the Soviet Union, Yugoslavia, Czechoslovakia (India increasingly looks like another failure). Nevertheless, many persist in arguing that multinational democracy not only is possible but represents the wave of the future. Multinational despotisms, they argue, should not be partitioned into nation states that (in some cases) may become democracies. Rather, they should be transformed from multinational despotisms into multinational democracies.

As examples of successful multinational federations, proponents of multinational democracy usually point to three countries with elaborate ethnic power-sharing arrangements: Switzerland, Belgium and Canada. The very fact that only three successes can be found, out of dozens of multinational states, in itself suggests the difficulty of getting linguistically and culturally distinct nations to cohabit peacefully under a common democratic constitution. In reality, these three examples hurt the multinationalist case more than they help it. Switzerland, for example, is better described as a confederation of relatively homogeneous territorial nation states (the cantons) than as a truly multiethnic society. Belgium is a society deeply troubled by its linguistic and political divisions, and Canada recently almost came apart over the Quebec question. The two "founding nations" of Canada may yet go their separate ways, like the Czechs and Slovaks did.

The fact that Switzerland and Belgium are small countries (and Canada a huge country with a small population) tends to contradict another argument made in favor of holding multinational entities together: the argument that more populous states benefit from economies of scale. While there are economic and military returns to scale, these may be neutralized if they are accompanied by the costs of increased ethnic diversity accompanied by ethnic conflict. All other things being equal, a large homogeneous nation state may well be preferable to a small homogeneous nation state. But a small nation state may be better off, in terms of prosperity and governability if not necessarily defense, than a gigantic state riven by ethnic and linguistic conflicts.

Those who call on nondemocratic multinational states to adopt Swiss- or Canadian-type power-sharing arrangements as an alternative to partition seldom describe the policy to be pursued if their constitutional panaceas fail (as they have in most cases). If elaborate power-sharing schemes are rejected, or tried and found not to work, is partition or secession then in order, as a second-best option? Or should multinational states like Iraq that cannot be held together by democratic and federal means be held together by force and terror?

Those who seek to promote democracy and at the same time to preserve multinational entities intact will discover that in many cases these goals cannot be reconciled. A world of liberal nationalist states, including many that are nondemocratic, is much more likely to develop into a world of democracies, as Franco's Spain would attest. For this reason, proponents of democratization are justified in encouraging liberal nationalism even where democracy is not yet possible. This might be the case, for instance, in Algeria or Egypt. Conversely, it may be a waste of time to try to hold together and democratize a multinational state, even a relatively liberal one, where a common national identity is lacking. This might be the case in the future in South Africa. Instead, it often makes more sense to promote liberal and constitutional nationalism, with or without electoral democracy. First comes the nation state, then a liberal constitution reinforced by a liberal political culture, and only then, if at all, democracy. For many, living as the citizen of a liberal but nondemocratic nation state is preferable to being the subject of an illiberal multinational despotism that can only be held together by force.

NO LONGER A LAST RESORT

To substitute indiscriminate support for national self-determination for reflexive defense of the territorial status quo around the world would be a mistake. Rather than strict principles, a few rules of thumb are in order. To begin with, the United States should refrain from making gratuitous statements in favor of state unity.... Even if American policy is to favor state unity in a particular case, the United States might lose some of its leverage if this preference is too obvious. Even worse, the United States may appear to license vicious repression, as the Bush administration's statements in favor of Yugoslav unity may have convinced Serb nationalists that they would not be penalized seriously for attacking Slovenia and Croatia.

In the civil wars where ethnic or cultural differences are at issue, partition should no longer be considered the last resort. It might sometimes be wise to stress national self-determination above free elections, during the terminal crisis of a state that is both multinational and undemocratic. Oppressed nations seeking to escape from a multinational empire should not be told that they will be free to vote on everything except their independence. Since democracy and liberal constitutionalism work best in relatively homogeneous nation states, in most of the world democratic constitution-writing should follow national independence, not be promoted as an alternative to it. Indeed, it is not only futile but insulting for policymakers and academics in Western capitals and campuses to design democratic federal constitutions like the Vance-Owen plan for Bosnia and try to impose them on Kurds, Kosovars or Kashmiris as alternatives to national independence. Where a multiethnic federation has utterly collapsed, it may be better to create two or more new, relatively homogeneous nation states than to try to piece the wreckage together with ingenious but unworkable power-sharing schemes.

The corollary of support for national self-determination in the form of secession is support for the enlargement of nation states through peaceful and democratic accession or annexation, like the unification of Germany. The United States enlarged itself in this manner as recently as 1958 (with the statehood of Alaska and Hawaii); President Bush called for statehood for Puerto Rico. If east Germany can join west Germany, by what reasoning can the 90 percent majority of ethnic Albanians in Kosovo [a province of Yugoslavia] be denied accession to Albania, if they choose and can make their choice effective? How can compact populations of Bosnian Croats be forbidden by the international community from voluntarily merging with Croatia (the very international borders of which are recent and fluid)? States should be allowed not only to shrink but to expand, so long as the expansion is undertaken peacefully and with the consent of majorities (or perhaps supermajorities) of those affected. The difficulties attending European unification suggest that we need not fear the creation of possibly overpowerful bureaucratic superstates like the Third Reich and the Soviet Union through purely voluntary mergers.

The United States may legitimately refuse to support nationalist movements that define the nation in narrow racial or religious terms, rather than in inclusive linguistic and cultural terms, as well as movements that threaten minorities with persecution or genocide. Also, as a condition of admitting new nation states to the international community, outsiders may legitimately insist that states protect the rights of association of individual members of cultural minorities, such as private religious or language instruction. It would be a mistake, however, for the international community to attempt to promulgate a general duty of states not only to tolerate but to subsidize and promote minority cultures. Such policies, whether undertaken as a result of international or purely domestic pressure, tend only to inflame majority resentment without accomplishing any important goals that cannot be achieved by less intrusive, more voluntary means.

The wave of disintegrative nationalism that ripped apart the former Soviet Union and the Yugoslav federation will not be the last. In all likelihood, the next few decades will see increasingly determined secessionist movements in the multiethnic successor states of the European empires: India, Pakistan, South Africa, Iraq, perhaps even the Russian federation. In such countries, as dominant elites, seeking new formulas for legitimacy to replace fading secular and socialist philosophies, make more concessions to the national and religious sentiments of ethnic majorities, minority nationalisms may grow more bitter and intense in response. The fact that in many, perhaps most, cases central authorities will prevail will not prevent secessionist nationalism from being a major source of terrorism and civil war in the 21st century. The United States does not need to become an exporter of secession. Washington should recognize, however, that in particular cases American values, as well as American interests, may be served by those who seek to break up multinational states rather than by those who seek to preserve them.

NO

Amitai Etzioni

THE EVILS OF SELF-DETERMINATION

Self-determination movements, a major historical force for more than 200 years, have largely exhausted their legitimacy as a means to create more strongly democratic states. While they long served to destroy empires and force governments to be more responsive to the governed, with rare exceptions self-determination movements now undermine the potential for democratic development in nondemocratic countries and threaten the foundations of democracy in the democratic ones. It is time to withdraw moral approval from most of the movements and see them for what they mainly are—destructive.

All people must develop more tolerance for those with different backgrounds and cultures; with compromise, ethnic identities can be expressed within existing national entities without threatening national unity. If tolerance between groups is not fostered, the resulting breakups will not lead to the formation of new stable democracies, but rather to further schisms and more ethnic strife, with few gains and many losses for proponents of self-government. The United States, then, should use moral approbation and diplomatic effort to support forces that enhance democratic determination and oppose those that seek fragmentation and tribalism.

Historically, the principle of self-determination served well those who sought to dissolve empires—governments of one people imposed on another that lacked economic reciprocity between the metropolitan center and the outlying colonies. While historians tend to treat as distinct the emergence of nation-states from the Ottoman and Hapsburg empires and the liberation of former colonies in Asia and Africa following World War II, there are actually great sociological similarities between the two movements. In the Balkan peninsula, foreign empires imposed themselves on the indigenous people, roughly in the area of the modern-day countries of Albania, Bulgaria, Greece, Romania, and what used to be Yugoslavia. The foreign imperialists gained dominance by conquest, and the metropolitan core drew significant economic benefit from the "colonies," although that term is not usually used. When nationalism strengthened the self-awareness of the Balkan people in the late nineteenth century, they rebelled against colonial rule. By 1914, Albanians,

From Amitai Etzioni, "The Evils of Self-Determination," *Foreign Policy,* no. 89 (Winter 1992/1993). Copyright © 1992 by The Carnegie Endowment for International Peace. Reprinted by permission of *Foreign Policy.*

Bulgarians, Greeks, Montenegrins, Romanians, and Serbians had established their independence. Similarly, undemocratic, imperially imposed governments in Africa and Asia led to demands for, and eventually the establishment of, more fully representative governments. In discussing Africa and Asia in the post–World War II era, historians argued that the quest for a new self-expression and self-awareness was at the heart of those self-determination movements. In retrospect, it seems that the metropolitan government's failure to represent and respond to the needs and demands of the various subgroups constituting the empire's population was at least as important.

Nationalism, then, functioned not only as a way to gain one's own flag, national hymn, and other symbols of selfhood, but, perhaps even more important, as a way to lay the foundations for a responsive government. It is true that not all emergent nation-states fashioned democratic governments, but where democracy was absent, the struggle for democratic self-determination continued. The wars of national liberation after World War II that yielded new countries from the former colonies of the British, Dutch, French, Germans, Italians, and Portuguese parallel the historical development of the Balkans in important ways. In both cases, the metropolitan countries were remote and at least in some ways exploitative. While some of the metropolitan governments, especially Britain's, were democratic, their democracy did not embrace the people of their colonies. Moreover, in Africa in particular, the demands for national self-expression were weak because the colonial borders drawn by the empires paid little attention to tribal, cultural, and linguistic lines. Most

of today's African nationalism was generated after independence. In short, the driving force behind the wars of liberation was the desire for democratization and a responsive government, not for ethnic self-determination.

That pursuit parallels the American quest for independence from Great Britain in the late eighteenth century. The American colonial rebellion was most openly and directly a call for representation, not for national expression. Many pre-independence "Americans" saw themselves as British. The American sense of nationhood remained rather tentative, even during the Revolutionary War period, and grew largely after independence. The remoteness and unresponsiveness of the British government, not strong American nationalism, motivated the colonists' revolt.

The world witnessed the final round of the thrust against imperial governments in a most dramatic fashion from 1989 to 1991, as the Soviet empire crumbled with a speed only possible because the imposed government lacked legitimacy. The breakaway of Bulgaria, Czechoslovakia, East Germany, Hungary, Poland, and Romania can easily, though mistakenly, be understood simply as a result of repressed nationalism. Closer examination, however, reveals that another factor was the unresponsiveness of remote and exploitative Muscovite rule. The unresponsiveness of the "local" East European governments explains the collapse of Communist regimes in each of those countries; however, the breakdown of the Soviet-led system was rooted in the member countries' overwhelming sense that the system was dominated by an exploitative USSR that ignored their needs. The same must be said about the breakaway of Estonia, Latvia, and Lithuania.

With the latest attempts at independence, though, there are signs of a new and unproductive strain of self-determination. Far from enhancing democratic government, the drive to dismember the USSR has so far resulted in a shift of power away from the reforming parliament, the most freely elected to date, and toward a small group of republic heads, many of whom were not democratically elected.

There are so far precious few indications that the governments of the 12 non-Baltic republics will be more democratic than the Soviet government they replace. Uzbekistan, for example, remains firmly under control of the former Communist leadership, and even by late 1992 it showed very few signs that it would soon institute the kinds of democratic reforms evident at the federal level. Georgia also remains under one-party rule, and rebels ousted a president who was elected with 87 per cent of the popular vote. Several of the new republics outlawed the main opposition party (the Communist party), and in some the press is often muzzled. President Boris Yeltsin has reminded the Russian parliament that it contains many Communists, and he demands that his powers be increased whenever the parliament does not favor his policies. In short, self-determination in the former USSR often weakens democracy.

INDEPENDENCE WITHOUT DEMOCRACY

Those concerned with promoting responsive governments, by and for the people, can no longer assume that breaking up larger entities provides movement in the desired direction. One may favor or oppose replacement of an empire with a group of local tyrannies; some-

times, it is said, at least they are "ours." But replacing a metropolitan democratic government, into which, for instance, the USSR was beginning to evolve, with a bunch of local autocrats hardly constitutes progress toward genuine self-determination.

True, some pockets of empire remain. The people of Tibet and Inner Mongolia may well need to break away from the remote, imposed, exploitative, and undemocratic Chinese empire. And the Kurds may never find a responsive government in tyrannical Iraq or authoritarian Iran. Turkey, however, given its close relationship to the United States and its interest in democracy, may be persuaded to be more tolerant of and responsive to the Kurds, and to grant them more local autonomy. If it becomes clear that the international community would discourage a Kurdish drive for independence from Turkey, reconciliation and compromise between the Turks and the Kurds would be more likely....

The need to tilt in favor of fuller representation, responsiveness, and democratization—and against self-determination by fragmentation—is most evident in those countries that are already basically democratic but within which one subgroup is, or feels that it is, underrepresented or isolated. African Americans were among the first to understand that point. While some flirted with the notion of a separate black state within the United States during the 1960s, and while others had previously promoted a separate state in Liberia, most African Americans quickly realized that their needs would be better served by a racially mixed state—as long as discrimination could be brought to a end. In India, with many ethnic groups competing for resources and recognition, democracy continues to be far from perfect; however, few can expect it to benefit if more territories, such as Kashmir, were to break away and form their own states. The peoples of India desire and deserve a government that is responsive to them, but not necessarily a separatist one. Areas such as Kashmir should be allowed more autonomy and proper participation in national politics, but they should not be encouraged to break up the country into a jigsaw puzzle of hostile, undemocratic, and potentially warring territories.

Yugoslavia was at best a partial democracy; it required much restructuring to make its government responsive to the groups that made up the country—to allow a truly free press, free elections, and the other elements of democracy. However, one thing stands out so far: The governments of the new, fragmented countries that dismembered the Yugoslav federation are even less democratic, and more murderous. . . .

The Parti Québécois self-determination movement in Canada, though not now violent, poses similar dangers to the Canadian federation and Canadian citizens. However legitimate one judges the complaints of French-speaking Canadians to be, it is hard to compare their lot to that of Czechs or Hungarians under Soviet occupation, or even to that of Indians under British colonial rule. One must consider the danger of less democracy in a separatist Quebec, if not for the French-speaking Québécois, then for the English speakers. The merits of enhancing Ottawa's responsiveness and allowing for some redefinition of the central government's role far outweigh the benefits of dismembering the union.

The success of the Flemings and the Walloons in Belgium provides a paradigm for other countries. While the Flemings and the Walloons do not live together in what might be characterized as one big happy community, a democratic government, responsive to both major ethnic groups, has enabled them to avoid the terrible fate of the people of Lebanon, who were relieved from years of horrendous interethnic civil war only by Syrian occupation. Indeed, changes in the structure of the Belgian government in recent years led its two groups toward more satisfactory self-expression—without separation and within the framework of a shared, democratic government. Switzerland, now held up as a model of a country containing people of different origins, ethnicities, languages and cultures, was possible only after the ethnic groups that fought each other for nearly 1,000 years were able to agree on a common democratic government.

Self-determinists often say that they seek to preserve a separate ethnic culture, tradition, religion, or language. They argue, for instance, that Macedonian distinctiveness is threatened within a Greek state. However, as the preceding examples suggest, within a truly democratic state patterns of integration can be created that preserve distinct identities without breaking up the encompassing societies. In a truly democratic state, there is no reason for one culture to try to suppress others, as long as the others seek self-expression rather than cultural dominance or territorial separatism.

It is impossible to sustain the notion that every ethnic group can find its expression in a full-blown nation-state, fly its flag at the United Nations, and have its ambassadors accredited by other nation-states; the process of ethnic separation and the breakdown of existing states will then never be exhausted. Many countries in the world continue to contain numerous ethnic enclaves. Even within those enclaves, further ethnic splinters exist. Moreover, new ethnic "selves" can be generated quite readily, drawing on fracture lines now barely noticeable. Subtle differences in geography, religion, culture, and loyalty can be fanned into new separatist movements, each seeking their own symbols and powers of statehood. Few saw the potential for three countries in Iraq until it nearly broke into a Shiite southern state, a northern Kurdish state, and a central Iraqi Sunni state after the 1991 Persian Gulf war. In the United Kingdom, Scots and Welsh are again asserting themselves. The former Yugoslavia, already riddled by division, may fragment further still; for instance, Albanians, Yugoslavia's third largest and Serbia's second largest ethnic minority, have elected a shadow government in Kosovo and are agitating for independence but have so far stopped short of armed rebellion. And so it goes throughout the world. In most places centrifugal forces, forever present, are accelerating.

Indeed, as most drives to break away from existing states or coalesce in new ones advance, groups line up to tear the emergent state into segments. New divisions often take place long before ethnic groups accord the new entity even a limited opportunity to develop a responsive, democratic government.

A good example would be the Sorbians in eastern Germany who want to establish the state of Lusatia. Though one may not take their claims seriously, Alfred Symank, a Sorbian and the chief lobbyist for a group known as Sorbian Nationality for Autonomous Lusatia, argues that Sorbians "are a legitimate nation" and "want the world to recognize that Germany isn't just made up of Germans.

The Sorbs are here too!" Symank speaks of the oppression of the Sorbs at the hands of the Prussians, Saxons, Nazis, communists, and now unified Germany. He wonders, "If Lithuania succeeds, if Slovenia succeeds, why can't we?" All that before the ink had even dried on German unification.

Much more serious are the demands of various groups within the former Soviet Union's republics. For example, the southern Ossetians in Georgia are in violent battle with the majority Georgians, and the ethnically Turkish Gagauz have already proclaimed independence from the Moldovan majority in Moldova. Continued ethnic strife destablizes a region and makes it unlikely that the new states will survive as more ethnic groups emerge and demand further fragmentation.

Even the romantics of self-determination may pause before the prospect of a United Nations with thousands of members. The world may well survive the creation of ever more toy states, smaller than Liechtenstein and less populated than the South Pacific island-country of Nauru (population 9,300), but what meaning does self-determination have when minuscule countries are at the economic and military mercy, even whim, of larger states—states in whose government they have no representation at all?

If the world is to avoid such chaos, the call for self-determination should no longer elicit almost reflexive moral support. We should withhold political and moral support unless the movement faces one of the truly exceptional situations in which self-determination will enhance democracy rather than retard it. Generally, people who see themselves as oppressed put great value in gaining the moral support of others. As a rule, though, we should encourage groups to work out their differences within existing national communities. Also, to further discourage fragmentation, the economic disadvantages of separatism should be made evident. Finally, governments that face ethnic challenges, like Canada, should be urged to provide more local autonomy and more democratic federalism in order to prevent dissolution.

THE ECONOMICS OF SECESSION

Objectively assessed, the economic disadvantages of fragmentation stand out. Countries that fragment into smaller economies pay heavy economic penalties. For instance, Slovakia, a source of many raw materials, ... split from the Czech republic, a place where raw materials have been turned into finished products. Also, the pipelines that carry oil from the former USSR to the Czech republic run through Slovakia, and Slovakian independence [could] pose a potential security threat to the Czechs' oil supply. ... [Conversely,] the Czechs supply much of the Slovaks' electricity. ...

In another case, Quebec's ardor for separation seems to have cooled recently as its business leaders have recognized the great economic losses independence could entail. Even the mere possibility that Quebec could secede has pushed up the cost of its credit. When it issued bonds in 1990, it had to offer higher interest rates than the other Canadian provinces.

Theoretically, in a world of truly free trade, it does not matter where national borders are drawn. However, under existing conditions, national borders retain considerable economic significance, ranging from the subtle—such as the tendency of citizens to buy domestically pro-

duced products, even when there are no legal restrictions on imports—to overt industrial policies aimed at giving domestic producers a competitive advantage. National borders continue to affect not only the economy, but also the environment. Many environmental issues cannot be dealt with by fragments of countries: The acid rain produced in one rains on the other; the pollution dumped into a river by one country can appear in the drinking water of another downstream. Of course environmental issues also pose a problem for long-established countries, but their new prominence demonstrates the need for more cross-national community building and the difficulties posed by additional fragmentation.

Some argue that groups like the Croatians and Slovenians will first find their nationalist self-expression and later form common markets. However, the argument is akin to suggesting that a married couple running a mom-and-pop store will, after divorce, be more able to work together on behalf of their joint business than during marriage. It rarely happens that way. Indeed, the African experience makes evident the great difficulty, indeed near impossibility, of forming new unions once various territories have become independent states. Some experts once considered independent states a transitional stage between Western colonialism and African unity. Instead, the African states have been independent for decades now and show very few signs of moving toward a new political African union.

Providing yet another argument for the large, multiethnic state and the development of international communities, economies of scale are becoming increasingly important. Economists long stressed the efficiency of large-scale divisions of labor and exchange. However, it is only in the last decades that we have developed the technologies of communication and management that allow us to run enterprises on a truly continental, even inter-continental, scale. In recent years, even many of the world's strongest economies, like those of Western Europe, have found it advantageous to join together and have cooperated on high-tech and industrial ventures. For its part, the United States has responded to economic competition by forming a free-trade area with Canada and... Mexico.

It must be acknowledged that economies of scale are not the only factor in determining economic success. Some small countries, like Singapore, are doing relatively well, while much larger ones, like Brazil, are doing poorly. Holding all other factors constant, though, few would contend that countries like Brazil would benefit from being broken into parts—or that smaller countries would not benefit from economic mergers. Economics has motivated many countries to form, or at least to try to form, economic unions. (Brazil is hoping to join with Argentina, Paraguay, and Uruguay by 1995.) From a sheer economic viewpoint, the way to well-being is not fragmentation but its opposite: community.

Moreover, it is highly questionable whether groups of autonomous countries successfully develop common economies, a process that entails far more than shared markets and trade zones. The European Community is now considering, albeit with difficulty, varying degrees of political union because of the difficulty of maintaining an economic union without broader integration. Because governments routinely seek to affect the rate of inflation, interest rates, unemployment, economic growth, and other economic

fundamentals, a successful economic policy requires a political consensus and a specification of shared goals. It would be the ultimate irony of history for countries to dismember existing states, such as India, only to discover that the resulting entities must reunite politically to provide their citizens with the blessings of a modern economy. Though such irony may satisfy the observer and provide social scientists with a fascinating experiment, it would impose pervasive suffering on the people involved.

Although the economic penalties paid by splinter states may be painful, they are not the primary cost of disunion. Excessive self-determination works against democratization and threatens democracy in countries that have already attained it. Self-determination movements challenge democracy by chipping away at its structural and socio-psychological foundations.

Structurally, democracy depends on more than regular elections. Elections were conducted frequently by... the communist USSR. A true democratic structure requires that nonviolent change of those in power can be made in response to the people's changing preferences. Such changes ensure that the government can continue to respond to the needs and desires of the people, and that if the government becomes unresponsive it will be replaced without undue difficulties.

To ensure that the variety of needs within a population find effective political expression, democracies require that the sitting government not "homogenize" the population in some artificial manner, like imposing one state-approved religion. Only a plurality of social, cultural, and economic loyalties and power centers within society make it possible for new groups to break upon the political scene, find allies, build coalitions, and effect change. The Great Society reforms of the mid-1960s in the United States demonstrate the importance of a plural, fluid system. Rising African American groups formed a coalition with white liberals and labor unions to advance a common agenda, increasing political participation and preventing a political explosion.

Aside from keeping the government and its closest allies in the population in check, the pluralistic array of groups that thrive in a truly democratic society also keep one another in check. When historical processes or deliberate government policies leave only one group of supporters organized and weaken all other groups, as the Nazis did in post–World War I Germany, they undermine the foundations of democracy. In short, social pluralism supports democratic government.

While there are many ways the coalitions needed for social pluralism can be built, the best are those that cut across existing lines of division, dampening the power of each and allowing for a large number of possible combinations of social bases to build political power. Thus, a society rigidly divided into two or three economic classes may have a structure that is somewhat more conducive to democratic government than a society with only one class. However, the potential for democracy in such a society increases when there are other groups that draw on members from various classes, so that loyalty to them cuts across class lines.

In the United States, ethnic loyalties have historically cut across socioeconomic strata, dampening both class and ethnic divisions. Thus, American Jews may be largely middle and upper-middle class, but most people in those classes are not Jewish, and there are Jews in the other classes. White Anglo-Saxon Protestants may be over-represented in the upper classes, but they are also found in large numbers in all other classes, and so on. The fact that both economic and ethnic loyalties cut across regional boundaries further cements the foundations of pluralism and, hence, of democracy.

In contrast, breakaway states based on ethnicity tend to fashion communities that are more sociologically monolithic than their parent states. Quebec, obviously, would be more "French"— and the remaining Canada more "English"—than the current composite. The great intolerance breakaway states tend to display toward minority ethnic groups heightens the polarization. Ethnically based breakaway states generally result in more ethnic homogeneity and less pluralism, meaning that they often lack the deeper sociological foundations of democracy.

Democracy requires tolerance to function because tolerance provides the socio-psychological bases for compromise, such as the willingness to accept the outcome of an election even if it favors a party one opposes. Community requires the same basic psychological mindset because tolerance is inherent in the ability to work out differences with people whose religions, histories, and habits one does not share and is vital to the process of uniting people of different backgrounds and traditions. When tolerance is absent, as it often is in breakaway states, the predisposition toward further fragmentation is strong. Since the ultimate purpose of self-determination is not self-determination per se but a responsive government, mutual tolerance might be what many countries and ethnic groups need most and first.

At least before self-determination groups take a wrecking ball to their countries, it seems reasonable to expect them to try to work out their differences by reforming the existing government to render it more responsive, for example changing its structures to make it less unitary and more federal. If that truly doesn't work, we must insist that the newly formed communities take special pains to nurture the tolerance they will need to stay together.

In earlier historical periods the people favoring self-determination tended to be internationalist. As long as the leaders of various national movements were largely poets, philosophers, and intellectuals rallying against dominant empires, their causes seemed appealing and just. However, as nationalism—and especially micronationalism—has spread increasing hostility, ethnic fragmentation has opened the door to great new violence. In Moldova, the Russian minority and the Gagauz people face discrimination and outright violence. The same holds for the ethnic Turkish minority in Bulgaria, Romanians in Hungary, and Hungarians in Romania. Civil wars among ethnic entities within the newly independent African states are commonplace. And in India, though the Sikhs have not yet obtained independence for Punjab, subgroups are already at each other's throats.

A DEMOCRATIC MOSAIC

Self-determination should not be treated as an absolute value, trumping all others. Self-determination is meant to enhance justice in the world through self-government. However, in spite of its positive role in previous periods, the violence and destruction—even war —it now incites greatly undercut its legitimacy.

Pluralism can exist, even flourish, within a unified state; ethnic groups and other subgroups need not be suppressed or dissolved to maintain community. The best solution to the worldwide ethnic crumble is not total assimilation. In fact, ethnic groups should continue not only to exist, but to thrive and enrich the cultural mosaic. They form the foundation of democratic pluralism, as long as their sociological scope does not expand to the point where it cuts into the community's sustaining bonds.

Ethnic expressions can include many things: the maintenance of traditional cuisine, music, dance, religious rituals, and mutual aid associations. Ethnic groups should accept those values embedded in the shared national constitution (like respect for individual and minority rights), a limited set of ultimate values (like the defense of one's country), and, in most countries, a shared language. However, those minimum requirements still leave room for free cultural expression, assuming ethnic groups coexist in an environment of mutual tolerance. The preservation of a national community or democracy does not demand the assimilation or the elimination of ethnic groups, though it does require that some basic limits be placed upon them.

Those who seek to bolster national unity often argue for the imposition of one language while those seeking to maintain their own ethnic cultures strongly oppose the introduction of a language other than their own, and they see efforts to do so as a major attack on their unique cultural identity.

They may point to the experiences of Belgium and Switzerland, which show that a country can sustain government responsiveness and unity even in face of separate languages.

The principle of pluralism within unity provides a guideline for consideration. Countries that encourage their citizens to acquire one common language facilitate communication and community building. But they should not discourage subgroups from maintaining their own languages. Quebec can encourage its citizens to learn and speak French but should not make taboo the use of English as a second language on its shop and restaurant signs. The Soviet government, after all, oppressed Jews not by expecting them to learn Russian but by prohibiting the teaching of Yiddish and Hebrew.

Clearly, the moral support historically granted to self-determination movements was based on the often-correct belief that empires deny minorities their right to a responsive, democratic government forcing them to break away. Self-determination movements gained support because they fought against oppression, not because they fought for separatism.

Now, in most states of the world, further fragmentation is likely to imperil democratic forces and endanger economic development. Only when secessionist movements seek to break out of empires—and only when those empires refuse to democratize—does self-determination deserve our support. Otherwise, democratic government and community building, not fragmentation, should be accorded the highest standing.

POSTSCRIPT

Is Self-Determination a Right of All Nationalities?

The issue of self-determination presents a particularly emotional conundrum. On one hand, the idea that people should be free to govern themselves is very appealing. Also, for Americans and others, opposing self-determination puts them in a position of arguing against the very principle that once led them to independence.

On the other hand, self-determination has its drawbacks. First, countries are becoming integrated economic units, and rendering them asunder often creates great hardship for all. Second, the various claims of nations/ethnic groups/tribes are hard to unravel in an even-handed and just manner. In central Africa, the Tutsis have recently suffered amazing cruelty at the hands of the Hutus. But the Hutus, a majority, were long dominated by the Tutsis, who invaded the region, probably from Ethiopia, in the sixteenth century. The Tutsis were also used by European colonial powers as the local enforcers of their oppressive rule. Then again, the Hutus also are invaders who long ago conquered the area and its indigenous people, the Twa. Would it be reasonable to return control of Rwanda and Burundi to the Twa? A third drawback of self-determination is that it leads to so-called microstates. There are some 38 countries with populations of less than 1 million. Many of these microstates have marginal economies that are too small to sustain the diverse base necessary to build a modern economy and compete in world commerce. Also, the ability of these microstates to defend themselves against outside domination is negligible. In an ideal world, size would not be an issue. In the real world, microstates tempt the powerful, and an ensuing struggle could set off a wave of conflict among the major powers. As one scholar has put it, "microstates can cause macropolitical havoc."

Few people advocate unrestrained self-determination or absolutely oppose it. Lind and Etzioni both avoid those extremes. Yet, once one begins to make choices between the two, other issues arise. Most of us might readily agree, for example, that the white minority in South Africa should not be able to break away and establish a white state, as some there want to do. How about the Zulus, though? Should that black nation be supported in a claim for independence?

Further complicating the debate is whether or not the tolerance that Etzioni laudably advocates is even possible. For more on the origins and nature of ethnicity and nationalism, you may wish to read George M.Scholl, Jr.,

"A Resynthesis of the Primordial and Circumstantial Approaches to Ethnic Group Solidarity," *Ethnic and Racial Studies* (April 1990); Paul Brass, *Ethnicity and Nationalism* (Sage Publications, 1991); Liah Greenfeld, *Nationalism* (Harvard University Press, 1992); and Walker Connor, "Beyond Reason: The Nature of the Ethnonational Bond," *Ethnic and Racial Studies* (July 1993).

CONTRIBUTORS
TO THIS VOLUME

EDITOR

JOHN T. ROURKE, Ph.D., is a professor of political science at the University of Connecticut for campuses in Storrs and Hartford, Connecticut. He has written numerous articles and papers, and he is the author of *Congress and the Presidency in U.S. Foreign Policymaking* (Westview Press, 1985); *The United States, the Soviet Union, and China: Comparative Foreign Policymaking and Implementation* (Brooks/Cole, 1989); and *International Politics on the World Stage*, 5th ed. (Dushkin Publishing Group/Brown & Benchmark Publishers, 1995). He is also the coauthor, with Ralph G. Carter and Mark A. Boyer, of *Making American Foreign Policy*, 2d. ed. (Dushkin Publishing Group/Brown & Benchmark Publishers, 1996). Professor Rourke enjoys teaching introductory political science classes—which he does each semester—and he plays an active role in the university's internship program as well as advises one of its political clubs. In addition, he has served as a staff member of Connecticut's legislature and has been involved in political campaigns on the local, state, and national levels.

STAFF

Mimi Egan Publisher
David Dean List Manager
David Brackley Developmental Editor
Brenda S. Filley Production Manager
Libra Ann Cusack Typesetting Supervisor
Juliana Arbo Typesetter
Lara Johnson Graphics
Diane Barker Proofreader
Richard Tietjen Systems Manager

AUTHORS

AUNG SAN SUU KYI is the recipient of the 1991 Nobel Prize for Peace and the leader of Burma's National League for Democracy. She has been held under house arrest by the Burmese dictatorship since July 1989.

DOUG BANDOW is a senior fellow of the Cato Institute in Washington, D.C., a public policy research foundation, and a member of the State of California Bar Association and the U.S. Court of Appeals for the District of Columbia. He is the author of *Beyond Good Intentions* (Crossway Books, 1988) and *The Politics of Plunder: Misgovernment in Washington* (Transaction Publishers, 1990).

GEORGE J. BORJAS is a professor of economics at the University of California, San Diego, and the author of *Labor Economics*, forthcoming from McGraw-Hill.

MICHAEL E. BROWN is a senior fellow of the Center for Science and International Affairs at Harvard University in Cambridge, Massachusetts. He is also coeditor of the center's *International Security*.

ZBIGNIEW BRZEZINSKI is a counselor at the Center for Strategic and International Studies and a professor of foreign policy at the Paul H. Nitze School of Advanced International Studies at Johns Hopkins University. He was national security adviser to President Jimmy Carter.

HODDING CARTER is a syndicated columnist and cochairman of the Action Council for Peace in the Balkans. He was also the U.S. State Department spokesman for the Carter administration.

JOHN L. ESPOSITO is a professor of religion and international affairs at Georgetown University in Washington, D.C., and the director of the Center for Muslim-Christian Understanding: History and International Affairs at Georgetown University's Edmund A. Walsh School of Foreign Service. He is a former president of the Middle East Studies Association of North America and of the American Council for the Study of Islamic Societies. His publications include *Islam and Politics* (Syracuse University Press, 1991) and *The Islamic Threat: Myth or Reality?* (Oxford University Press, 1992).

AMITAI ETZIONI, a senior adviser to the White House from 1979 to 1980, is a professor in the Department of Sociology at George Washington University in Washington, D.C., where he has been teaching since 1968. He is also the founder of the Society for the Advancement of Socio-Economics and the founder and director of the Center for Policy Research, a nonprofit organization dedicated to public policy. His publications include *A Responsive Society: Collected Essays on Guiding Deliberate Social Change* (Jossey-Bass, 1991).

HILARY F. FRENCH is a senior researcher at the Worldwatch Institute in Washington, D.C. She is the author of *Clearing the Air: Worldwatch Paper 94.*

FRANCIS FUKUYAMA, a former deputy director of the U.S. State Department's policy planning staff, is a consultant for the RAND Corporation in Santa Monica, California. He is the author of *The End of History and the Last Man* (Free Press, 1992).

MICHAEL G. GALLAGHER holds a doctorate in international studies from the University of Miami. He has lived and taught in Hong Kong, China, as well as at the University of Miami and Florida International University in Miami, Florida. His published articles have focused on Chinese environment and technology issues.

PATRICK GLYNN is a resident scholar at the American Enterprise Institute in Washington, D.C., a privately funded public policy research organization. His publications include *Closing Pandora's Box: Arms Races, Arms Control, and the History of the Cold War* (Basic Books, 1992).

JAMES P. GRANT is the executive director of the United Nations Children's Fund.

LUKAS HAYNES, a former assistant to the president of the Carnegie Endowment for International Peace, is now doing doctoral research on U.S. policy toward the United Nations at Oxford University.

JOHN F. HILLEN III is a defense analyst at the Heritage Foundation and the author of *The Strategy of UN Military Operations.*

SAMUEL P. HUNTINGTON is the Eaton Professor of the Science of Government and director of the John M. Olin Institute for Strategic Studies at Harvard University.

DONALD KAGAN is the Hillhouse Professor of History and Classics at Yale University. His most recent book is *On the Origins of War and the Preservation of Peace,* and he has also written a four-volume history of the Peloponnesian War.

MICHAEL KANTOR, a U.S. trade representative, was a Democratic Party official from 1975 to 1992 and the presidential campaign chairman for Bill Clinton

in 1992. He served as a lieutenant in the U.S. Navy for over 17 years, and he was a partner in the law firm of Manatt, Phelps, Phillips, and Kantor until 1992.

JAMES KURTH is a professor of political science at Swarthmore College.

ANTHONY LAKE is the assistant to the president for National Security Affairs for the Clinton administration.

MICHAEL LIND is executive editor of *The National Interest.*

KISHORE MAHBUBANI is deputy secretary of foreign affairs and dean of the Civil Service College in Singapore. He last served overseas as Singapore's permanent representative to the United Nations (1984–1989)

CLOVIS MAKSOUD is director of the Center for the Study of the Global South and a professor of international relations in the School of International Service at the American University in Washington, D.C. He served as ambassador to and permanent observer for the League of Arab States at the United Nations and as the league's chief representative in the United States from 1979 to 1990.

STEPHEN MOORE is an economist with the Cato Institute in Washington, D.C., a public policy research foundation.

RALPH NADER is a lawyer and a public advocate. He heads the Center for Study of Responsive Law.

DANIEL PIPES is the editor of the new journal *Middle East Quarterly* and the author of three books on Islam and politics.

MICHAEL POSNER is executive director of the Lawyers Committee for Human Rights.

WILLIAM RATLIFF is a senior research fellow at the Hoover Institution at Stanford University in Stanford, California. He has written and edited several books and many articles on Cuba, and he is coauthor of *The Civil War in Nicaragua: Inside the Sandinistas* (Transaction, 1993), with Roger Miranda.

JOHN RAWLS, a political philosopher at Harvard University, is the author of *A Theory of Justice* (Belknap Press, 1971) and *Two Concepts of Rules* (Irvington, 1991).

ALEX ROLAND is a professor of history at Duke University, where he teaches military history and the history of technology.

JOSEPH ROTBLAT is an emeritus professor of physics at the University of London. He worked on the Manhattan Project in the 1940s, and he now serves as president of the Pugwash Conferences on Science and World Affairs, which was founded by members of the scientific community in 1957 in response to the threat posed by nuclear weapons.

DENNY ROY teaches in the Department of Political Science at the National University of Singapore.

ROBERT SATLOFF is executive director of the Washington Institute for Near East Policy.

JULIAN L. SIMON is a professor of economics and business administration in the College of Business and Management at the University of Maryland at Col-

lege Park. His research interests focus on population economics, and his publications include *The Economic Consequences of Immigration* (Basil Blackwell, 1989), *Population Matters: People, Resources, Environment, and Immigration* (Transaction Publishers, 1990), and *The Ultimate Resource*, 2d ed. (Princeton University Press, 1994).

TIMOTHY W. STANLEY is vice president for policy of the United Nations Association–National Capital Area. He had 10 years of active and reserve military service prior to holding senior civilian defense posts in four administrations. He is also president of the International Economic Studies Institute in Washington, D.C.

ALAN TONELSON is a fellow of the Economic Strategy Institute, a Washington, D.C.–based policy research organization that studies trade policy, technology policy, and national security.

MARTIN VAN HEUVEN is a retired U.S. Foreign Service officer and a former national intelligence officer for Europe. He is currently a senior consultant at the RAND Corporation and a senior associate at the Center for Strategic and International Studies.

NANCY WARTIK is a contributing editor for *American Health*.

MICHAEL G. WILSON is a senior analyst for inter-American affairs and trade policy at the Heritage Foundation in Washington, D.C., a public policy research and education institute whose programs are intended to apply a conservative philosophy to current policy questions.

INDEX